WAR STORIES

GARTH ENNIS

WRITER

CHRIS WESTON
GARY ERSKINE
JOHN HIGGINS
DAVE GIBBONS
DAVID LLOYD

ARTISTS

PAMELA RAMBO
DAVID LLOYD

COLORISTS

CLEM ROBINS

LETTERER

JOHN VAN FLEET

ORIGINAL
SERIES
COVERS

VOL. 1

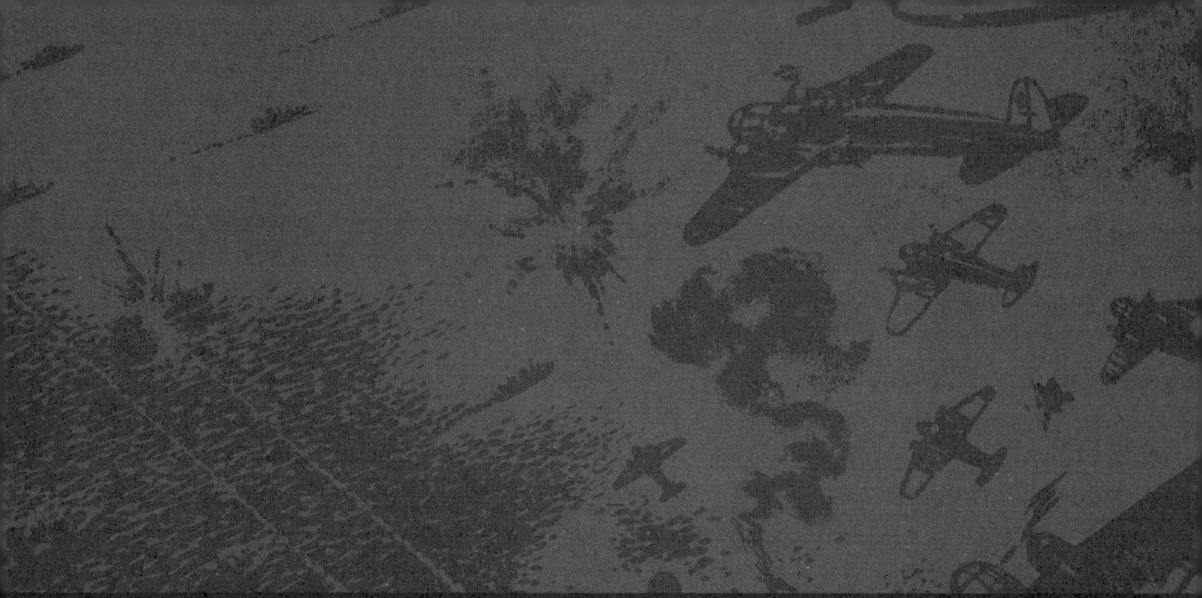

WAR STORIES VOL. 1 Published by DC Comics. Cover and
compilation copyright © 2004 DC Comics. Afterword copyright ©
2004 Garth Ennis. All Rights Reserved. Originally published in single
magazine form as WAR STORY: JOHANN'S TIGER, WAR STORY:
D-DAY DODGERS, WAR STORY: SCREAMING EAGLES and WAR
STORY: NIGHTINGALE. WAR STORY: JOHANN'S TIGER copyright ©
2001 Garth Ennis and Chris Weston. All Rights Reserved. WAR
STORY: D-DAY DODGERS copyright © 2001 Garth Ennis and John
Higgins. All Rights Reserved. WAR STORY: SCREAMING EAGLES
copyright © 2002 Garth Ennis and Dave Gibbons. All Rights
Reserved. WAR STORY: NIGHTINGALE copyright © 2002 Garth
Ennis and David Lloyd. All Rights Reserved. All characters, their
distinctive likenesses and related elements featured in this
publication are trademarks of their respective copyright holders.
VERTIGO is a trademark of DC Comics. The stories, characters, and
incidents featured in this publication are entirely fictional.
DC Comics does not read or accept unsolicited submissions of ideas,
stories or artwork.

DC Comics, 1700 Broadway, New York, NY 10019
A Warner Bros. Entertainment Company
Printed in Canada. Second Printing.
ISBN: 1-4012-0328-0. ISBN 13: 978-1-4012-0328-3.
Cover illustrations by Chris Weston & Gary Erskine,
John Higgins, Dave Gibbons, and David Lloyd.
Publication design by John J. Hill

CONTENTS

"THERE WAS A TIME, NOT LONG AGO, WHEN WE GAVE THIS WORLD A WAR IT HAD NOT DREAMED OF."

WAR STORY

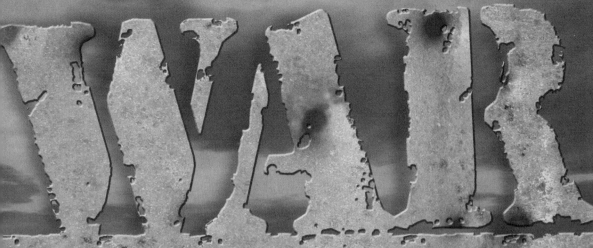

JOHANN'S TIGER

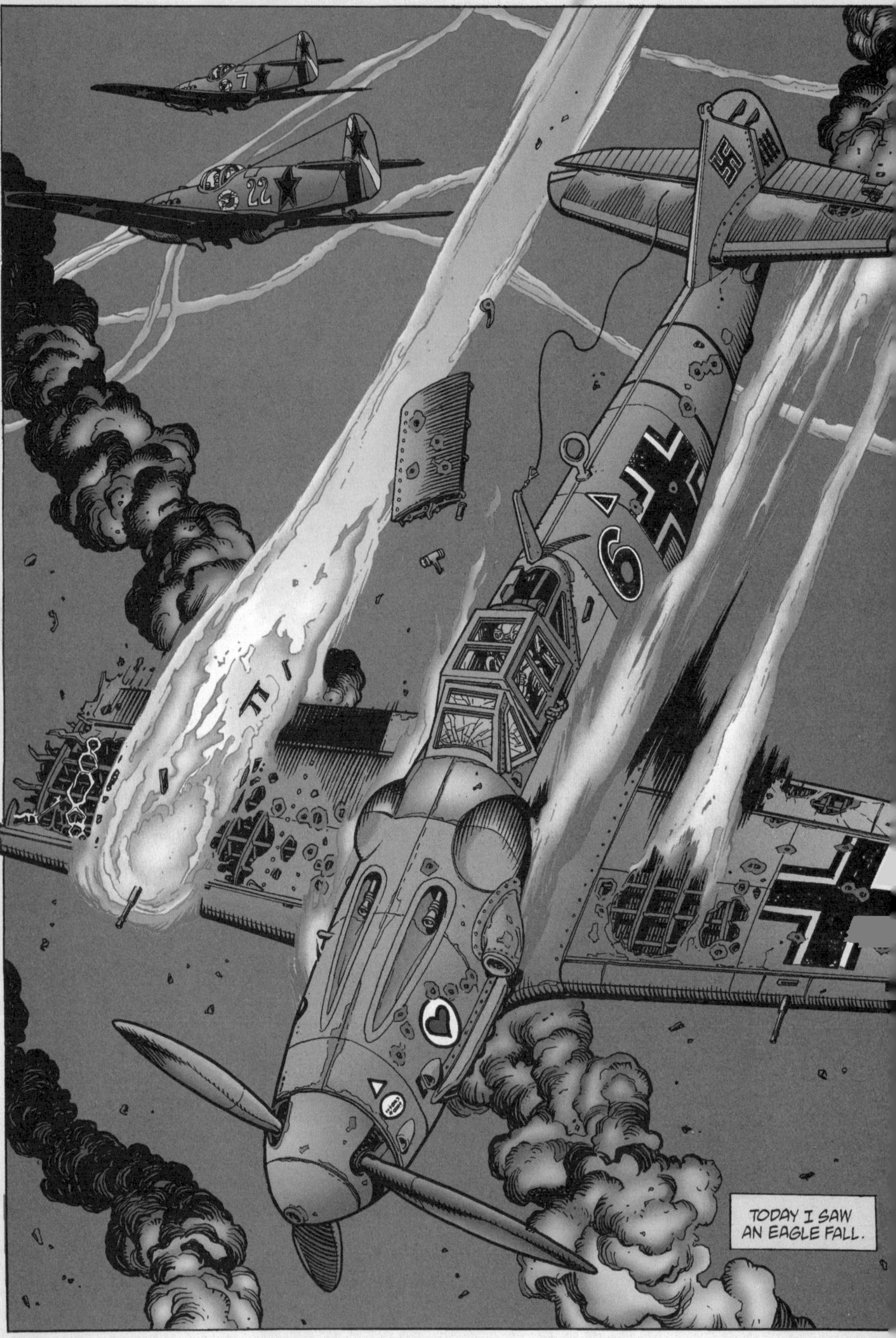
TODAY I SAW AN EAGLE FALL.

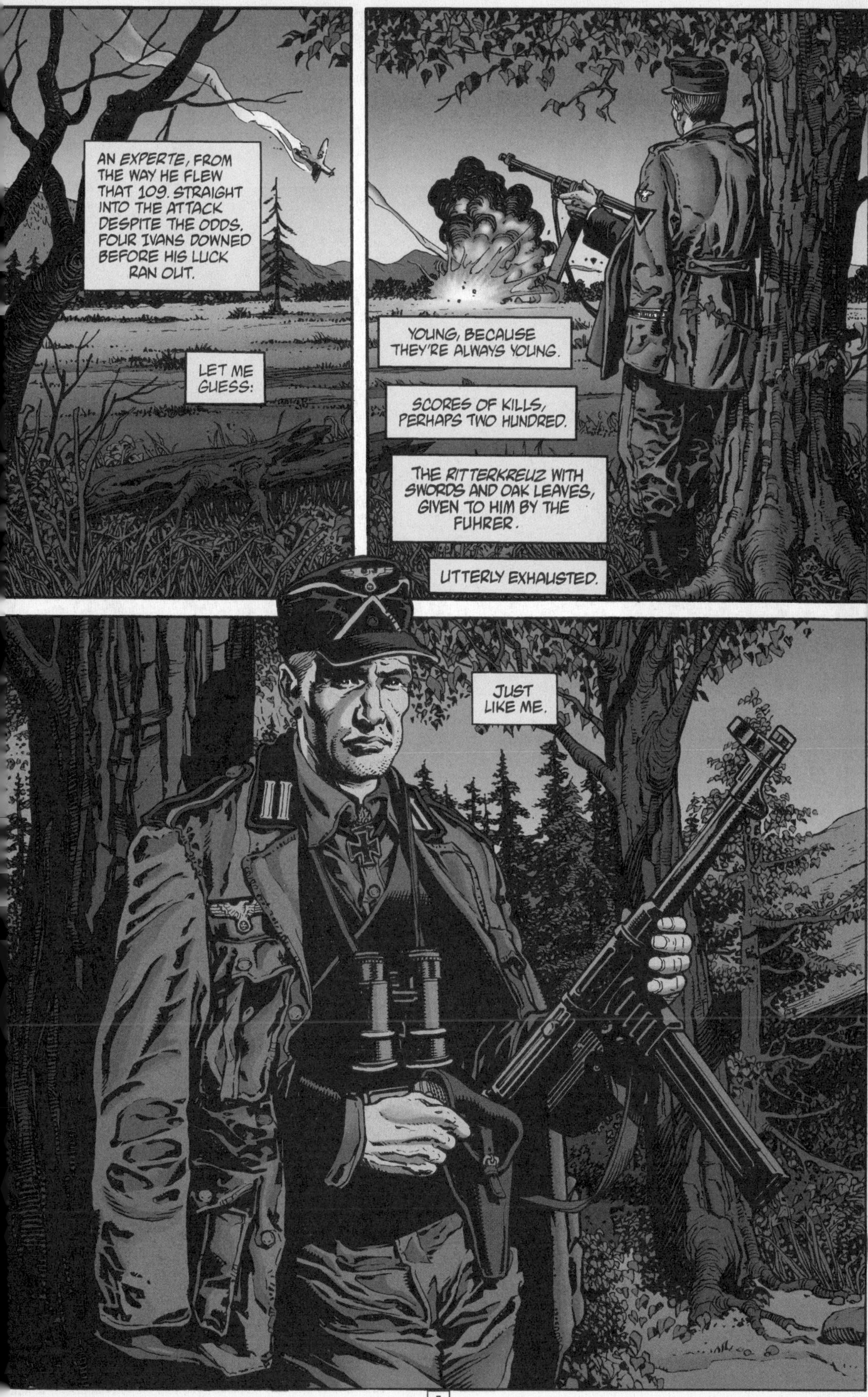
AN EXPERTE, FROM THE WAY HE FLEW THAT 109. STRAIGHT INTO THE ATTACK DESPITE THE ODDS. FOUR IVANS DOWNED BEFORE HIS LUCK RAN OUT.
LET ME GUESS:
YOUNG, BECAUSE THEY'RE ALWAYS YOUNG.
SCORES OF KILLS, PERHAPS TWO HUNDRED.
THE RITTERKREUZ WITH SWORDS AND OAK LEAVES, GIVEN TO HIM BY THE FUHRER.
UTTERLY EXHAUSTED.
JUST LIKE ME.

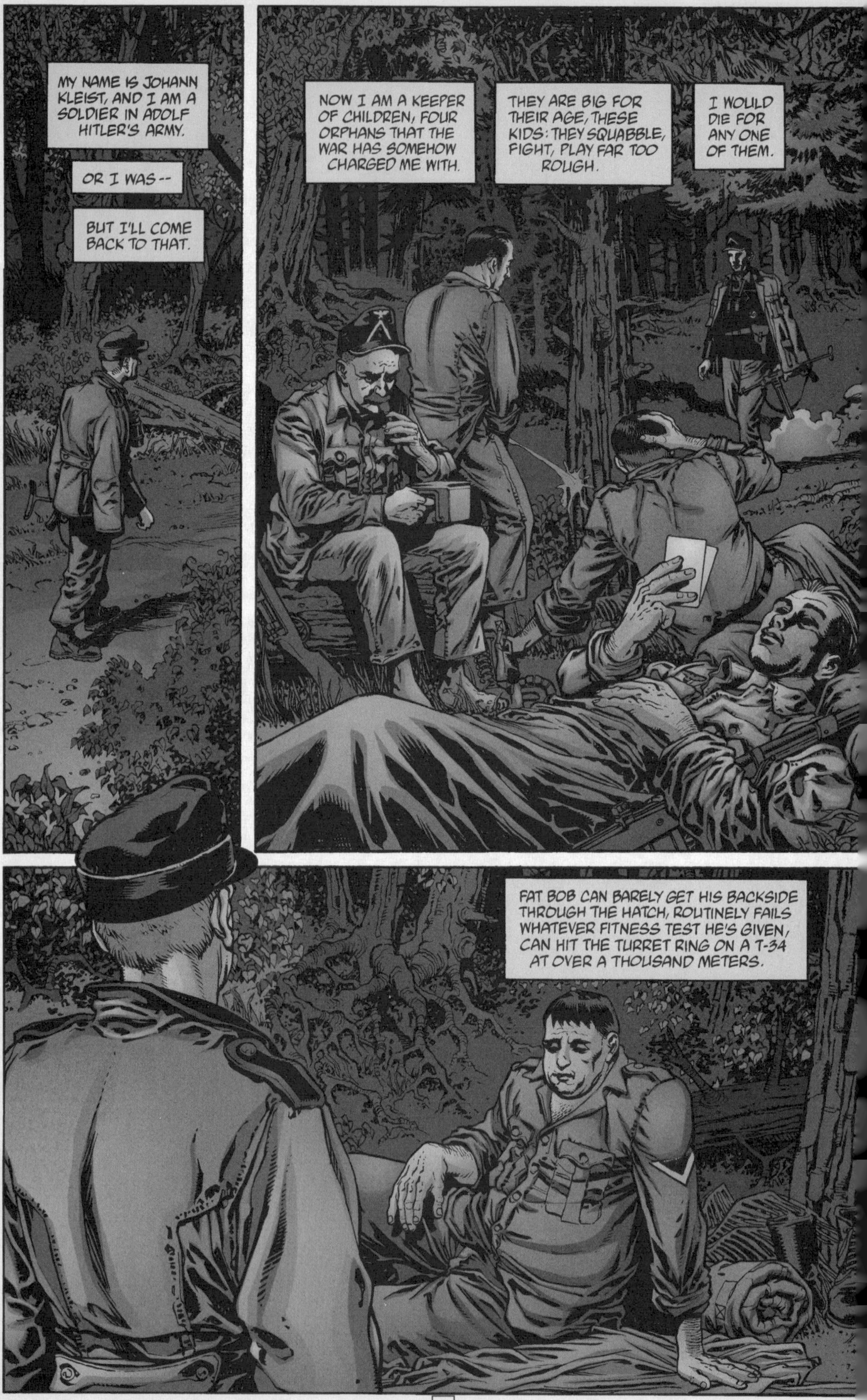
MY NAME IS JOHANN KLEIST, AND I AM A SOLDIER IN ADOLF HITLER'S ARMY.
OR I WAS--
BUT I'LL COME BACK TO THAT.
NOW I AM A KEEPER OF CHILDREN, FOUR ORPHANS THAT THE WAR HAS SOMEHOW CHARGED ME WITH.
THEY ARE BIG FOR THEIR AGE, THESE KIDS: THEY SQUABBLE, FIGHT, PLAY FAR TOO ROUGH.
I WOULD DIE FOR ANY ONE OF THEM.
FAT BOB CAN BARELY GET HIS BACKSIDE THROUGH THE HATCH, ROUTINELY FAILS WHATEVER FITNESS TEST HE'S GIVEN, CAN HIT THE TURRET RING ON A T-34 AT OVER A THOUSAND METERS.

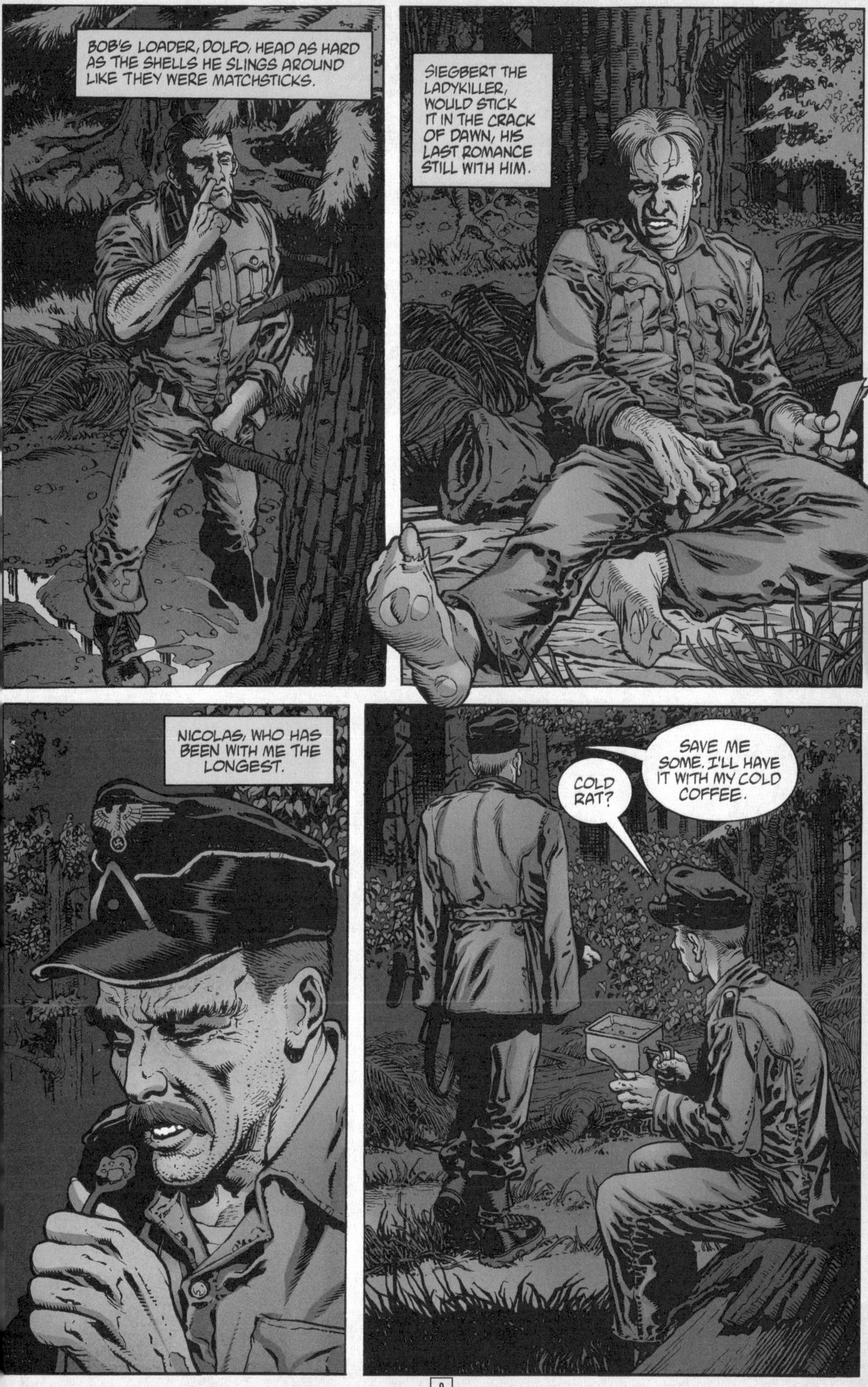
BOB'S LOADER, DOLFO, HEAD AS HARD AS THE SHELLS HE SLINGS AROUND LIKE THEY WERE MATCHSTICKS.
SIEGBERT THE LADYKILLER, WOULD STICK IT IN THE CRACK OF DAWN, HIS LAST ROMANCE STILL WITH HIM.
NICOLAS, WHO HAS BEEN WITH ME THE LONGEST.
SAVE ME SOME. I'LL HAVE IT WITH MY COLD COFFEE.
COLD RAT?

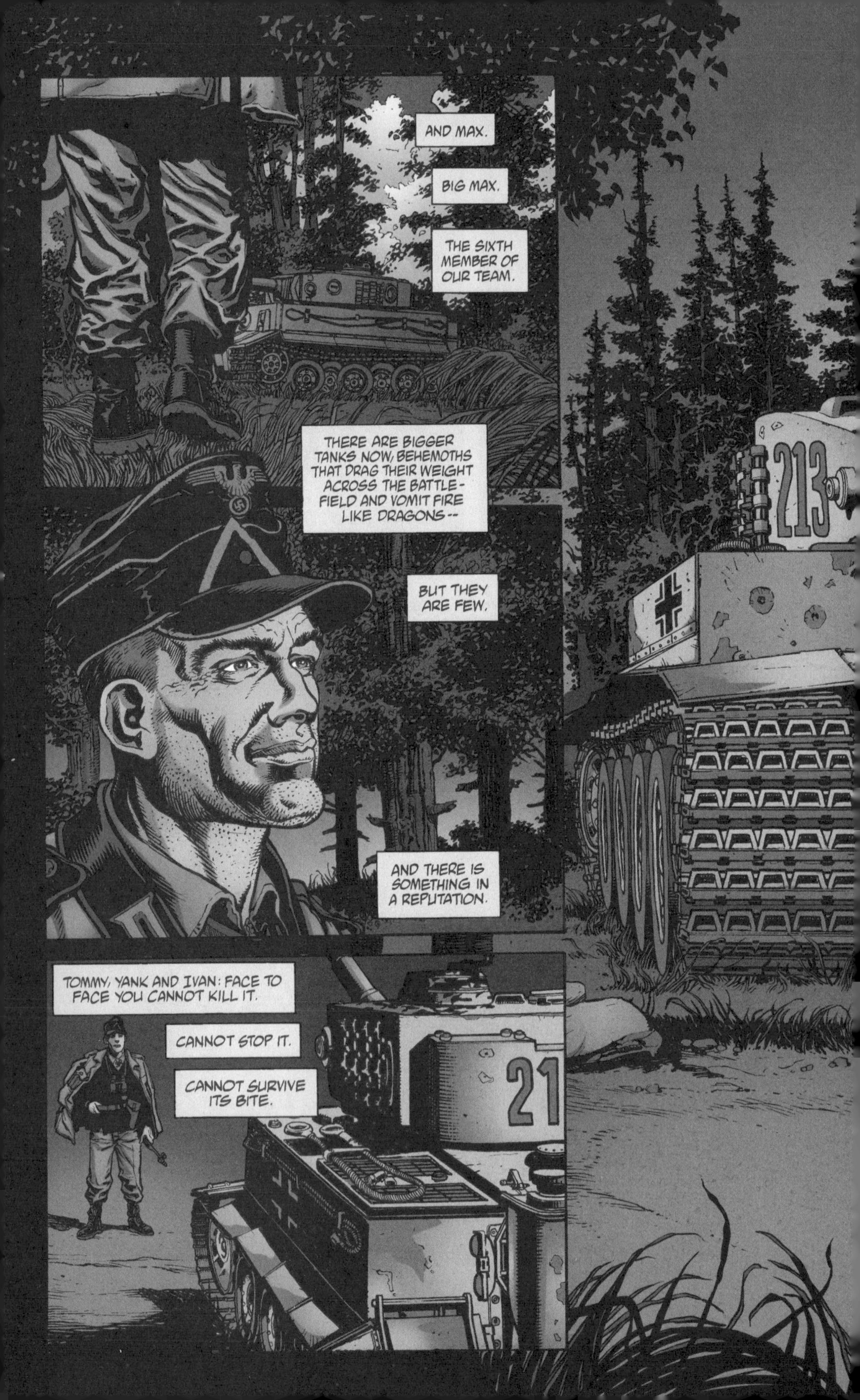
AND MAX.
BIG MAX.
THE SIXTH MEMBER OF OUR TEAM.
THERE ARE BIGGER TANKS NOW, BEHEMOTHS THAT DRAG THEIR WEIGHT ACROSS THE BATTLE-FIELD AND VOMIT FIRE LIKE DRAGONS--
BUT THEY ARE FEW.
AND THERE IS SOMETHING IN A REPUTATION.
TOMMY, YANK AND IVAN: FACE TO FACE YOU CANNOT KILL IT.
CANNOT STOP IT.
CANNOT SURVIVE ITS BITE.
213
21

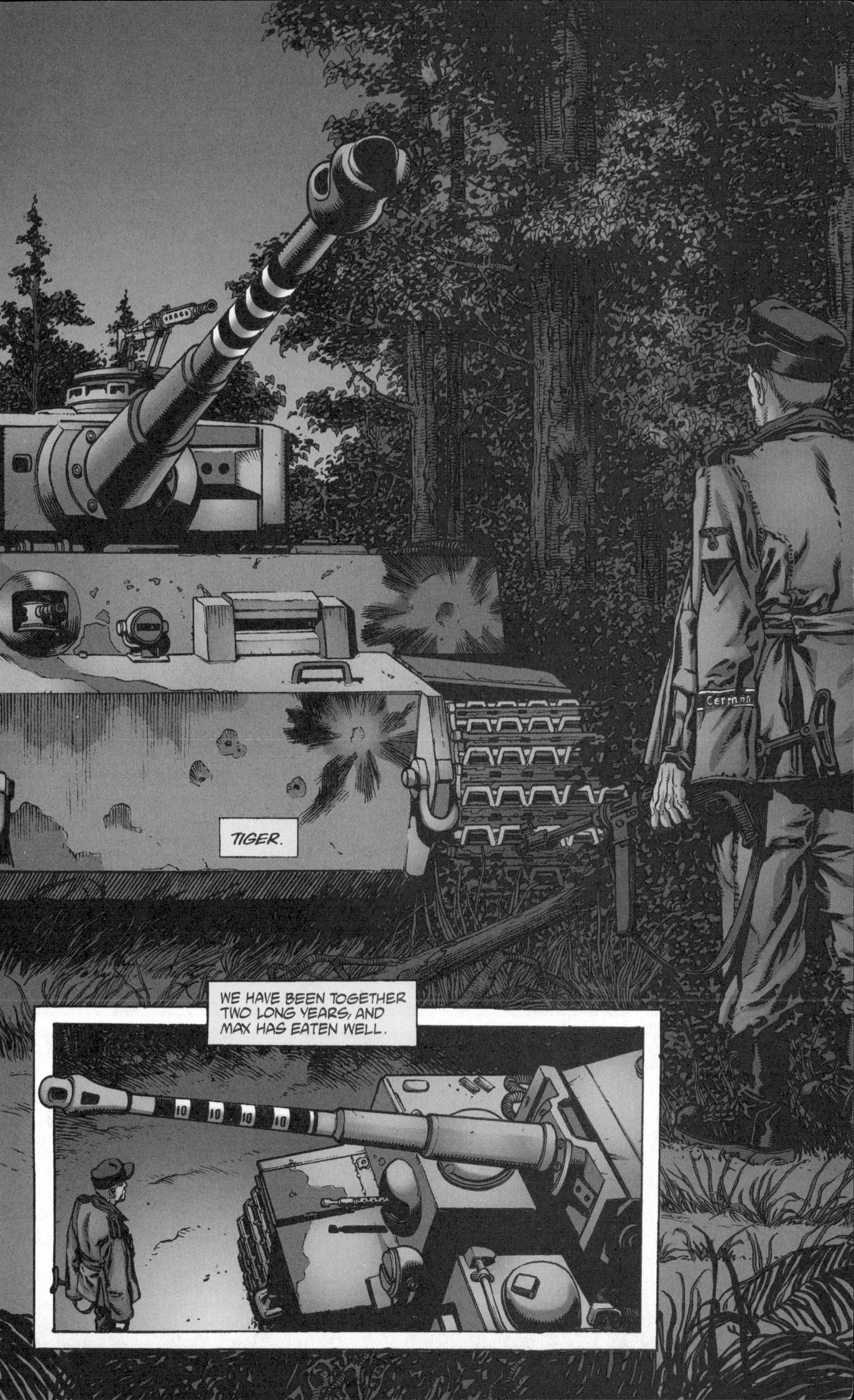
TIGER.
WE HAVE BEEN TOGETHER TWO LONG YEARS, AND MAX HAS EATEN WELL.

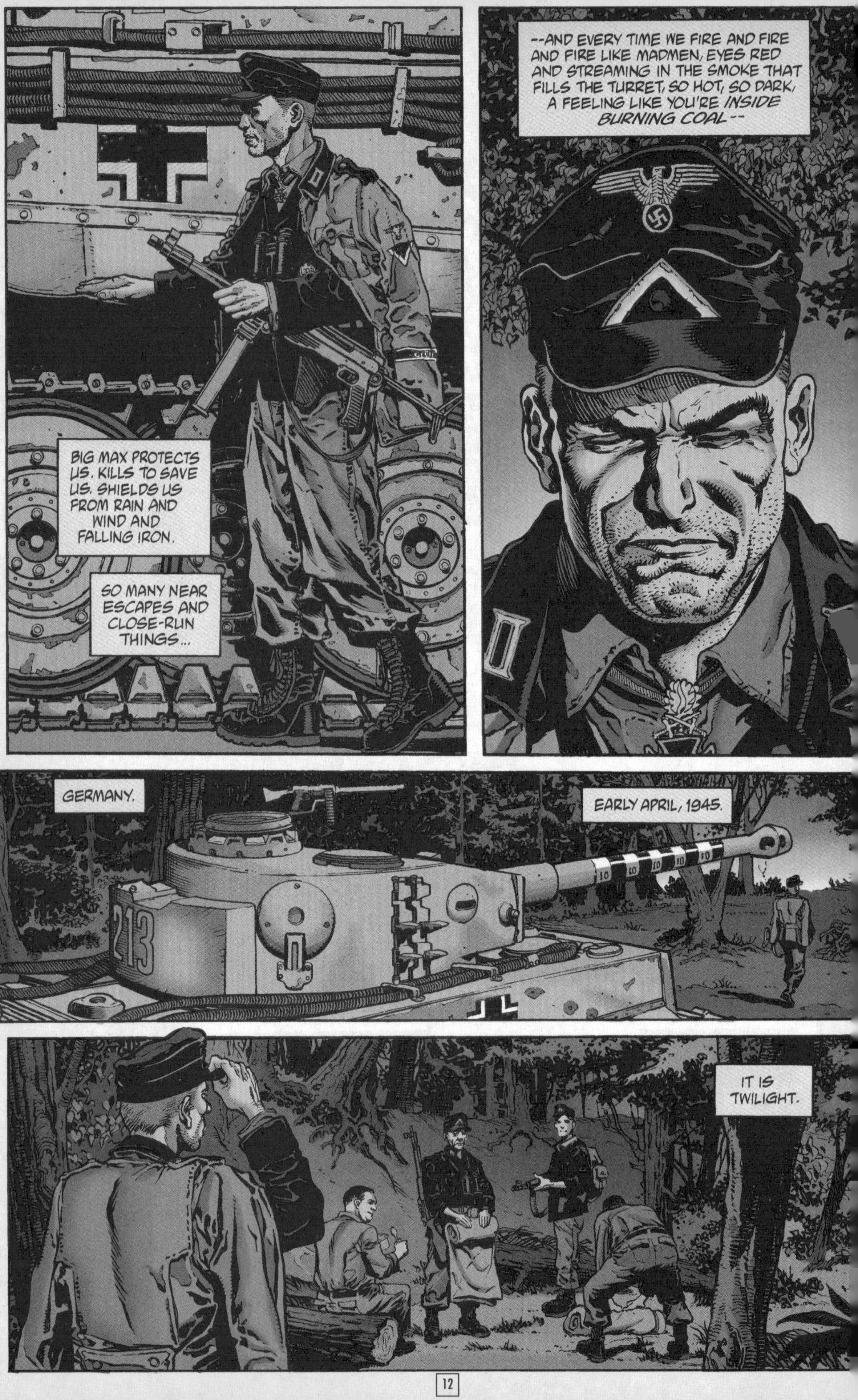
BIG MAX PROTECTS US. KILLS TO SAVE US. SHIELDS US FROM RAIN AND WIND AND FALLING IRON.
SO MANY NEAR ESCAPES AND CLOSE-RUN THINGS...
--AND EVERY TIME WE FIRE AND FIRE AND FIRE LIKE MADMEN, EYES RED AND STREAMING IN THE SMOKE THAT FILLS THE TURRET, SO HOT, SO DARK, A FEELING LIKE YOU'RE *INSIDE BURNING COAL*--
GERMANY.
EARLY APRIL, 1945.
IT IS TWILIGHT.

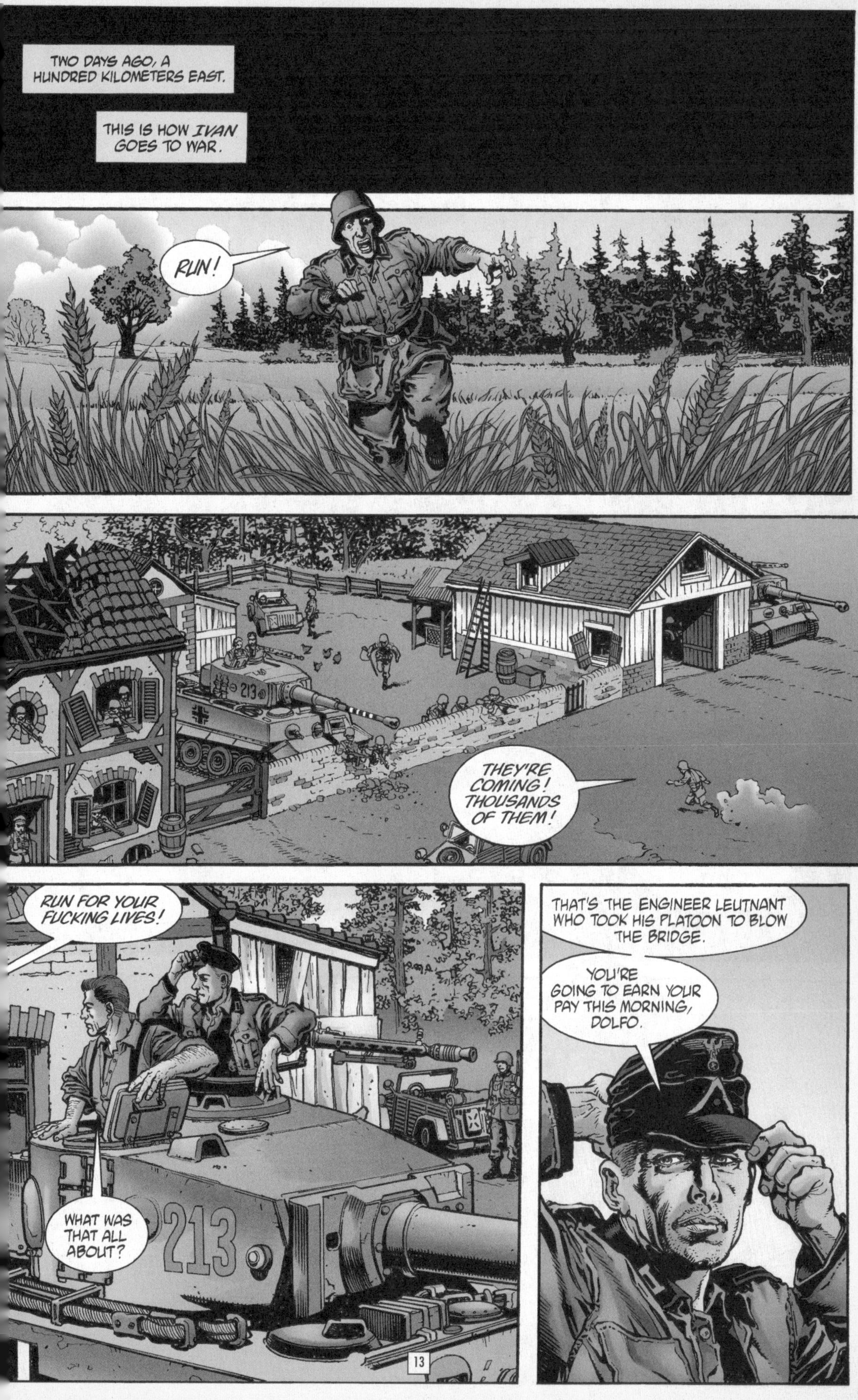
TWO DAYS AGO, A HUNDRED KILOMETERS EAST.
THIS IS HOW IVAN GOES TO WAR.
RUN!
THEY'RE COMING! THOUSANDS OF THEM!
RUN FOR YOUR FUCKING LIVES!
WHAT WAS THAT ALL ABOUT?
THAT'S THE ENGINEER LEUTNANT WHO TOOK HIS PLATOON TO BLOW THE BRIDGE.
YOU'RE GOING TO EARN YOUR PAY THIS MORNING, DOLFO.

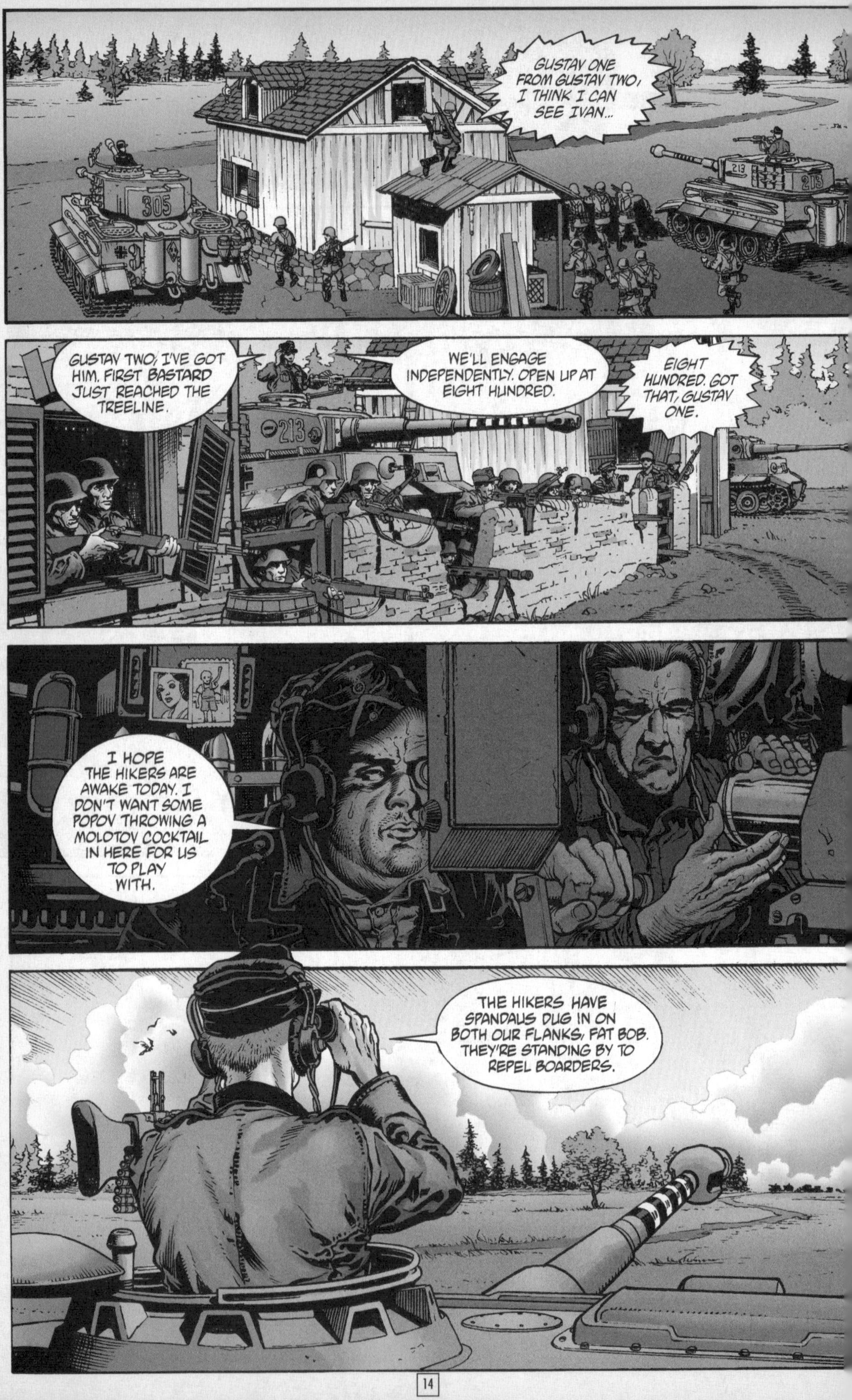
GUSTAV ONE FROM GUSTAV TWO, I THINK I CAN SEE IVAN...
GUSTAV TWO, I'VE GOT HIM. FIRST BASTARD JUST REACHED THE TREELINE.
WE'LL ENGAGE INDEPENDENTLY. OPEN UP AT EIGHT HUNDRED.
EIGHT HUNDRED. GOT THAT, GUSTAV ONE.
I HOPE THE HIKERS ARE AWAKE TODAY. I DON'T WANT SOME POPOV THROWING A MOLOTOV COCKTAIL IN HERE FOR US TO PLAY WITH.
THE HIKERS HAVE SPANDAUS DUG IN ON BOTH OUR FLANKS, FAT BOB. THEY'RE STANDING BY TO REPEL BOARDERS.
213
305

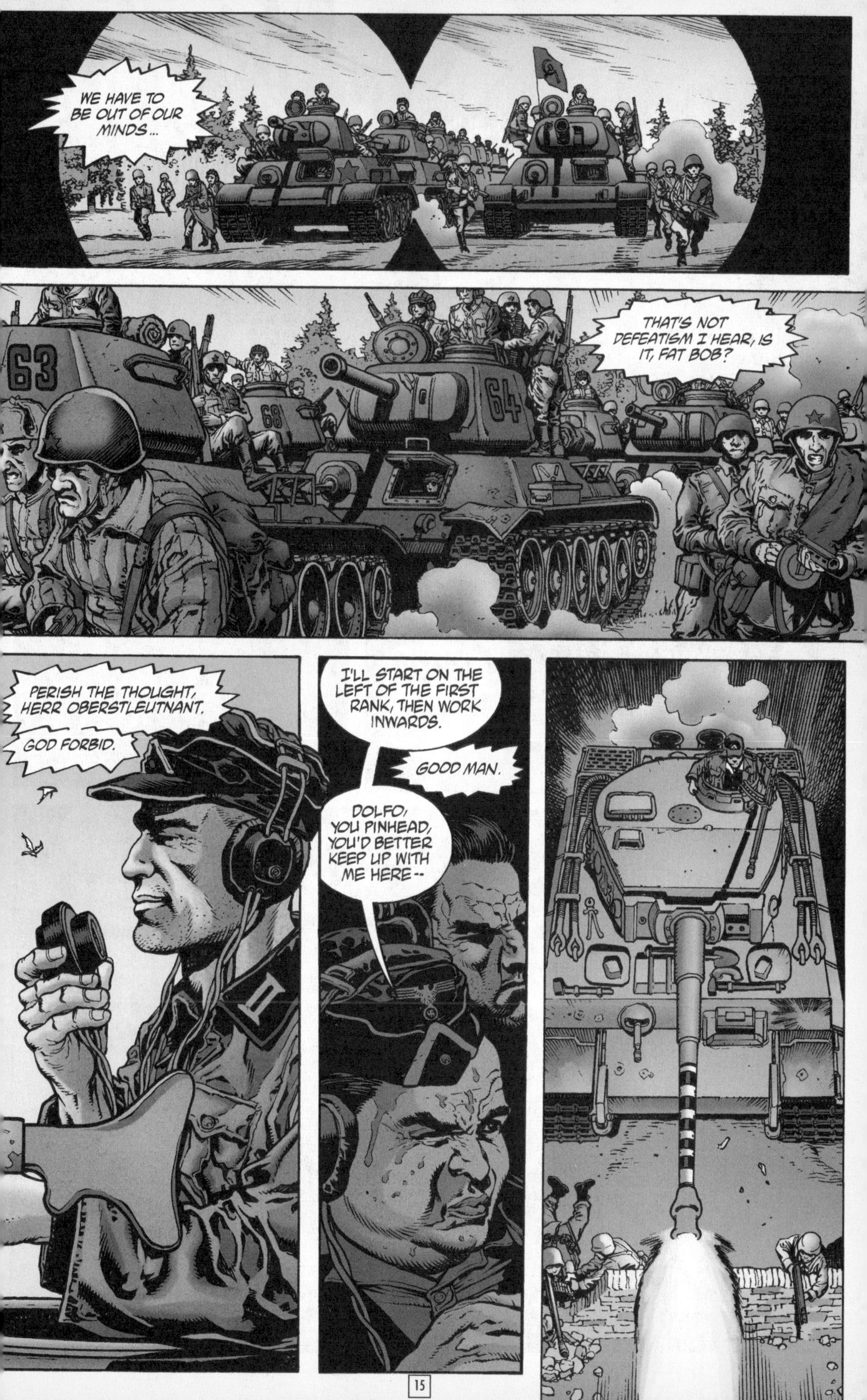

WE HAVE TO BE OUT OF OUR MINDS...
THAT'S NOT DEFEATISM I HEAR, IS IT, FAT BOB?
PERISH THE THOUGHT, HERR OBERSTLEUTNANT.
GOD FORBID.
I'LL START ON THE LEFT OF THE FIRST RANK, THEN WORK INWARDS.
GOOD MAN.
DOLFO, YOU PINHEAD, YOU'D BETTER KEEP UP WITH ME HERE--

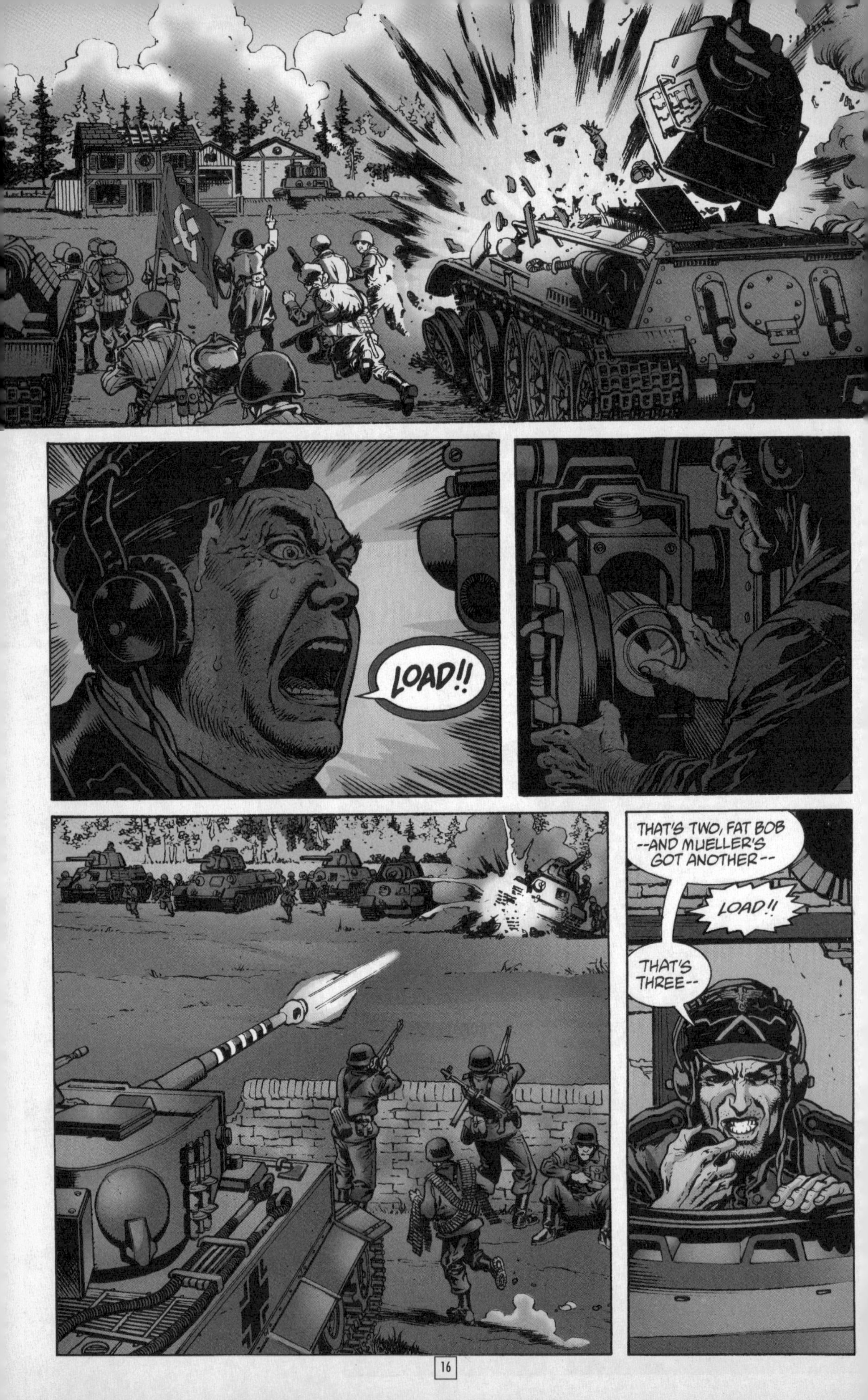
LOAD!!
THAT'S TWO, FAT BOB --AND MUELLER'S GOT ANOTHER--
LOAD!!
THAT'S THREE--

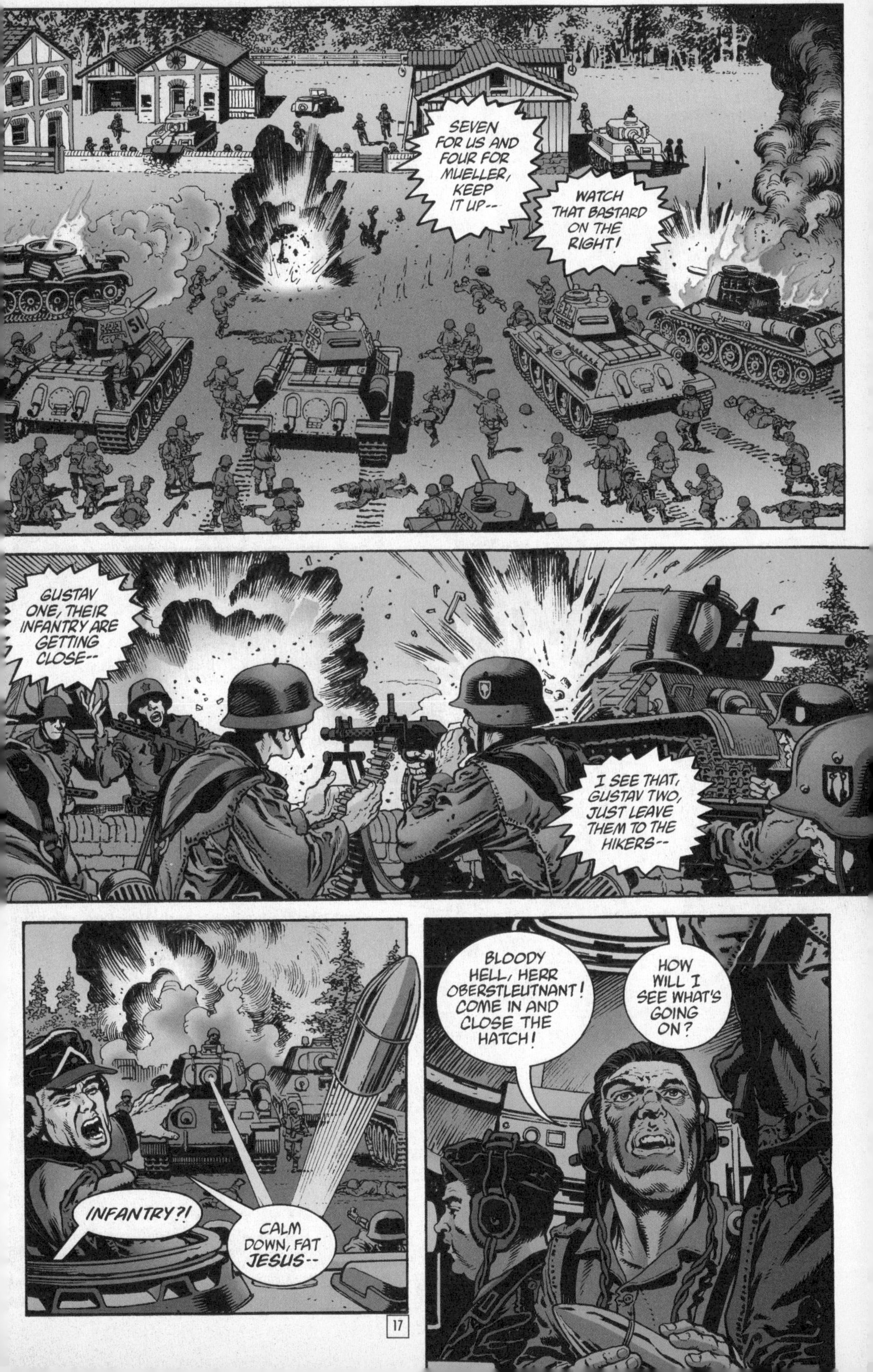
SEVEN FOR US AND FOUR FOR MUELLER, KEEP IT UP--
WATCH THAT BASTARD ON THE RIGHT!
GUSTAV ONE, THEIR INFANTRY ARE GETTING CLOSE--
I SEE THAT, GUSTAV TWO, JUST LEAVE THEM TO THE HIKERS--
INFANTRY?!
CALM DOWN, FAT JESUS--
BLOODY HELL, HERR OBERSTLEUTNANT! COME IN AND CLOSE THE HATCH!
HOW WILL I SEE WHAT'S GOING ON?

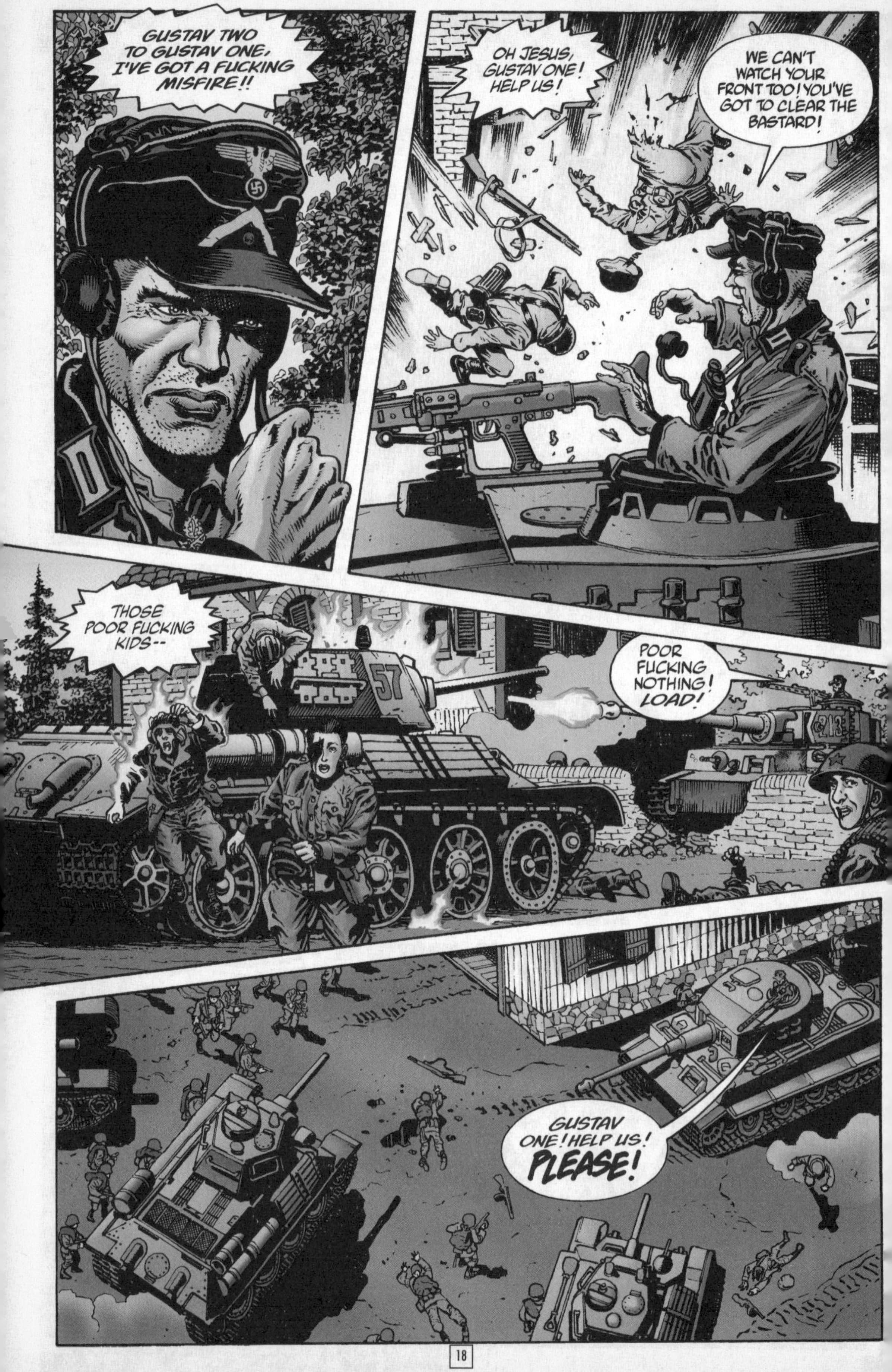
GUSTAV TWO TO GUSTAV ONE, I'VE GOT A FUCKING MISFIRE!!
OH JESUS, GUSTAV ONE! HELP US!
WE CAN'T WATCH YOUR FRONT TOO! YOU'VE GOT TO CLEAR THE BASTARD!
THOSE POOR FUCKING KIDS--
57
POOR FUCKING NOTHING! LOAD!
GUSTAV ONE! HELP US! PLEASE!

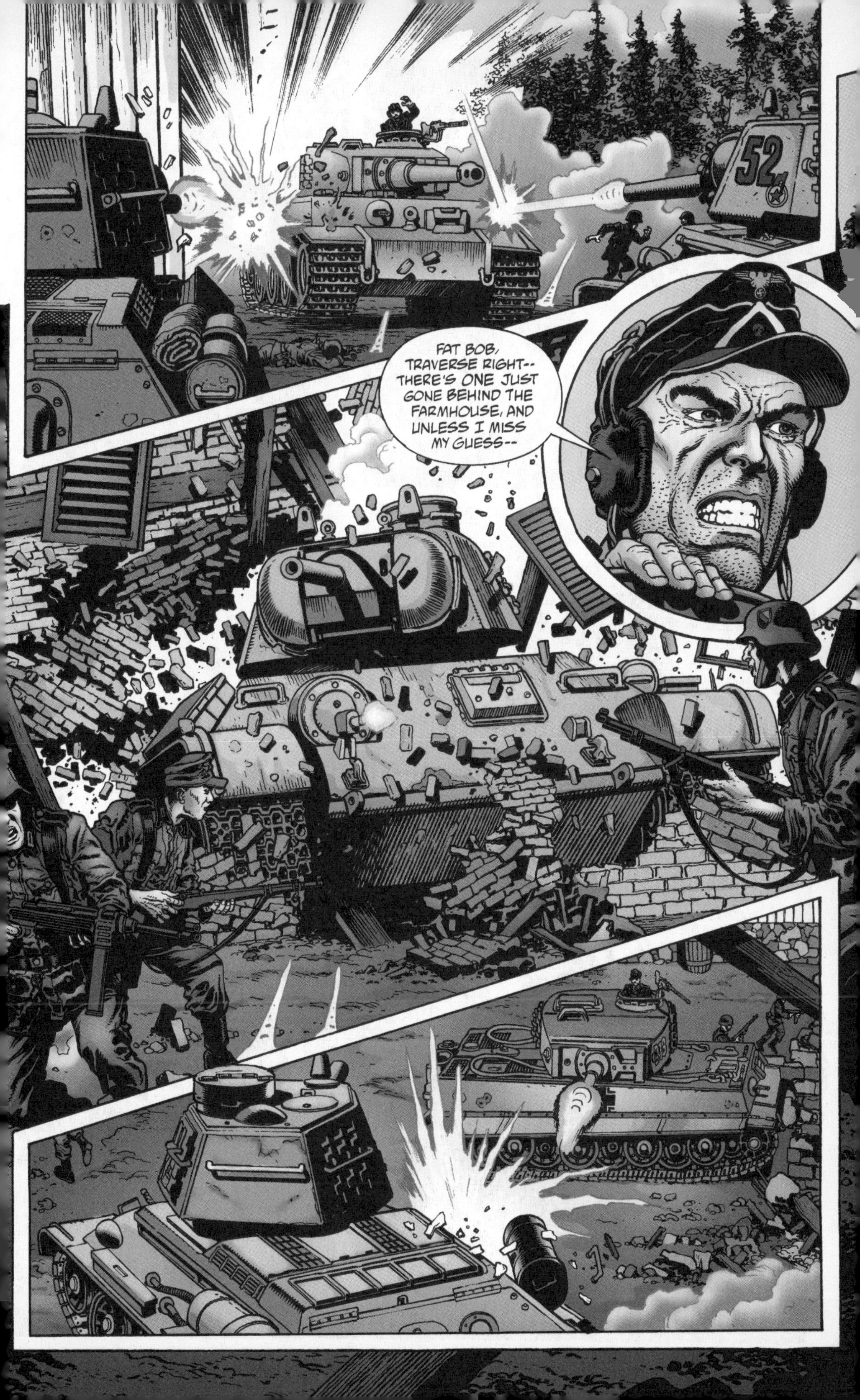
FAT BOB, TRAVERSE RIGHT-- THERE'S ONE JUST GONE BEHIND THE FARMHOUSE, AND UNLESS I MISS MY GUESS--

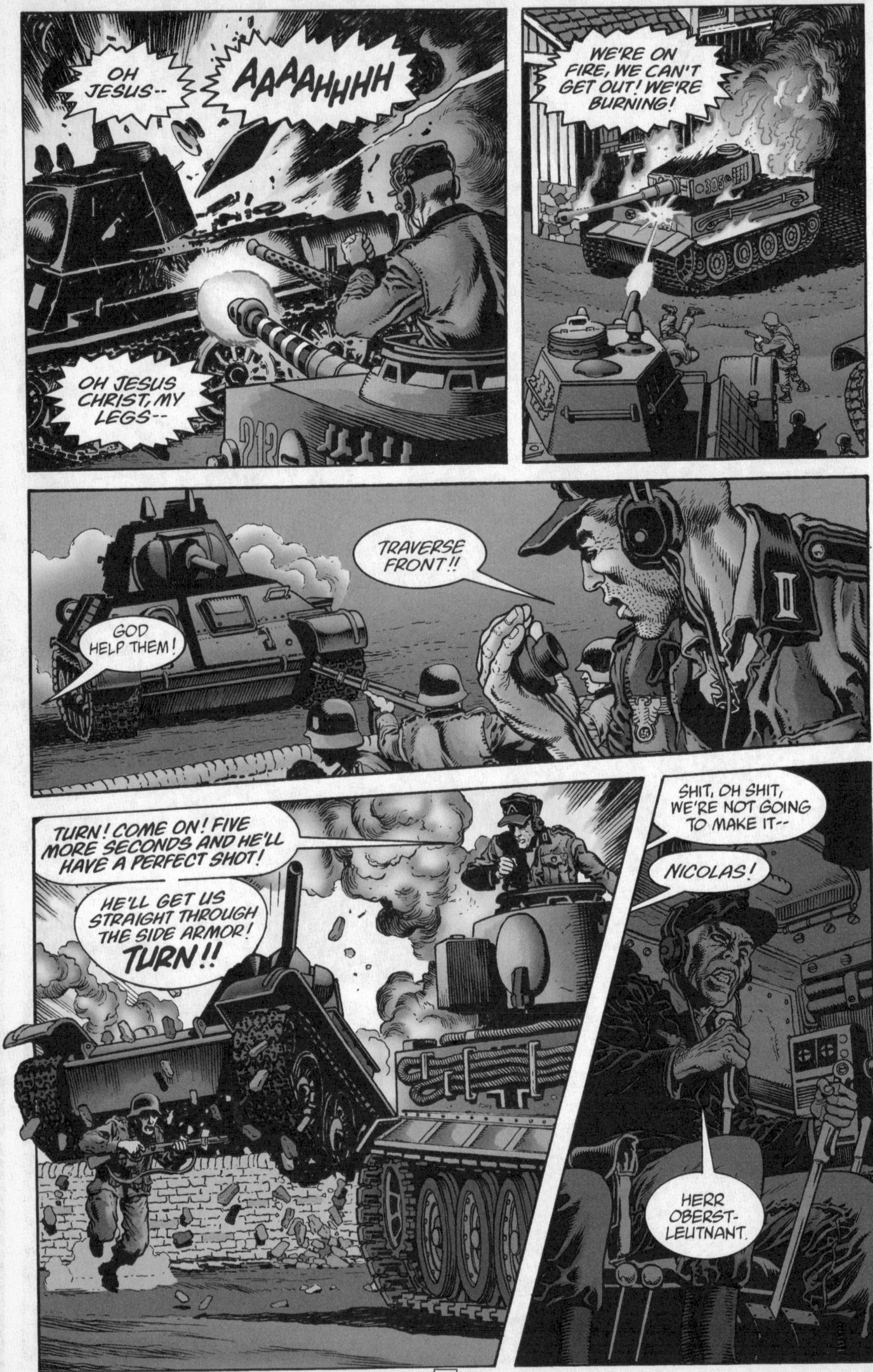
OH JESUS--
AAAAHHHH
OH JESUS CHRIST, MY LEGS--
WE'RE ON FIRE, WE CAN'T GET OUT! WE'RE BURNING!
TRAVERSE FRONT!!
GOD HELP THEM!
TURN! COME ON! FIVE MORE SECONDS AND HE'LL HAVE A PERFECT SHOT!
HE'LL GET US STRAIGHT THROUGH THE SIDE ARMOR! TURN!!
SHIT, OH SHIT, WE'RE NOT GOING TO MAKE IT--
NICOLAS!
HERR OBERST-LEUTNANT.

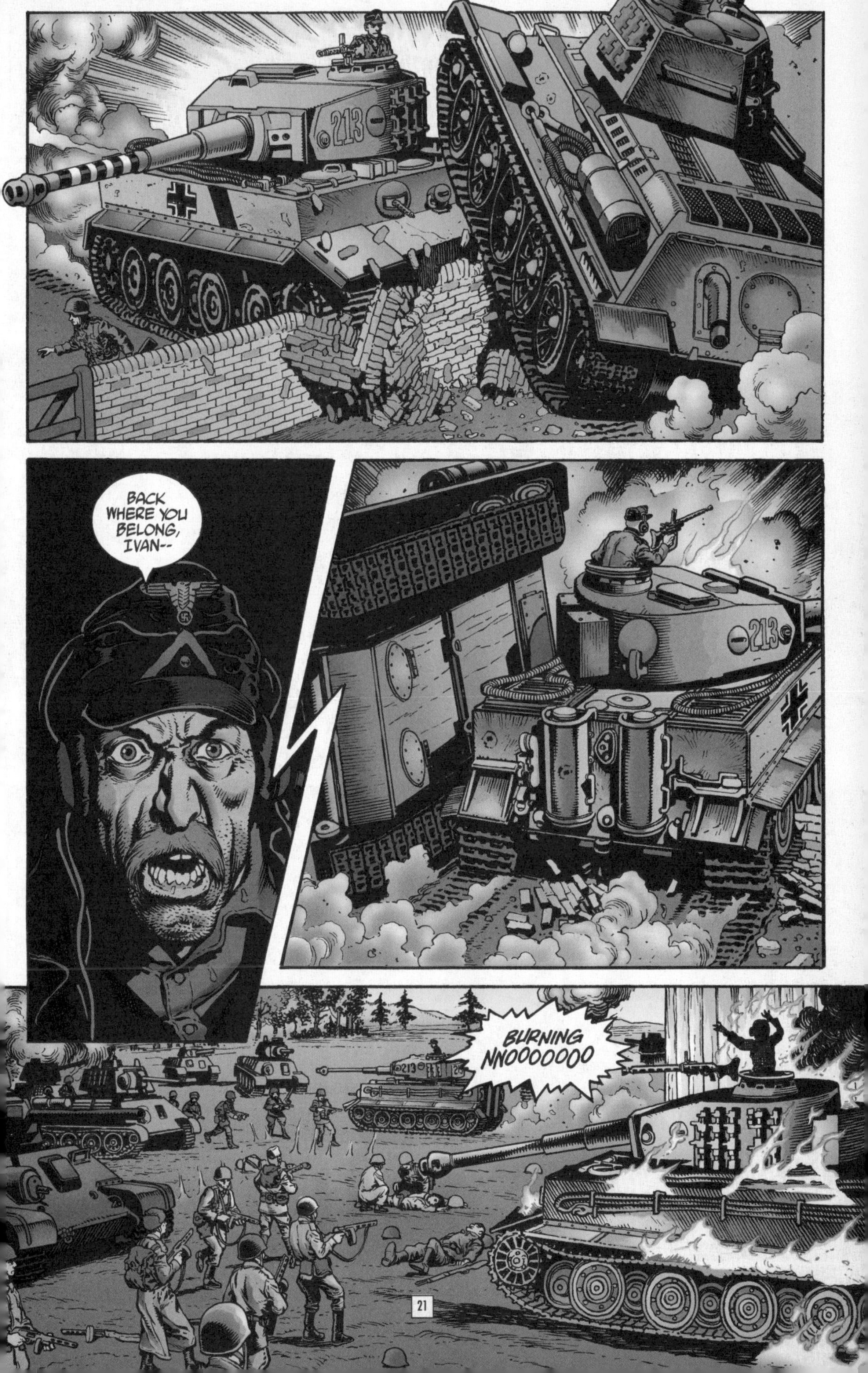
BACK WHERE YOU BELONG, IVAN--
BURNING
NNOOOOOOO

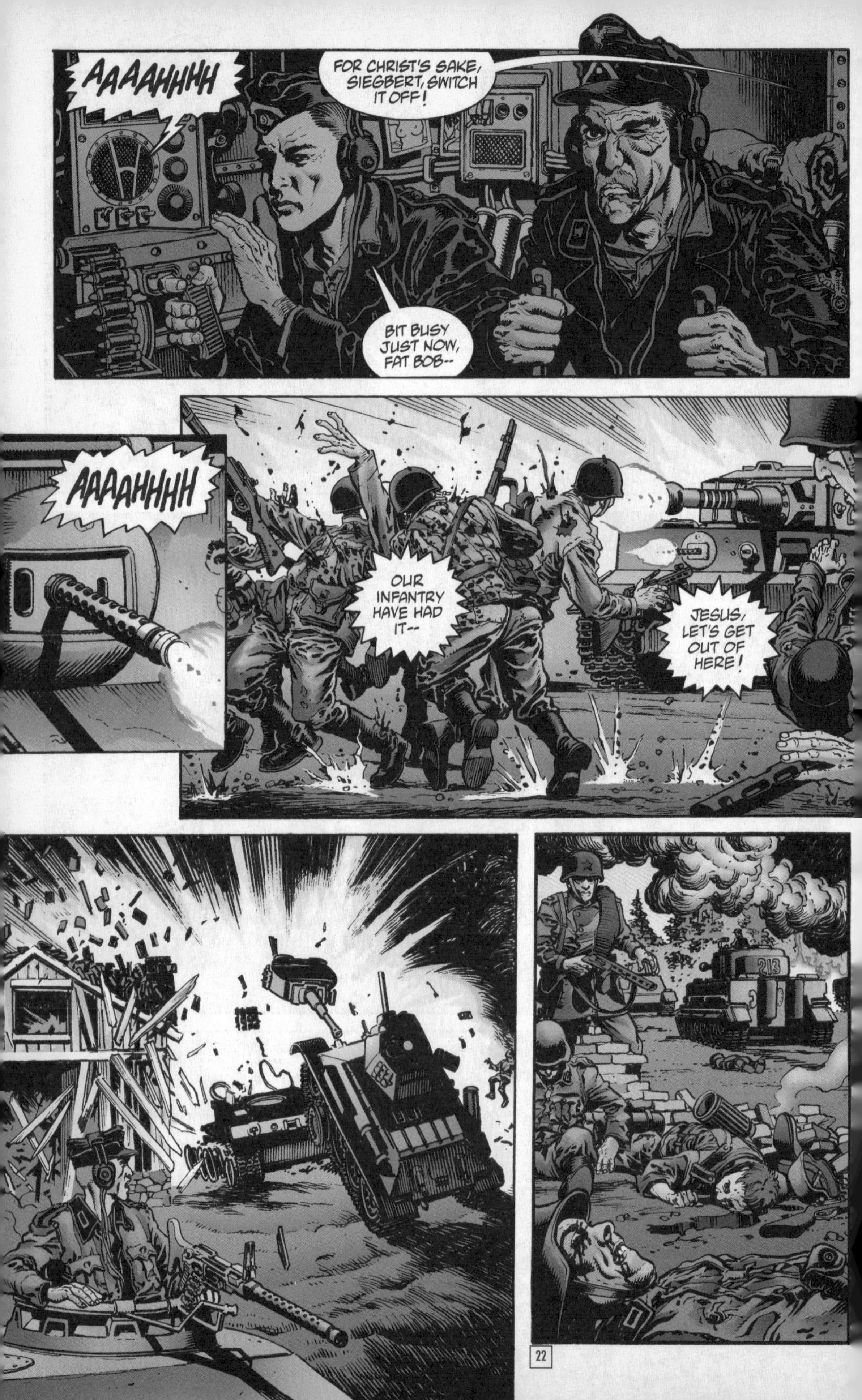
AAAAHHHH
FOR CHRIST'S SAKE, SIEGBERT, SWITCH IT OFF!
BIT BUSY JUST NOW, FAT BOB--
AAAAHHHH
OUR INFANTRY HAVE HAD IT--
JESUS, LET'S GET OUT OF HERE!
213

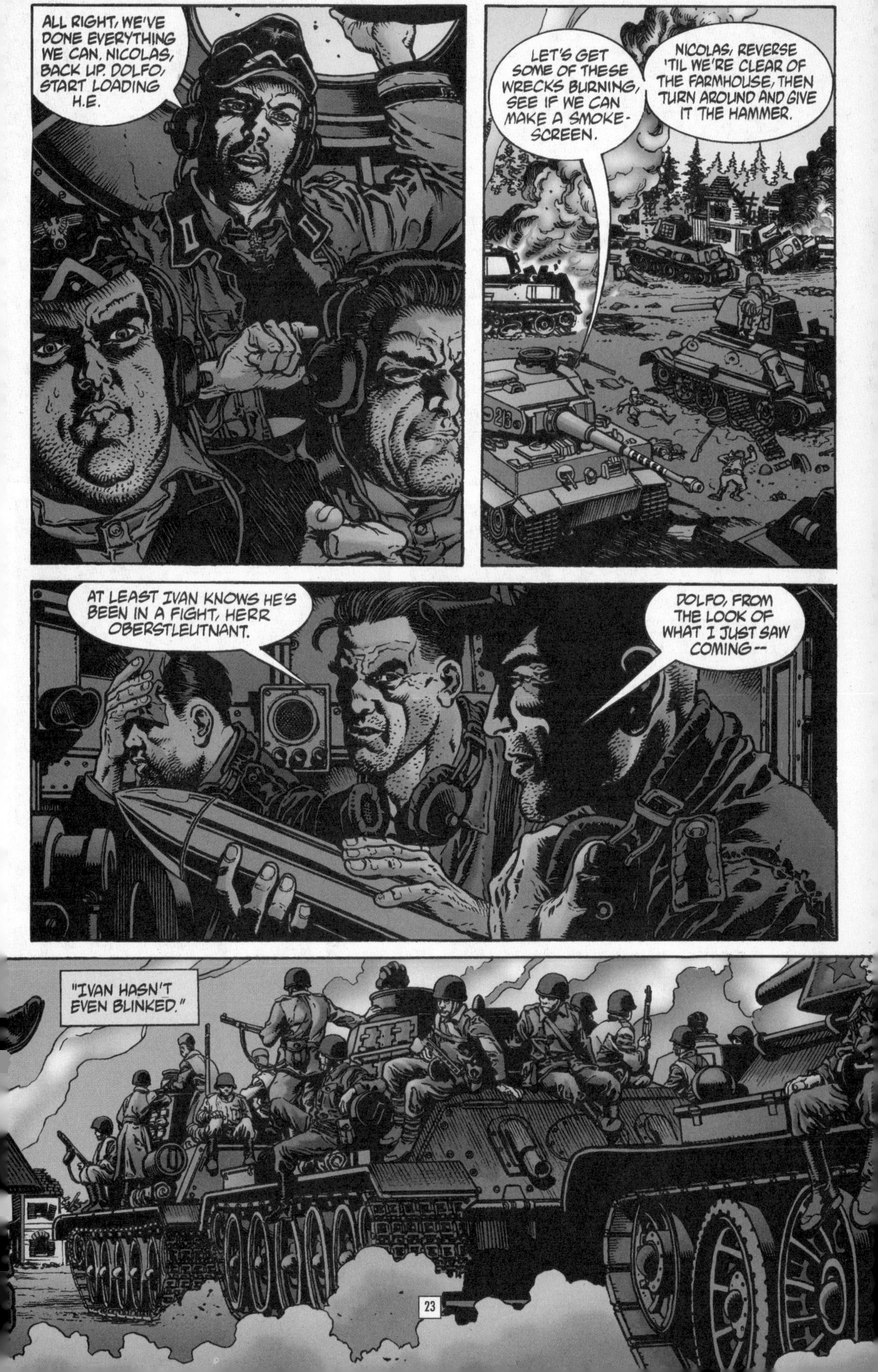
ALL RIGHT, WE'VE DONE EVERYTHING WE CAN. NICOLAS, BACK UP. DOLFO, START LOADING H.E.
LET'S GET SOME OF THESE WRECKS BURNING, SEE IF WE CAN MAKE A SMOKE-SCREEN.
NICOLAS, REVERSE 'TIL WE'RE CLEAR OF THE FARMHOUSE, THEN TURN AROUND AND GIVE IT THE HAMMER.
AT LEAST IVAN KNOWS HE'S BEEN IN A FIGHT, HERR OBERSTLEUTNANT.
DOLFO, FROM THE LOOK OF WHAT I JUST SAW COMING--
"IVAN HASN'T EVEN BLINKED."

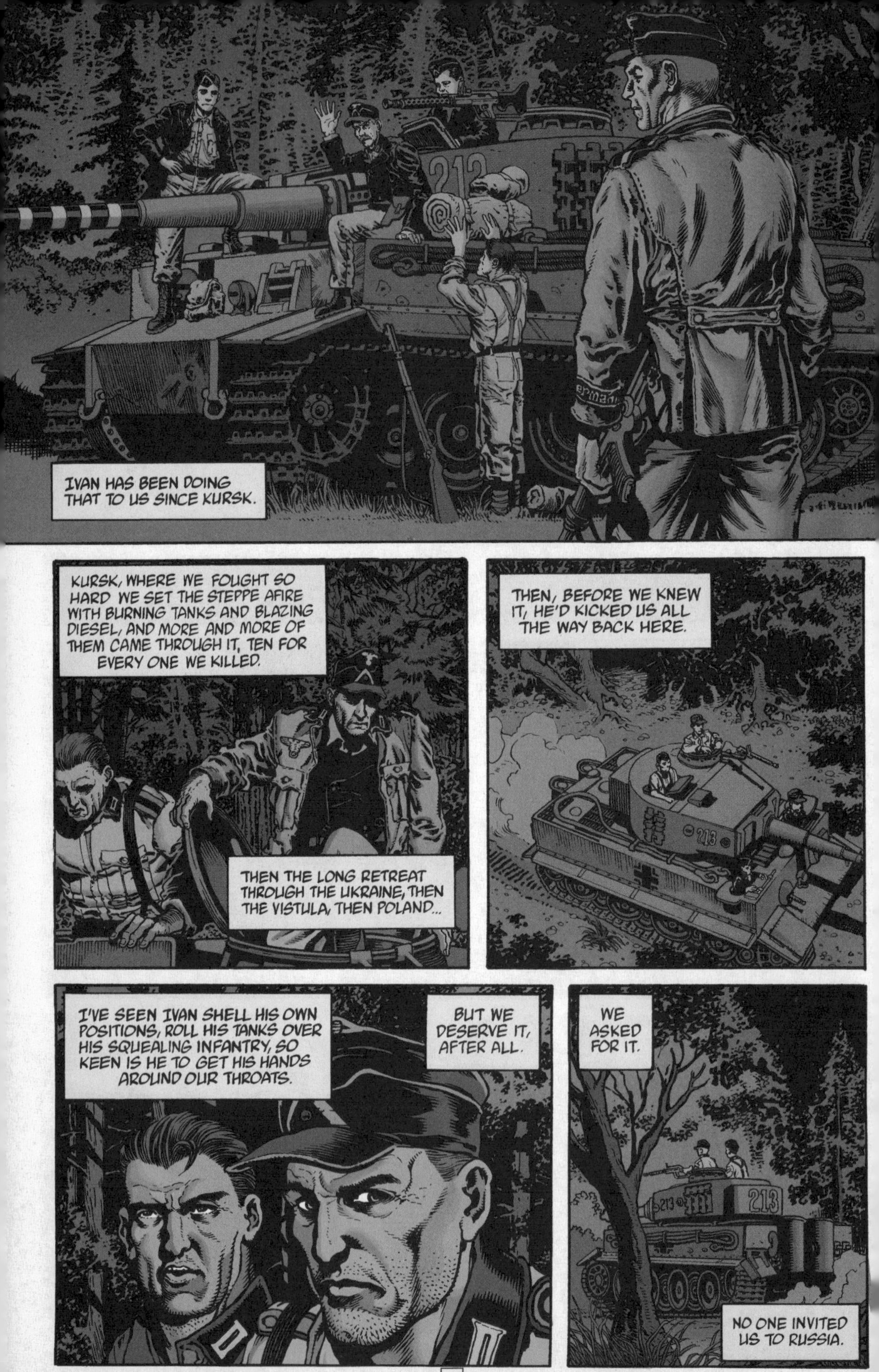
IVAN HAS BEEN DOING THAT TO US SINCE KURSK.
KURSK, WHERE WE FOUGHT SO HARD WE SET THE STEPPE AFIRE WITH BURNING TANKS AND BLAZING DIESEL, AND MORE AND MORE OF THEM CAME THROUGH IT, TEN FOR EVERY ONE WE KILLED.
THEN THE LONG RETREAT THROUGH THE UKRAINE, THEN THE VISTULA, THEN POLAND...
THEN, BEFORE WE KNEW IT, HE'D KICKED US ALL THE WAY BACK HERE.
213
I'VE SEEN IVAN SHELL HIS OWN POSITIONS, ROLL HIS TANKS OVER HIS SQUEALING INFANTRY, SO KEEN IS HE TO GET HIS HANDS AROUND OUR THROATS.
BUT WE DESERVE IT, AFTER ALL.
WE ASKED FOR IT.
213
NO ONE INVITED US TO RUSSIA.

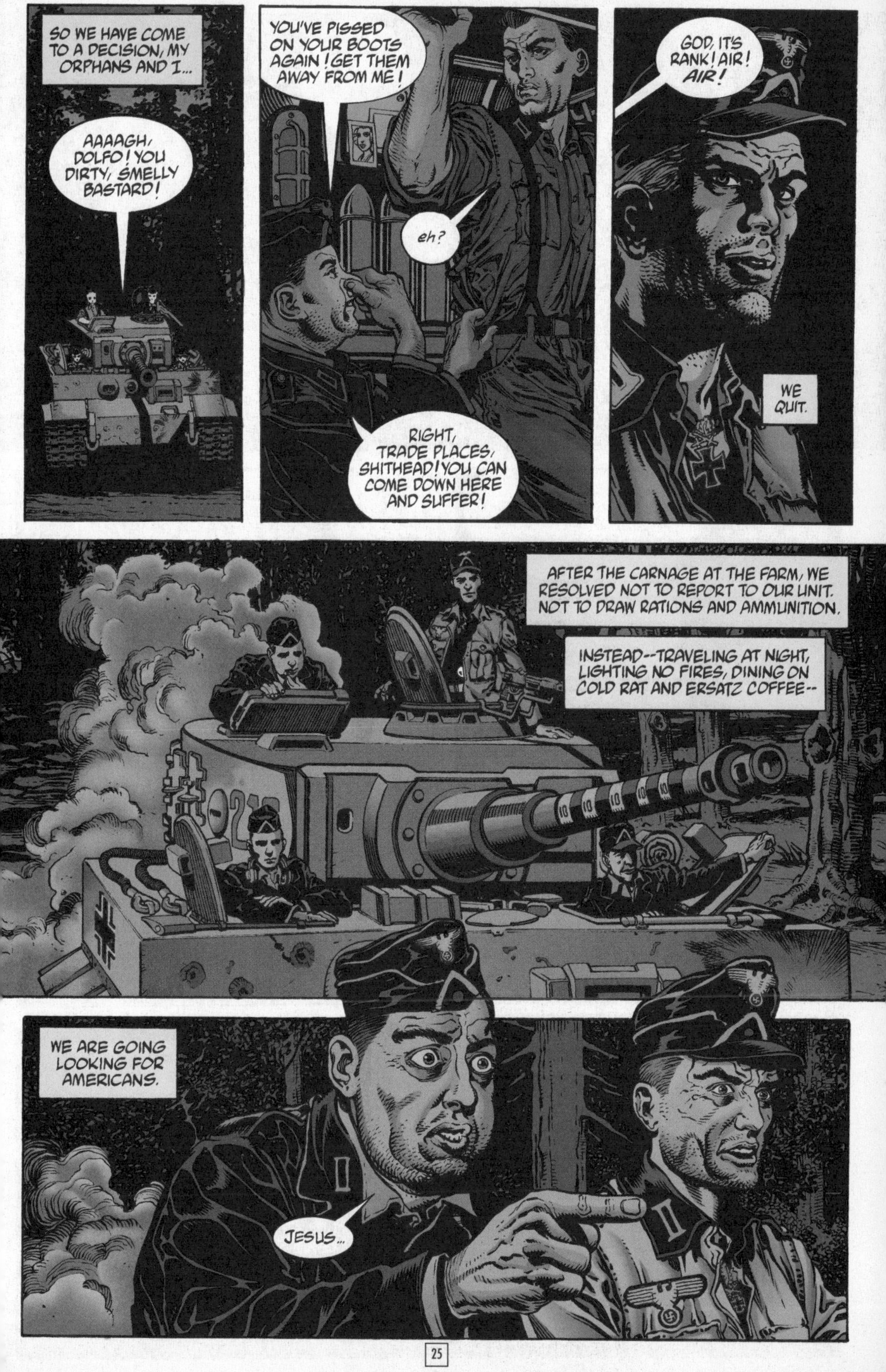
SO WE HAVE COME TO A DECISION, MY ORPHANS AND I...
AAAAGH, DOLFO! YOU DIRTY, SMELLY BASTARD!
YOU'VE PISSED ON YOUR BOOTS AGAIN! GET THEM AWAY FROM ME!
eh?
RIGHT, TRADE PLACES, SHITHEAD! YOU CAN COME DOWN HERE AND SUFFER!
GOD, IT'S RANK! AIR! AIR!
WE QUIT.
AFTER THE CARNAGE AT THE FARM, WE RESOLVED NOT TO REPORT TO OUR UNIT. NOT TO DRAW RATIONS AND AMMUNITION.
INSTEAD--TRAVELING AT NIGHT, LIGHTING NO FIRES, DINING ON COLD RAT AND ERSATZ COFFEE--
WE ARE GOING LOOKING FOR AMERICANS.
JESUS...

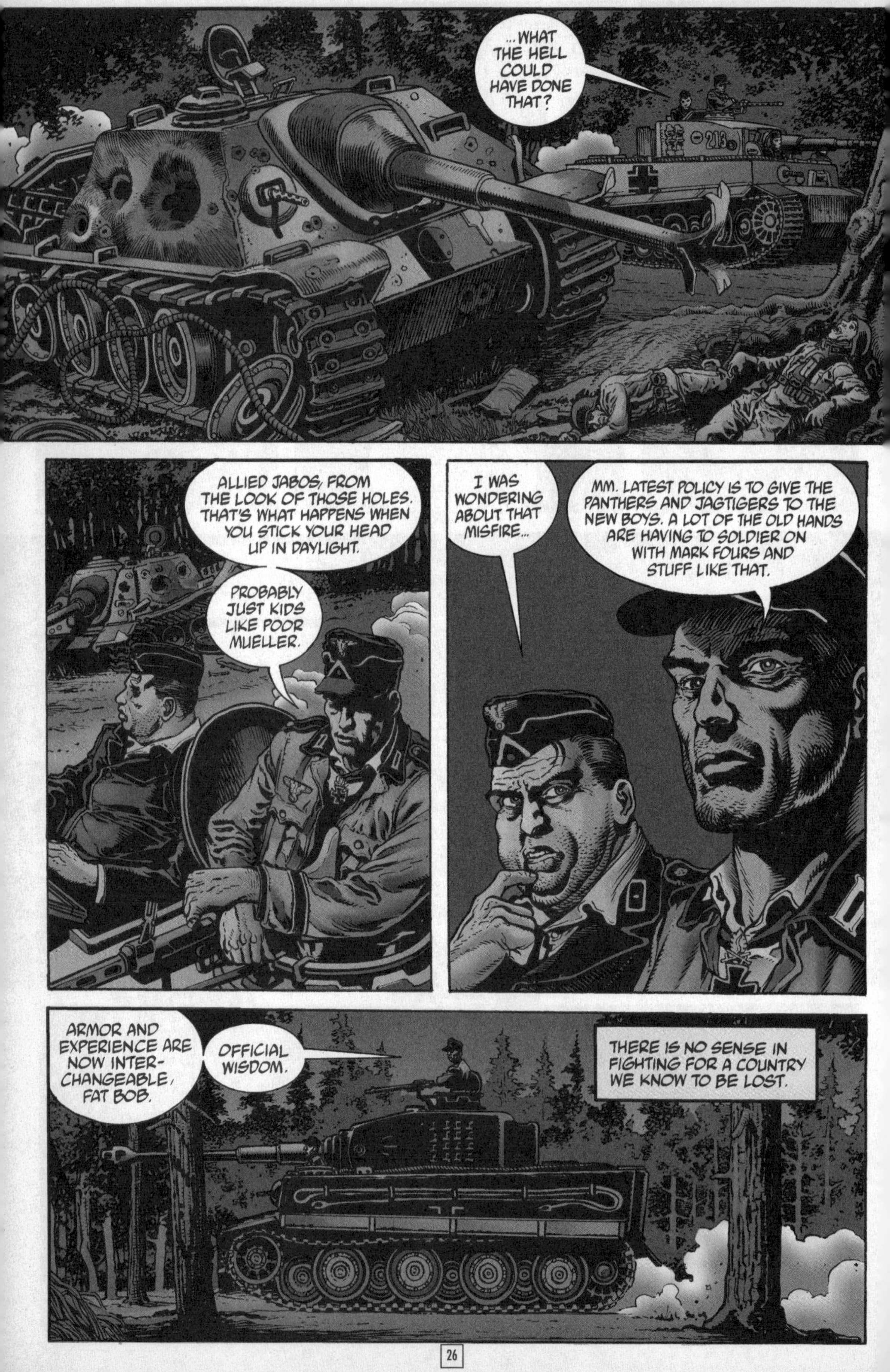
...WHAT THE HELL COULD HAVE DONE THAT?
ALLIED JABOS, FROM THE LOOK OF THOSE HOLES. THAT'S WHAT HAPPENS WHEN YOU STICK YOUR HEAD UP IN DAYLIGHT.
PROBABLY JUST KIDS LIKE POOR MUELLER.
I WAS WONDERING ABOUT THAT MISFIRE...
MM. LATEST POLICY IS TO GIVE THE PANTHERS AND JAGTIGERS TO THE NEW BOYS. A LOT OF THE OLD HANDS ARE HAVING TO SOLDIER ON WITH MARK FOURS AND STUFF LIKE THAT.
ARMOR AND EXPERIENCE ARE NOW INTER-CHANGEABLE, FAT BOB.
OFFICIAL WISDOM.
THERE IS NO SENSE IN FIGHTING FOR A COUNTRY WE KNOW TO BE LOST.

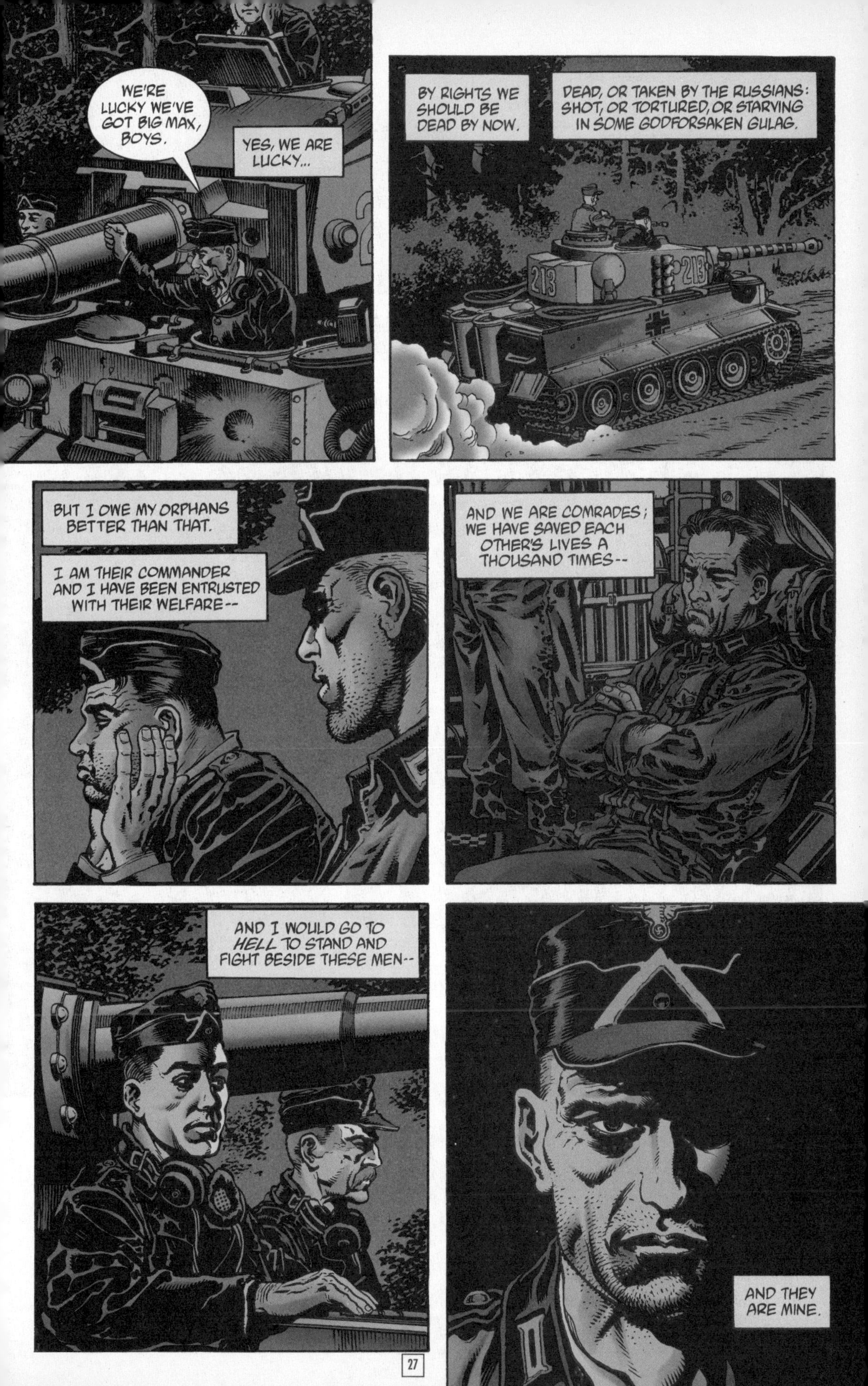

WE'RE LUCKY WE'VE GOT BIG MAX, BOYS.
YES, WE ARE LUCKY...
BY RIGHTS WE SHOULD BE DEAD BY NOW.
DEAD, OR TAKEN BY THE RUSSIANS: SHOT, OR TORTURED, OR STARVING IN SOME GODFORSAKEN GULAG.
213
213
BUT I OWE MY ORPHANS BETTER THAN THAT.
I AM THEIR COMMANDER AND I HAVE BEEN ENTRUSTED WITH THEIR WELFARE--
AND WE ARE COMRADES; WE HAVE SAVED EACH OTHER'S LIVES A THOUSAND TIMES--
AND I WOULD GO TO *HELL* TO STAND AND FIGHT BESIDE THESE MEN--
AND THEY ARE MINE.

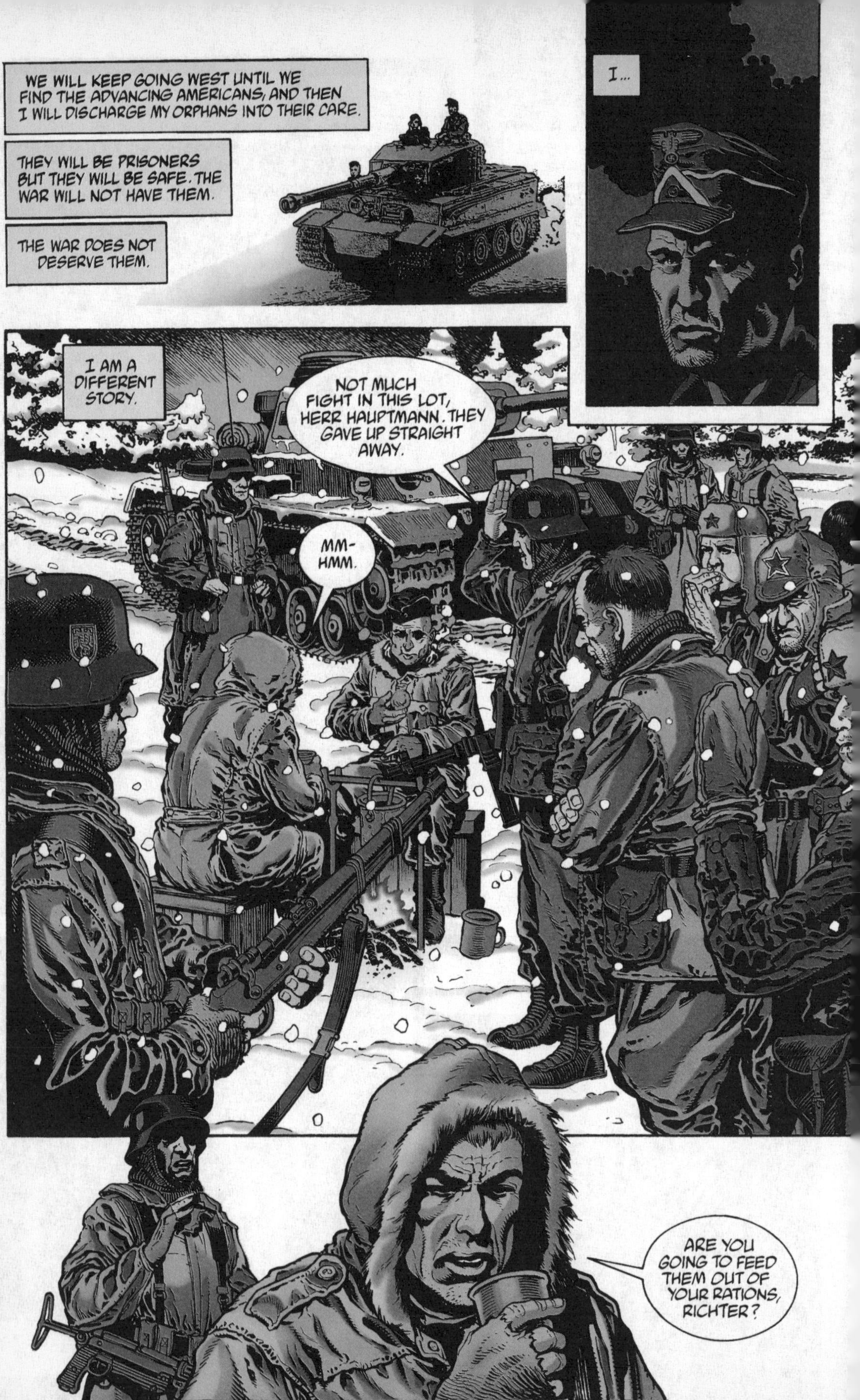
WE WILL KEEP GOING WEST UNTIL WE FIND THE ADVANCING AMERICANS, AND THEN I WILL DISCHARGE MY ORPHANS INTO THEIR CARE.
THEY WILL BE PRISONERS BUT THEY WILL BE SAFE. THE WAR WILL NOT HAVE THEM.
THE WAR DOES NOT DESERVE THEM.
I...
I AM A DIFFERENT STORY.
NOT MUCH FIGHT IN THIS LOT, HERR HAUPTMANN. THEY GAVE UP STRAIGHT AWAY.
MM-HMM.
ARE YOU GOING TO FEED THEM OUT OF YOUR RATIONS, RICHTER?

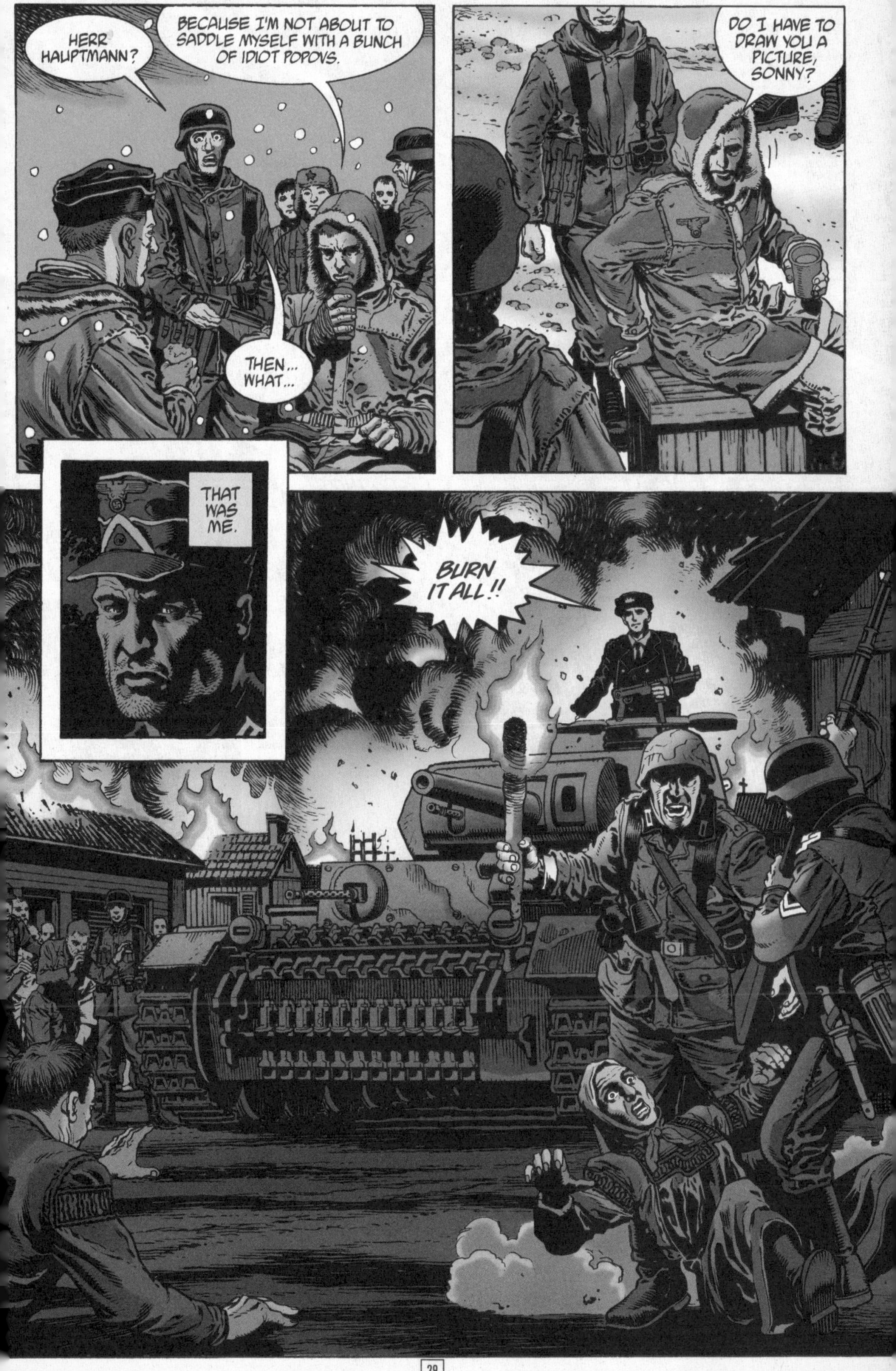
HERR HAUPTMANN?
BECAUSE I'M NOT ABOUT TO SADDLE MYSELF WITH A BUNCH OF IDIOT POPOVS.
THEN... WHAT...
DO I HAVE TO DRAW YOU A PICTURE, SONNY?
THAT WAS ME.
BURN IT ALL!!

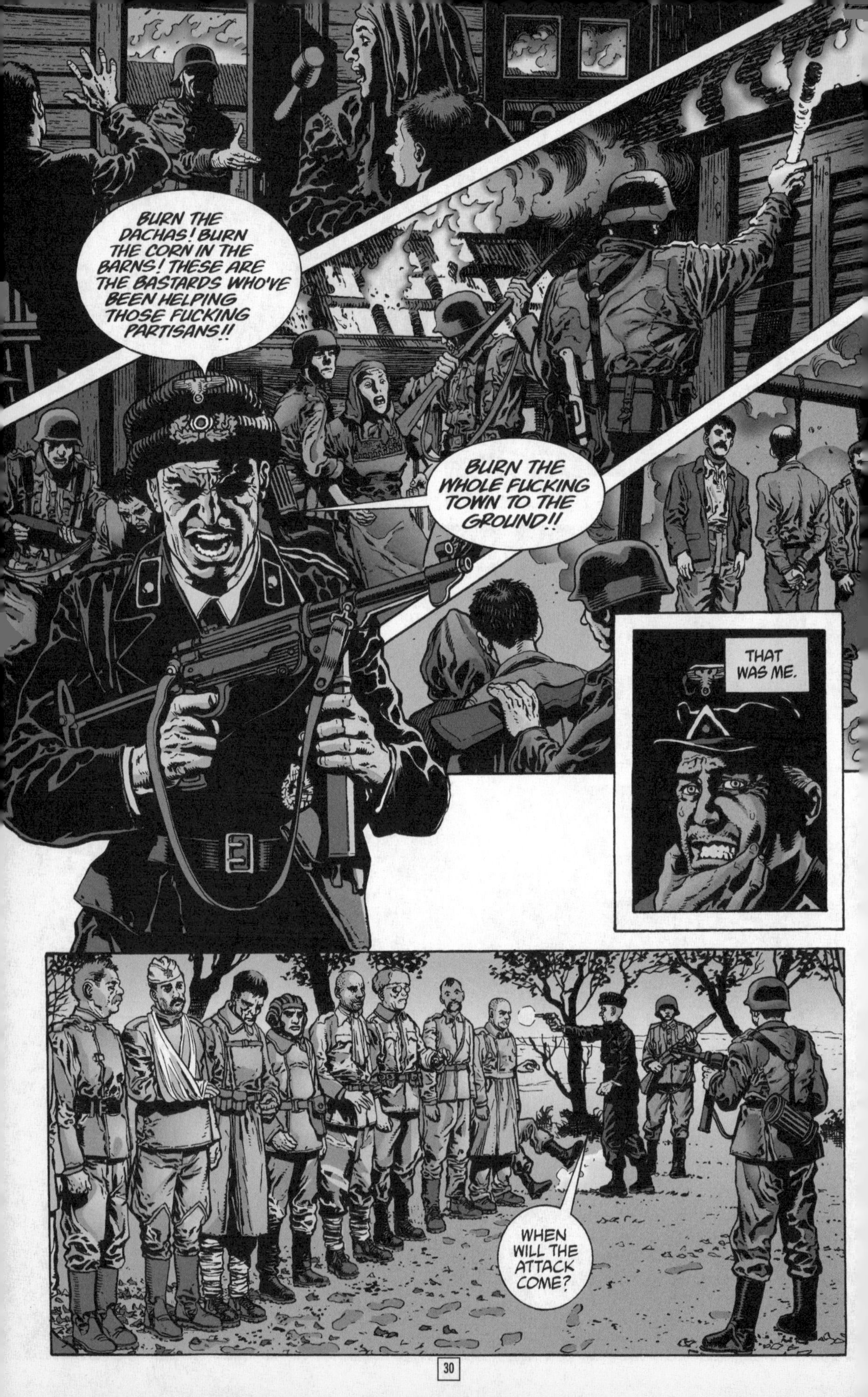
BURN THE DACHAS! BURN THE CORN IN THE BARNS! THESE ARE THE BASTARDS WHO'VE BEEN HELPING THOSE FUCKING PARTISANS!!
BURN THE WHOLE FUCKING TOWN TO THE GROUND!!
THAT WAS ME.
WHEN WILL THE ATTACK COME?

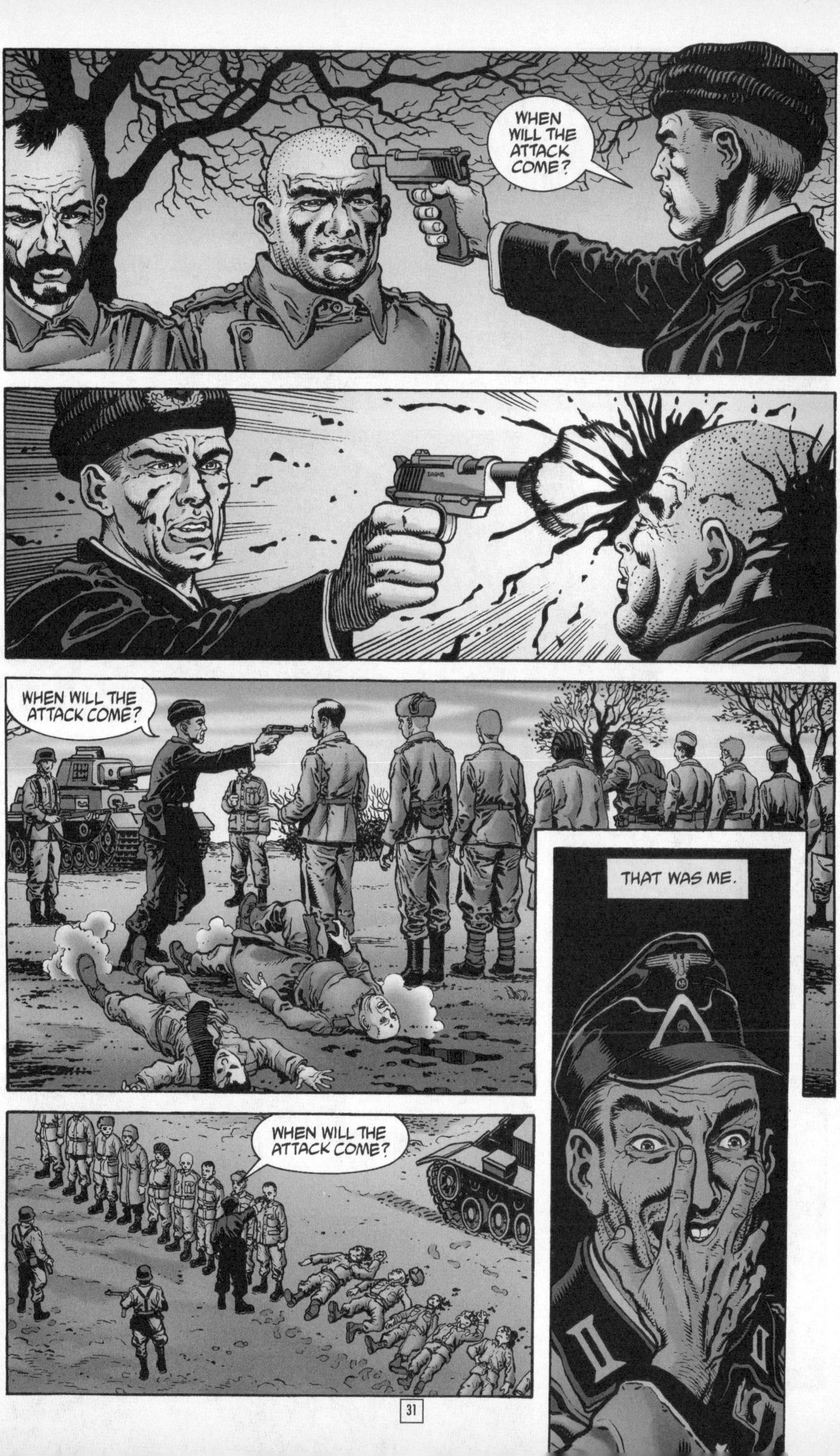
WHEN WILL THE ATTACK COME?
WHEN WILL THE ATTACK COME?
THAT WAS ME.
WHEN WILL THE ATTACK COME?

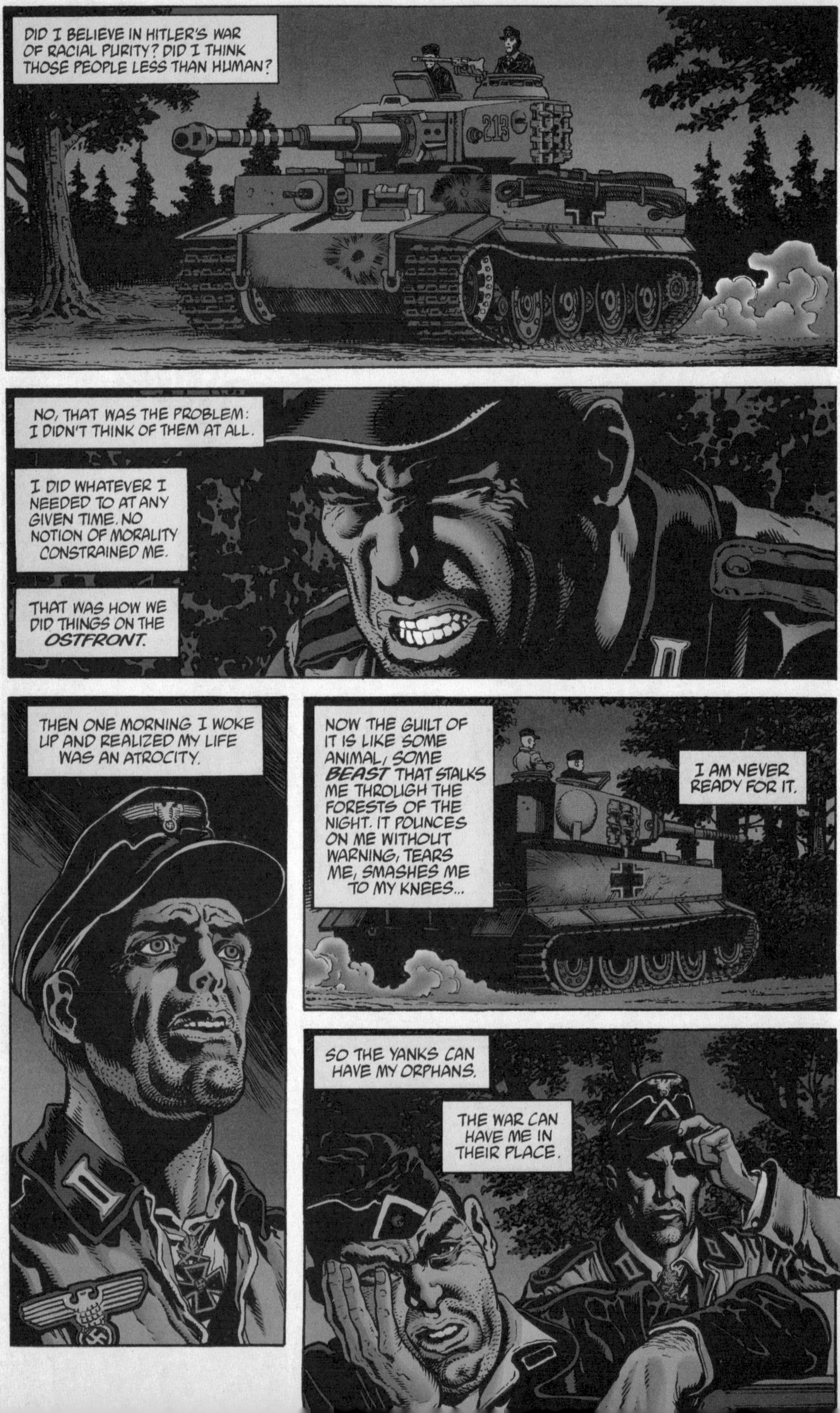
DID I BELIEVE IN HITLER'S WAR OF RACIAL PURITY? DID I THINK THOSE PEOPLE LESS THAN HUMAN?
213
NO, THAT WAS THE PROBLEM: I DIDN'T THINK OF THEM AT ALL.
I DID WHATEVER I NEEDED TO AT ANY GIVEN TIME. NO NOTION OF MORALITY CONSTRAINED ME.
THAT WAS HOW WE DID THINGS ON THE OSTFRONT.
THEN ONE MORNING I WOKE UP AND REALIZED MY LIFE WAS AN ATROCITY.
NOW THE GUILT OF IT IS LIKE SOME ANIMAL, SOME BEAST THAT STALKS ME THROUGH THE FORESTS OF THE NIGHT. IT POUNCES ON ME WITHOUT WARNING, TEARS ME, SMASHES ME TO MY KNEES...
I AM NEVER READY FOR IT.
SO THE YANKS CAN HAVE MY ORPHANS.
THE WAR CAN HAVE ME IN THEIR PLACE.

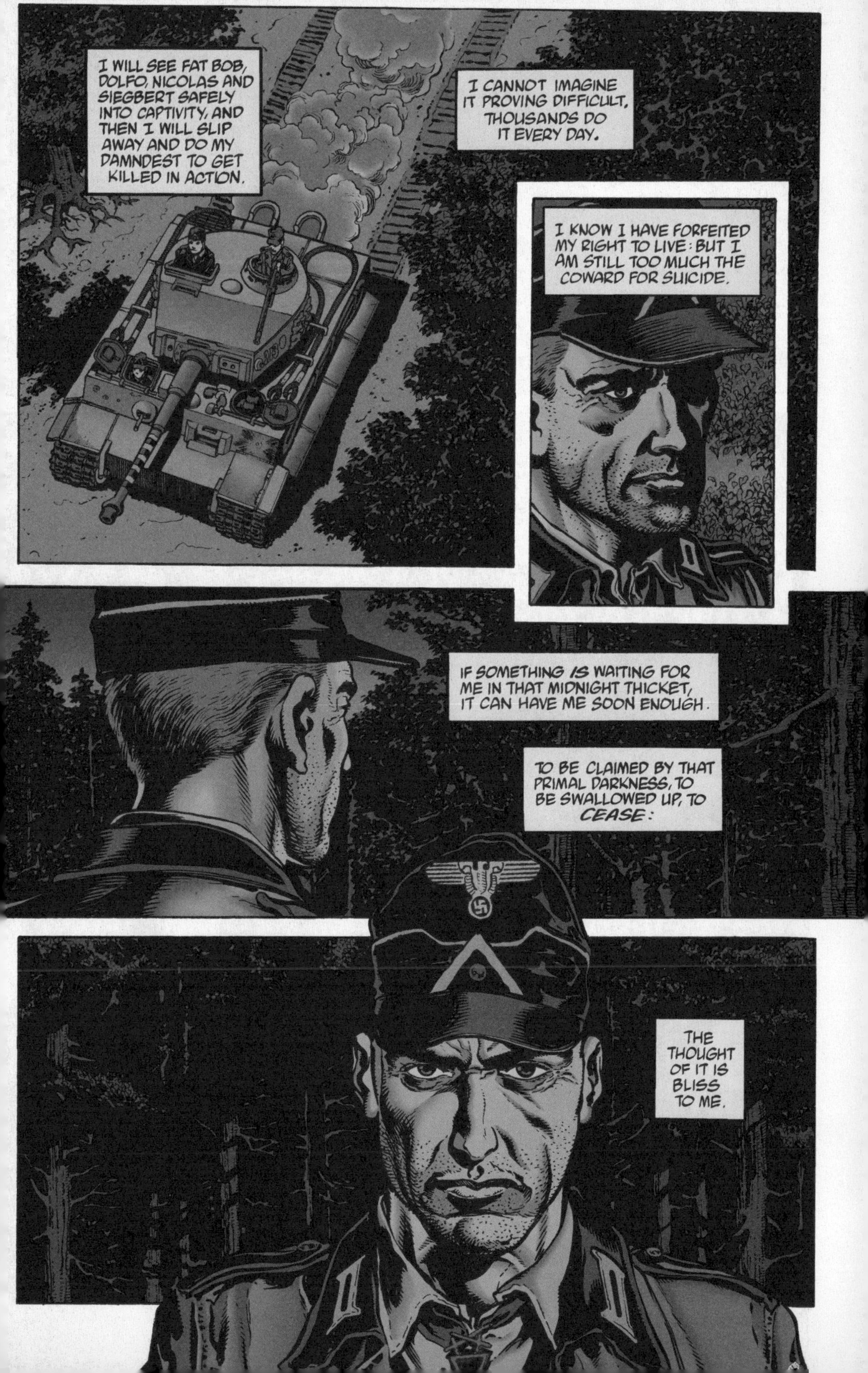
I WILL SEE FAT BOB, DOLFO, NICOLAS AND SIEGBERT SAFELY INTO CAPTIVITY, AND THEN I WILL SLIP AWAY AND DO MY DAMNDEST TO GET KILLED IN ACTION.
I CANNOT IMAGINE IT PROVING DIFFICULT, THOUSANDS DO IT EVERY DAY.
I KNOW I HAVE FORFEITED MY RIGHT TO LIVE: BUT I AM STILL TOO MUCH THE COWARD FOR SUICIDE.
IF SOMETHING IS WAITING FOR ME IN THAT MIDNIGHT THICKET, IT CAN HAVE ME SOON ENOUGH.
TO BE CLAIMED BY THAT PRIMAL DARKNESS, TO BE SWALLOWED UP, TO CEASE:
THE THOUGHT OF IT IS BLISS TO ME.

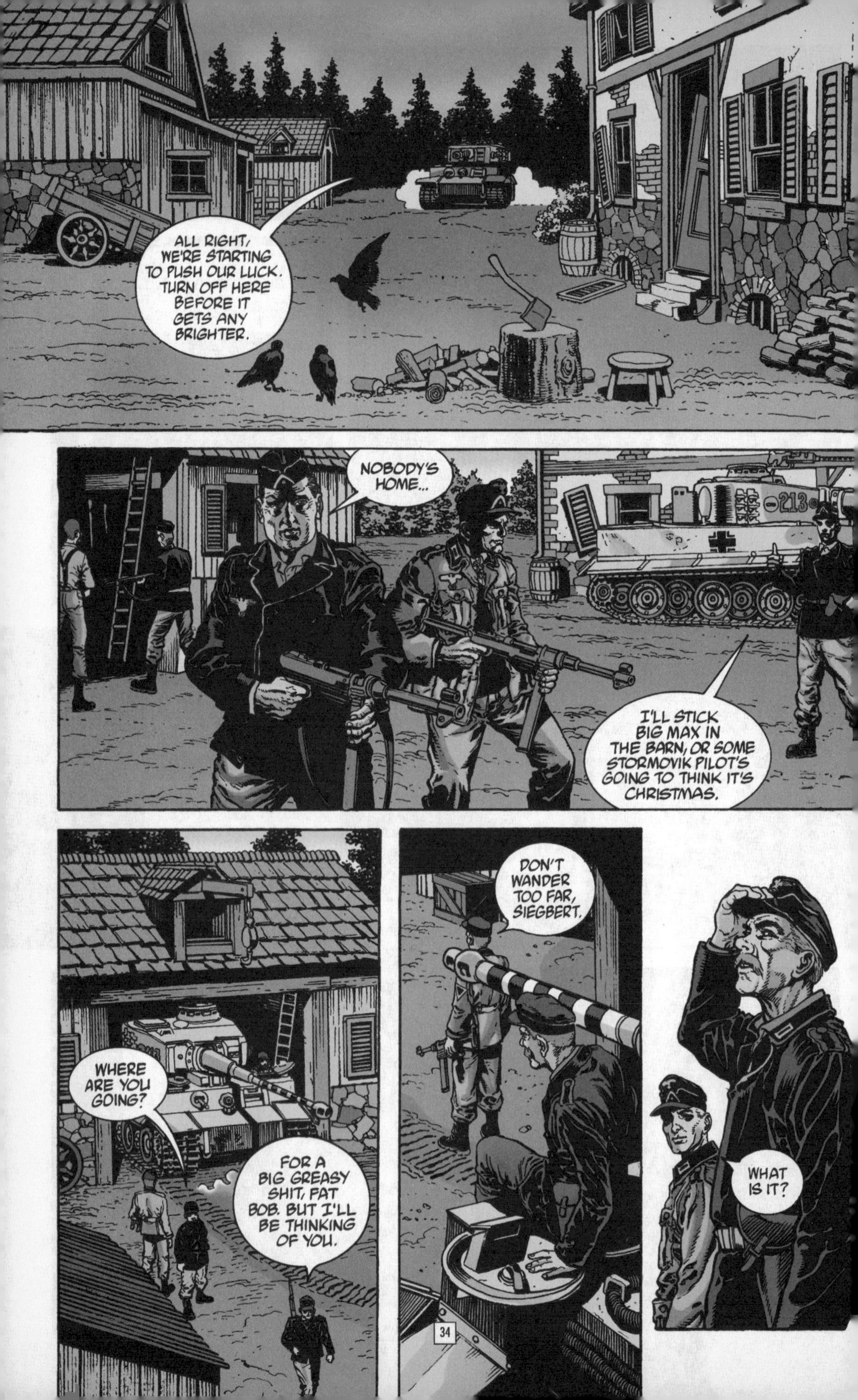
ALL RIGHT, WE'RE STARTING TO PUSH OUR LUCK. TURN OFF HERE BEFORE IT GETS ANY BRIGHTER.
NOBODY'S HOME...
I'LL STICK BIG MAX IN THE BARN, OR SOME STORMOVIK PILOT'S GOING TO THINK IT'S CHRISTMAS.
WHERE ARE YOU GOING?
FOR A BIG GREASY SHIT, FAT BOB. BUT I'LL BE THINKING OF YOU.
DON'T WANDER TOO FAR, SIEGBERT.
WHAT IS IT?

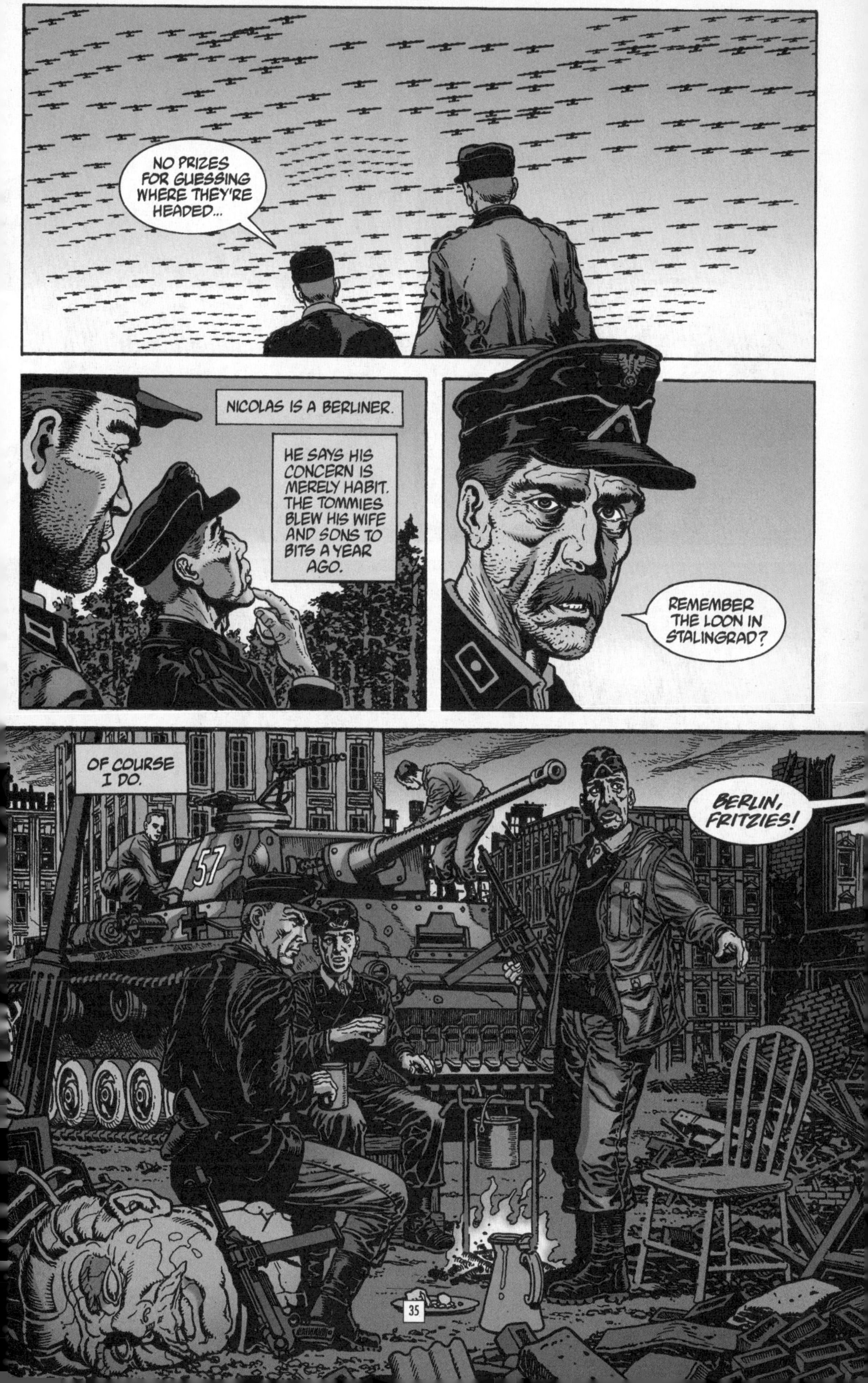
NO PRIZES FOR GUESSING WHERE THEY'RE HEADED...
NICOLAS IS A BERLINER.
HE SAYS HIS CONCERN IS MERELY HABIT. THE TOMMIES BLEW HIS WIFE AND SONS TO BITS A YEAR AGO.
REMEMBER THE LOON IN STALINGRAD?
OF COURSE I DO.
BERLIN, FRITZIES!
57

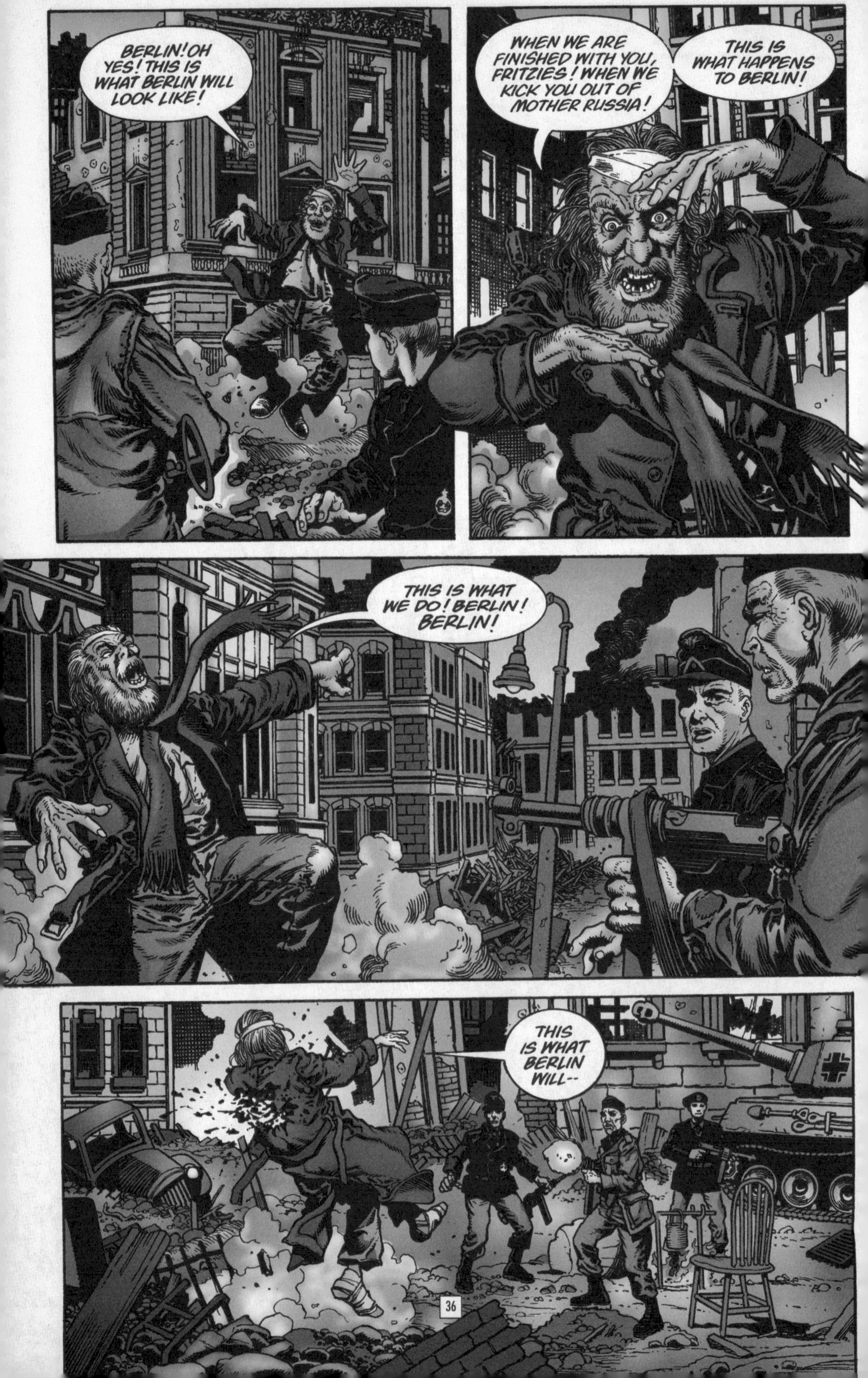
BERLIN! OH YES! THIS IS WHAT BERLIN WILL LOOK LIKE!
WHEN WE ARE FINISHED WITH YOU, FRITZIES! WHEN WE KICK YOU OUT OF MOTHER RUSSIA!
THIS IS WHAT HAPPENS TO BERLIN!
THIS IS WHAT WE DO! BERLIN! BERLIN!
THIS IS WHAT BERLIN WILL--

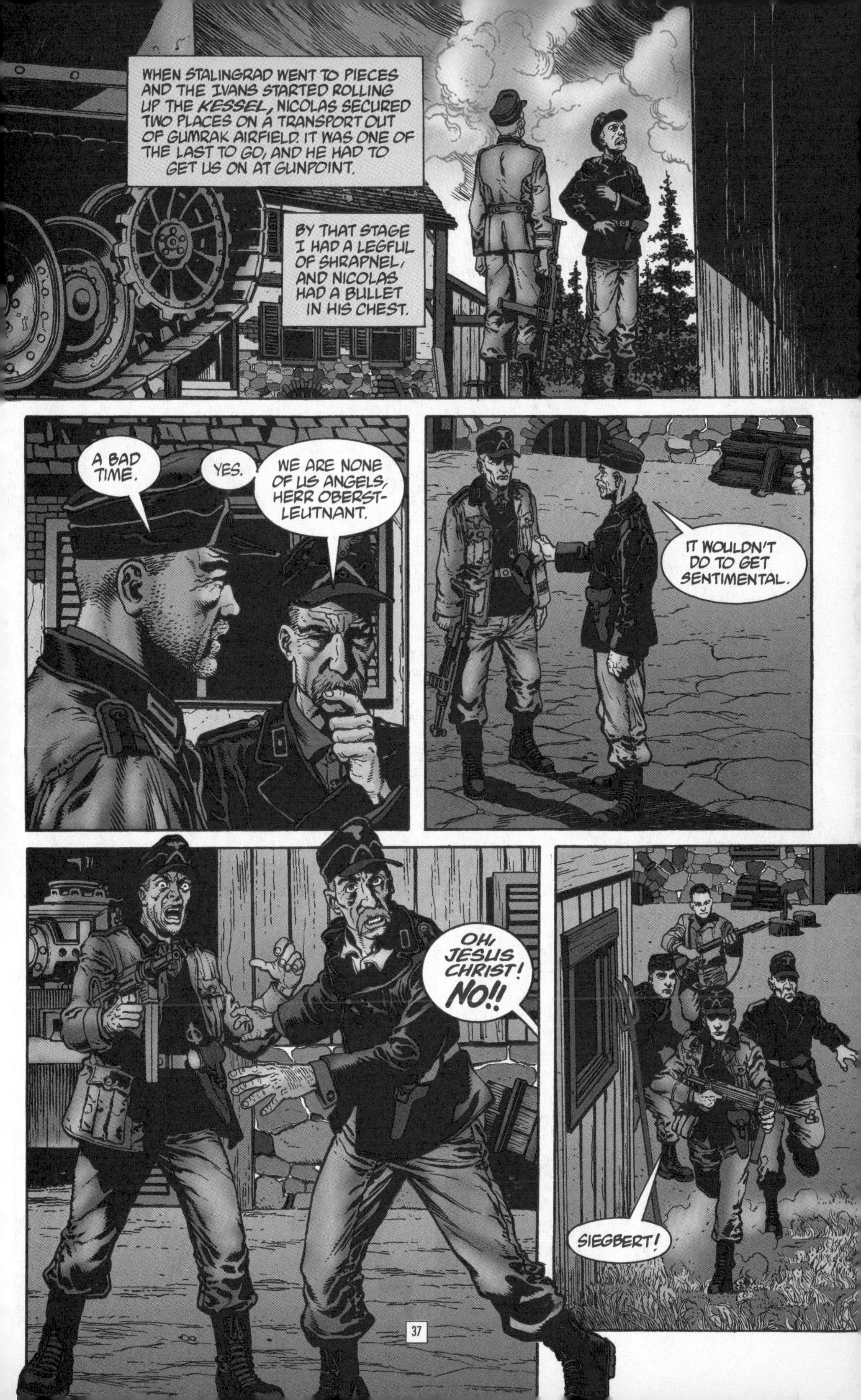
WHEN STALINGRAD WENT TO PIECES AND THE IVANS STARTED ROLLING UP THE *KESSEL*, NICOLAS SECURED TWO PLACES ON A TRANSPORT OUT OF GUMRAK AIRFIELD. IT WAS ONE OF THE LAST TO GO, AND HE HAD TO GET US ON AT GUNPOINT.
BY THAT STAGE I HAD A LEGFUL OF SHRAPNEL, AND NICOLAS HAD A BULLET IN HIS CHEST.
A BAD TIME.
YES.
WE ARE NONE OF US ANGELS, HERR OBERST-LEUTNANT.
IT WOULDN'T DO TO GET SENTIMENTAL.
OH, JESUS CHRIST! NO!!
SIEGBERT!

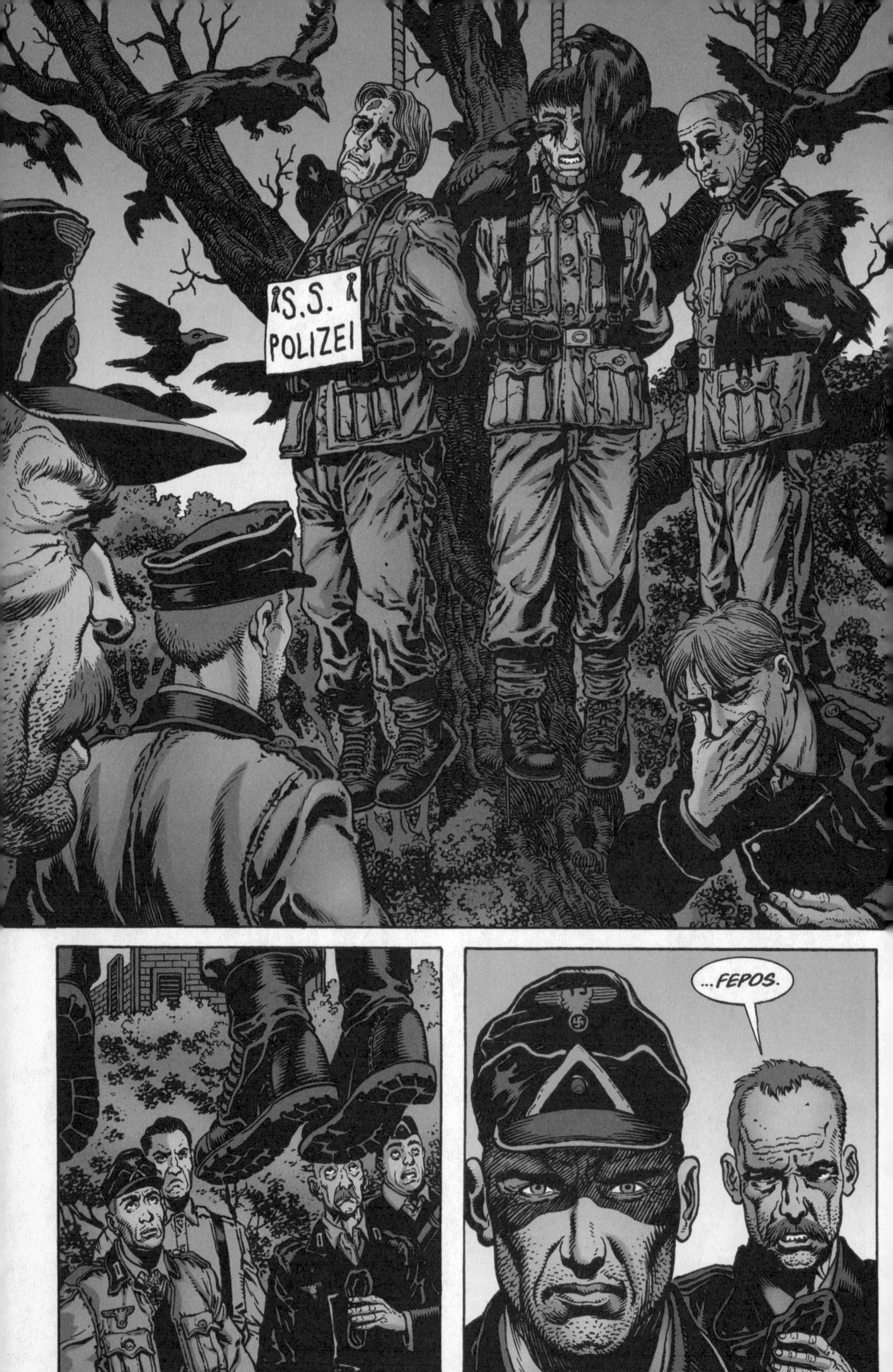
S.S.
POLIZEI
...FEPOS.

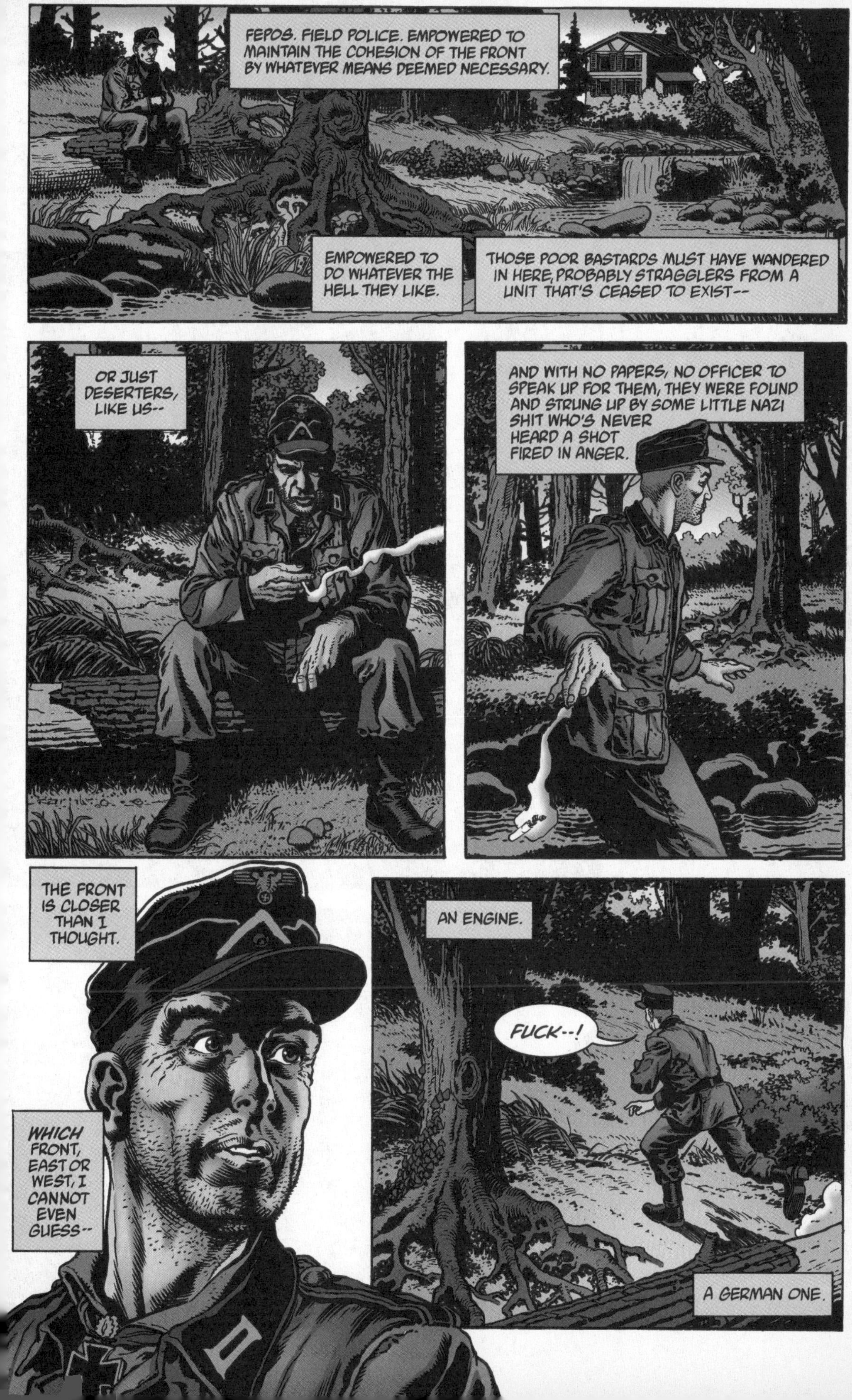
FEPOS. FIELD POLICE. EMPOWERED TO MAINTAIN THE COHESION OF THE FRONT BY WHATEVER MEANS DEEMED NECESSARY.
EMPOWERED TO DO WHATEVER THE HELL THEY LIKE.
THOSE POOR BASTARDS MUST HAVE WANDERED IN HERE, PROBABLY STRAGGLERS FROM A UNIT THAT'S CEASED TO EXIST--
OR JUST DESERTERS, LIKE US--
AND WITH NO PAPERS, NO OFFICER TO SPEAK UP FOR THEM, THEY WERE FOUND AND STRUNG UP BY SOME LITTLE NAZI SHIT WHO'S NEVER HEARD A SHOT FIRED IN ANGER.
THE FRONT IS CLOSER THAN I THOUGHT.
WHICH FRONT, EAST OR WEST, I CANNOT EVEN GUESS--
AN ENGINE.
FUCK--!
A GERMAN ONE.

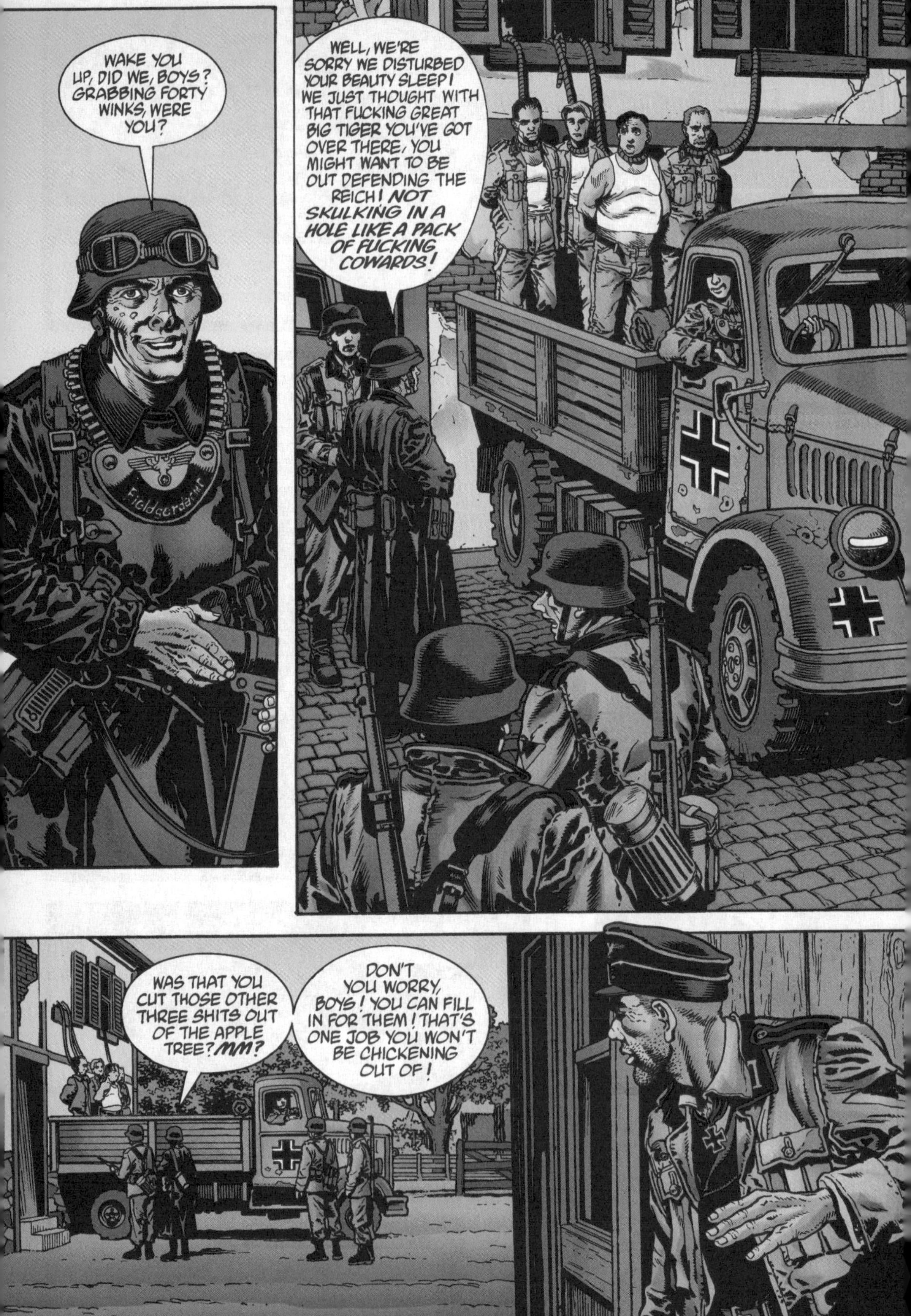
WAKE YOU UP, DID WE, BOYS? GRABBING FORTY WINKS, WERE YOU?
WELL, WE'RE SORRY WE DISTURBED YOUR BEAUTY SLEEP! WE JUST THOUGHT WITH THAT FUCKING GREAT BIG TIGER YOU'VE GOT OVER THERE, YOU MIGHT WANT TO BE OUT DEFENDING THE REICH! NOT SKULKING IN A HOLE LIKE A PACK OF FUCKING COWARDS!
WAS THAT YOU CUT THOSE OTHER THREE SHITS OUT OF THE APPLE TREE? MM?
DON'T YOU WORRY, BOYS! YOU CAN FILL IN FOR THEM! THAT'S ONE JOB YOU WON'T BE CHICKENING OUT OF!

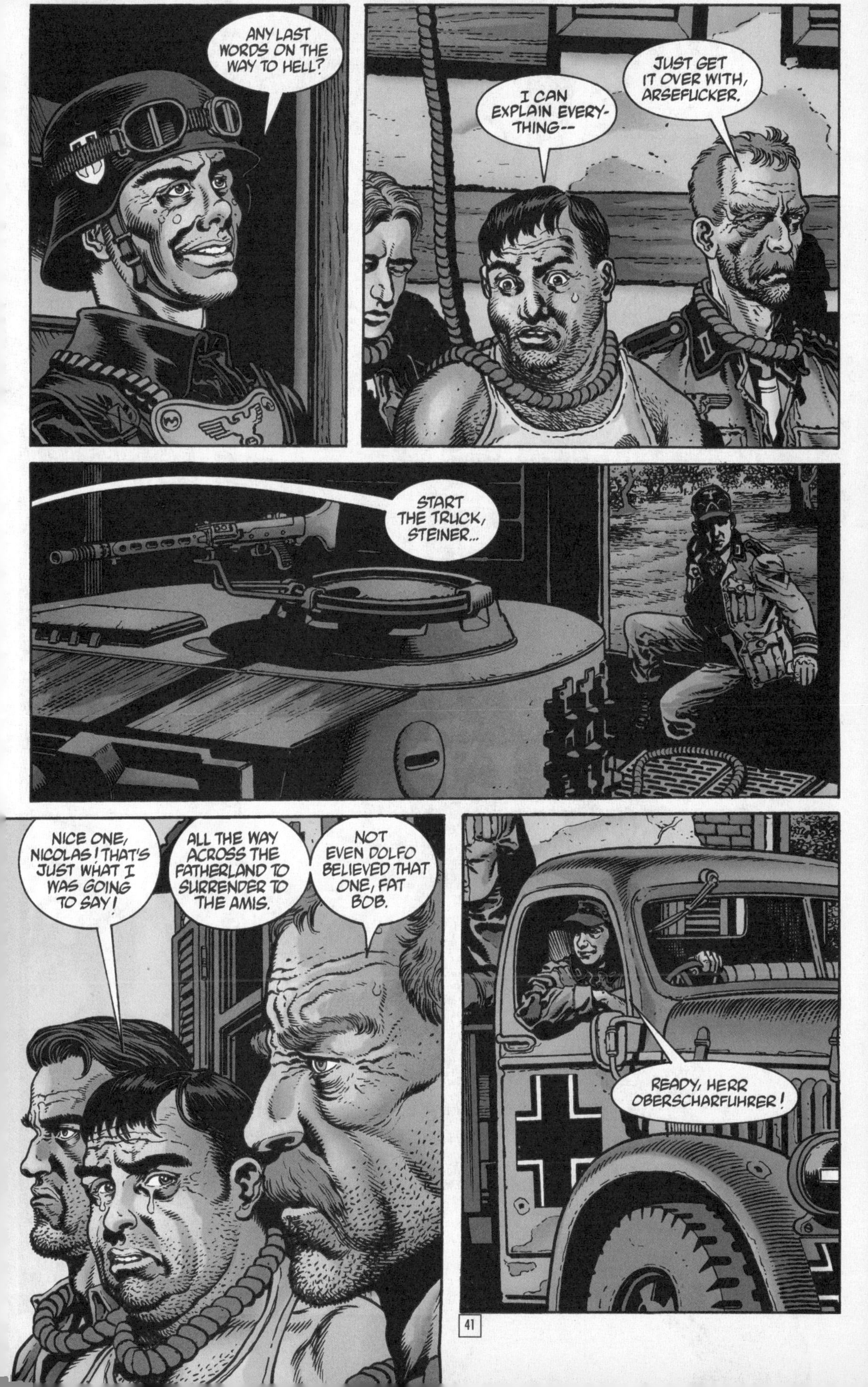
ANY LAST WORDS ON THE WAY TO HELL?
I CAN EXPLAIN EVERY-THING--
JUST GET IT OVER WITH, ARSEFUCKER.
START THE TRUCK, STEINER...
NICE ONE, NICOLAS! THAT'S JUST WHAT I WAS GOING TO SAY!
ALL THE WAY ACROSS THE FATHERLAND TO SURRENDER TO THE AMIS.
NOT EVEN DOLFO BELIEVED THAT ONE, FAT BOB.
READY, HERR OBERSCHARFUHRER!

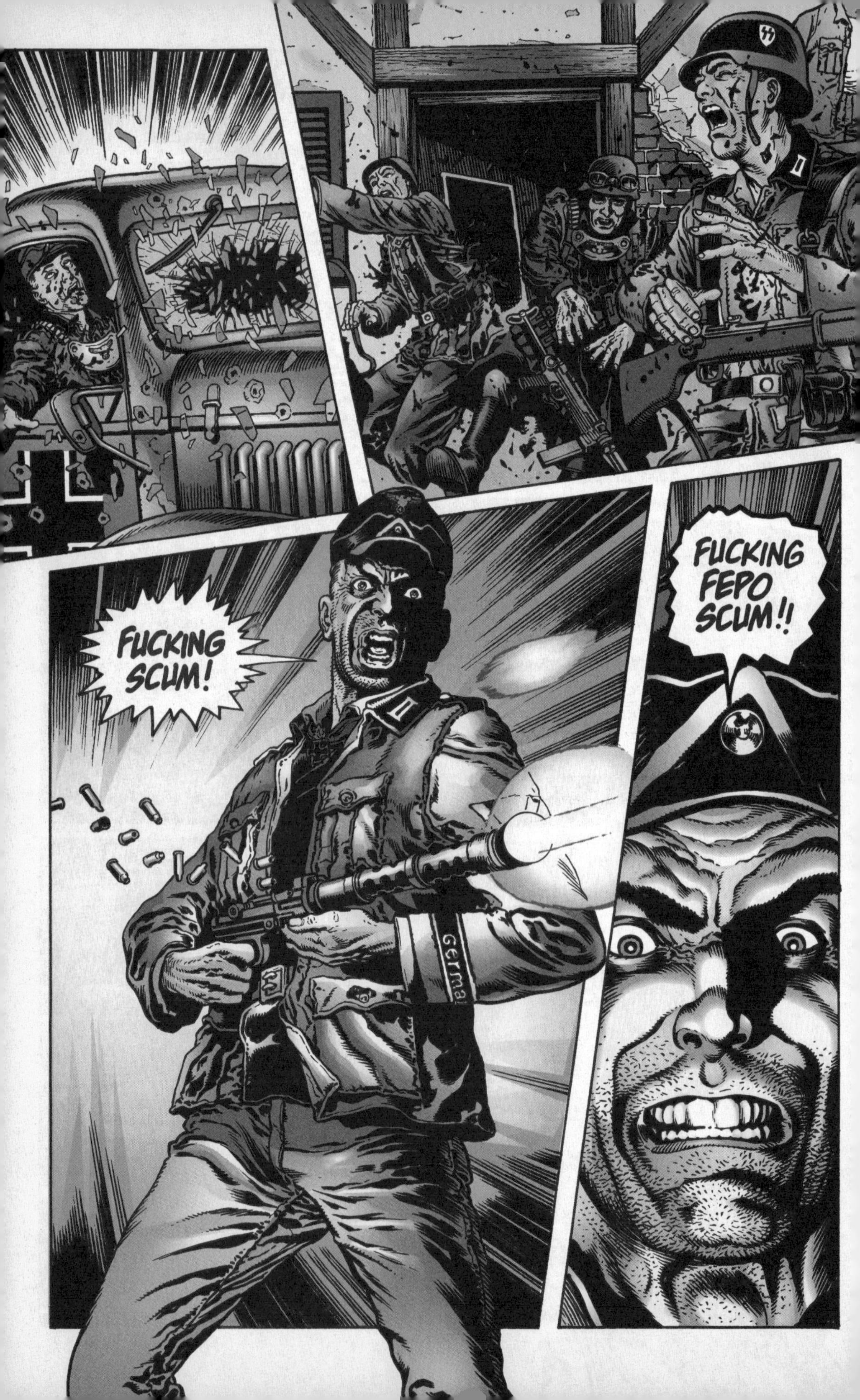
FUCKING SCUM!
FUCKING FEPO SCUM!!

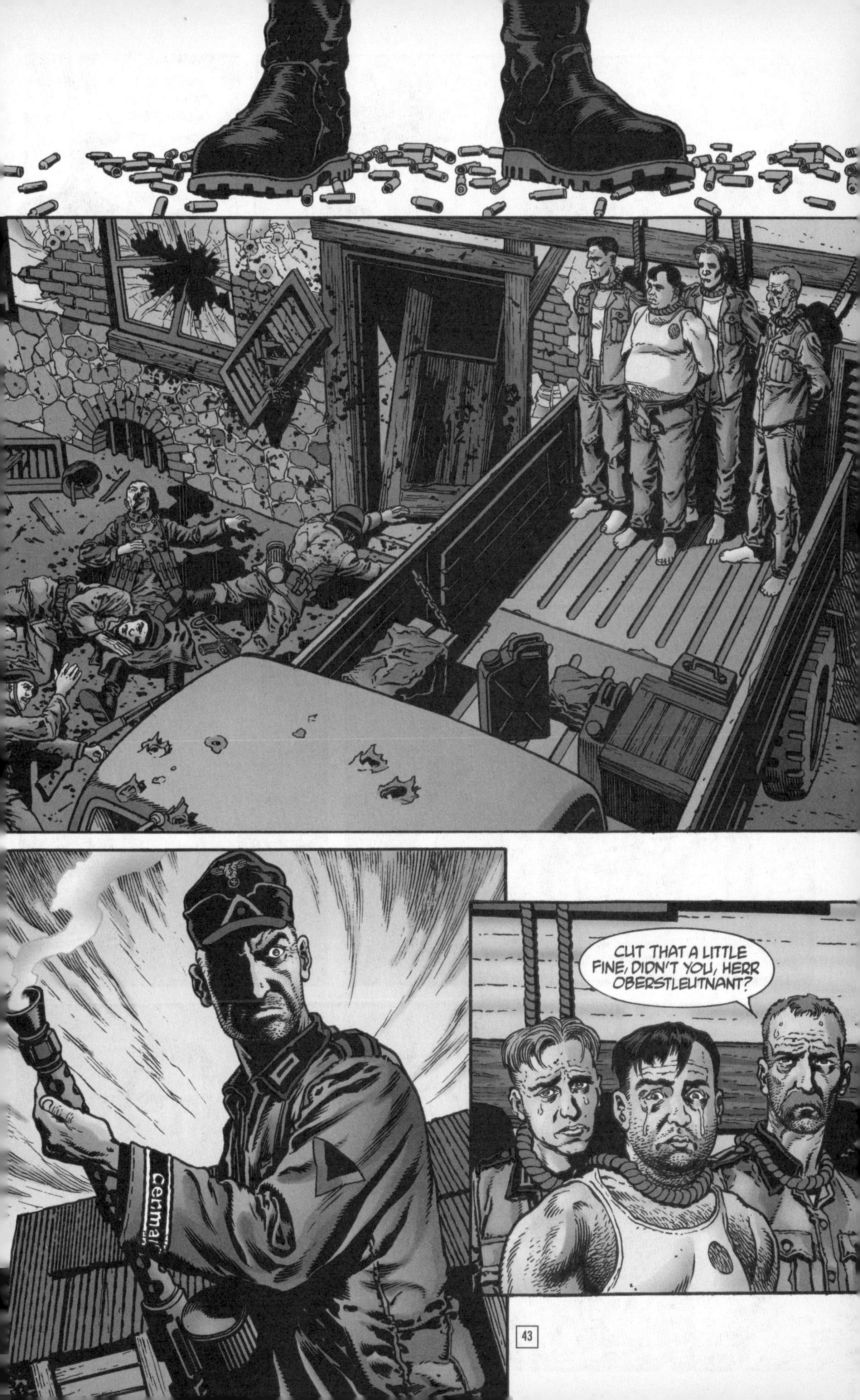
CUT THAT A LITTLE FINE, DIDN'T YOU, HERR OBERSTLEUTNANT?

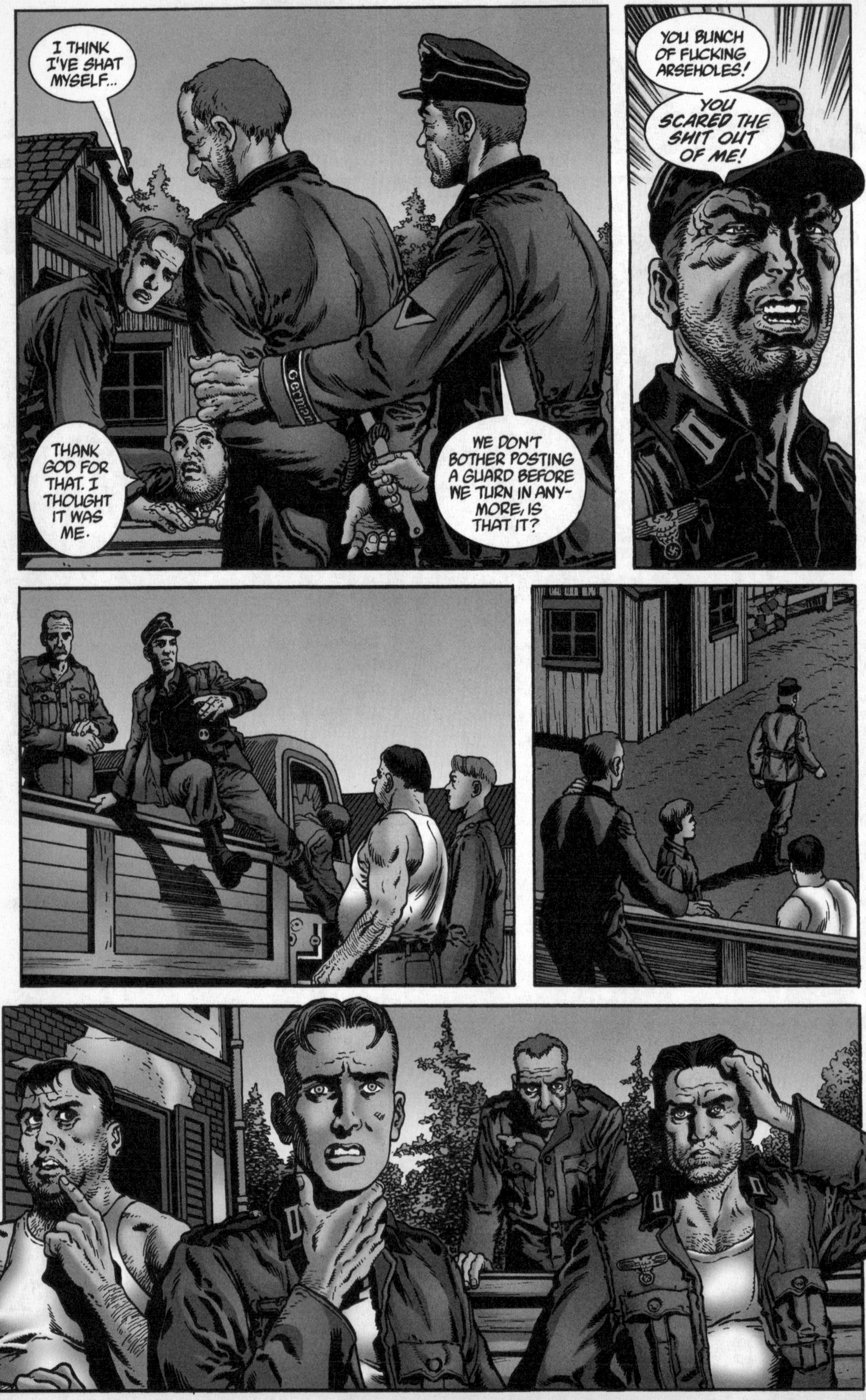
I THINK I'VE SHAT MYSELF...
THANK GOD FOR THAT. I THOUGHT IT WAS ME.
German
WE DON'T BOTHER POSTING A GUARD BEFORE WE TURN IN ANYMORE, IS THAT IT?
YOU BUNCH OF FUCKING ARSEHOLES!
YOU SCARED THE SHIT OUT OF ME!

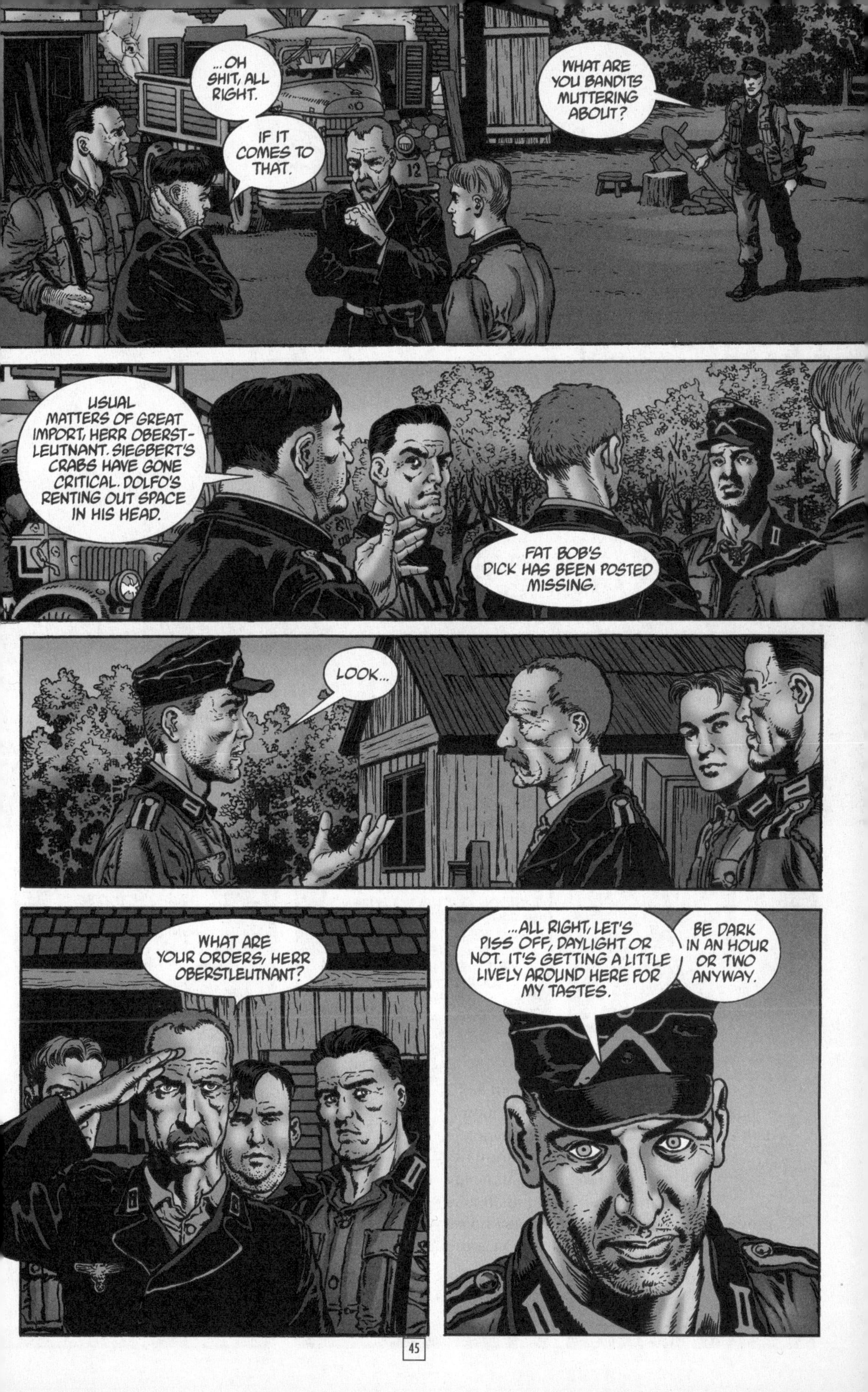
...OH SHIT, ALL RIGHT.
IF IT COMES TO THAT.
WHAT ARE YOU BANDITS MUTTERING ABOUT?
USUAL MATTERS OF GREAT IMPORT, HERR OBERST-LEUTNANT. SIEGBERT'S CRABS HAVE GONE CRITICAL. DOLFO'S RENTING OUT SPACE IN HIS HEAD.
FAT BOB'S DICK HAS BEEN POSTED MISSING.
LOOK...
WHAT ARE YOUR ORDERS, HERR OBERSTLEUTNANT?
...ALL RIGHT, LET'S PISS OFF, DAYLIGHT OR NOT. IT'S GETTING A LITTLE LIVELY AROUND HERE FOR MY TASTES.
BE DARK IN AN HOUR OR TWO ANYWAY.

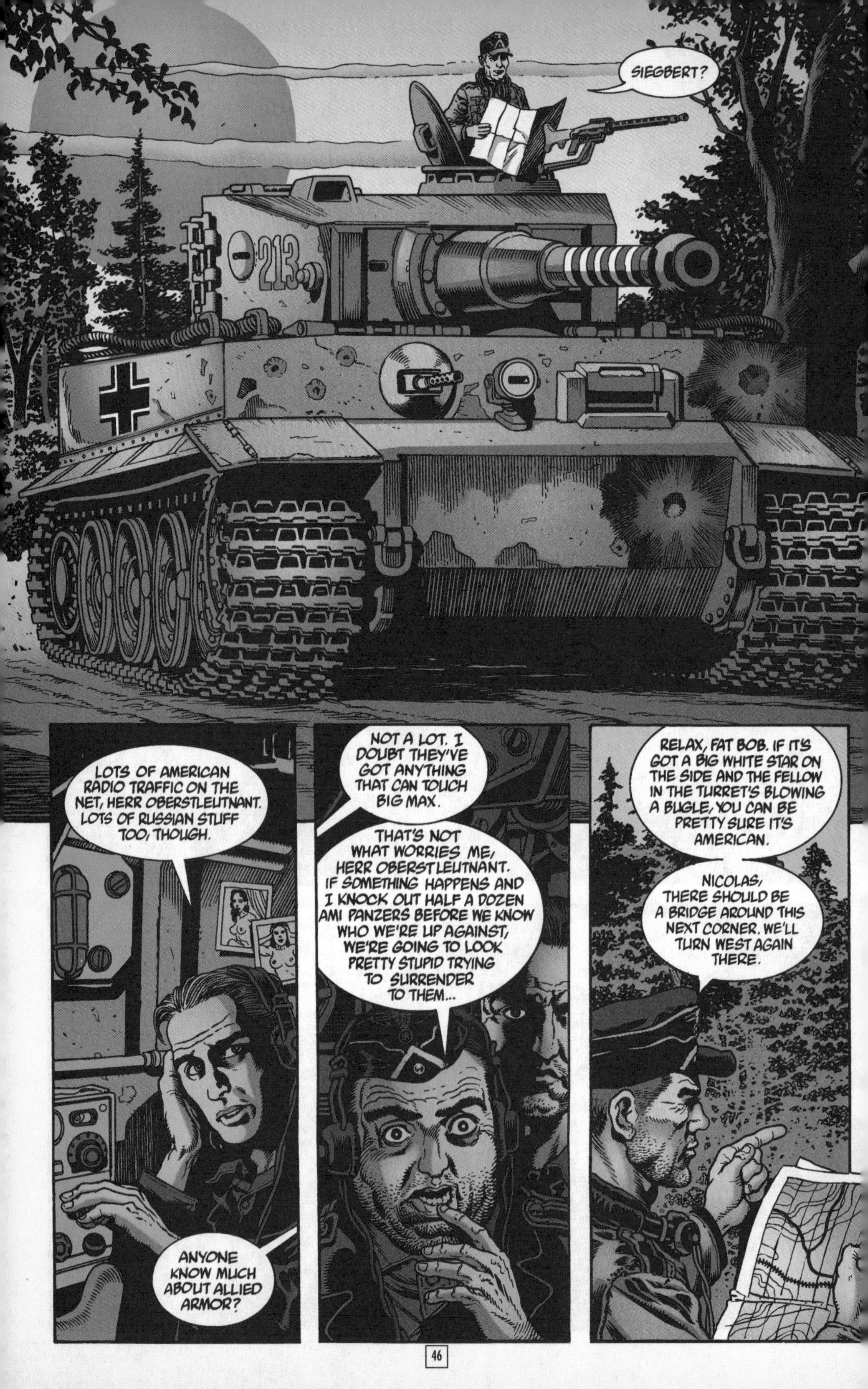
SIEGBERT?
LOTS OF AMERICAN RADIO TRAFFIC ON THE NET, HERR OBERSTLEUTNANT. LOTS OF RUSSIAN STUFF TOO, THOUGH.
ANYONE KNOW MUCH ABOUT ALLIED ARMOR?
NOT A LOT. I DOUBT THEY'VE GOT ANYTHING THAT CAN TOUCH BIG MAX.
THAT'S NOT WHAT WORRIES ME, HERR OBERSTLEUTNANT. IF SOMETHING HAPPENS AND I KNOCK OUT HALF A DOZEN AMI PANZERS BEFORE WE KNOW WHO WE'RE UP AGAINST, WE'RE GOING TO LOOK PRETTY STUPID TRYING TO SURRENDER TO THEM...
RELAX, FAT BOB. IF IT'S GOT A BIG WHITE STAR ON THE SIDE AND THE FELLOW IN THE TURRET'S BLOWING A BUGLE, YOU CAN BE PRETTY SURE IT'S AMERICAN.
NICOLAS, THERE SHOULD BE A BRIDGE AROUND THIS NEXT CORNER. WE'LL TURN WEST AGAIN THERE.

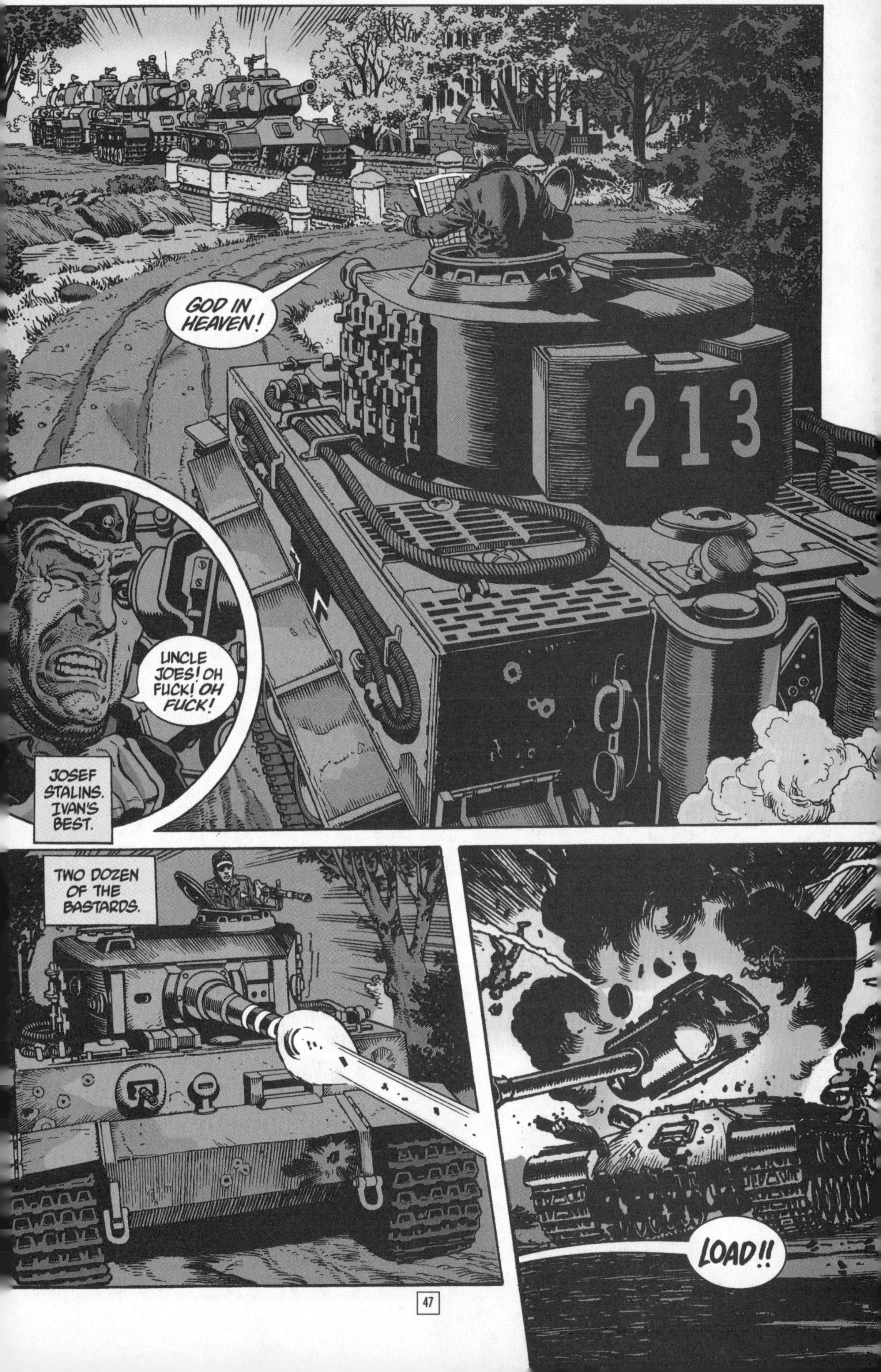
GOD IN HEAVEN!
UNCLE JOES! OH FUCK! OH FUCK!
JOSEF STALINS. IVAN'S BEST.
TWO DOZEN OF THE BASTARDS.
LOAD!!

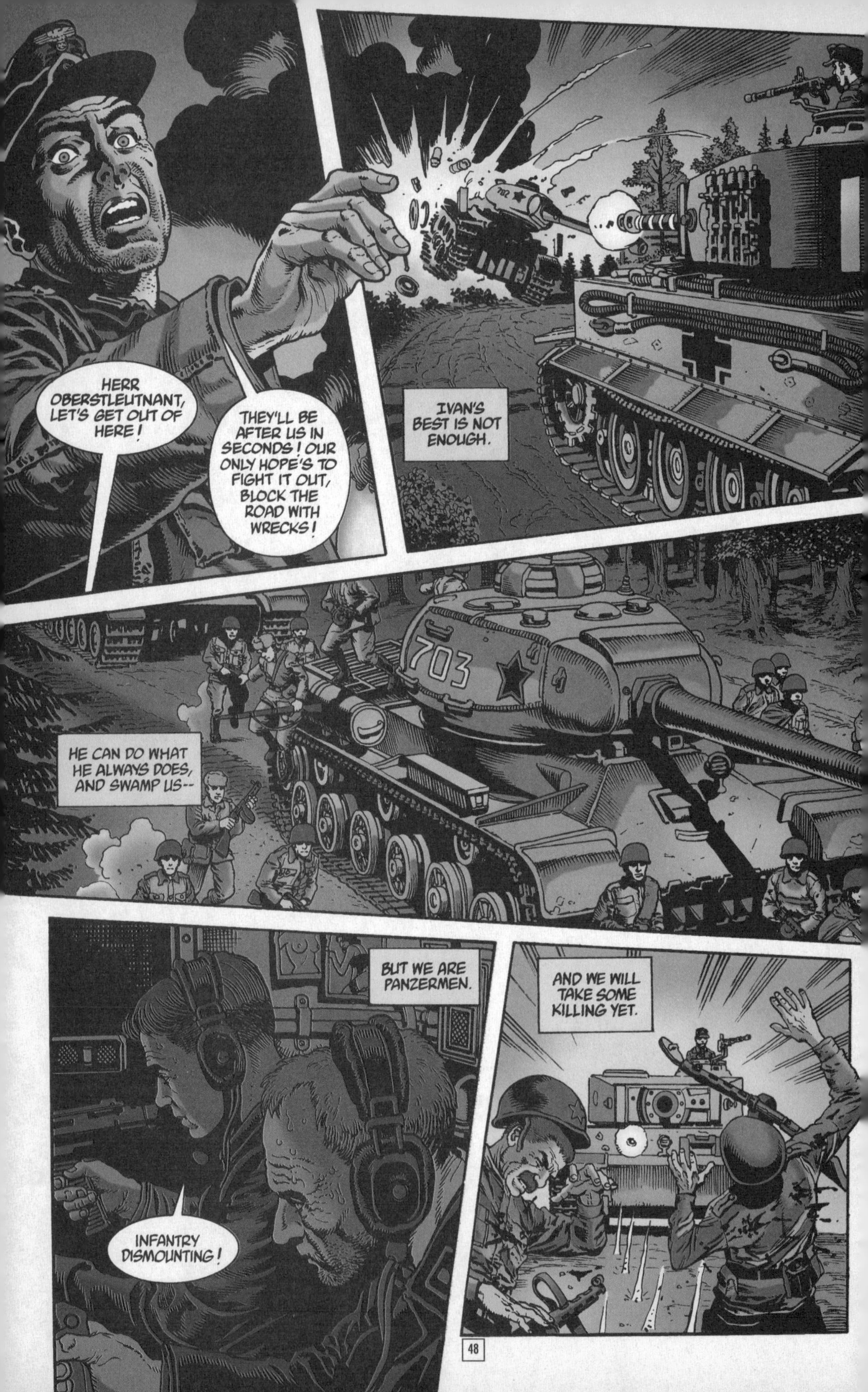

HERR OBERSTLEUTNANT, LET'S GET OUT OF HERE!
THEY'LL BE AFTER US IN SECONDS! OUR ONLY HOPE'S TO FIGHT IT OUT, BLOCK THE ROAD WITH WRECKS!
IVAN'S BEST IS NOT ENOUGH.
703
HE CAN DO WHAT HE ALWAYS DOES, AND SWAMP US--
BUT WE ARE PANZERMEN.
INFANTRY DISMOUNTING!
AND WE WILL TAKE SOME KILLING YET.

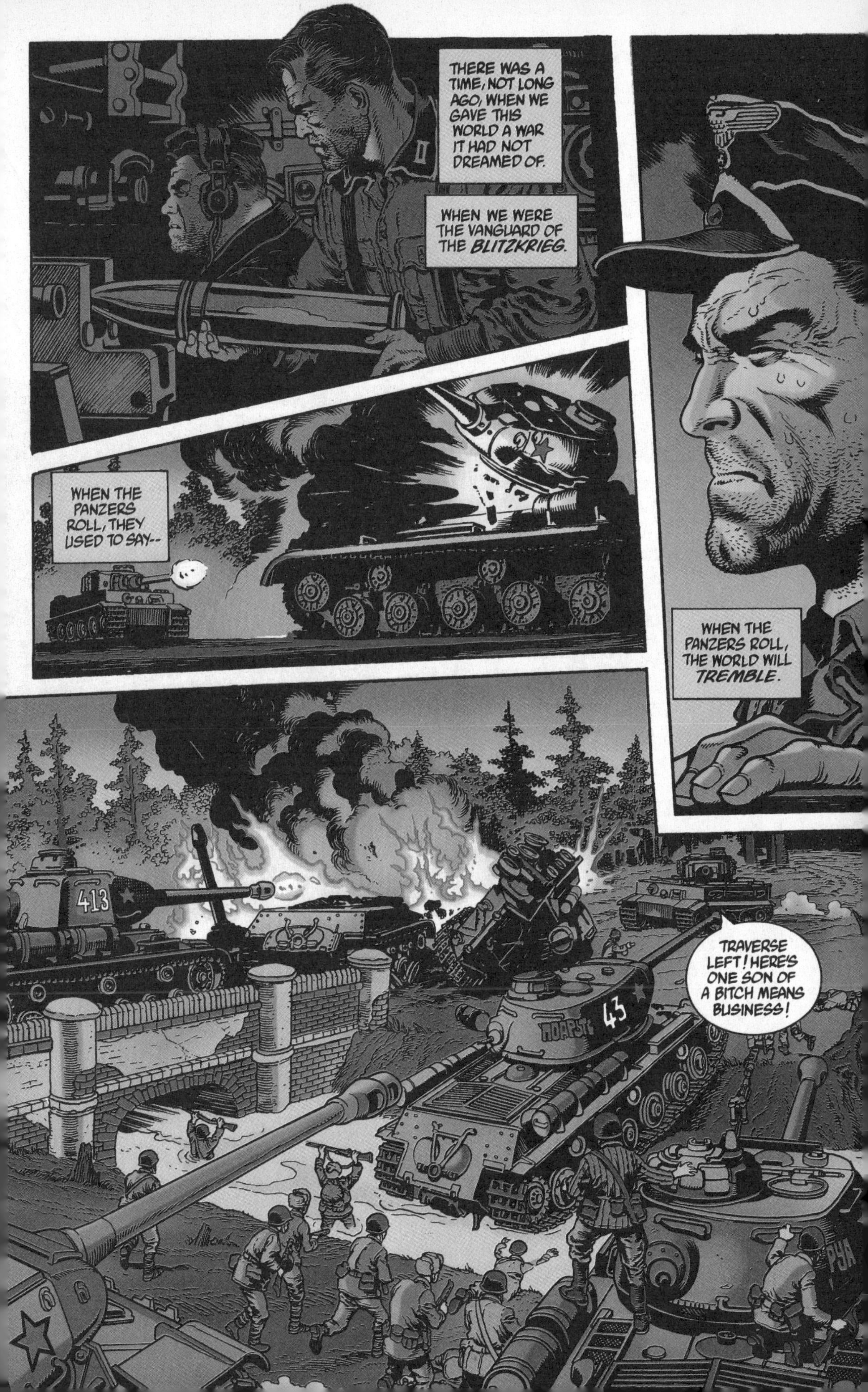
THERE WAS A TIME, NOT LONG AGO, WHEN WE GAVE THIS WORLD A WAR IT HAD NOT DREAMED OF.
WHEN WE WERE THE VANGUARD OF THE *BLITZKRIEG*.
WHEN THE PANZERS ROLL, THEY USED TO SAY--
WHEN THE PANZERS ROLL, THE WORLD WILL *TREMBLE*.
413
43
TRAVERSE LEFT! HERE'S ONE SON OF A BITCH MEANS BUSINESS!

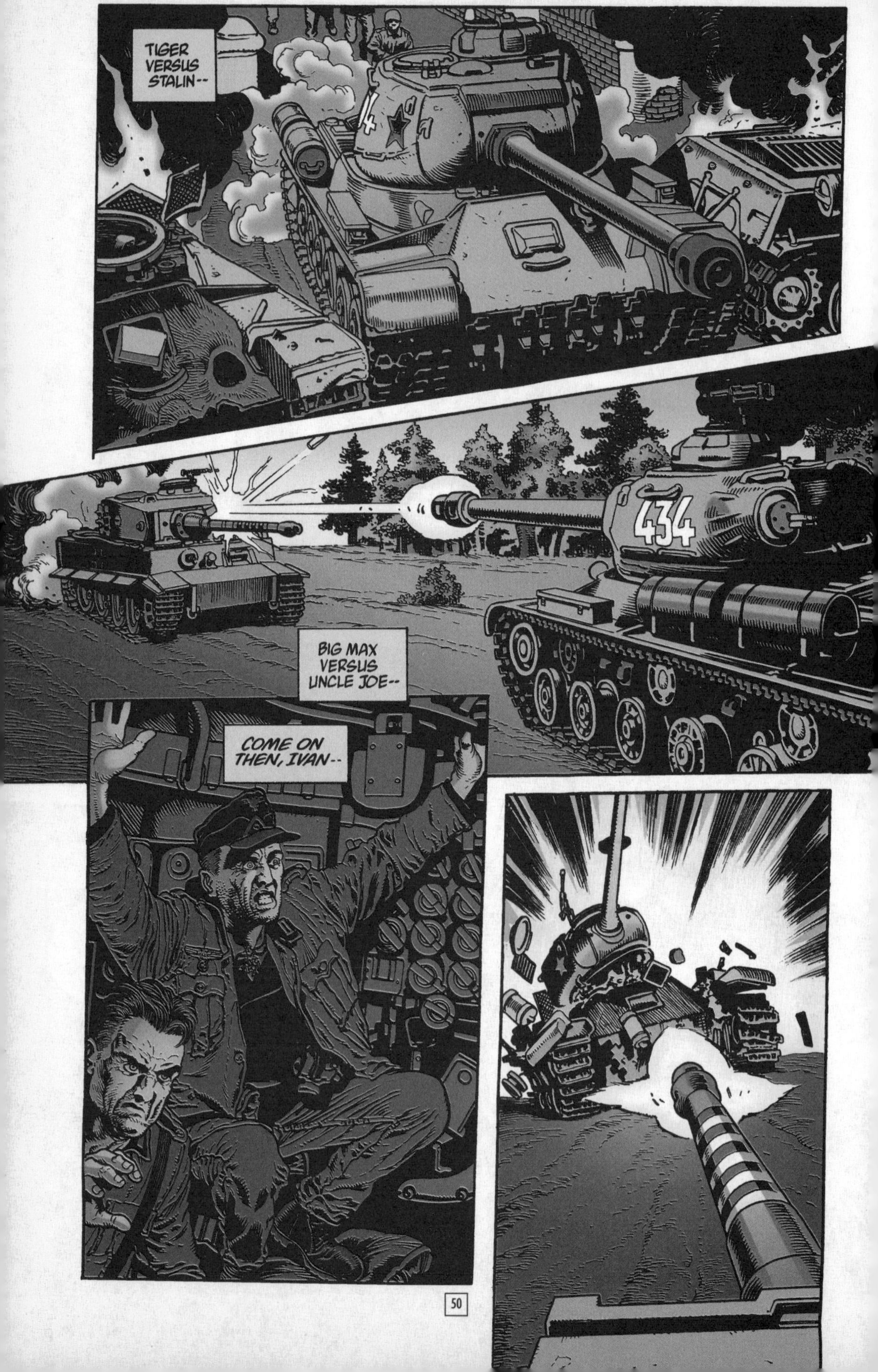
TIGER VERSUS STALIN--
BIG MAX VERSUS UNCLE JOE--
COME ON THEN, IVAN--
434

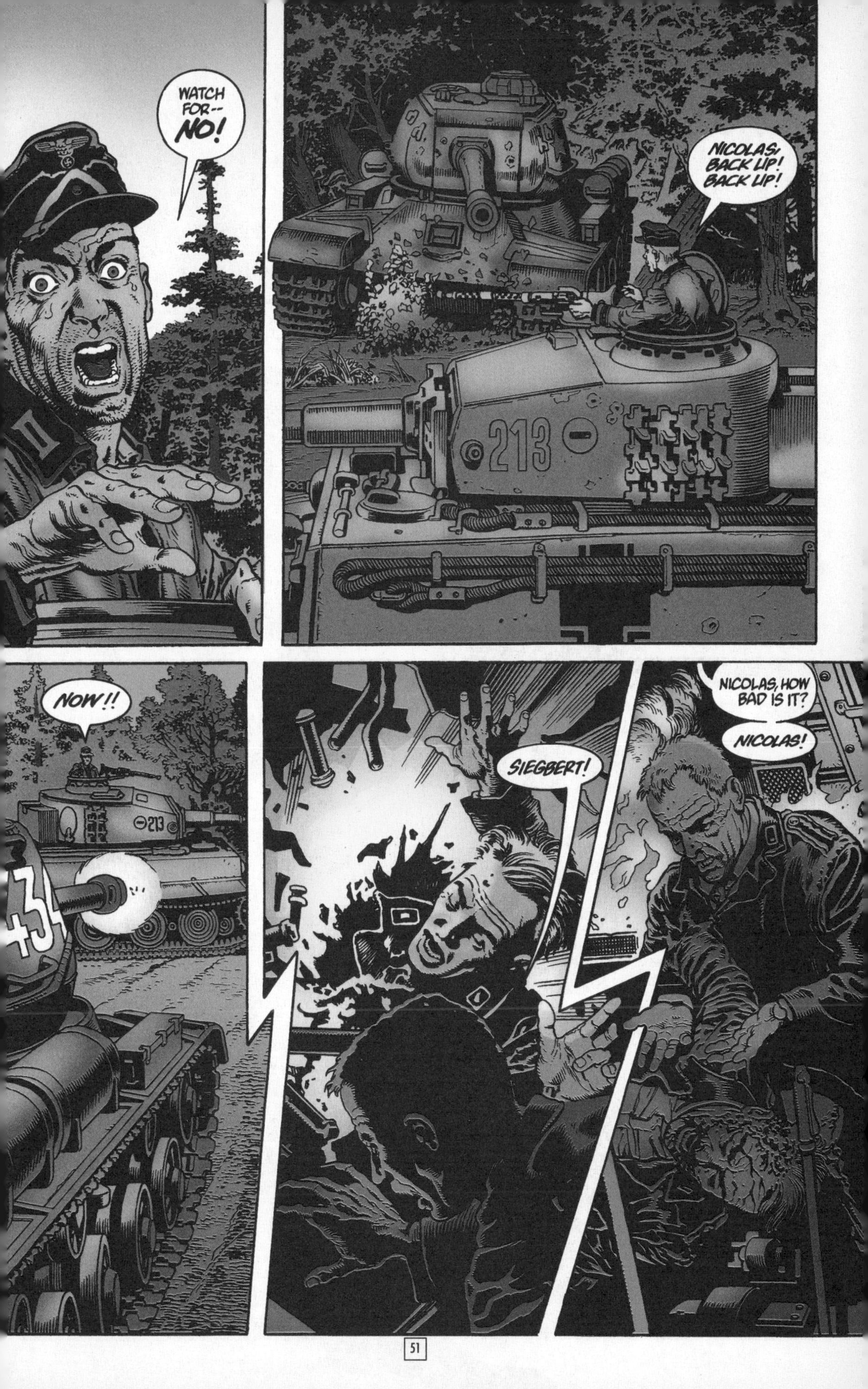
WATCH FOR-- NO!
NICOLAS, BACK UP! BACK UP!
213
NOW!!
213
SIEGBERT!
NICOLAS, HOW BAD IS IT?
NICOLAS!

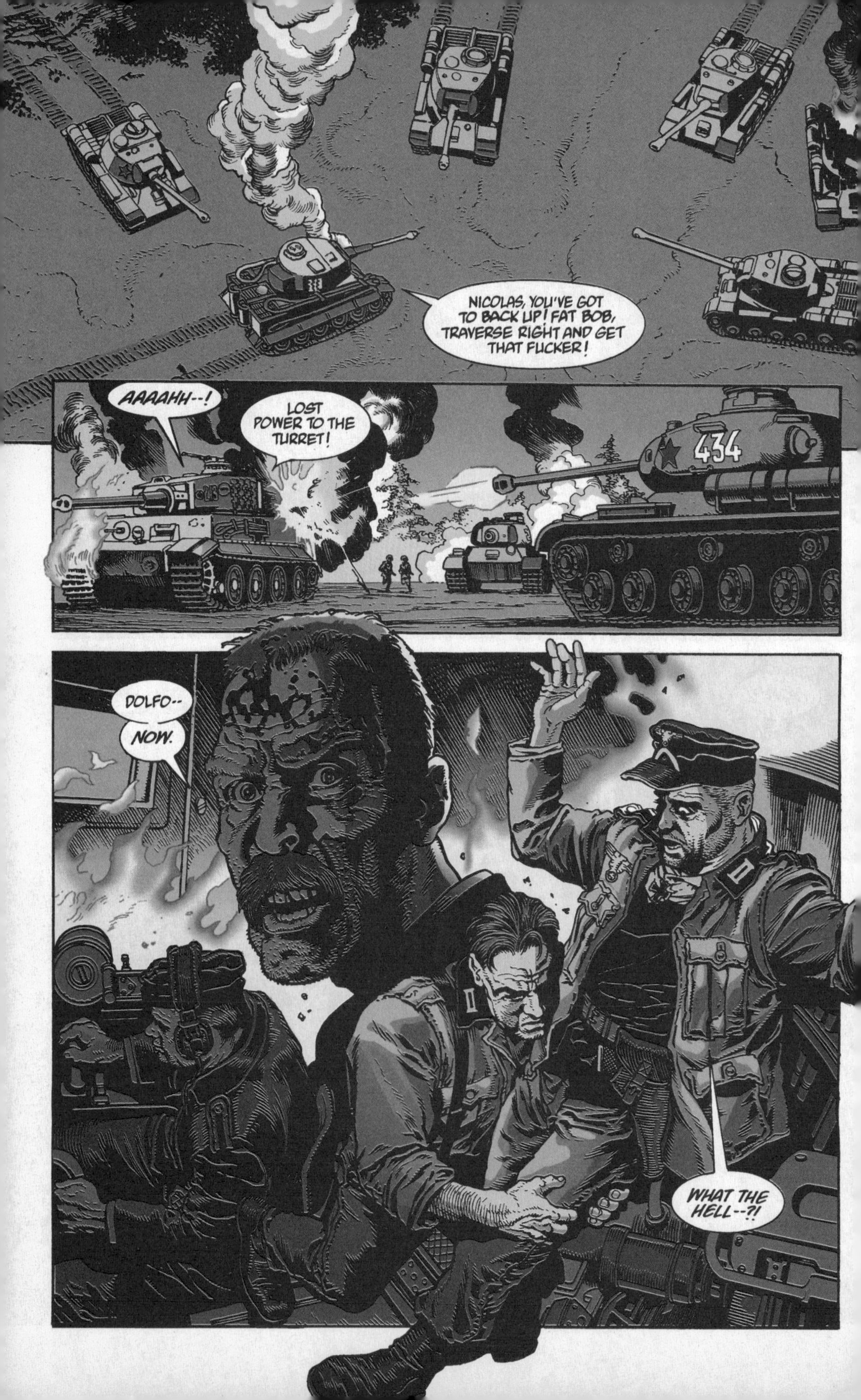
NICOLAS, YOU'VE GOT TO BACK UP! FAT BOB, TRAVERSE RIGHT AND GET THAT FUCKER!
AAAAHH--!
LOST POWER TO THE TURRET!
434
DOLFO--
NOW.
WHAT THE HELL--?!

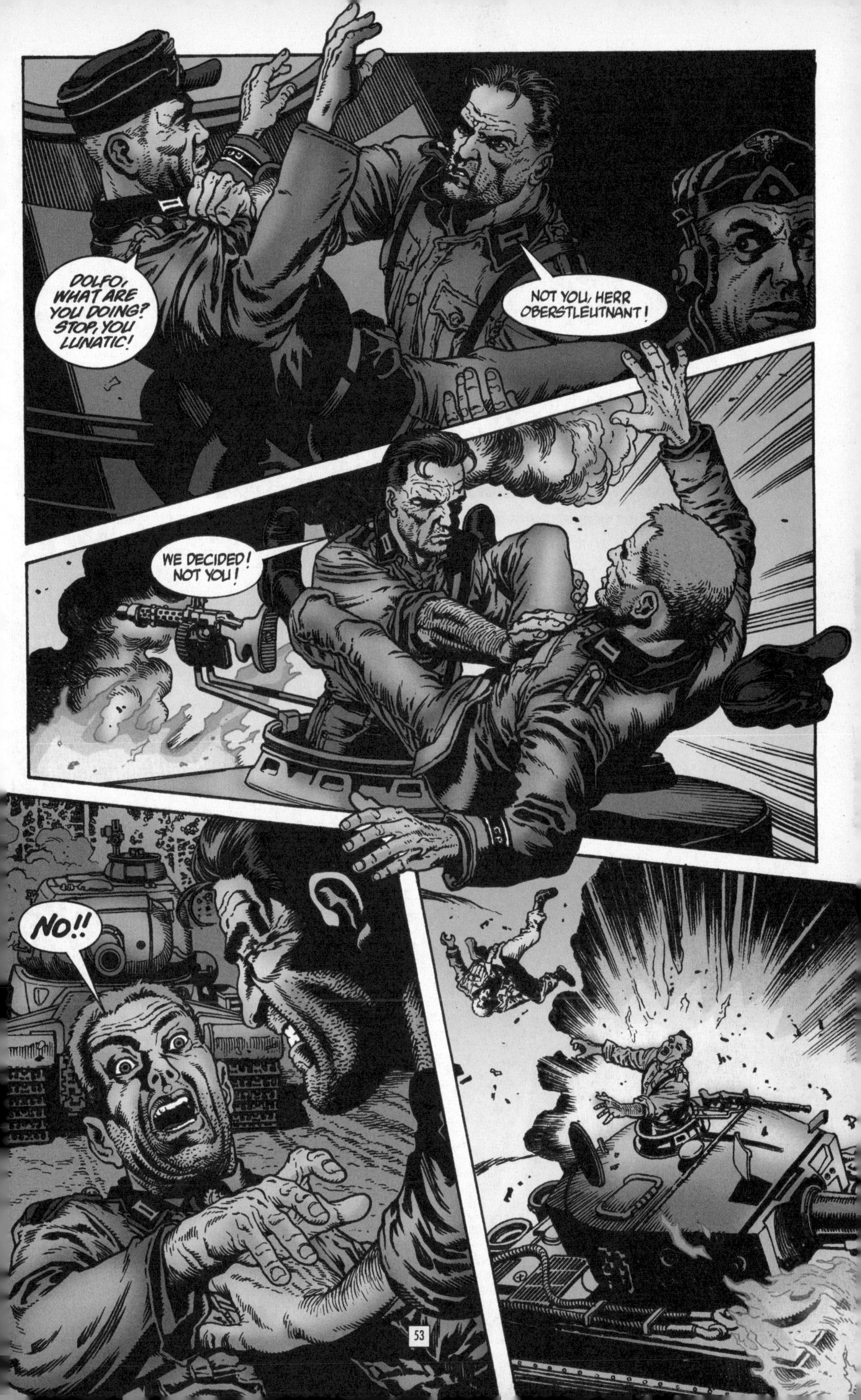
DOLFO, WHAT ARE YOU DOING? STOP, YOU LUNATIC!
NOT YOU, HERR OBERSTLEUTNANT!
WE DECIDED! NOT YOU!
NO!!

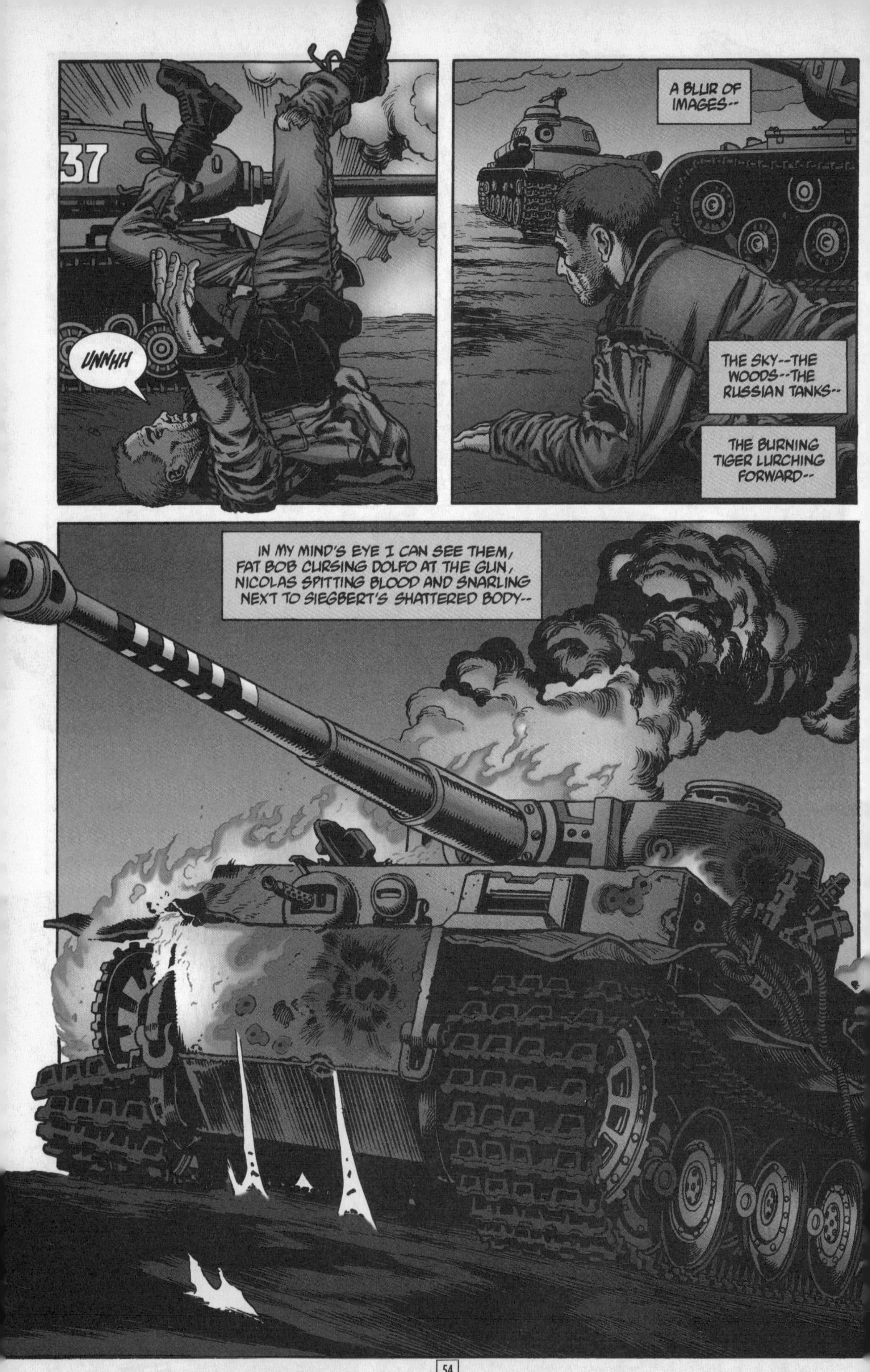
37
UNNHH
A BLUR OF IMAGES--
THE SKY--THE WOODS--THE RUSSIAN TANKS--
THE BURNING TIGER LURCHING FORWARD--
IN MY MIND'S EYE I CAN SEE THEM, FAT BOB CURSING DOLFO AT THE GUN, NICOLAS SPITTING BLOOD AND SNARLING NEXT TO SIEGBERT'S SHATTERED BODY--

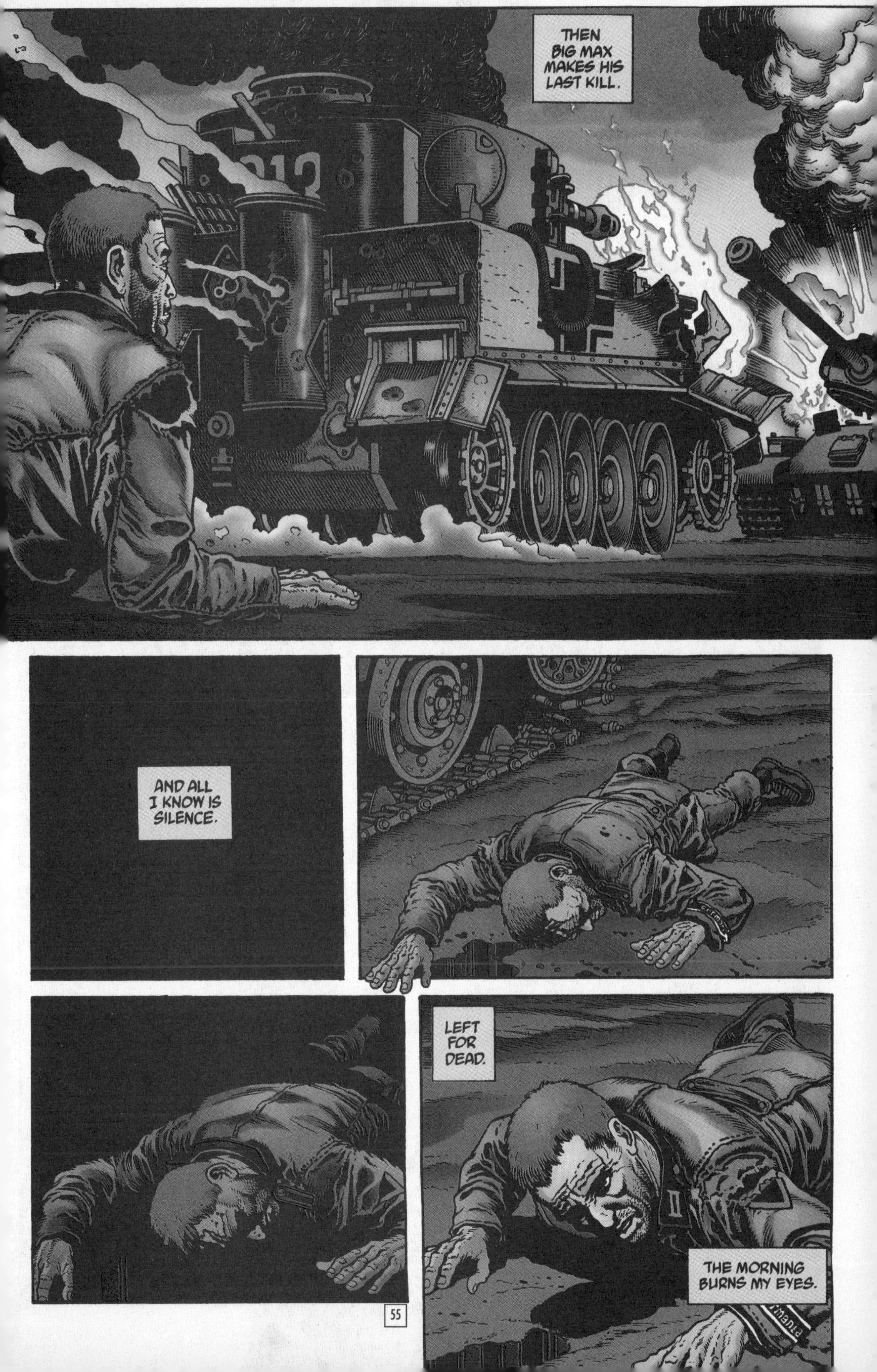
THEN BIG MAX MAKES HIS LAST KILL.
AND ALL I KNOW IS SILENCE.
LEFT FOR DEAD.
THE MORNING BURNS MY EYES.

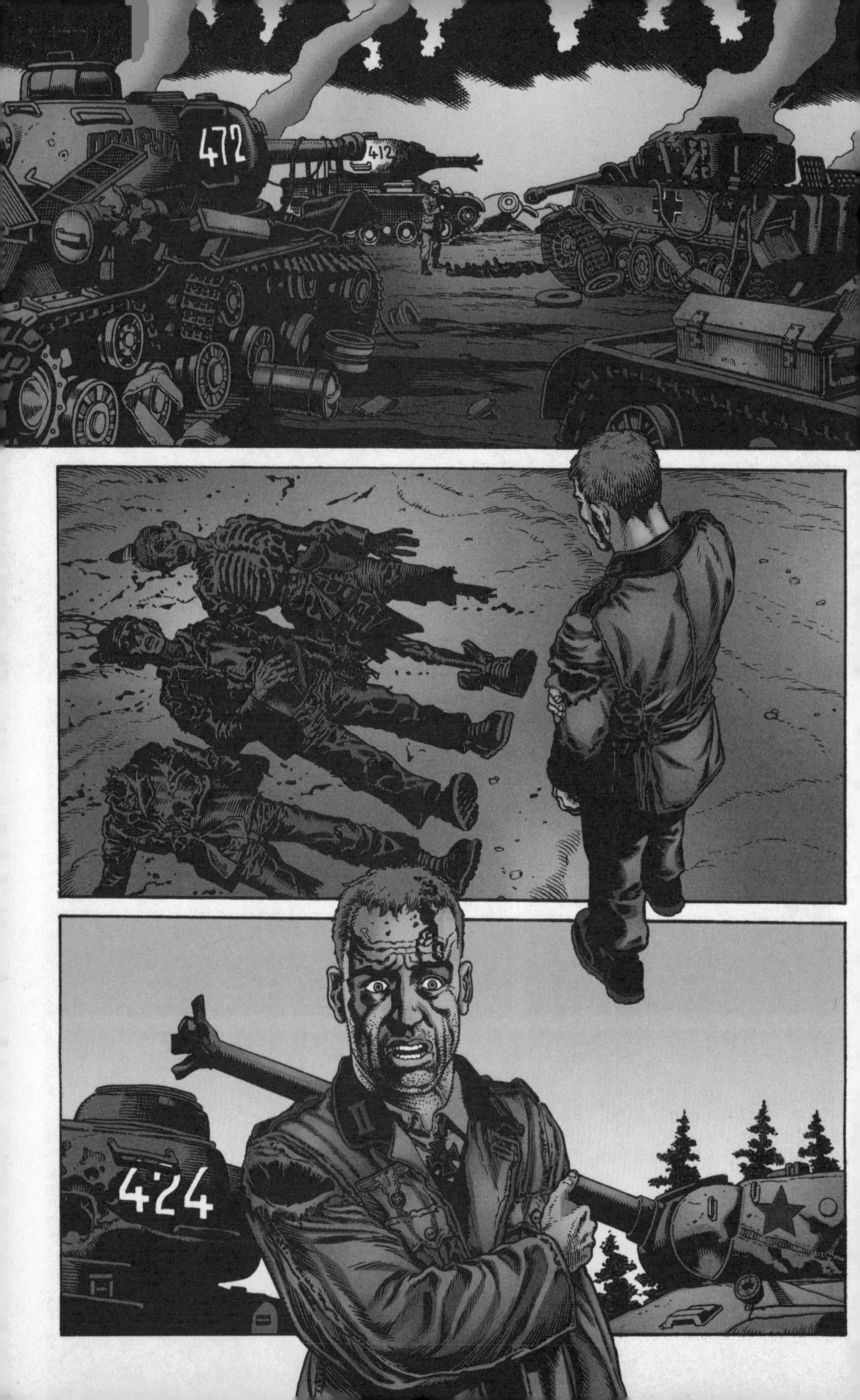

ПОДРУГА
472
412
424

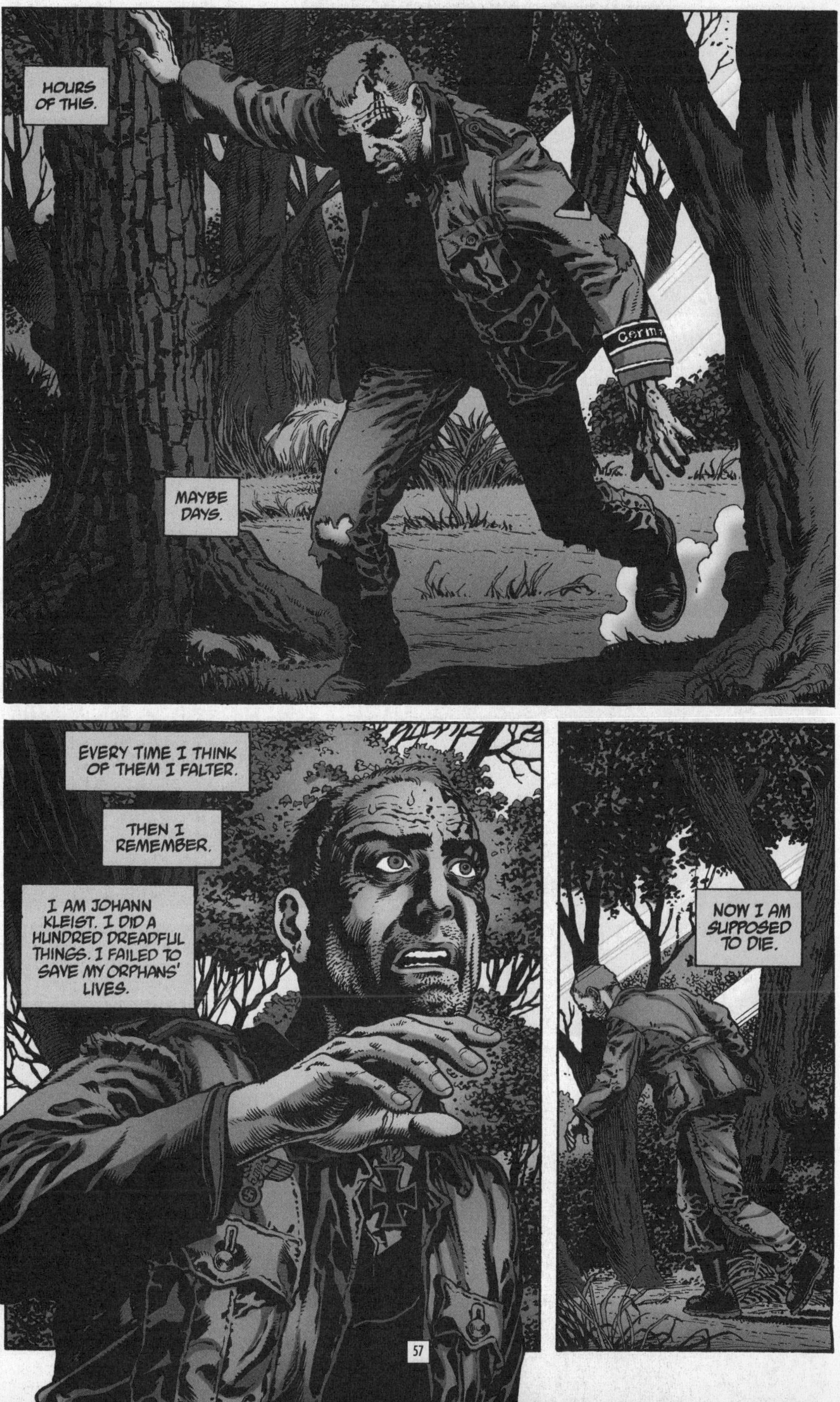
HOURS OF THIS.
Germ
MAYBE DAYS.
EVERY TIME I THINK OF THEM I FALTER.
THEN I REMEMBER.
I AM JOHANN KLEIST. I DID A HUNDRED DREADFUL THINGS. I FAILED TO SAVE MY ORPHANS' LIVES.
NOW I AM SUPPOSED TO DIE.

WHAT WAS IT I SAID, WITH A WRY LITTLE SMILE? THAT IT WOULD NOT BE DIFFICULT? THAT THOUSANDS DO IT EVERY DAY?

HOW VERY CLEVER OF ME.

WELL, JOHANN, THE MOMENT HAS ARRIVED.

LET'S SEE HOW CLEVER YOU ARE NOW.

SO WITH THE SICK FREEDOM GRANTED TO A DEAD MAN--

THE TOTAL ABSENCE OF RESPONSIBILITY--

I GO TO LOOK FOR IVAN.

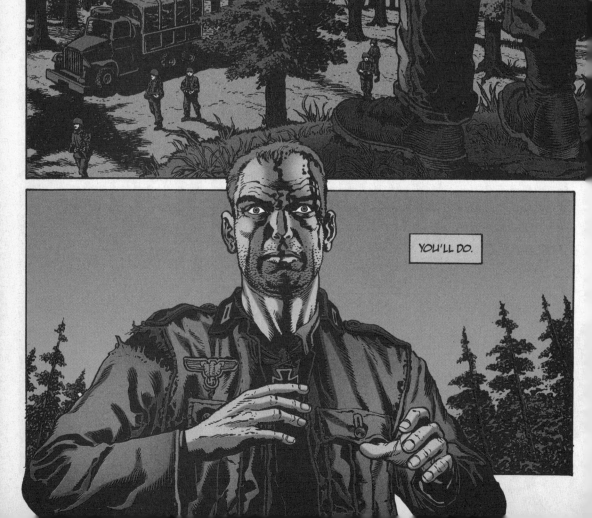

YOU'LL DO.

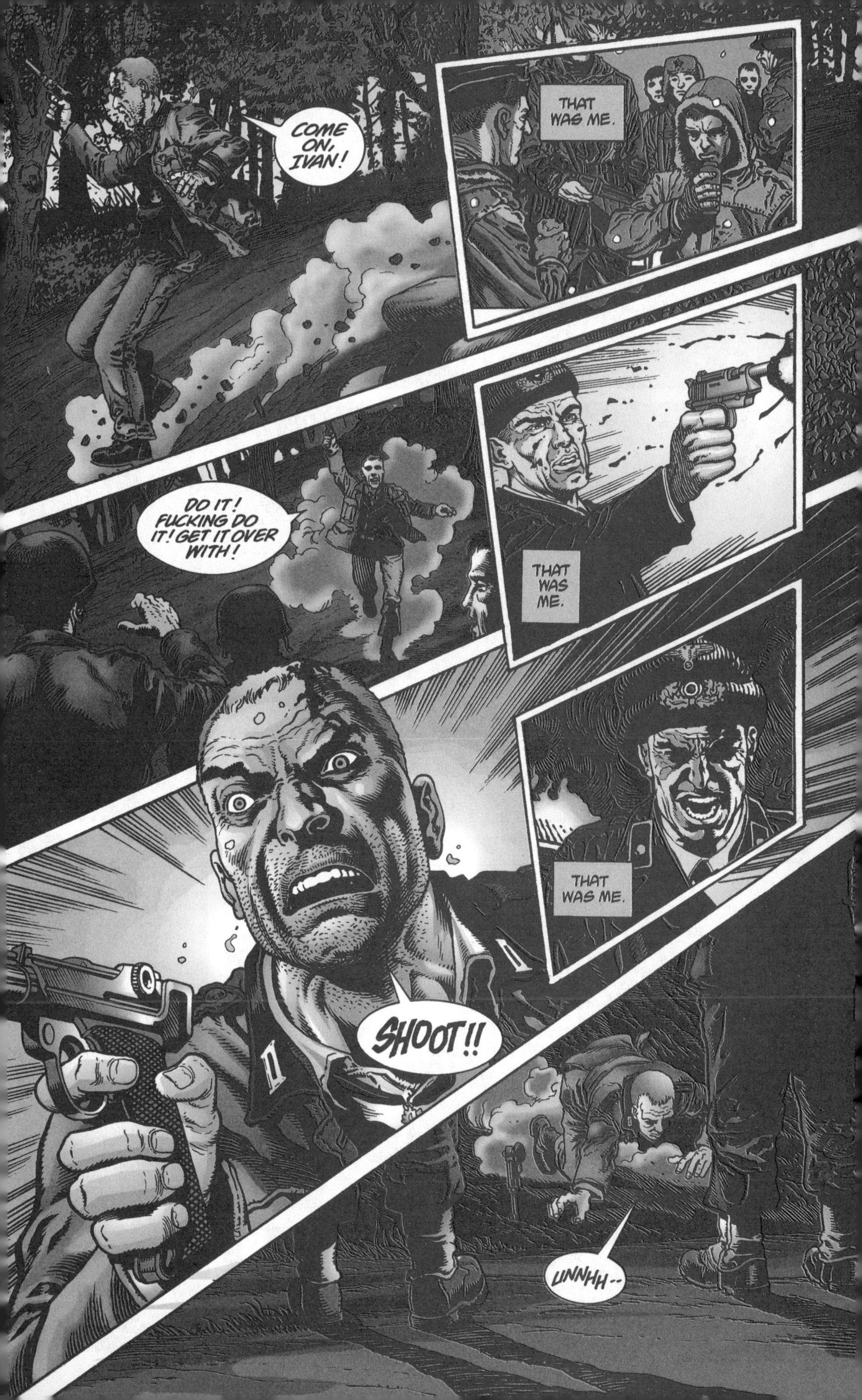
COME ON, IVAN!
THAT WAS ME.
THAT WAS ME.
DO IT! FUCKING DO IT! GET IT OVER WITH!
THAT WAS ME.
SHOOT!!
UNNHH--

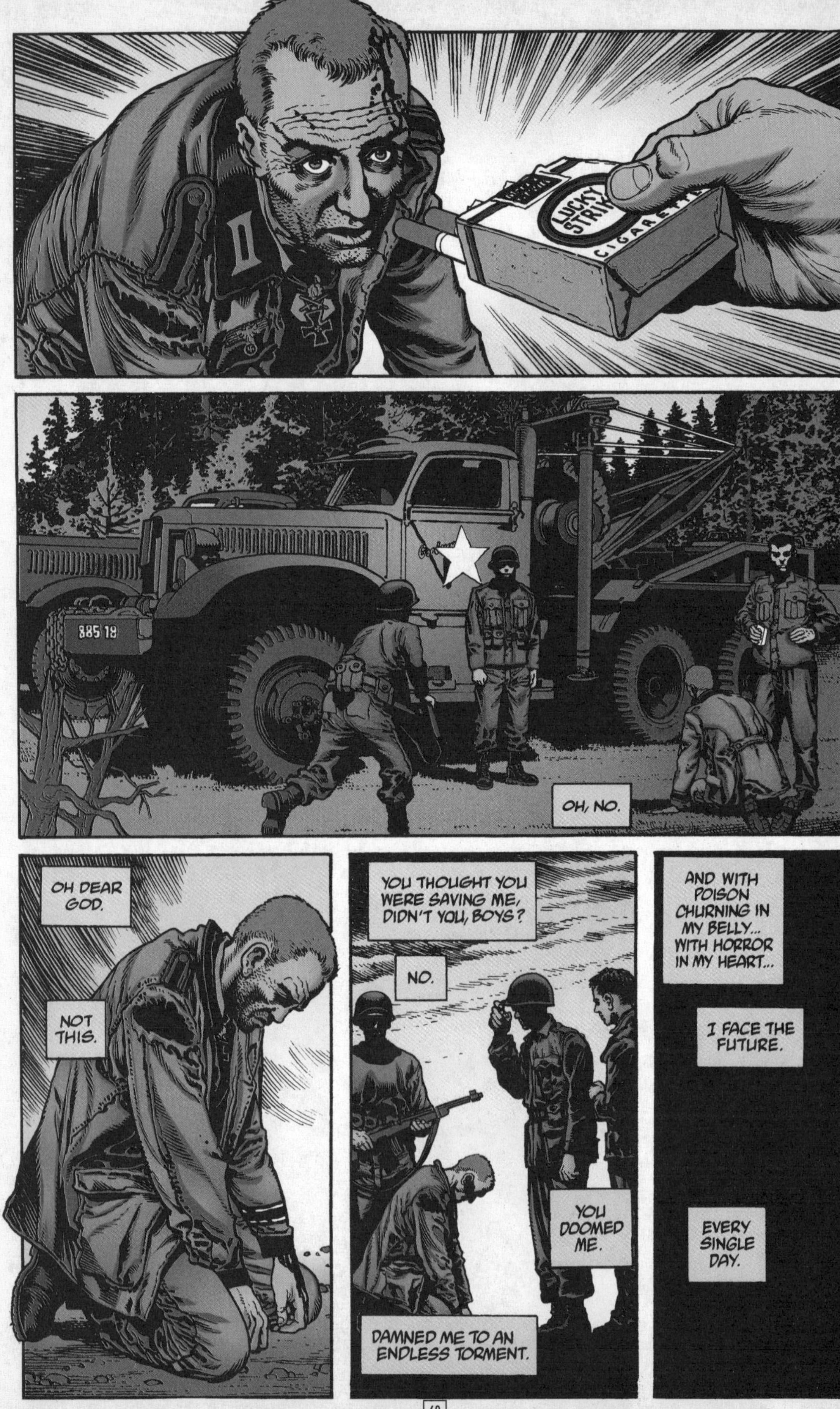
OH, NO.
OH DEAR GOD.
NOT THIS.
YOU THOUGHT YOU WERE SAVING ME, DIDN'T YOU, BOYS?
NO.
YOU DOOMED ME.
DAMNED ME TO AN ENDLESS TORMENT.
AND WITH POISON CHURNING IN MY BELLY... WITH HORROR IN MY HEART...
I FACE THE FUTURE.
EVERY SINGLE DAY.

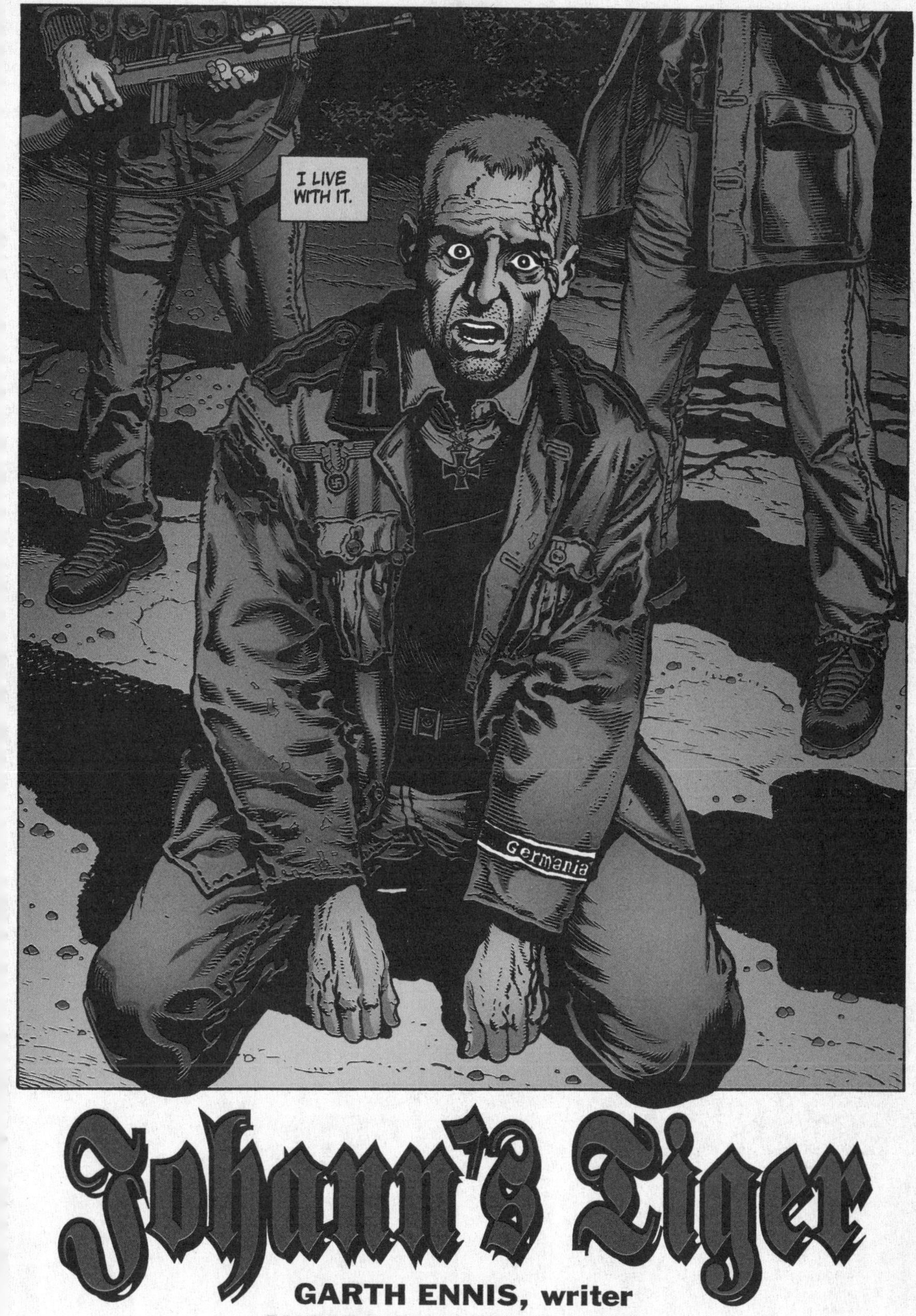
I LIVE WITH IT.
Germania

Johann's Tiger

GARTH ENNIS, writer
CHRIS WESTON, penciller
GARY ERSKINE, inker

PAMELA RAMBO, colorist CLEM ROBINS, letterer HEROIC AGE, separations JOHN VAN FLEET, cover artist
TONY BEDARD & WILL DENNIS, editors Special thanks to AXEL ALONSO Cover photo courtesy of the Tank Museum

"THE LAST VERSE TO BE SUNG WITH VINO ON YOUR LIPS AND TEARS IN YOUR EYES."

WAR STORY

STORY

D-DAY DODGERS

On third September, 1943, on the beaches of Reggio Calabria, the ramps on the landing craft slammed down and the boys went back to work.

They were English and Irish and Scots and Canadian; there were Americans among them, and Australians, and Poles and Moroccans and French and New Zealanders, and Indians and South Africans and later Brazilians, and they fought their way up Italy for twenty long and unexpected months.

They were bound for Germany in the north, Germany via Rimini and Anzio and the Gothic Line and a place called Monte Cassino, Germany with nothing but the Panzers and *Fallschirmjager* and the ridges and valleys and mountains of Italy to stop them: what could have taken them so long?

They were still hard at it when the Second Front began and all eyes turned to the great crusade in the west, and their commanders thinned their ranks to send men and guns and tanks to France. They soldiered on, forgotten for the most part, while other Allied armies inched toward the Rhine and the vengeful Russian behemoth drew ever nearer to Berlin.

Their lot was blood and dust and snow and mud and nasty little springmines rigged amongst the olive groves; and when they were remembered, it was not always as they might have hoped.

D-DAY DODGERS

Garth Ennis, writer   **John Higgins**, artist

Pamela Rambo, colorist   Clem Robins, letterer
Digital Chameleon, separations   John Van Fleet, cover artist
Tony Bedard & Will Dennis, editors

Special thanks to Axel Alonso

Cover image, Imperial War Museum (SE 3860)

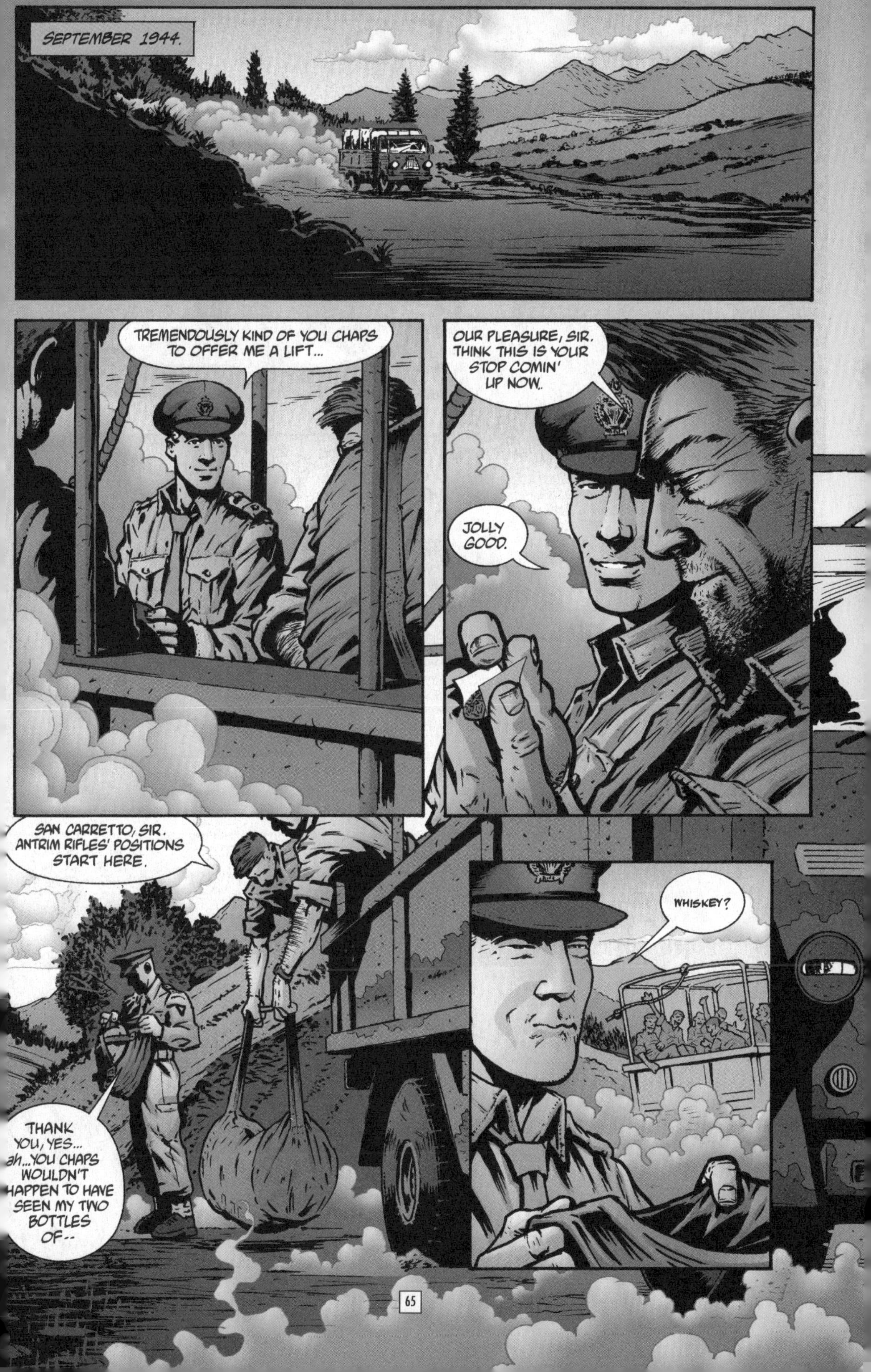
SEPTEMBER 1944.
TREMENDOUSLY KIND OF YOU CHAPS TO OFFER ME A LIFT...
OUR PLEASURE, SIR. THINK THIS IS YOUR STOP COMIN' UP NOW..
JOLLY GOOD.
SAN CARRETTO, SIR. ANTRIM RIFLES' POSITIONS START HERE.
THANK YOU, YES... ah...YOU CHAPS WOULDN'T HAPPEN TO HAVE SEEN MY TWO BOTTLES OF--
WHISKEY?

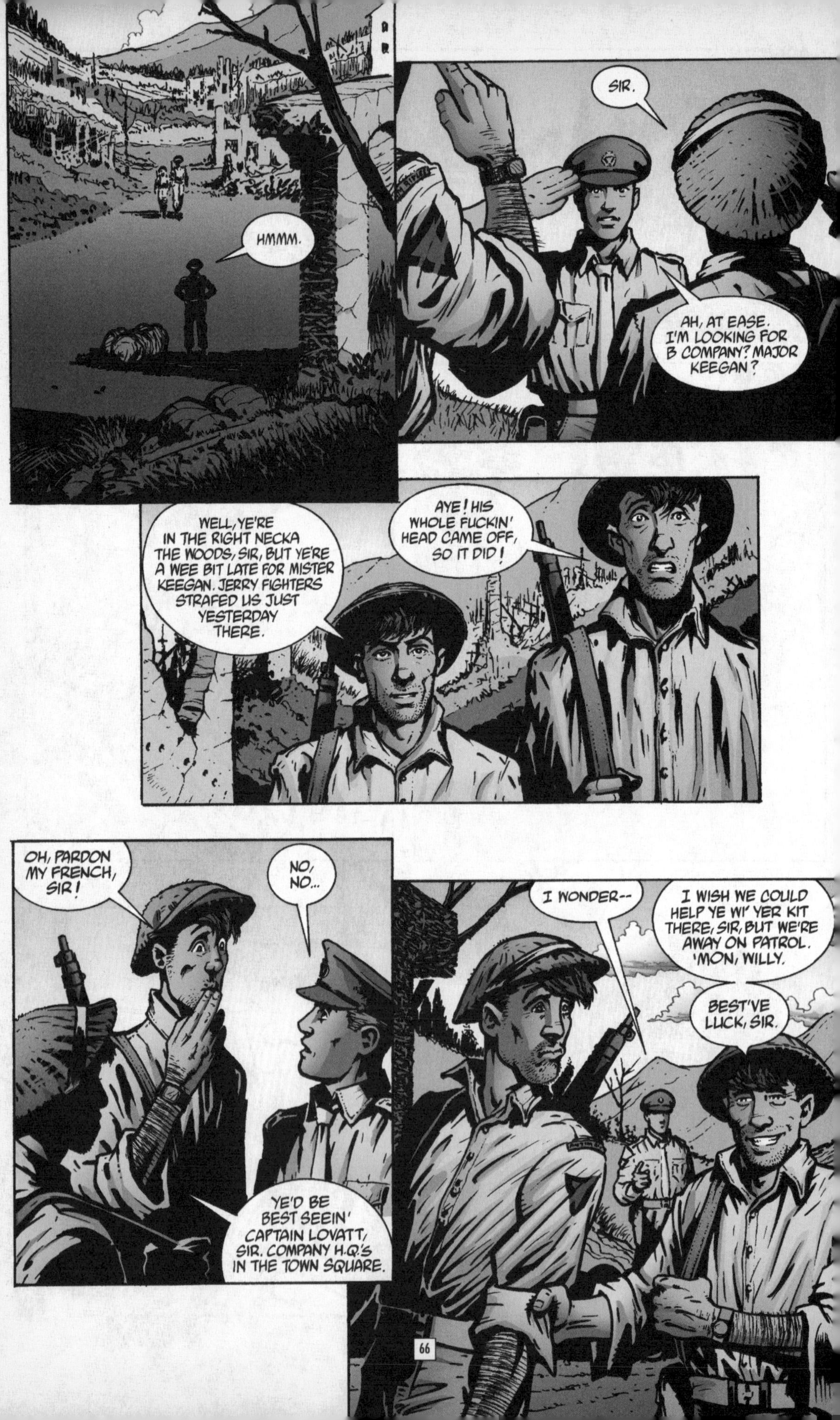
HMMM.
SIR.
AH, AT EASE. I'M LOOKING FOR B COMPANY? MAJOR KEEGAN?
WELL, YE'RE IN THE RIGHT NECKA THE WOODS, SIR, BUT YE'RE A WEE BIT LATE FOR MISTER KEEGAN. JERRY FIGHTERS STRAFED US JUST YESTERDAY THERE.
AYE! HIS WHOLE FUCKIN' HEAD CAME OFF, SO IT DID!
OH, PARDON MY FRENCH, SIR!
NO, NO...
YE'D BE BEST SEEIN' CAPTAIN LOVATT, SIR. COMPANY H.Q.'S IN THE TOWN SQUARE.
I WONDER--
I WISH WE COULD HELP YE WI' YER KIT THERE, SIR, BUT WE'RE AWAY ON PATROL. 'MON, WILLY.
BEST'VE LUCK, SIR.

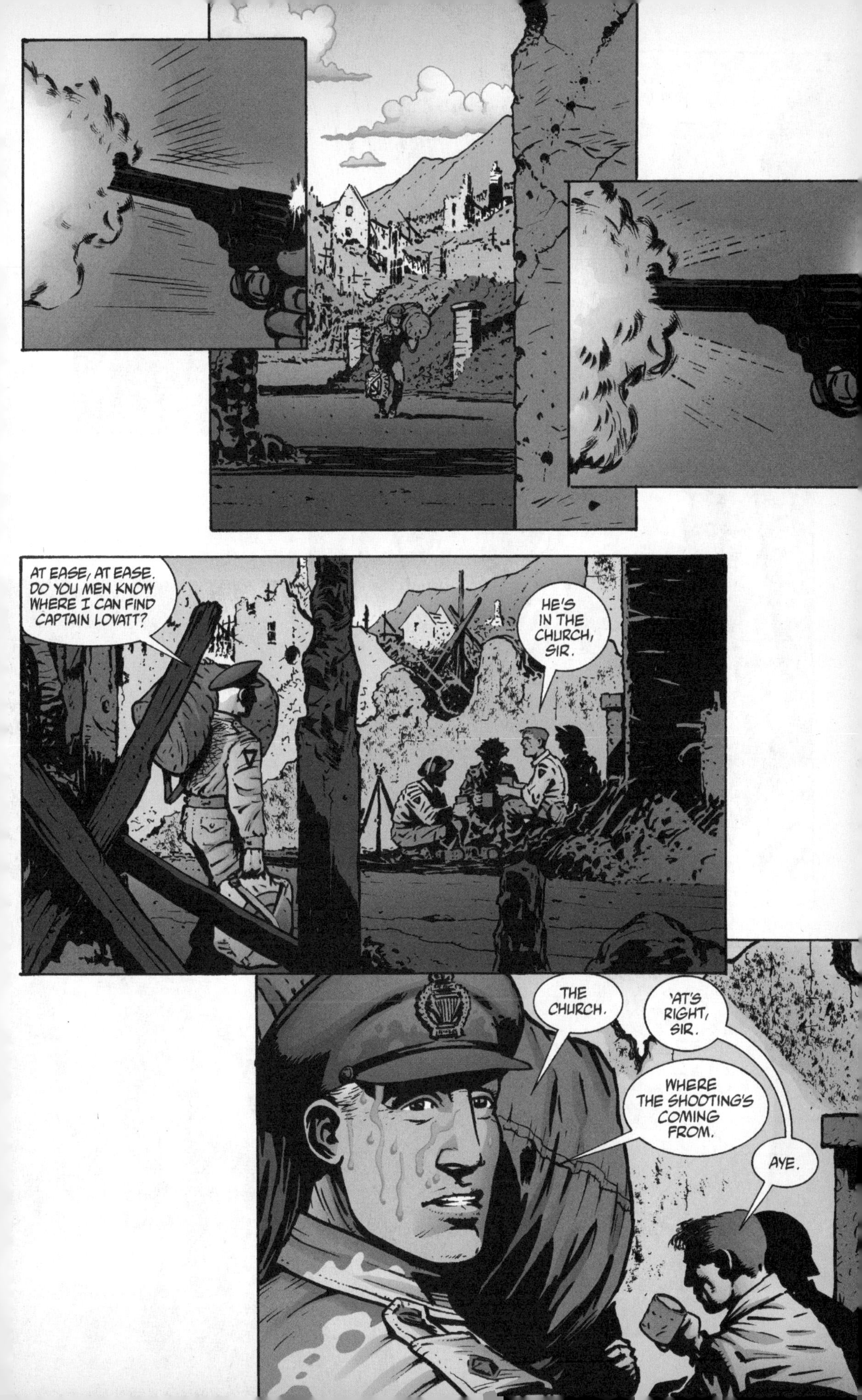
AT EASE, AT EASE. DO YOU MEN KNOW WHERE I CAN FIND CAPTAIN LOVATT?
HE'S IN THE CHURCH, SIR.
THE CHURCH.
'AT'S RIGHT, SIR.
WHERE THE SHOOTING'S COMING FROM.
AYE.

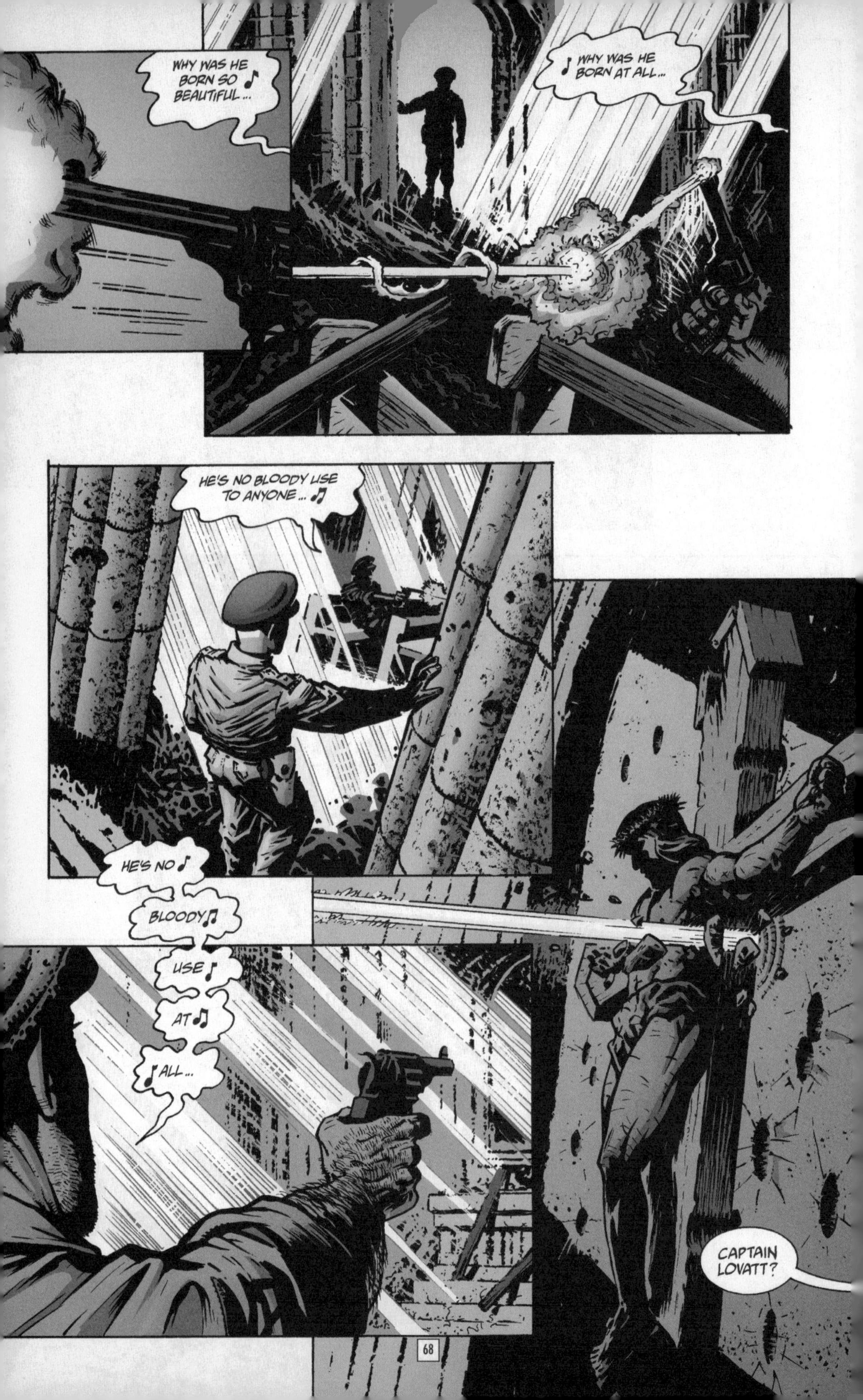
WHY WAS HE BORN SO ♪ BEAUTIFUL...
♪ WHY WAS HE BORN AT ALL...
HE'S NO BLOODY USE TO ANYONE... ♫
HE'S NO ♪
BLOODY ♫
USE ♪
AT ♫
♪ ALL...
CAPTAIN LOVATT?

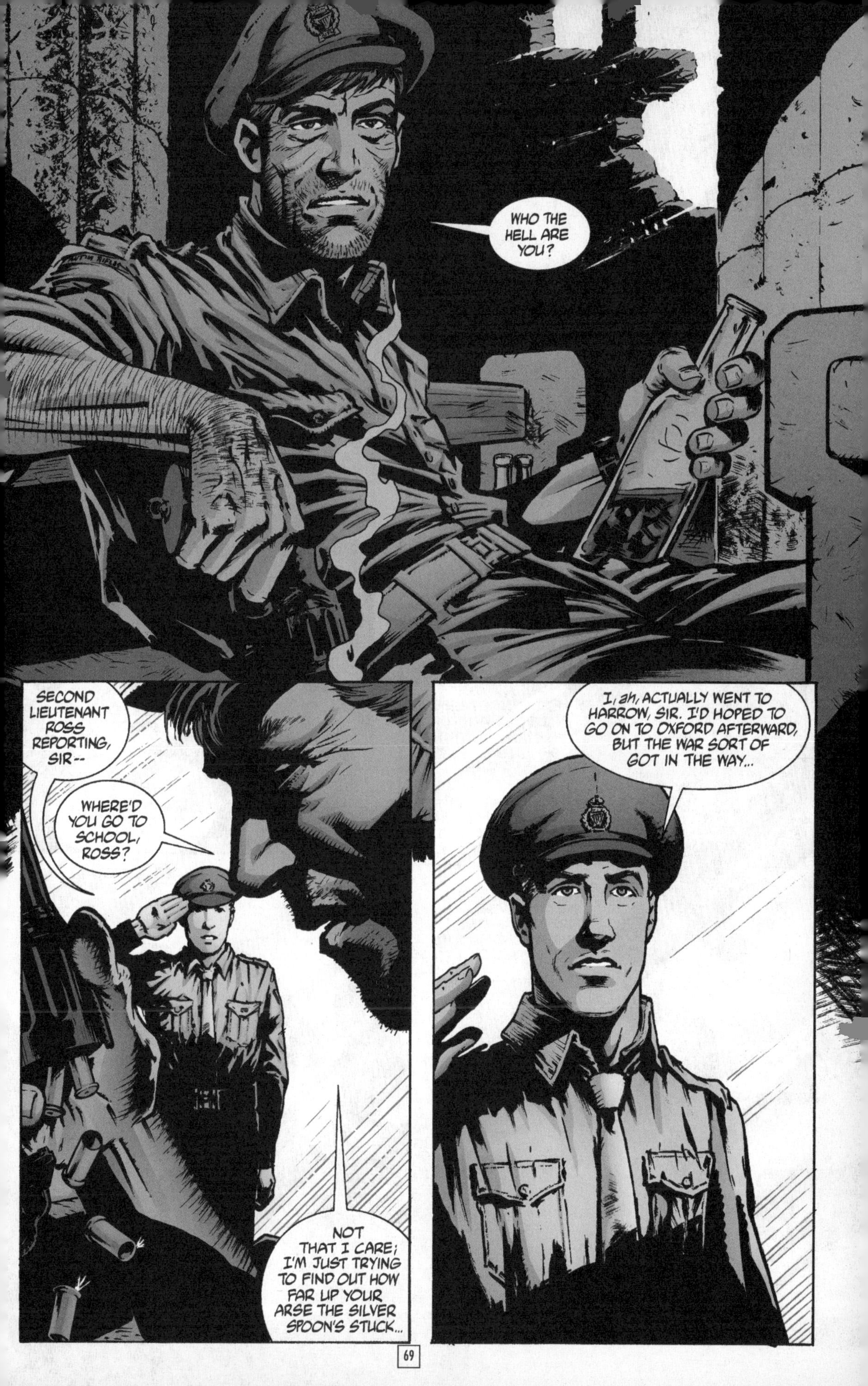
WHO THE HELL ARE YOU?
SECOND LIEUTENANT ROSS REPORTING, SIR--
WHERE'D YOU GO TO SCHOOL, ROSS?
NOT THAT I CARE; I'M JUST TRYING TO FIND OUT HOW FAR UP YOUR ARSE THE SILVER SPOON'S STUCK...
I, *ah,* ACTUALLY WENT TO HARROW, SIR. I'D HOPED TO GO ON TO OXFORD AFTERWARD, BUT THE WAR SORT OF GOT IN THE WAY...

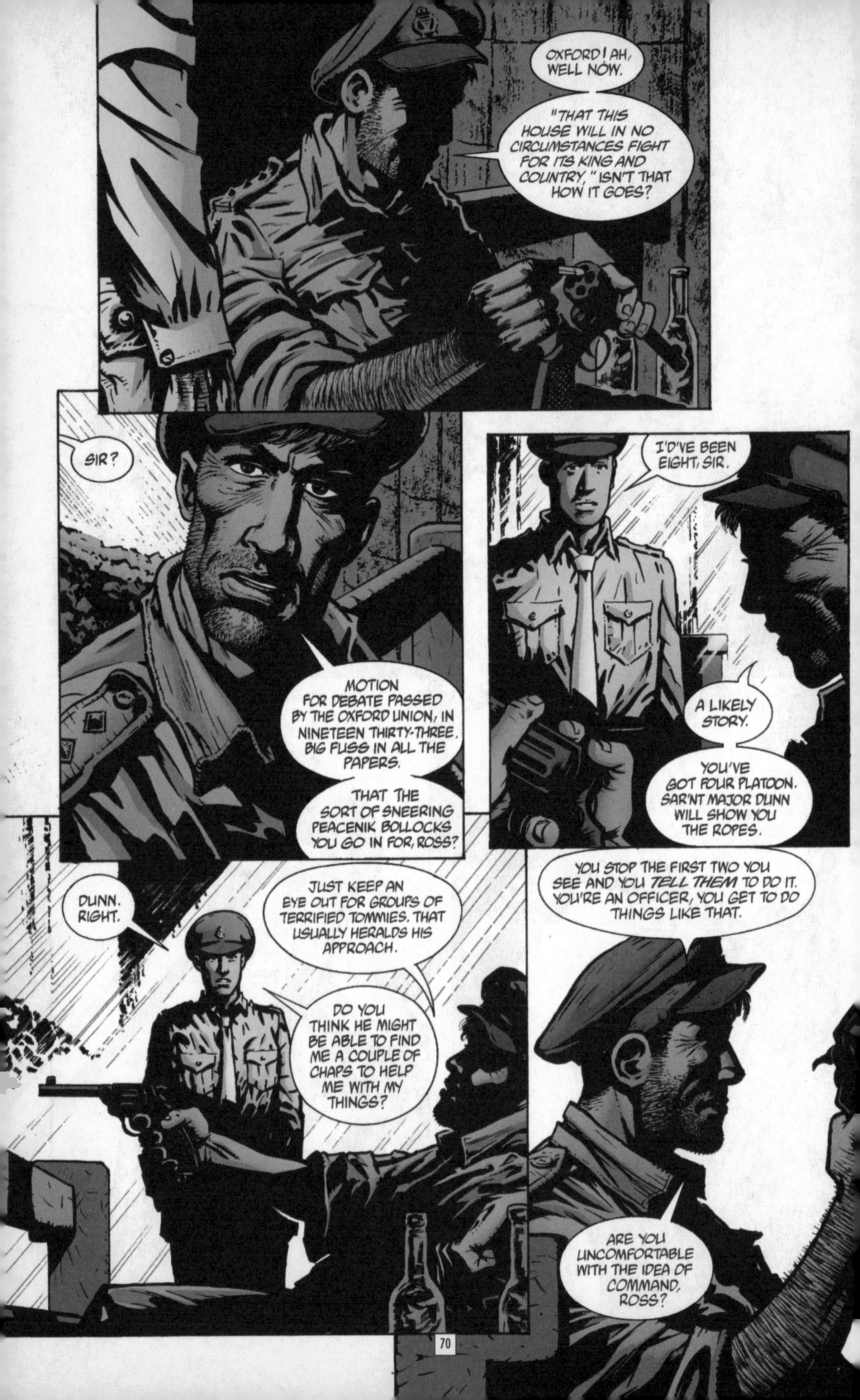
OXFORD! AH, WELL NOW.
"THAT THIS HOUSE WILL IN NO CIRCUMSTANCES FIGHT FOR ITS KING AND COUNTRY," ISN'T THAT HOW IT GOES?
SIR?
MOTION FOR DEBATE PASSED BY THE OXFORD UNION, IN NINETEEN THIRTY-THREE. BIG FUSS IN ALL THE PAPERS.
THAT THE SORT OF SNEERING PEACENIK BOLLOCKS YOU GO IN FOR, ROSS?
I'D'VE BEEN EIGHT, SIR.
A LIKELY STORY.
YOU'VE GOT FOUR PLATOON. SAR'NT MAJOR DUNN WILL SHOW YOU THE ROPES.
DUNN. RIGHT.
JUST KEEP AN EYE OUT FOR GROUPS OF TERRIFIED TOMMIES. THAT USUALLY HERALDS HIS APPROACH.
DO YOU THINK HE MIGHT BE ABLE TO FIND ME A COUPLE OF CHAPS TO HELP ME WITH MY THINGS?
YOU STOP THE FIRST TWO YOU SEE AND YOU *TELL THEM* TO DO IT. YOU'RE AN OFFICER, YOU GET TO DO THINGS LIKE THAT.
ARE YOU UNCOMFORTABLE WITH THE IDEA OF COMMAND, ROSS?

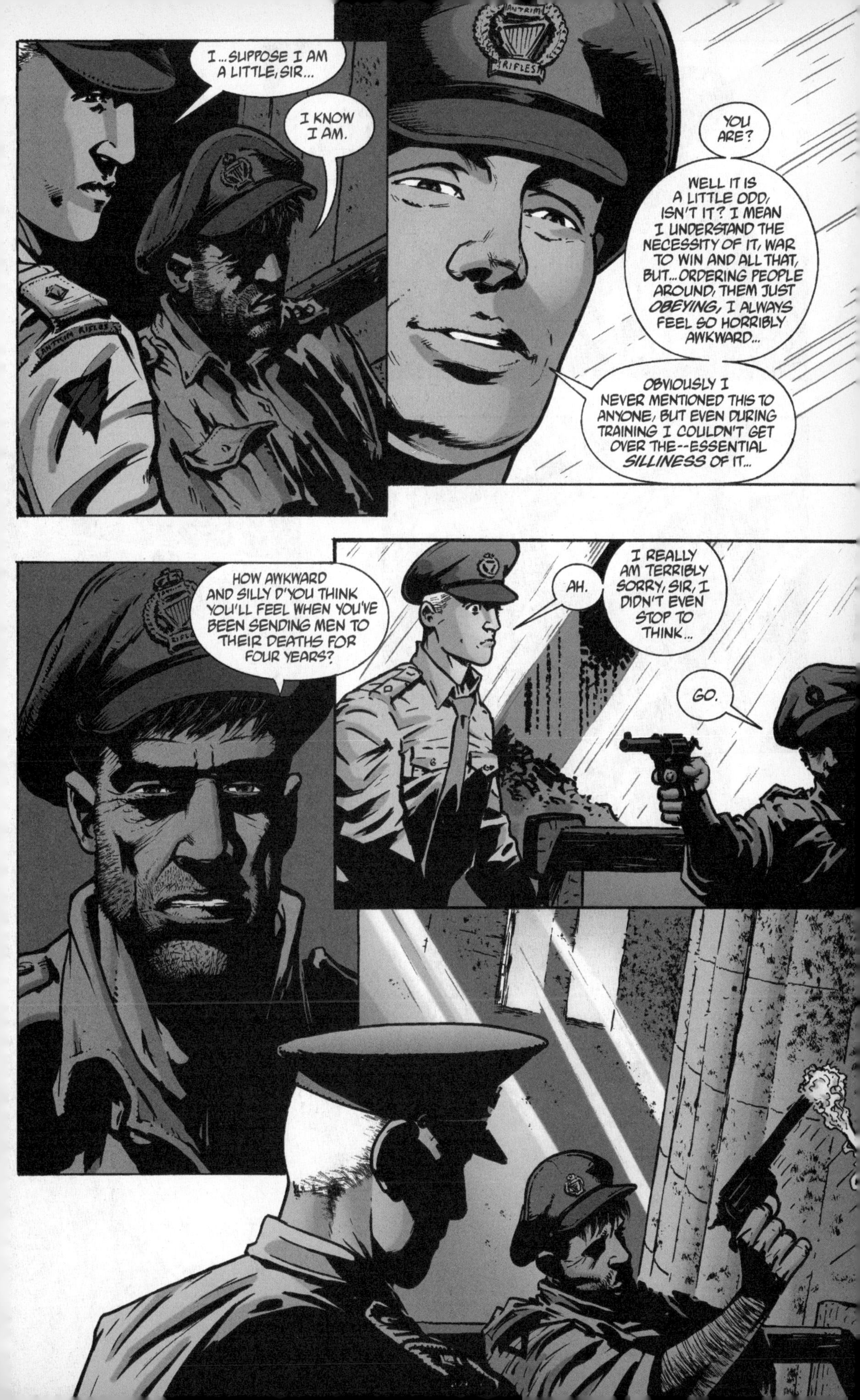

I...SUPPOSE I AM A LITTLE, SIR...
I KNOW I AM.
YOU ARE?
WELL IT IS A LITTLE ODD, ISN'T IT? I MEAN I UNDERSTAND THE NECESSITY OF IT, WAR TO WIN AND ALL THAT, BUT...ORDERING PEOPLE AROUND, THEM JUST *OBEYING*, I ALWAYS FEEL SO HORRIBLY AWKWARD...
OBVIOUSLY I NEVER MENTIONED THIS TO ANYONE, BUT EVEN DURING TRAINING I COULDN'T GET OVER THE--ESSENTIAL *SILLINESS* OF IT...
HOW AWKWARD AND SILLY D'YOU THINK YOU'LL FEEL WHEN YOU'VE BEEN SENDING MEN TO THEIR DEATHS FOR FOUR YEARS?
AH.
I REALLY AM TERRIBLY SORRY, SIR, I DIDN'T EVEN STOP TO THINK...
GO.

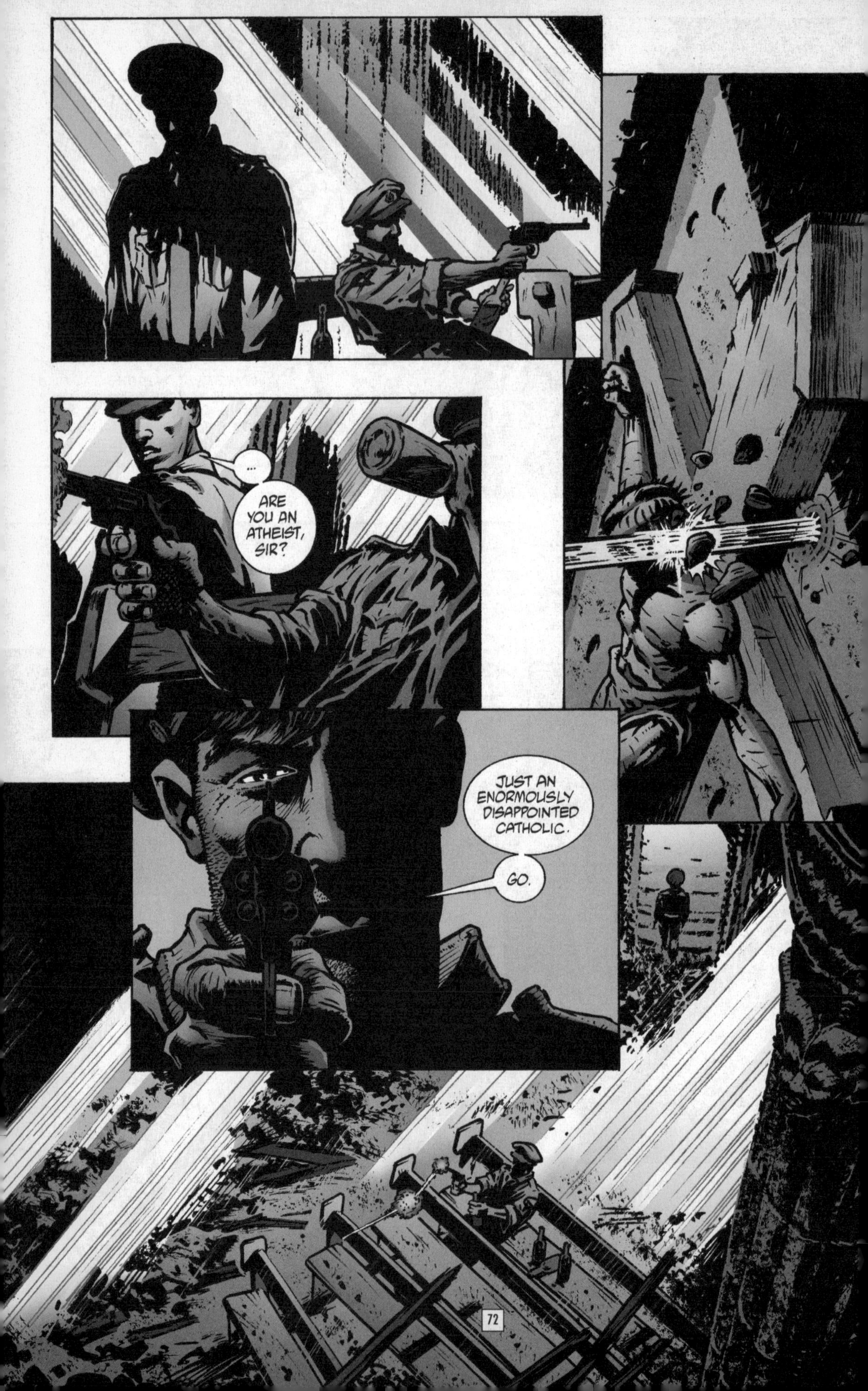
...
ARE YOU AN ATHEIST, SIR?
JUST AN ENORMOUSLY DISAPPOINTED CATHOLIC.
GO.

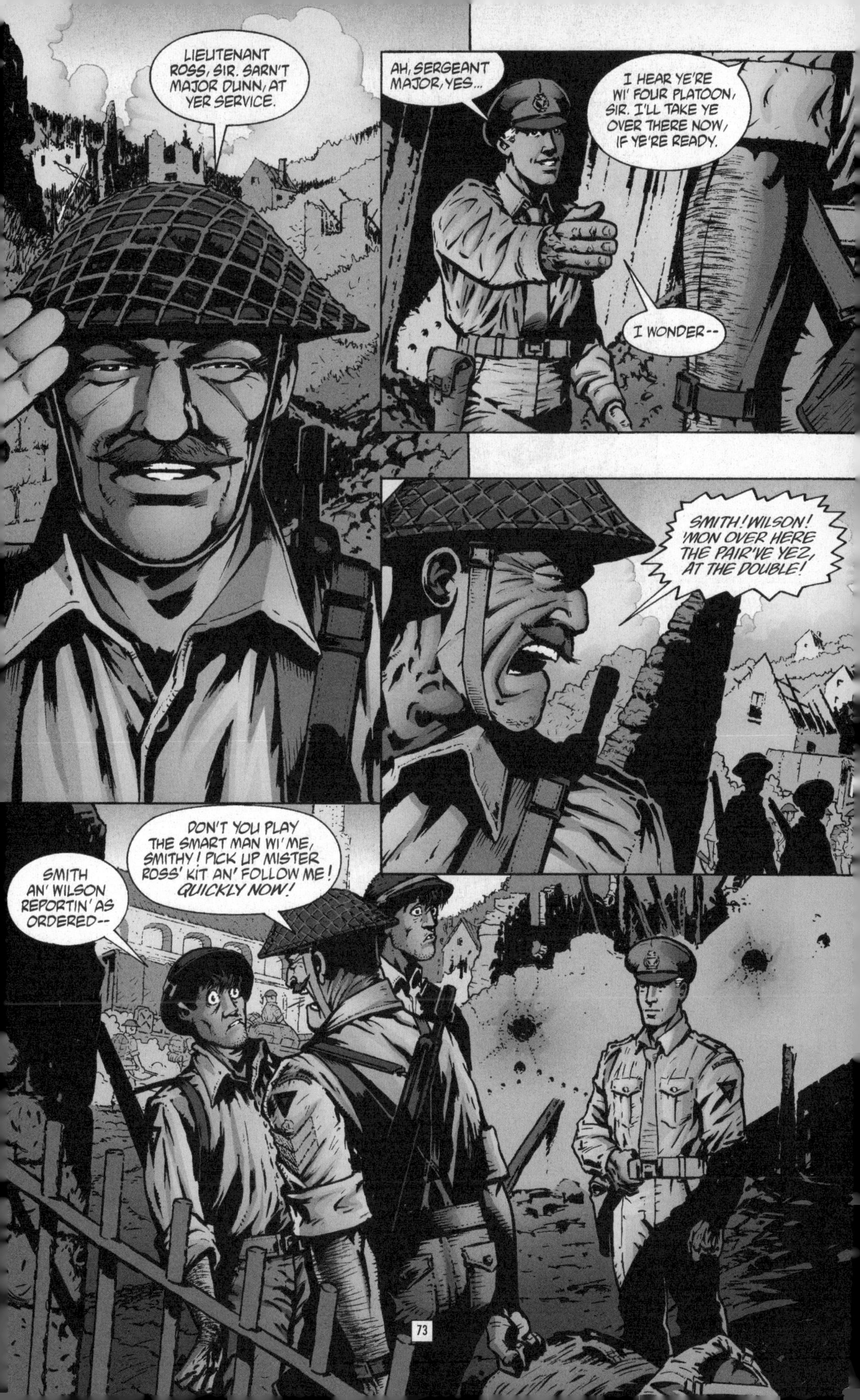
LIEUTENANT ROSS, SIR. SARN'T MAJOR DUNN, AT YER SERVICE.
AH, SERGEANT MAJOR, YES...
I HEAR YE'RE WI' FOUR PLATOON, SIR. I'LL TAKE YE OVER THERE NOW, IF YE'RE READY.
I WONDER--
SMITH! WILSON! 'MON OVER HERE THE PAIR'VE YEZ, AT THE DOUBLE!
SMITH AN' WILSON REPORTIN' AS ORDERED--
DON'T YOU PLAY THE SMART MAN WI' ME, SMITHY! PICK UP MISTER ROSS' KIT AN' FOLLOW ME! *QUICKLY NOW!*

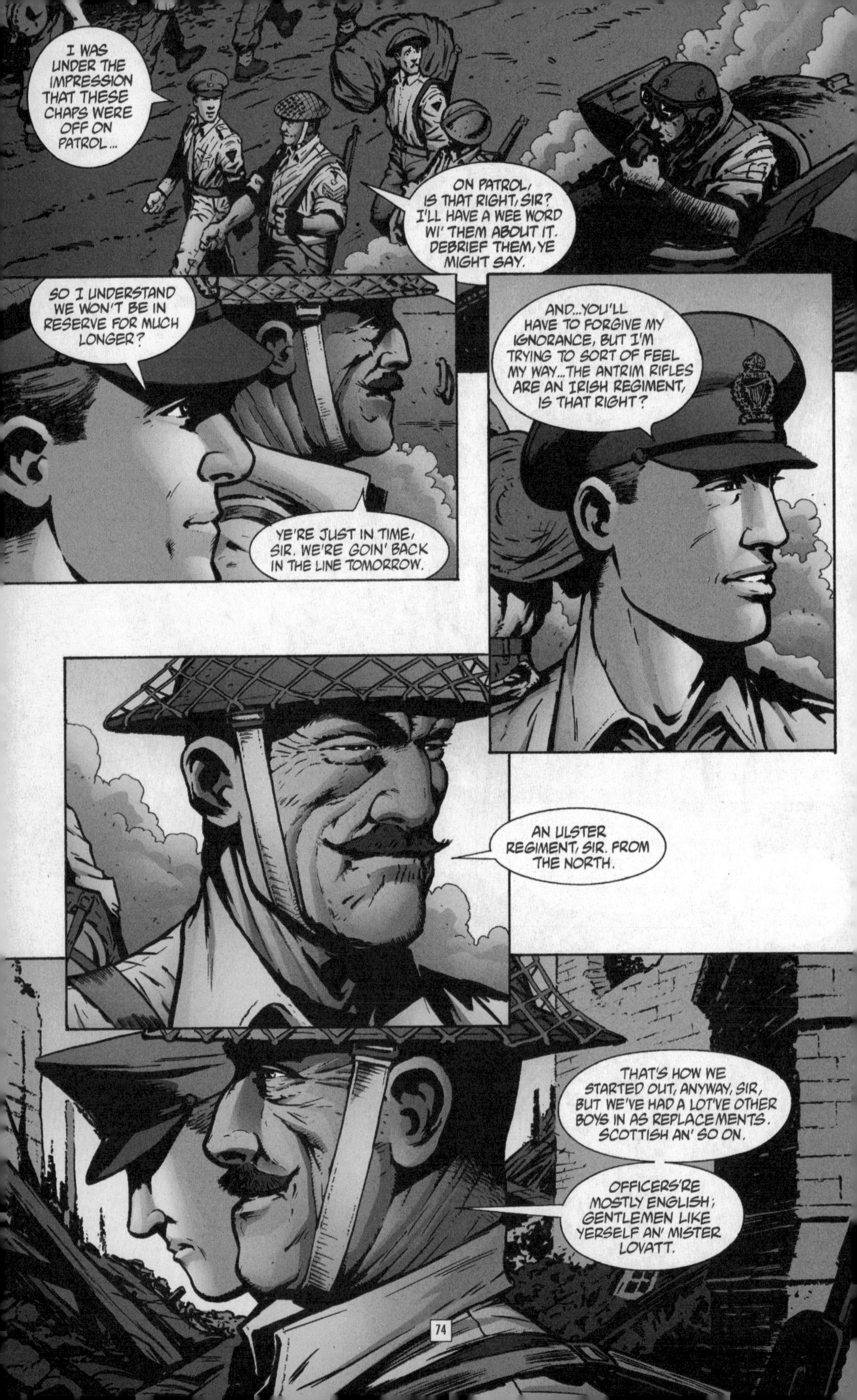
I WAS UNDER THE IMPRESSION THAT THESE CHAPS WERE OFF ON PATROL...
ON PATROL, IS THAT RIGHT, SIR? I'LL HAVE A WEE WORD WI' THEM ABOUT IT. DEBRIEF THEM, YE MIGHT SAY.
SO I UNDERSTAND WE WON'T BE IN RESERVE FOR MUCH LONGER?
YE'RE JUST IN TIME, SIR. WE'RE GOIN' BACK IN THE LINE TOMORROW.
AND...YOU'LL HAVE TO FORGIVE MY IGNORANCE, BUT I'M TRYING TO SORT OF FEEL MY WAY...THE ANTRIM RIFLES ARE AN IRISH REGIMENT, IS THAT RIGHT?
AN ULSTER REGIMENT, SIR. FROM THE NORTH.
THAT'S HOW WE STARTED OUT, ANYWAY, SIR, BUT WE'VE HAD A LOT'VE OTHER BOYS IN AS REPLACEMENTS. SCOTTISH AN' SO ON.
OFFICERS'RE MOSTLY ENGLISH; GENTLEMEN LIKE YERSELF AN' MISTER LOVATT.

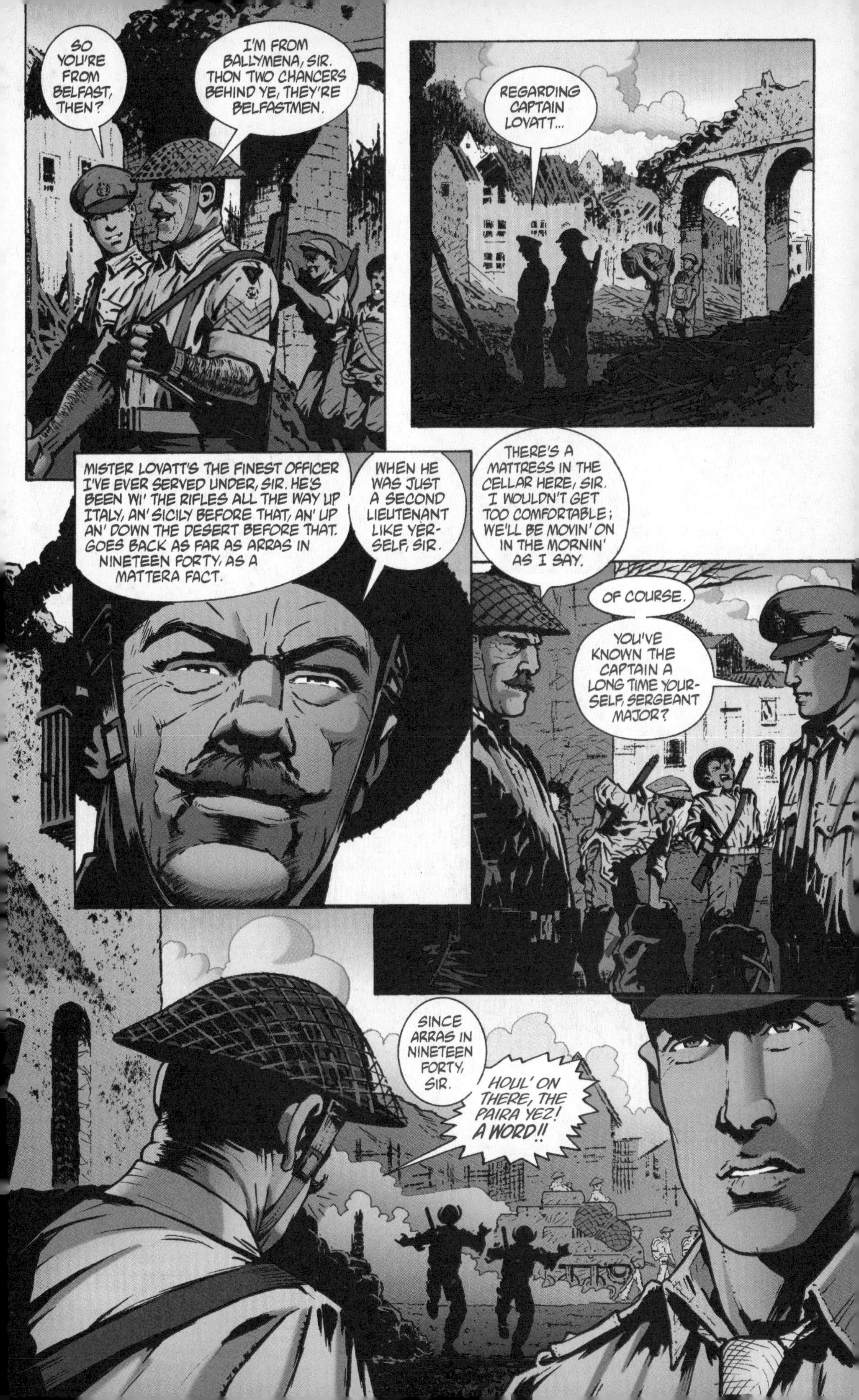
SO YOU'RE FROM BELFAST, THEN?
I'M FROM BALLYMENA, SIR. THON TWO CHANCERS BEHIND YE, THEY'RE BELFASTMEN.
REGARDING CAPTAIN LOVATT...
MISTER LOVATT'S THE FINEST OFFICER I'VE EVER SERVED UNDER, SIR. HE'S BEEN WI' THE RIFLES ALL THE WAY UP ITALY, AN' SICILY BEFORE THAT, AN' UP AN' DOWN THE DESERT BEFORE THAT. GOES BACK AS FAR AS ARRAS IN NINETEEN FORTY, AS A MATTERA FACT.
WHEN HE WAS JUST A SECOND LIEUTENANT LIKE YER-SELF, SIR.
THERE'S A MATTRESS IN THE CELLAR HERE, SIR. I WOULDN'T GET TOO COMFORTABLE; WE'LL BE MOVIN' ON IN THE MORNIN' AS I SAY.
OF COURSE.
YOU'VE KNOWN THE CAPTAIN A LONG TIME YOUR-SELF, SERGEANT MAJOR?
SINCE ARRAS IN NINETEEN FORTY, SIR.
HOUL' ON THERE, THE PAIRA YEZ! A WORD!!

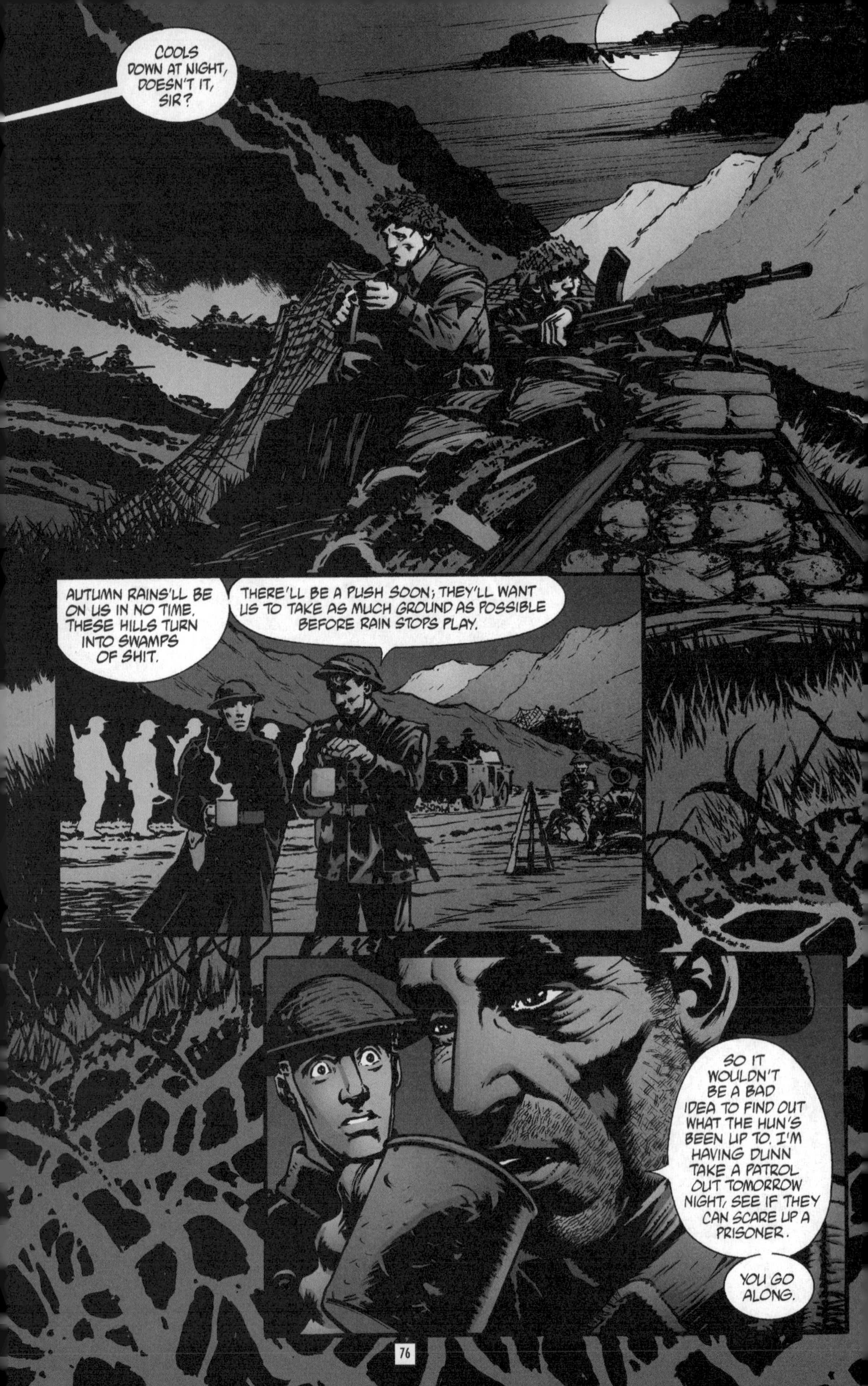
COOLS DOWN AT NIGHT, DOESN'T IT, SIR?
AUTUMN RAINS'LL BE ON US IN NO TIME. THESE HILLS TURN INTO SWAMPS OF SHIT.
THERE'LL BE A PUSH SOON; THEY'LL WANT US TO TAKE AS MUCH GROUND AS POSSIBLE BEFORE RAIN STOPS PLAY.
SO IT WOULDN'T BE A BAD IDEA TO FIND OUT WHAT THE HUN'S BEEN UP TO. I'M HAVING DUNN TAKE A PATROL OUT TOMORROW NIGHT, SEE IF THEY CAN SCARE UP A PRISONER.
YOU GO ALONG.

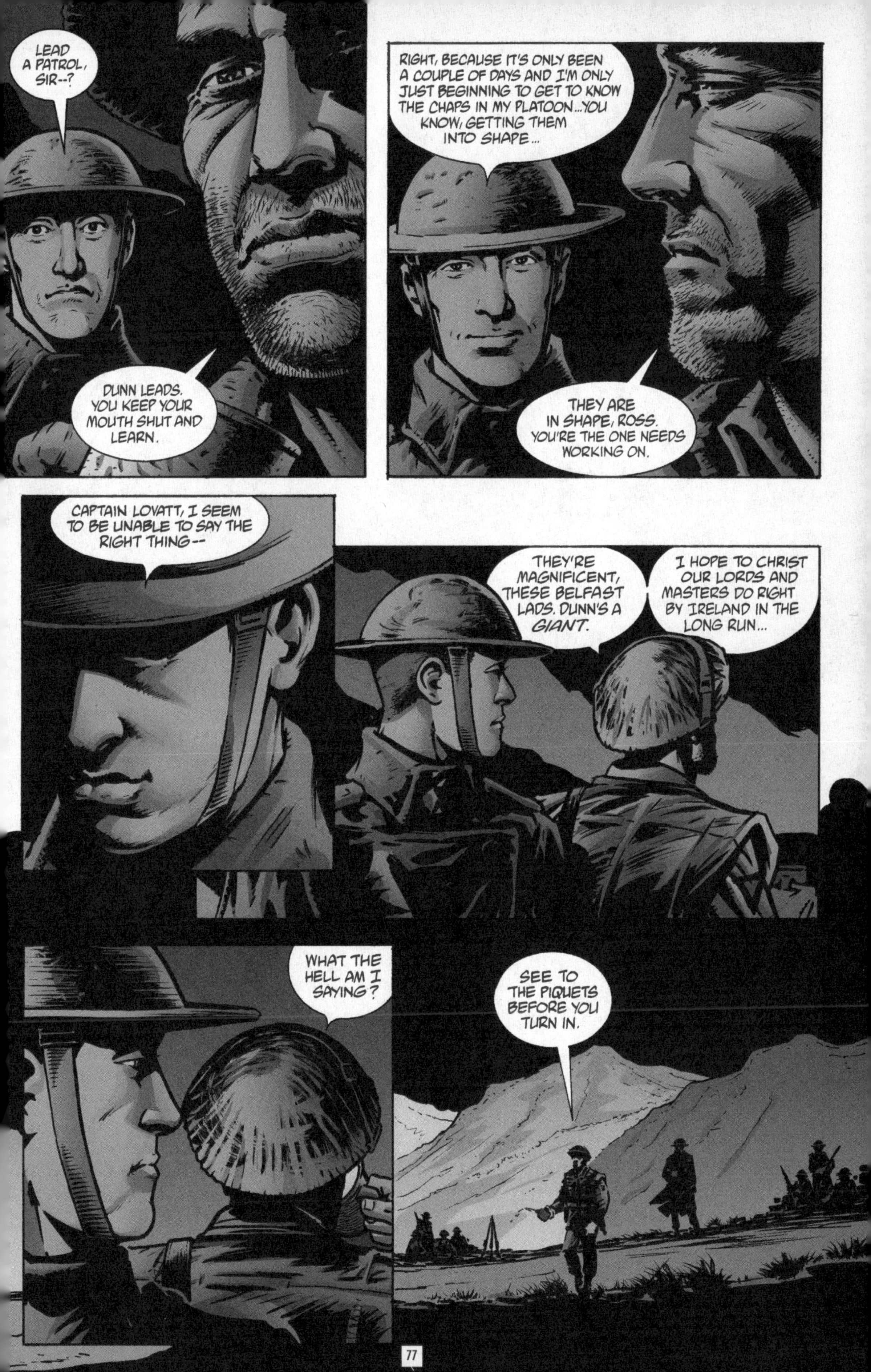
LEAD A PATROL, SIR--?
DUNN LEADS. YOU KEEP YOUR MOUTH SHUT AND LEARN.
RIGHT, BECAUSE IT'S ONLY BEEN A COUPLE OF DAYS AND I'M ONLY JUST BEGINNING TO GET TO KNOW THE CHAPS IN MY PLATOON...YOU KNOW, GETTING THEM INTO SHAPE...
THEY ARE IN SHAPE, ROSS. YOU'RE THE ONE NEEDS WORKING ON.
CAPTAIN LOVATT, I SEEM TO BE UNABLE TO SAY THE RIGHT THING--
THEY'RE MAGNIFICENT, THESE BELFAST LADS. DUNN'S A *GIANT*.
I HOPE TO CHRIST OUR LORDS AND MASTERS DO RIGHT BY IRELAND IN THE LONG RUN...
WHAT THE HELL AM I SAYING?
SEE TO THE PIQUETS BEFORE YOU TURN IN.

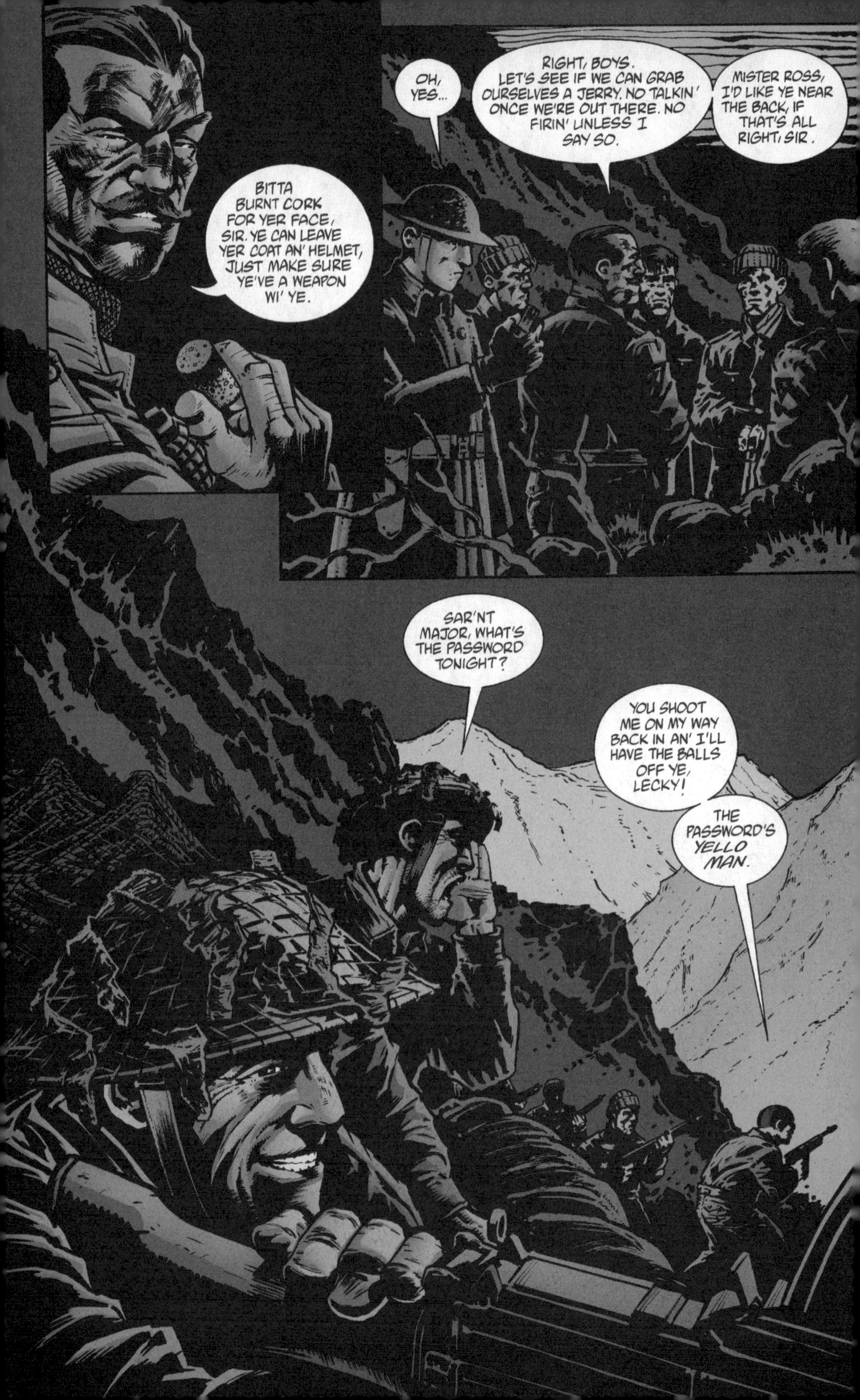
BITTA BURNT CORK FOR YER FACE, SIR. YE CAN LEAVE YER COAT AN' HELMET, JUST MAKE SURE YE'VE A WEAPON WI' YE.
OH, YES...
RIGHT, BOYS. LET'S SEE IF WE CAN GRAB OURSELVES A JERRY. NO TALKIN' ONCE WE'RE OUT THERE. NO FIRIN' UNLESS I SAY SO.
MISTER ROSS, I'D LIKE YE NEAR THE BACK, IF THAT'S ALL RIGHT, SIR.
SAR'NT MAJOR, WHAT'S THE PASSWORD TONIGHT?
YOU SHOOT ME ON MY WAY BACK IN AN' I'LL HAVE THE BALLS OFF YE, LECKY!
THE PASSWORD'S *YELLO MAN*.

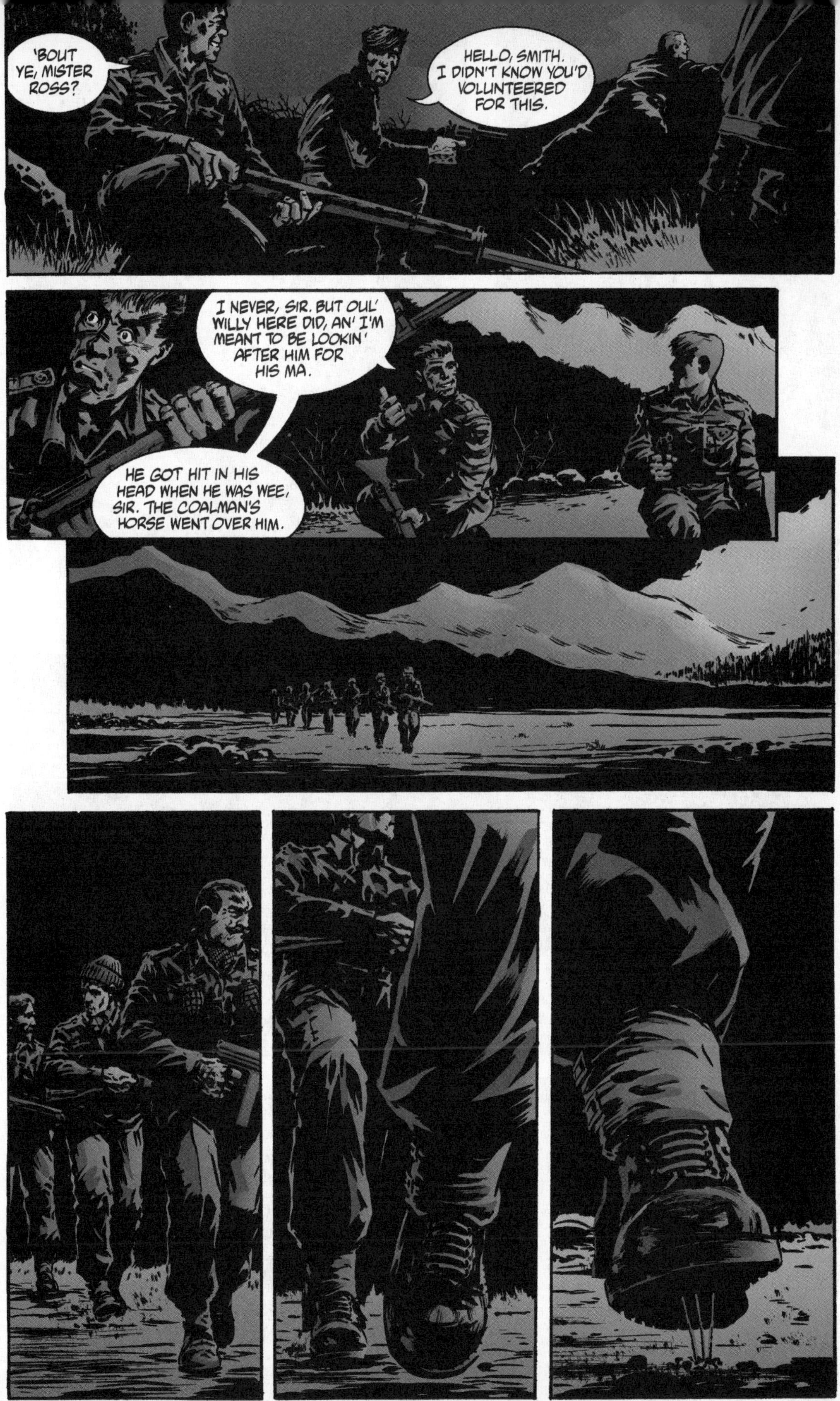
'BOUT YE, MISTER ROSS?
HELLO, SMITH. I DIDN'T KNOW YOU'D VOLUNTEERED FOR THIS.
I NEVER, SIR. BUT OUL' WILLY HERE DID, AN' I'M MEANT TO BE LOOKIN' AFTER HIM FOR HIS MA.
HE GOT HIT IN HIS HEAD WHEN HE WAS WEE, SIR. THE COALMAN'S HORSE WENT OVER HIM.

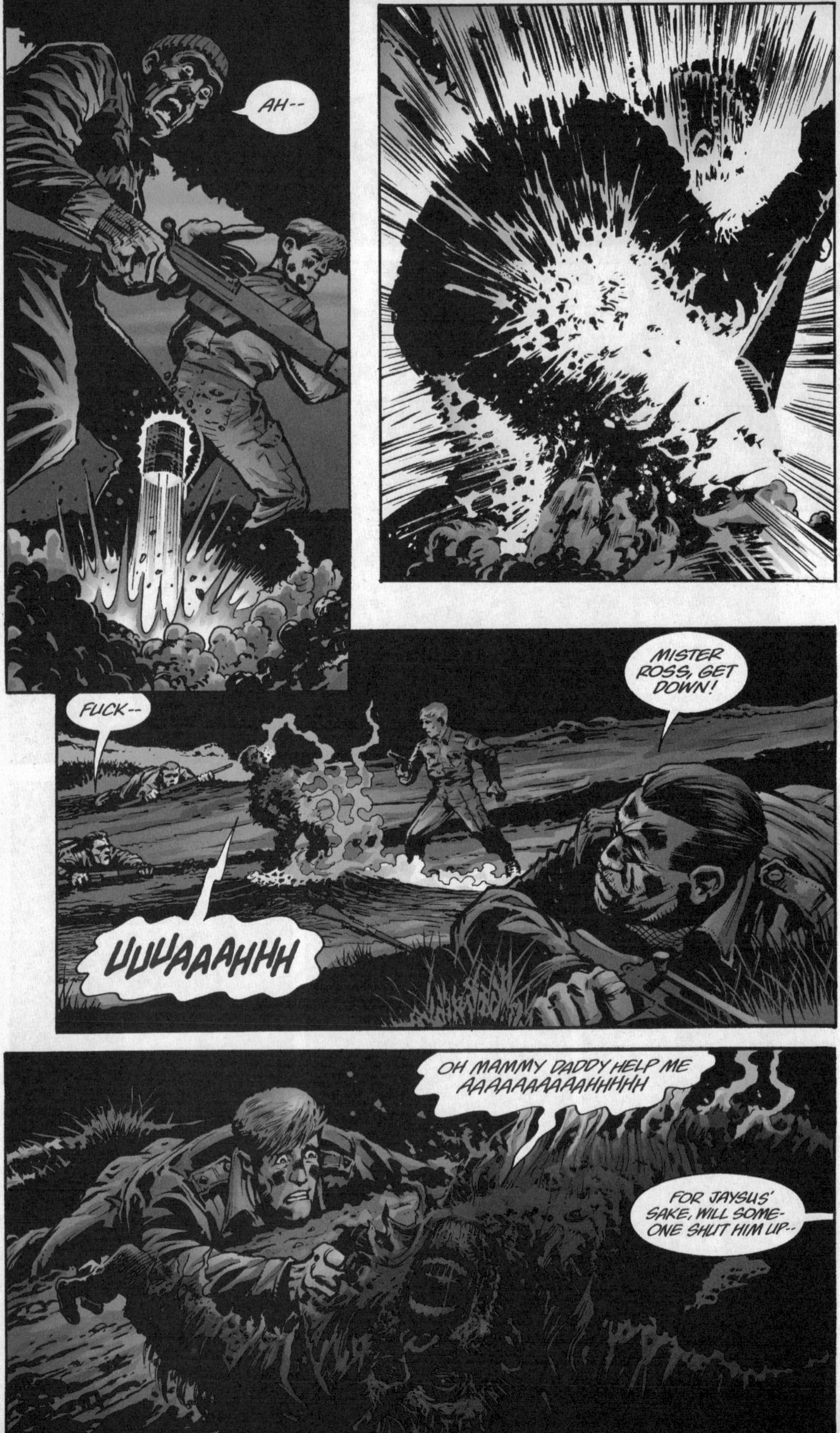
AH--
MISTER ROSS, GET DOWN!
FUCK--
UUUAAAAHHH
OH MAMMY DADDY HELP ME AAAAAAAAAHHHHH
FOR JAYSUS' SAKE, WILL SOME-ONE SHUT HIM UP--

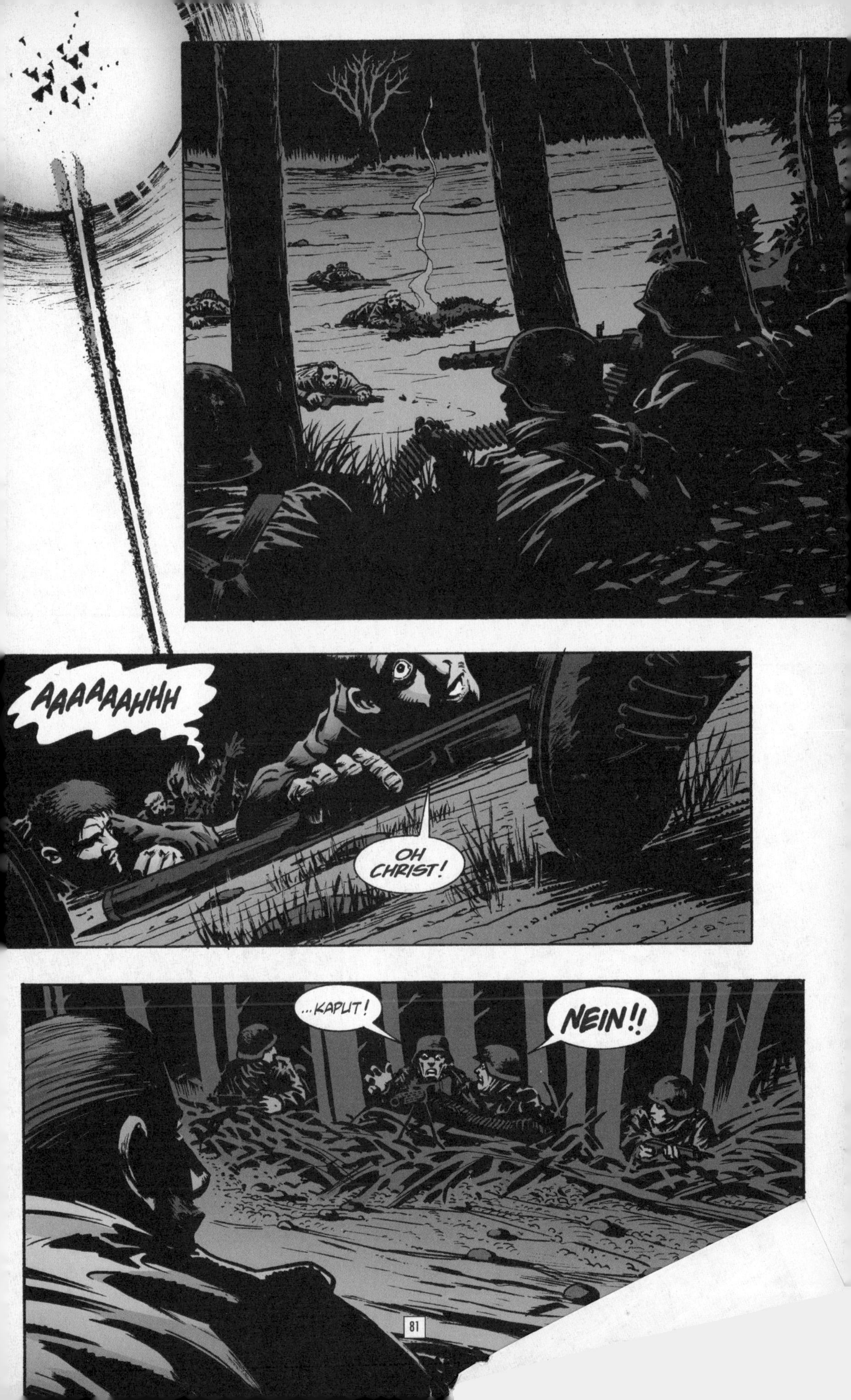
AAAAAAHHH
OH CHRIST!
...KAPUT!
NEIN!!

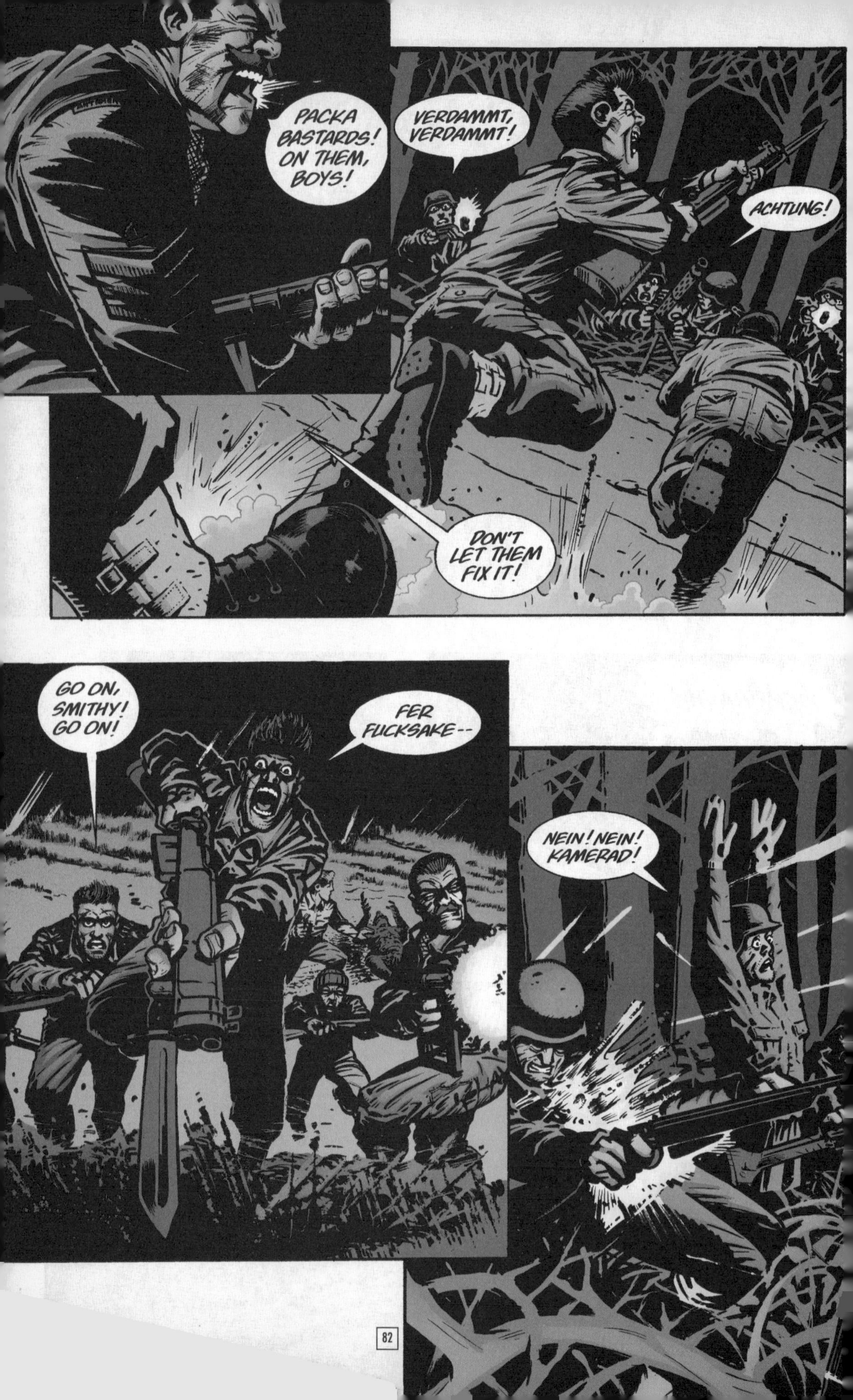
PACKA BASTARDS! ON THEM, BOYS!
VERDAMMT, VERDAMMT!
ACHTUNG!
DON'T LET THEM FIX IT!
GO ON, SMITHY! GO ON!
FER FUCKSAKE--
NEIN! NEIN! KAMERAD!

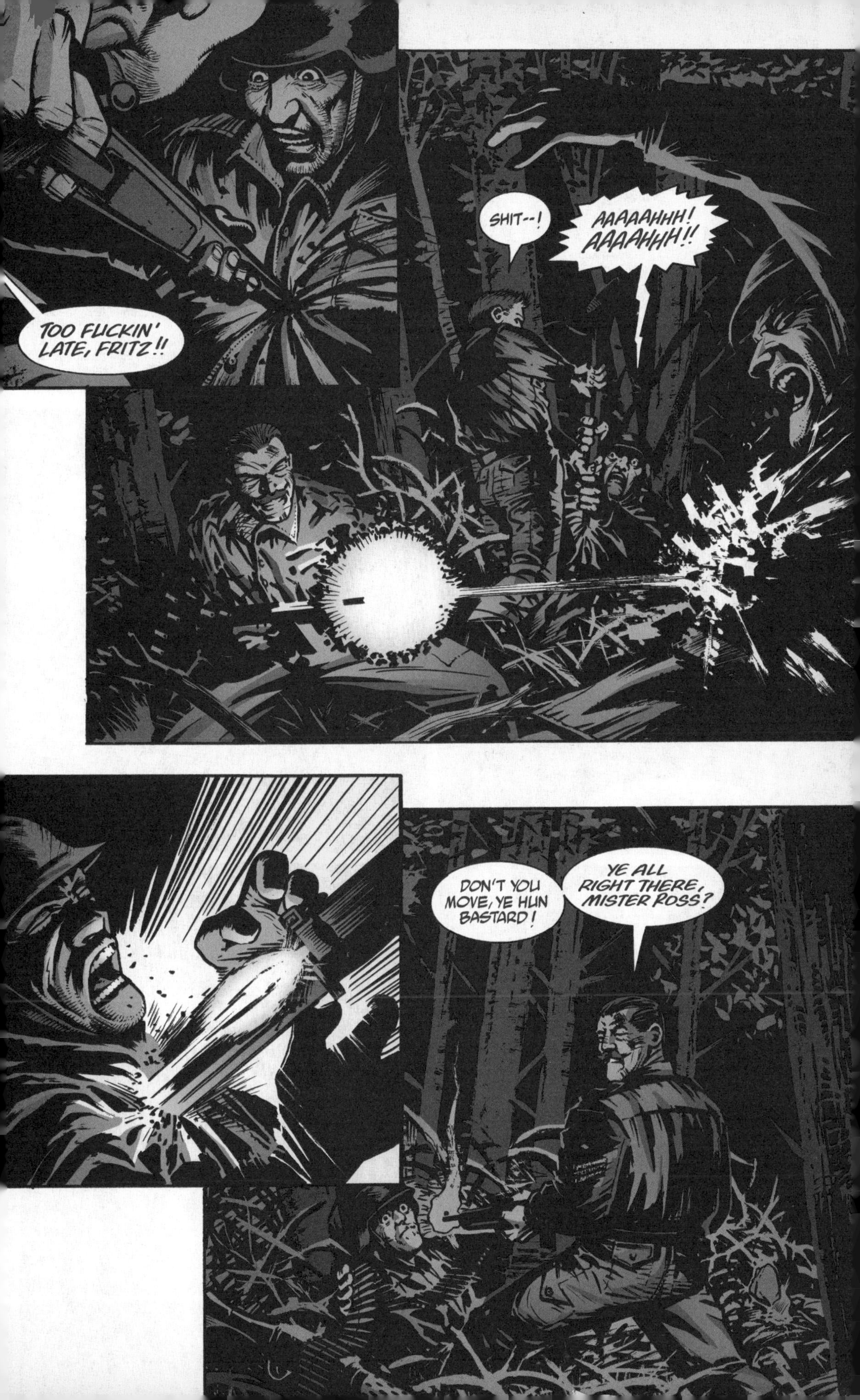
TOO FUCKIN' LATE, FRITZ!!
SHIT--!
AAAAAHHH! AAAAHHH!!
DON'T YOU MOVE, YE HUN BASTARD!
YE ALL RIGHT THERE, MISTER ROSS?

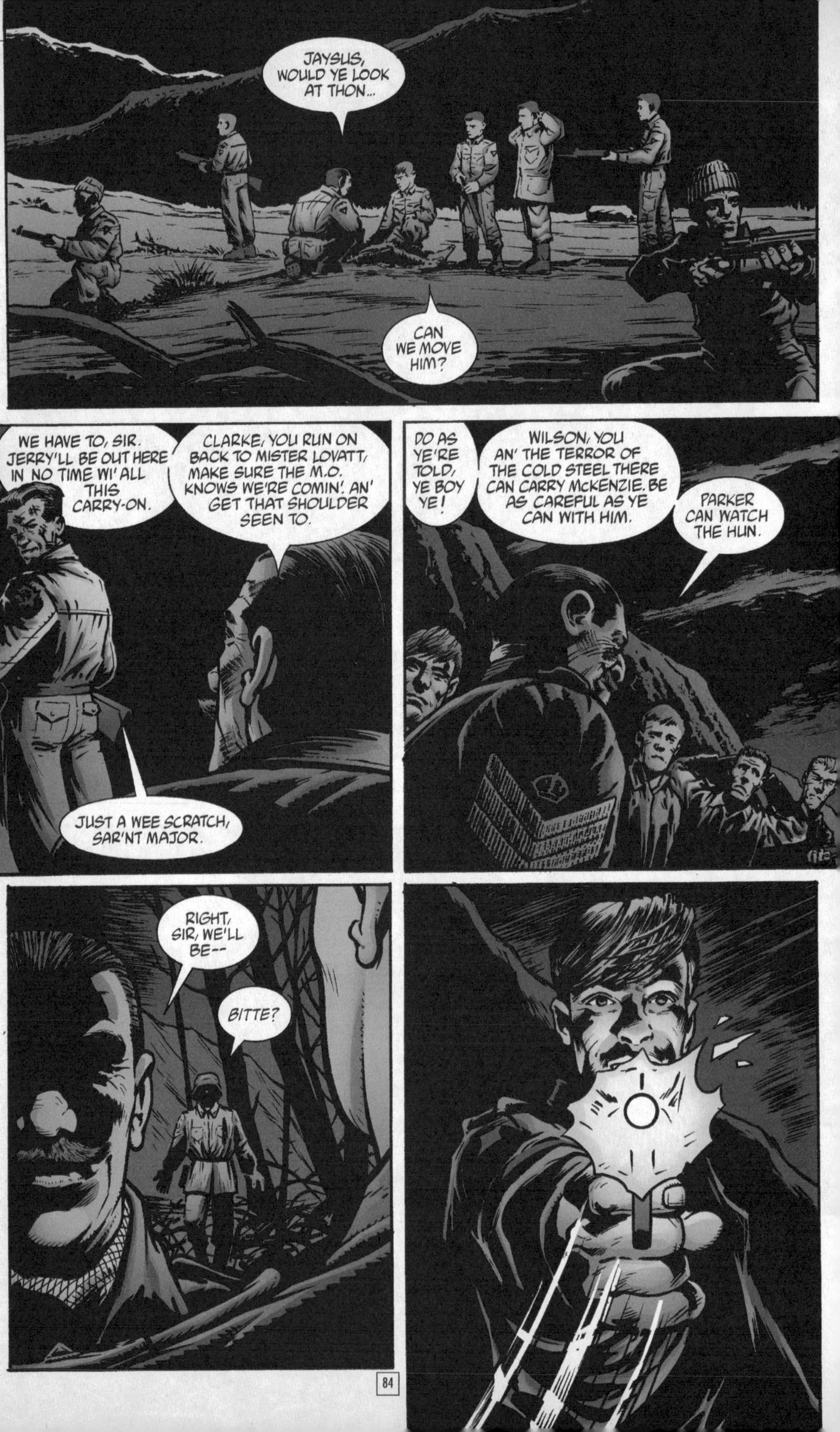
JAYSUS, WOULD YE LOOK AT THON...
CAN WE MOVE HIM?
WE HAVE TO, SIR. JERRY'LL BE OUT HERE IN NO TIME WI' ALL THIS CARRY-ON.
CLARKE, YOU RUN ON BACK TO MISTER LOVATT, MAKE SURE THE M.O. KNOWS WE'RE COMIN'. AN' GET THAT SHOULDER SEEN TO.
JUST A WEE SCRATCH, SAR'NT MAJOR.
DO AS YE'RE TOLD, YE BOY YE!
WILSON, YOU AN' THE TERROR OF THE COLD STEEL THERE CAN CARRY McKENZIE. BE AS CAREFUL AS YE CAN WITH HIM.
PARKER CAN WATCH THE HUN.
RIGHT, SIR, WE'LL BE--
BITTE?

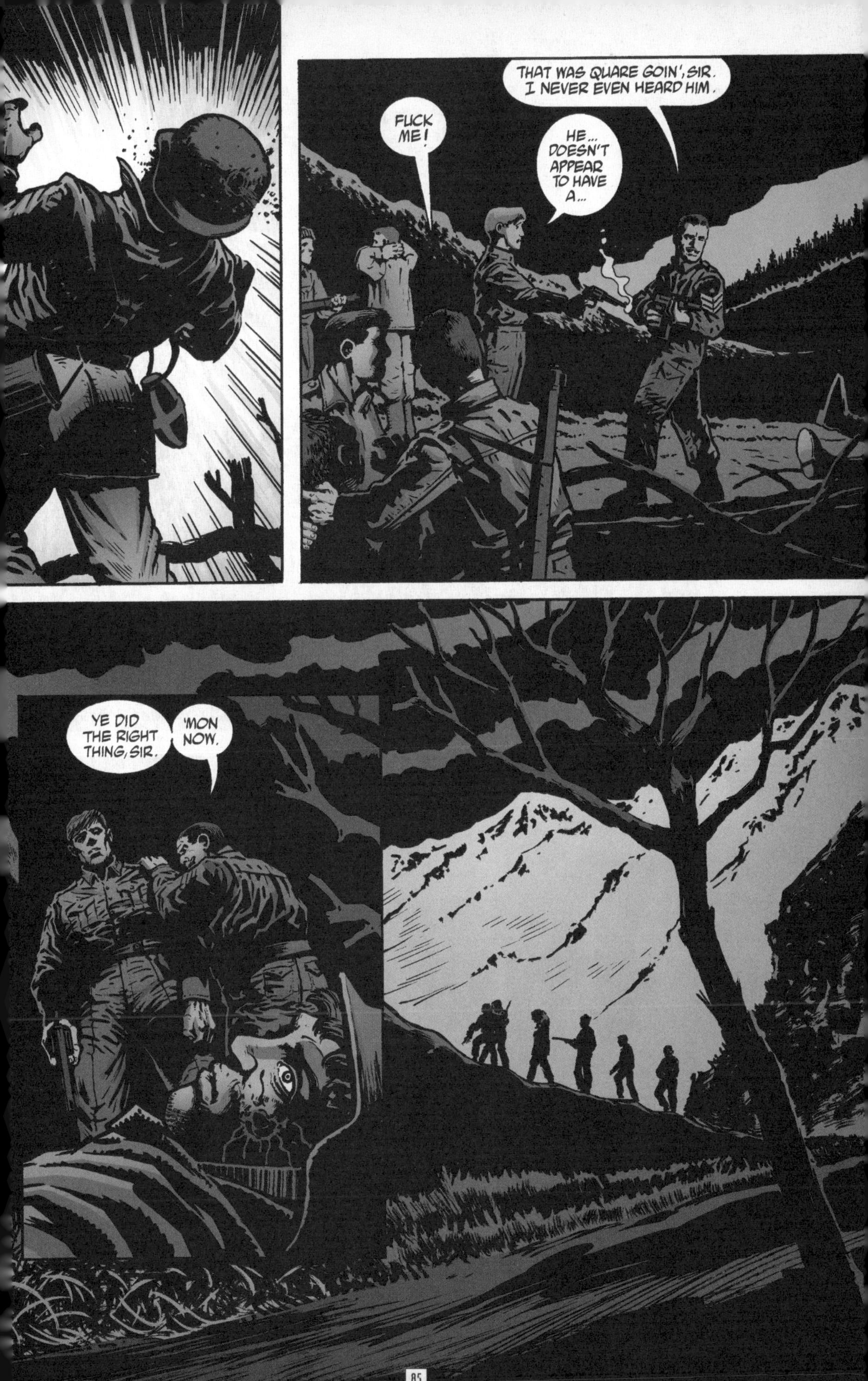
FUCK ME!
HE... DOESN'T APPEAR TO HAVE A...
THAT WAS QUARE GOIN', SIR. I NEVER EVEN HEARD HIM.
YE DID THE RIGHT THING, SIR.
'MON NOW.

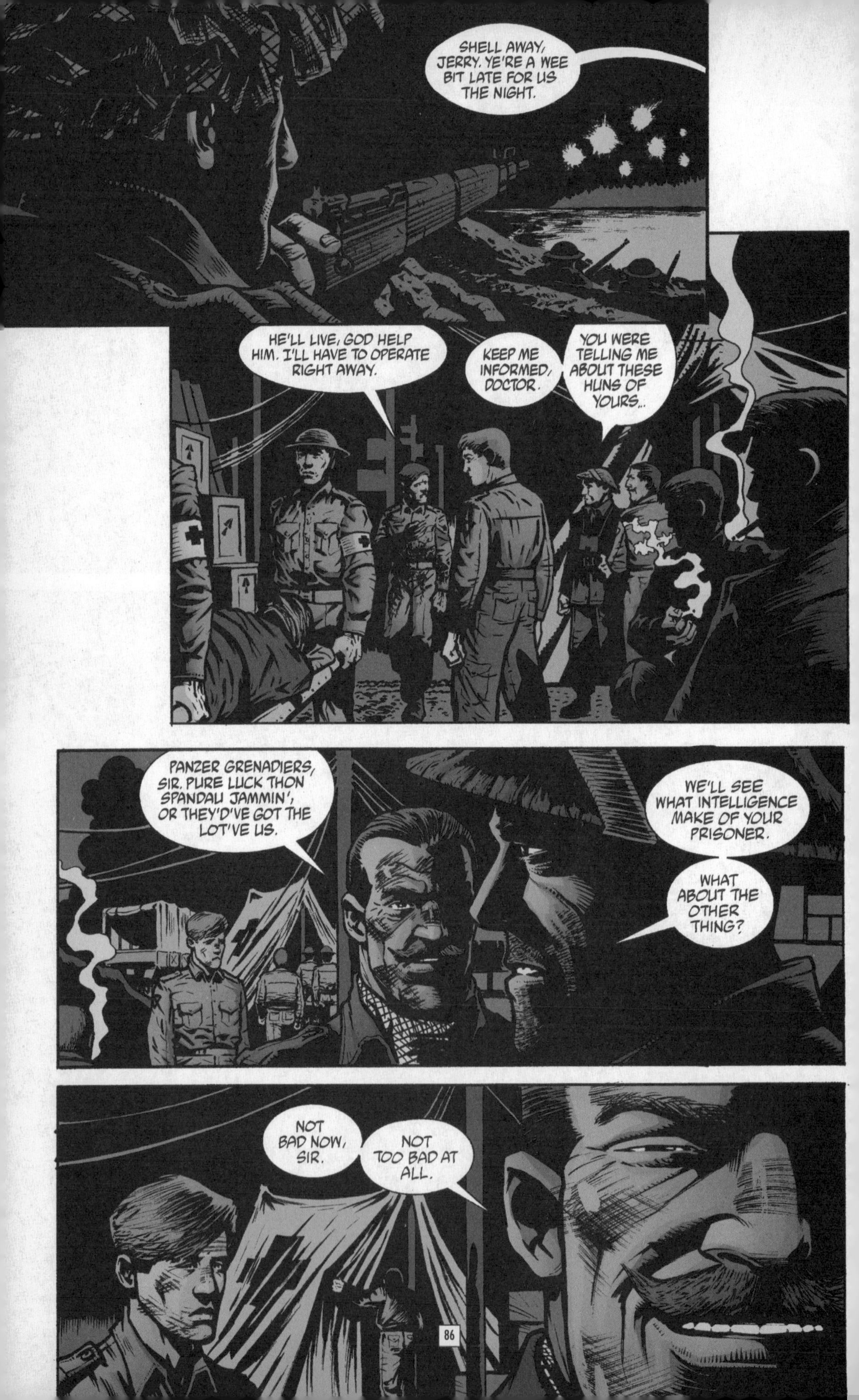
SHELL AWAY, JERRY. YE'RE A WEE BIT LATE FOR US THE NIGHT.
HE'LL LIVE, GOD HELP HIM. I'LL HAVE TO OPERATE RIGHT AWAY.
KEEP ME INFORMED, DOCTOR.
YOU WERE TELLING ME ABOUT THESE HUNS OF YOURS...
PANZER GRENADIERS, SIR. PURE LUCK THON SPANDAU JAMMIN', OR THEY'D'VE GOT THE LOT'VE US.
WE'LL SEE WHAT INTELLIGENCE MAKE OF YOUR PRISONER.
WHAT ABOUT THE OTHER THING?
NOT BAD NOW, SIR.
NOT TOO BAD AT ALL.

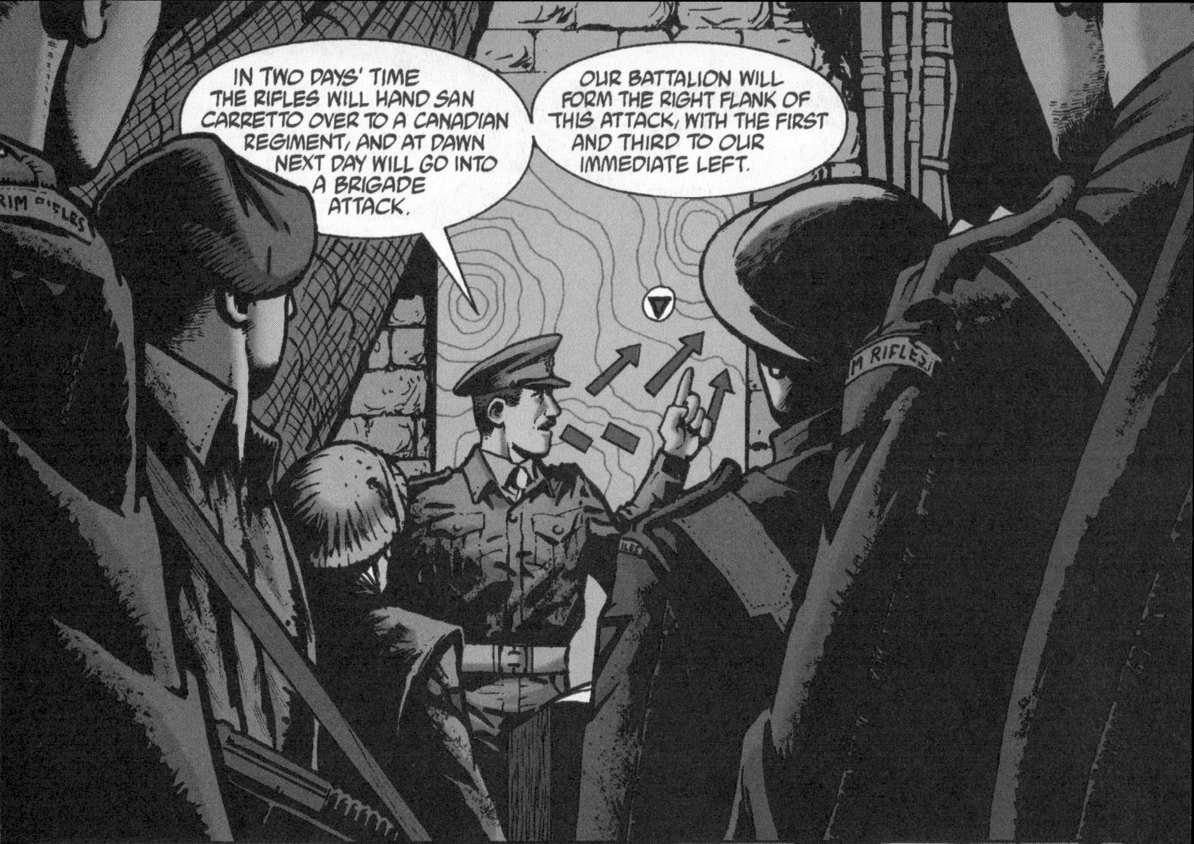
IN TWO DAYS' TIME THE RIFLES WILL HAND SAN CARRETTO OVER TO A CANADIAN REGIMENT, AND AT DAWN NEXT DAY WILL GO INTO A BRIGADE ATTACK.
OUR BATTALION WILL FORM THE RIGHT FLANK OF THIS ATTACK, WITH THE FIRST AND THIRD TO OUR IMMEDIATE LEFT.

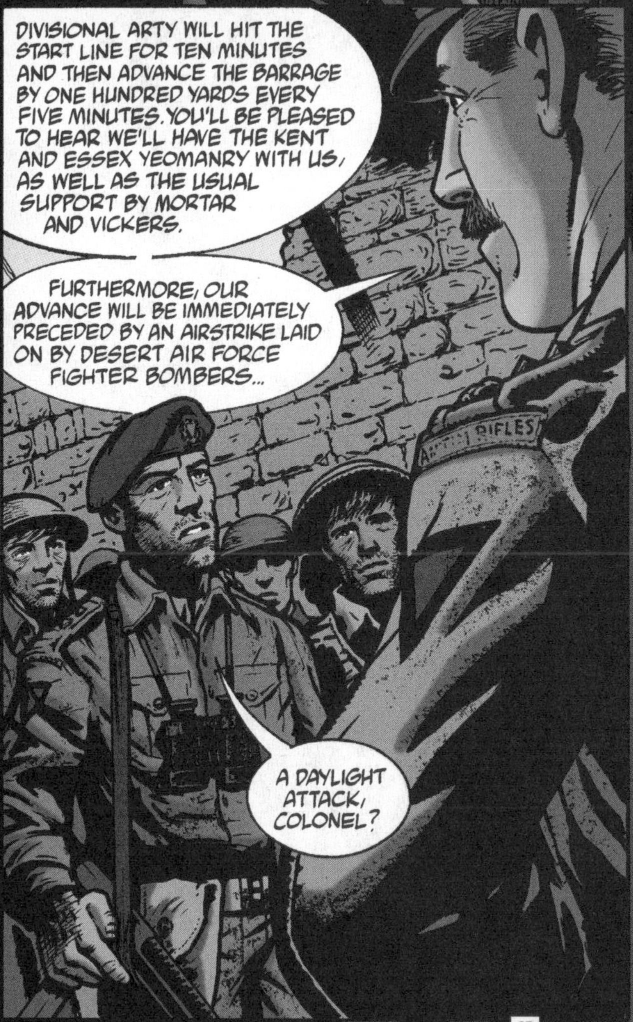
DIVISIONAL ARTY WILL HIT THE START LINE FOR TEN MINUTES AND THEN ADVANCE THE BARRAGE BY ONE HUNDRED YARDS EVERY FIVE MINUTES. YOU'LL BE PLEASED TO HEAR WE'LL HAVE THE KENT AND ESSEX YEOMANRY WITH US, AS WELL AS THE USUAL SUPPORT BY MORTAR AND VICKERS.
FURTHERMORE, OUR ADVANCE WILL BE IMMEDIATELY PRECEDED BY AN AIRSTRIKE LAID ON BY DESERT AIR FORCE FIGHTER BOMBERS...
A DAYLIGHT ATTACK, COLONEL?

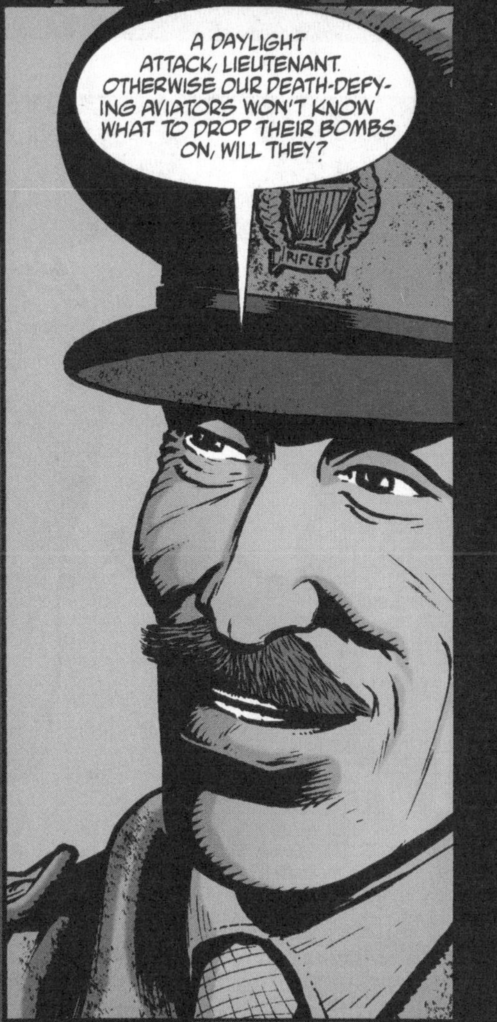
A DAYLIGHT ATTACK, LIEUTENANT. OTHERWISE OUR DEATH-DEFYING AVIATORS WON'T KNOW WHAT TO DROP THEIR BOMBS ON, WILL THEY?

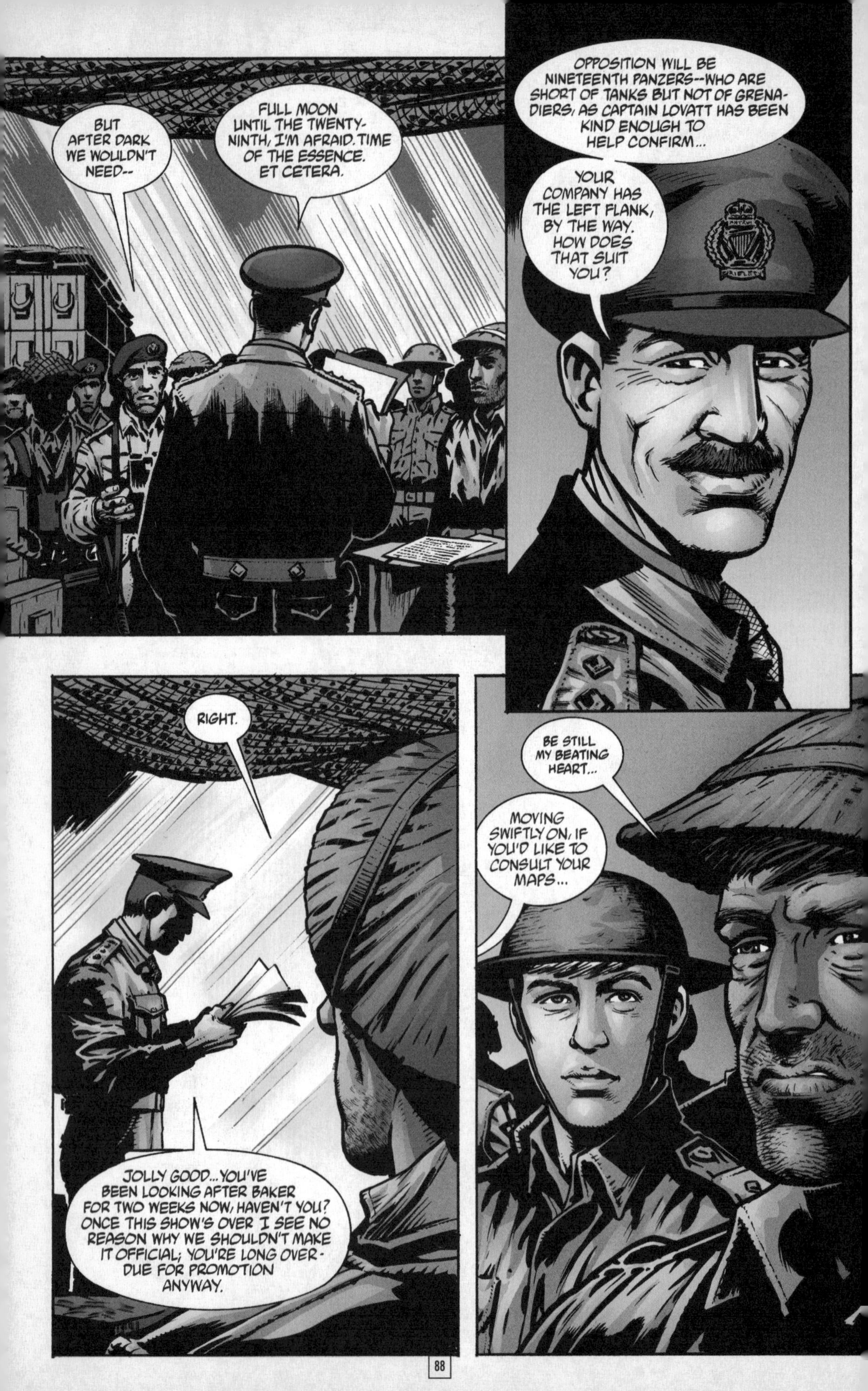
BUT AFTER DARK WE WOULDN'T NEED--
FULL MOON UNTIL THE TWENTY-NINTH, I'M AFRAID. TIME OF THE ESSENCE. ET CETERA.
OPPOSITION WILL BE NINETEENTH PANZERS--WHO ARE SHORT OF TANKS BUT NOT OF GRENADIERS, AS CAPTAIN LOVATT HAS BEEN KIND ENOUGH TO HELP CONFIRM...
YOUR COMPANY HAS THE LEFT FLANK, BY THE WAY. HOW DOES THAT SUIT YOU?
RIGHT.
JOLLY GOOD... YOU'VE BEEN LOOKING AFTER BAKER FOR TWO WEEKS NOW, HAVEN'T YOU? ONCE THIS SHOW'S OVER I SEE NO REASON WHY WE SHOULDN'T MAKE IT OFFICIAL; YOU'RE LONG OVERDUE FOR PROMOTION ANYWAY.
BE STILL MY BEATING HEART...
MOVING SWIFTLY ON, IF YOU'D LIKE TO CONSULT YOUR MAPS...

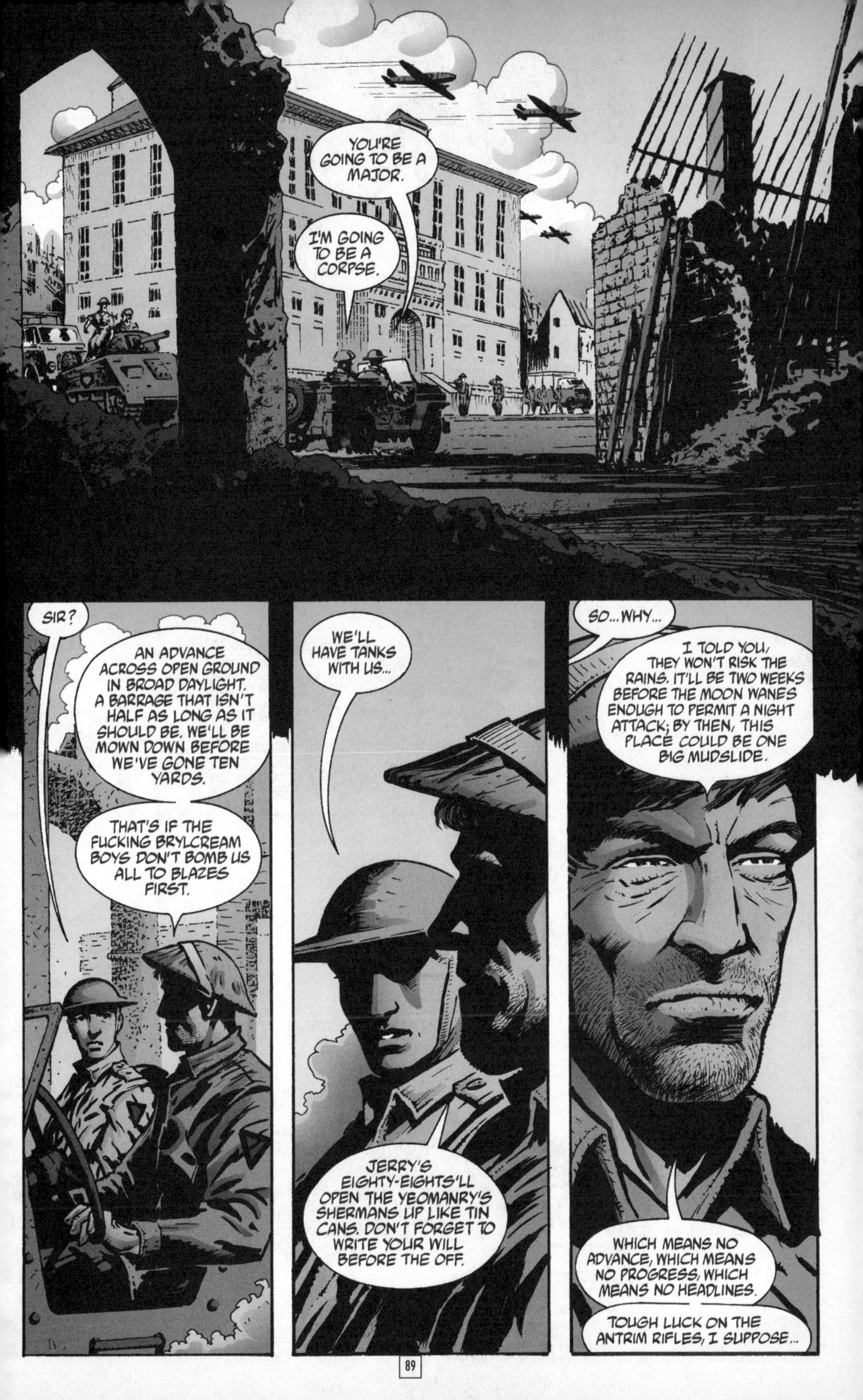

YOU'RE GOING TO BE A MAJOR.
I'M GOING TO BE A CORPSE.
SIR?
AN ADVANCE ACROSS OPEN GROUND IN BROAD DAYLIGHT. A BARRAGE THAT ISN'T HALF AS LONG AS IT SHOULD BE. WE'LL BE MOWN DOWN BEFORE WE'VE GONE TEN YARDS.
THAT'S IF THE FUCKING BRYLCREAM BOYS DON'T BOMB US ALL TO BLAZES FIRST.
WE'LL HAVE TANKS WITH US...
JERRY'S EIGHTY-EIGHTS'LL OPEN THE YEOMANRY'S SHERMANS UP LIKE TIN CANS. DON'T FORGET TO WRITE YOUR WILL BEFORE THE OFF.
SO... WHY...
I TOLD YOU, THEY WON'T RISK THE RAINS. IT'LL BE TWO WEEKS BEFORE THE MOON WANES ENOUGH TO PERMIT A NIGHT ATTACK; BY THEN, THIS PLACE COULD BE ONE BIG MUDSLIDE.
WHICH MEANS NO ADVANCE, WHICH MEANS NO PROGRESS, WHICH MEANS NO HEADLINES.
TOUGH LUCK ON THE ANTRIM RIFLES, I SUPPOSE...

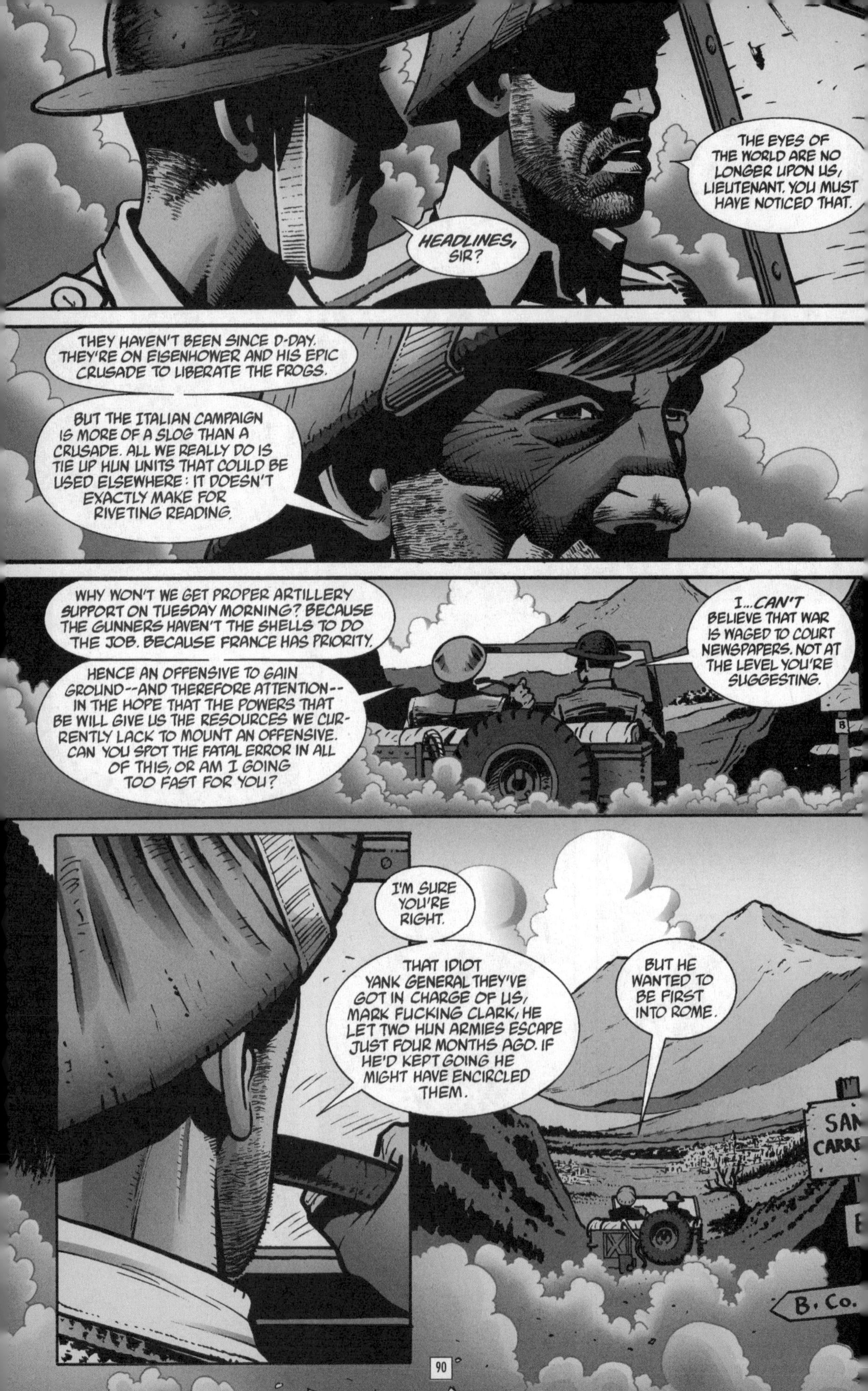
THE EYES OF THE WORLD ARE NO LONGER UPON US, LIEUTENANT. YOU MUST HAVE NOTICED THAT.
HEADLINES, SIR?
THEY HAVEN'T BEEN SINCE D-DAY. THEY'RE ON EISENHOWER AND HIS EPIC CRUSADE TO LIBERATE THE FROGS.
BUT THE ITALIAN CAMPAIGN IS MORE OF A SLOG THAN A CRUSADE. ALL WE REALLY DO IS TIE UP HUN UNITS THAT COULD BE USED ELSEWHERE: IT DOESN'T EXACTLY MAKE FOR RIVETING READING.
WHY WON'T WE GET PROPER ARTILLERY SUPPORT ON TUESDAY MORNING? BECAUSE THE GUNNERS HAVEN'T THE SHELLS TO DO THE JOB. BECAUSE FRANCE HAS PRIORITY.
HENCE AN OFFENSIVE TO GAIN GROUND--AND THEREFORE ATTENTION-- IN THE HOPE THAT THE POWERS THAT BE WILL GIVE US THE RESOURCES WE CURRENTLY LACK TO MOUNT AN OFFENSIVE. CAN YOU SPOT THE FATAL ERROR IN ALL OF THIS, OR AM I GOING TOO FAST FOR YOU?
I...*CAN'T* BELIEVE THAT WAR IS WAGED TO COURT NEWSPAPERS. NOT AT THE LEVEL YOU'RE SUGGESTING.
I'M SURE YOU'RE RIGHT.
THAT IDIOT YANK GENERAL THEY'VE GOT IN CHARGE OF US, MARK FUCKING CLARK, HE LET TWO HUN ARMIES ESCAPE JUST FOUR MONTHS AGO. IF HE'D KEPT GOING HE MIGHT HAVE ENCIRCLED THEM.
BUT HE WANTED TO BE FIRST INTO ROME.
B. Co.

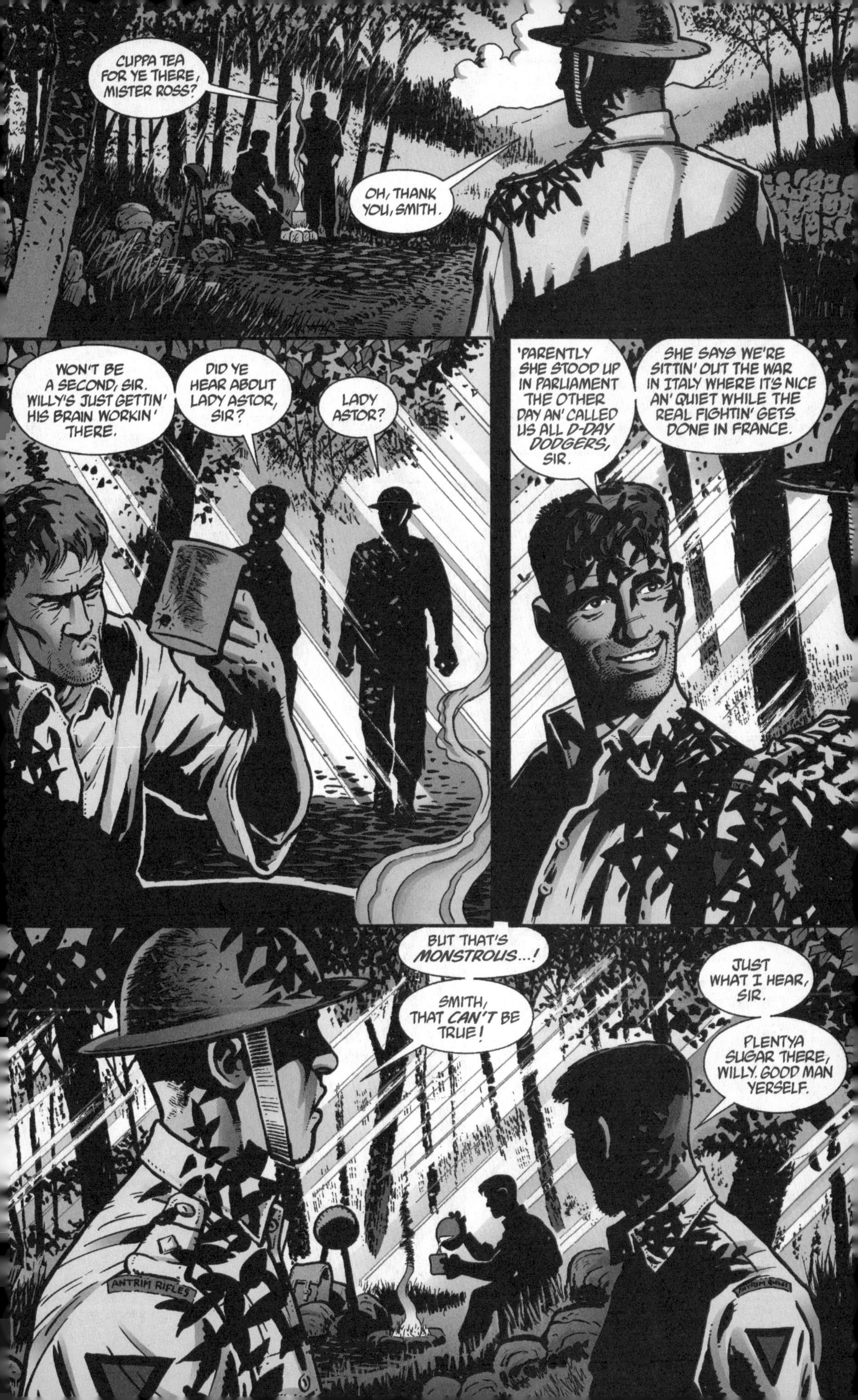

CUPPA TEA FOR YE THERE, MISTER ROSS?
OH, THANK YOU, SMITH.
WON'T BE A SECOND, SIR. WILLY'S JUST GETTIN' HIS BRAIN WORKIN' THERE.
DID YE HEAR ABOUT LADY ASTOR, SIR?
LADY ASTOR?
'PARENTLY SHE STOOD UP IN PARLIAMENT THE OTHER DAY AN' CALLED US ALL D-DAY DODGERS, SIR.
SHE SAYS WE'RE SITTIN' OUT THE WAR IN ITALY WHERE IT'S NICE AN' QUIET WHILE THE REAL FIGHTIN' GETS DONE IN FRANCE.
BUT THAT'S MONSTROUS...!
SMITH, THAT CAN'T BE TRUE!
JUST WHAT I HEAR, SIR.
PLENTYA SUGAR THERE, WILLY. GOOD MAN YERSELF.
ANTRIM RIFLES

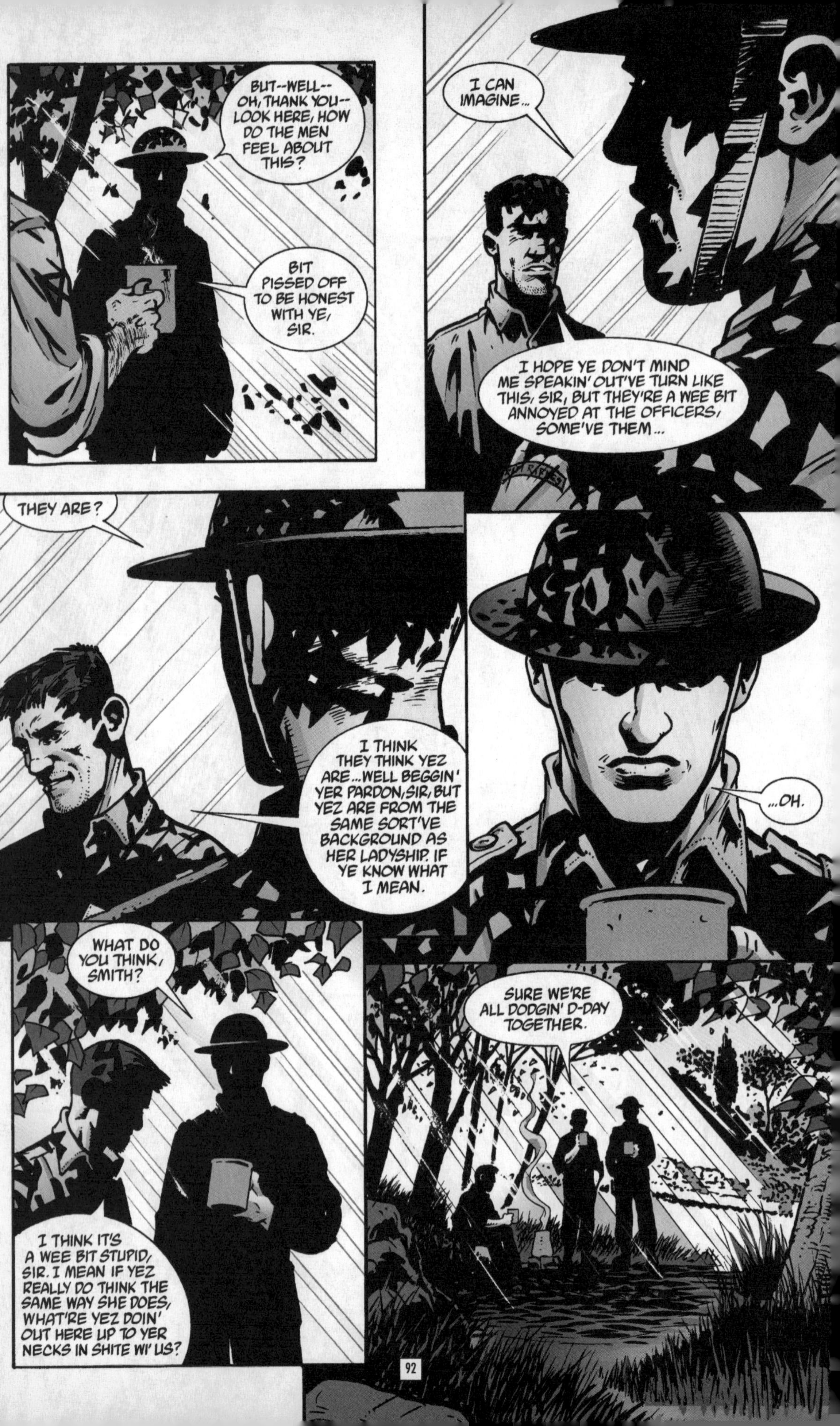
BUT--WELL--
OH, THANK YOU--
LOOK HERE, HOW
DO THE MEN
FEEL ABOUT
THIS?
BIT PISSED OFF TO BE HONEST WITH YE, SIR.
I CAN IMAGINE...
I HOPE YE DON'T MIND ME SPEAKIN' OUT'VE TURN LIKE THIS, SIR, BUT THEY'RE A WEE BIT ANNOYED AT THE OFFICERS, SOME'VE THEM...
THEY ARE?
I THINK THEY THINK YEZ ARE...WELL BEGGIN' YER PARDON, SIR, BUT YEZ ARE FROM THE SAME SORT'VE BACKGROUND AS HER LADYSHIP. IF YE KNOW WHAT I MEAN.
...OH.
WHAT DO YOU THINK, SMITH?
I THINK IT'S A WEE BIT STUPID, SIR. I MEAN IF YEZ REALLY DO THINK THE SAME WAY SHE DOES, WHAT'RE YEZ DOIN' OUT HERE UP TO YER NECKS IN SHITE WI' US?
SURE WE'RE ALL DODGIN' D-DAY TOGETHER.

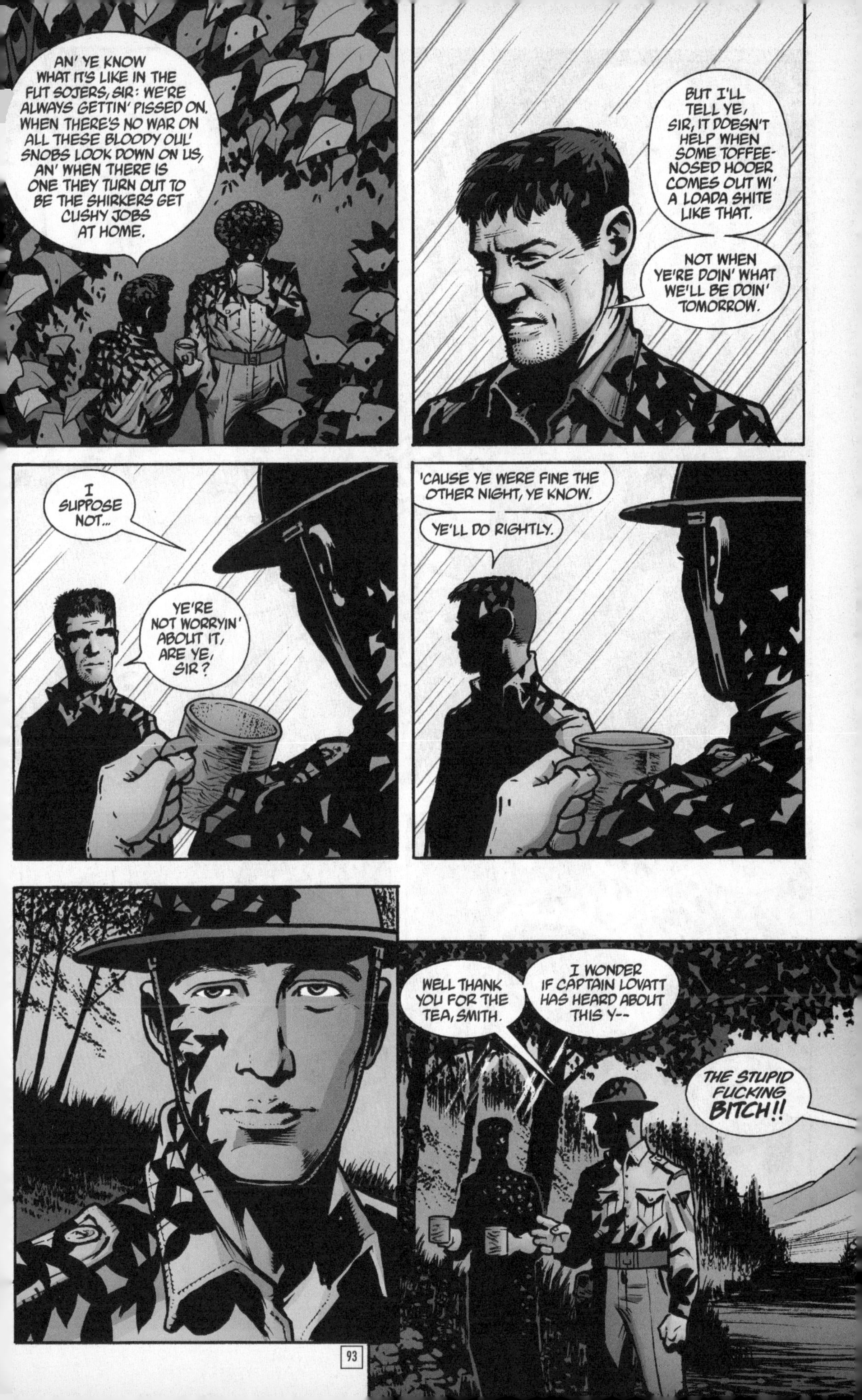
AN' YE KNOW WHAT IT'S LIKE IN THE FUT SOJERS, SIR: WE'RE ALWAYS GETTIN' PISSED ON. WHEN THERE'S NO WAR ON ALL THESE BLOODY OUL' SNOBS LOOK DOWN ON US, AN' WHEN THERE IS ONE THEY TURN OUT TO BE THE SHIRKERS GET CUSHY JOBS AT HOME.
BUT I'LL TELL YE, SIR, IT DOESN'T HELP WHEN SOME TOFFEE-NOSED HOOER COMES OUT WI' A LOADA SHITE LIKE THAT.
NOT WHEN YE'RE DOIN' WHAT WE'LL BE DOIN' TOMORROW.
I SUPPOSE NOT...
YE'RE NOT WORRYIN' ABOUT IT, ARE YE, SIR?
'CAUSE YE WERE FINE THE OTHER NIGHT, YE KNOW.
YE'LL DO RIGHTLY.
WELL THANK YOU FOR THE TEA, SMITH.
I WONDER IF CAPTAIN LOVATT HAS HEARD ABOUT THIS Y--
THE STUPID FUCKING BITCH!!

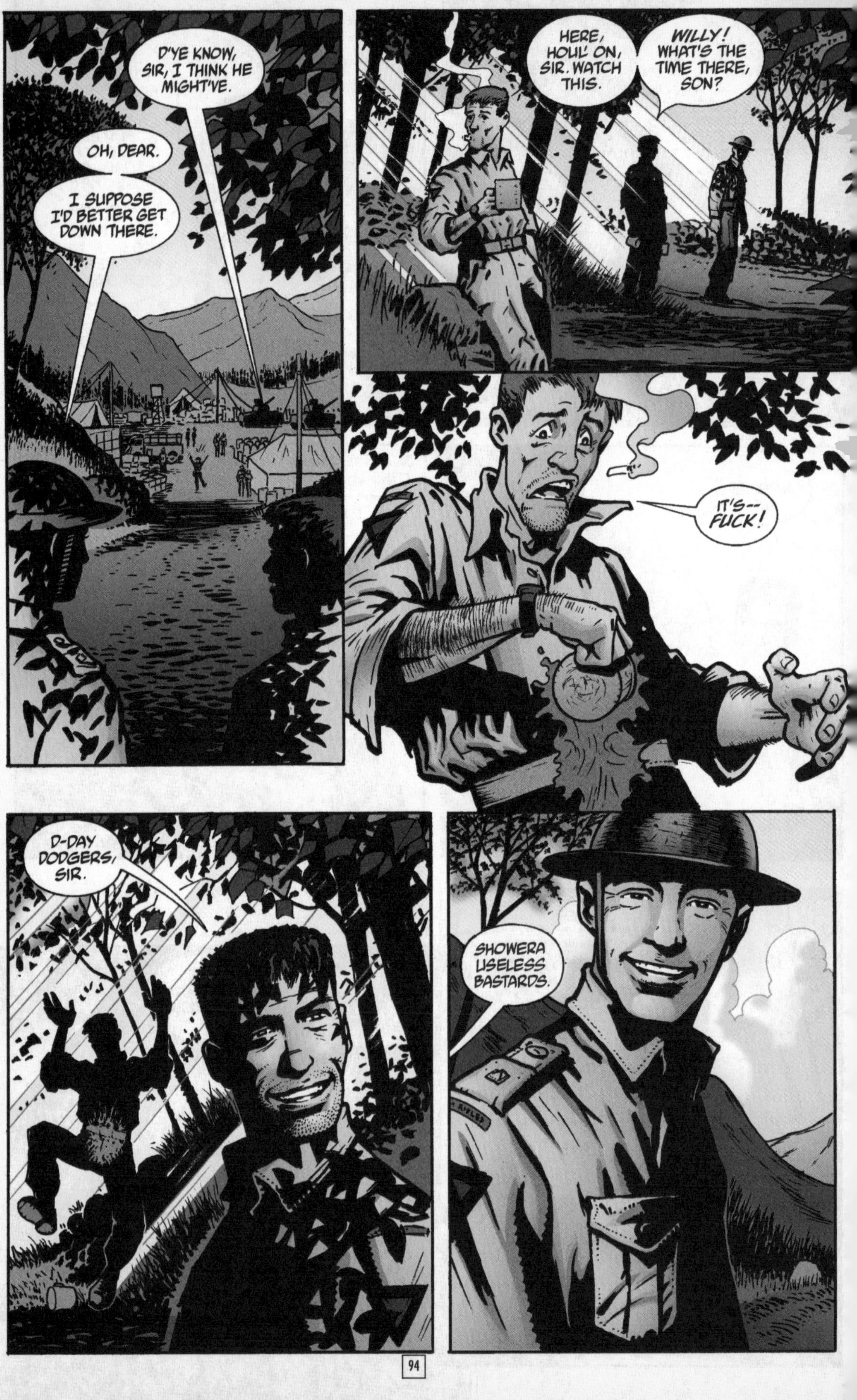
OH, DEAR.
D'YE KNOW, SIR, I THINK HE MIGHT'VE.
I SUPPOSE I'D BETTER GET DOWN THERE.
HERE, HOUL' ON, SIR. WATCH THIS.
WILLY! WHAT'S THE TIME THERE, SON?
IT'S-- FUCK!
D-DAY DODGERS, SIR.
SHOWERA USELESS BASTARDS.

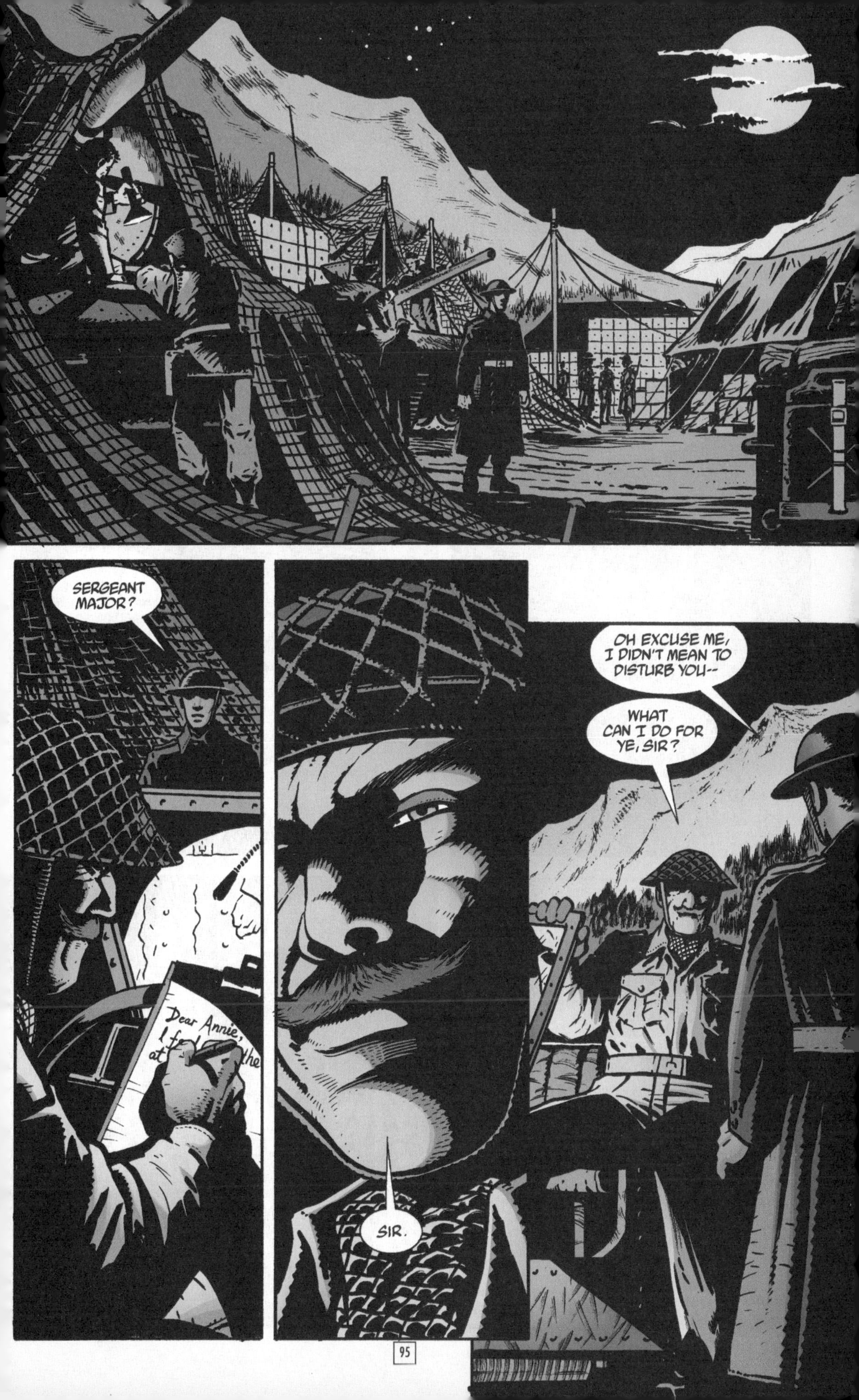
SERGEANT MAJOR?
Dear Annie,
SIR.
OH EXCUSE ME, I DIDN'T MEAN TO DISTURB YOU--
WHAT CAN I DO FOR YE, SIR?

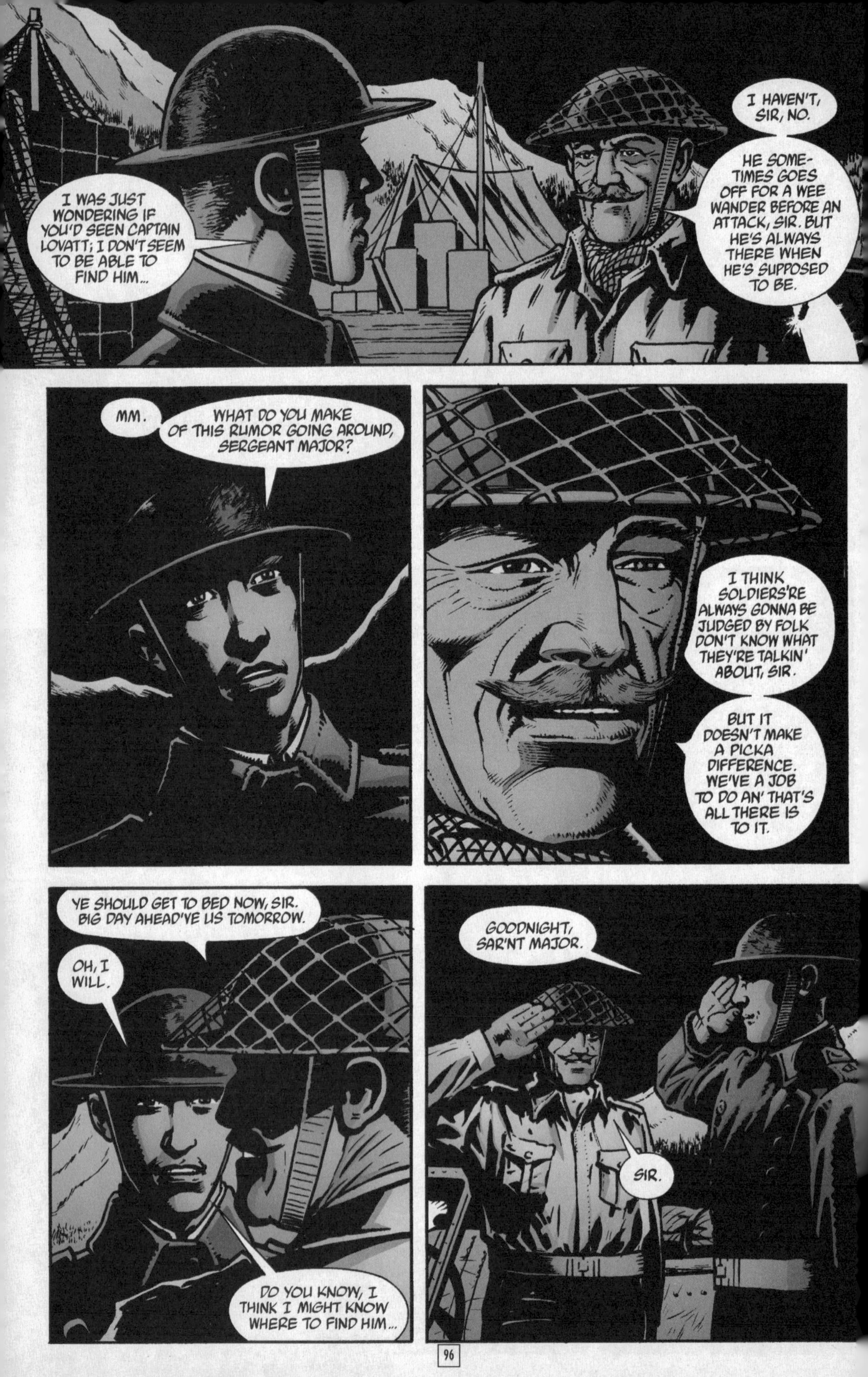
I WAS JUST WONDERING IF YOU'D SEEN CAPTAIN LOVATT; I DON'T SEEM TO BE ABLE TO FIND HIM...
I HAVEN'T, SIR, NO.
HE SOMETIMES GOES OFF FOR A WEE WANDER BEFORE AN ATTACK, SIR. BUT HE'S ALWAYS THERE WHEN HE'S SUPPOSED TO BE.
MM.
WHAT DO YOU MAKE OF THIS RUMOR GOING AROUND, SERGEANT MAJOR?
I THINK SOLDIERS'RE ALWAYS GONNA BE JUDGED BY FOLK DON'T KNOW WHAT THEY'RE TALKIN' ABOUT, SIR.
BUT IT DOESN'T MAKE A PICKA DIFFERENCE. WE'VE A JOB TO DO AN' THAT'S ALL THERE IS TO IT.
YE SHOULD GET TO BED NOW, SIR. BIG DAY AHEAD'VE US TOMORROW.
OH, I WILL.
DO YOU KNOW, I THINK I MIGHT KNOW WHERE TO FIND HIM...
GOODNIGHT, SAR'NT MAJOR.
SIR.

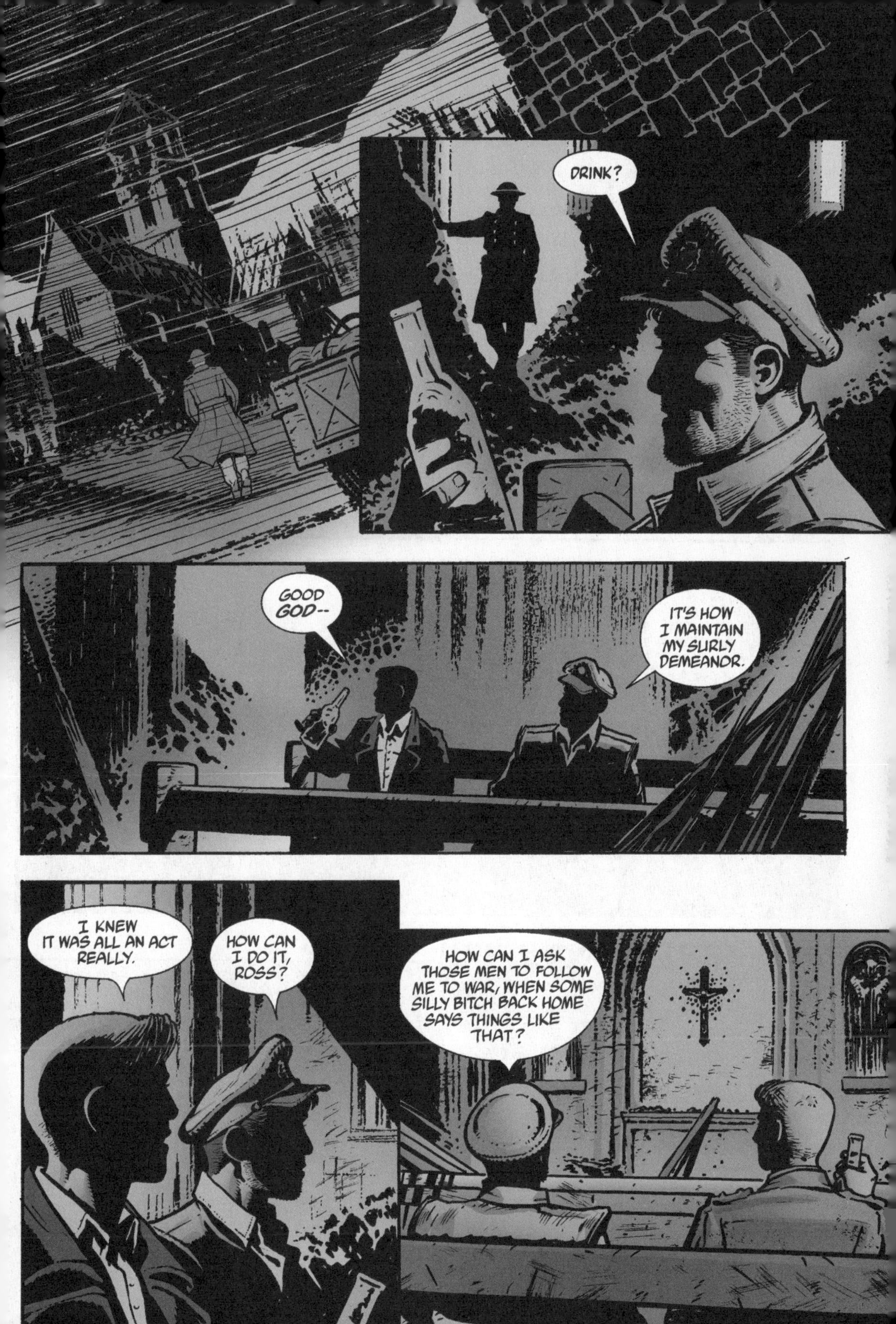
DRINK?
GOOD GOD--
IT'S HOW I MAINTAIN MY SURLY DEMEANOR.
I KNEW IT WAS ALL AN ACT REALLY.
HOW CAN I DO IT, ROSS?
HOW CAN I ASK THOSE MEN TO FOLLOW ME TO WAR, WHEN SOME SILLY BITCH BACK HOME SAYS THINGS LIKE THAT?

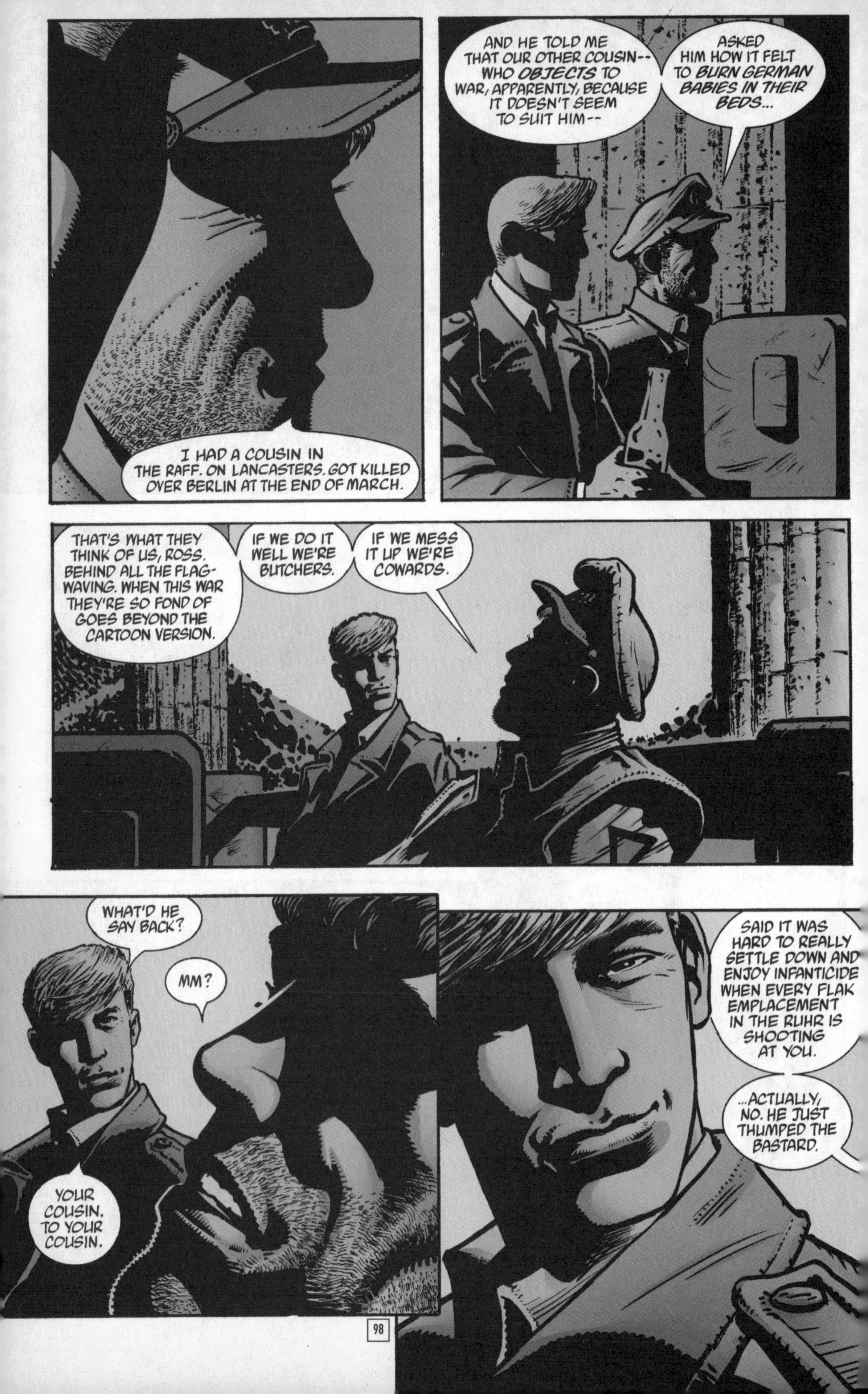
I HAD A COUSIN IN THE RAFF. ON LANCASTERS. GOT KILLED OVER BERLIN AT THE END OF MARCH.
AND HE TOLD ME THAT OUR OTHER COUSIN-- WHO *OBJECTS* TO WAR, APPARENTLY, BECAUSE IT DOESN'T SEEM TO SUIT HIM--
ASKED HIM HOW IT FELT TO *BURN GERMAN BABIES IN THEIR BEDS*...
THAT'S WHAT THEY THINK OF US, ROSS. BEHIND ALL THE FLAG-WAVING. WHEN THIS WAR THEY'RE SO FOND OF GOES BEYOND THE CARTOON VERSION.
IF WE DO IT WELL WE'RE BUTCHERS.
IF WE MESS IT UP WE'RE COWARDS.
WHAT'D HE SAY BACK?
MM?
YOUR COUSIN. TO YOUR COUSIN.
SAID IT WAS HARD TO REALLY SETTLE DOWN AND ENJOY INFANTICIDE WHEN EVERY FLAK EMPLACEMENT IN THE RUHR IS SHOOTING AT YOU.
...ACTUALLY, NO. HE JUST THUMPED THE BASTARD.

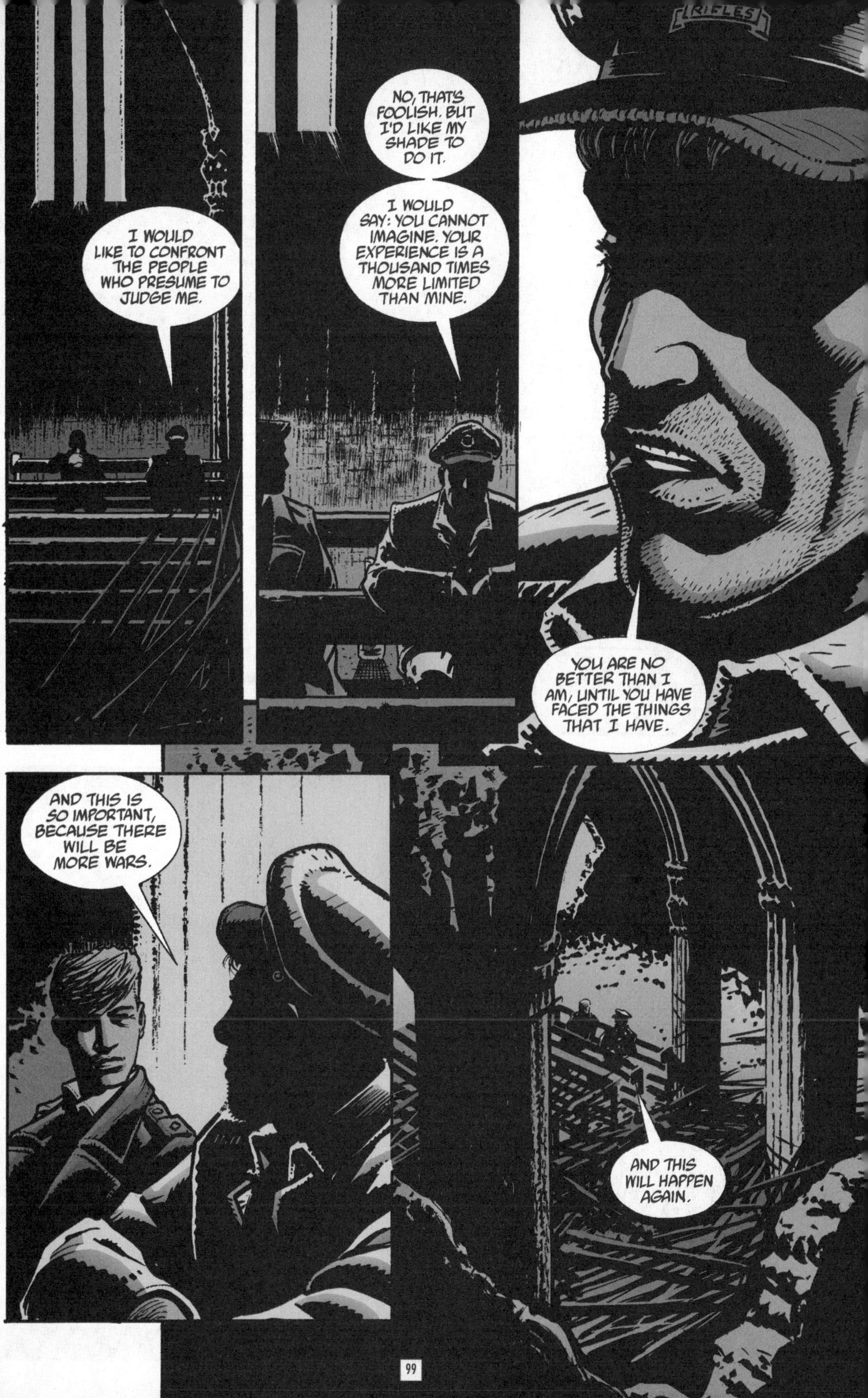
RIFLES
I WOULD LIKE TO CONFRONT THE PEOPLE WHO PRESUME TO JUDGE ME.
NO, THAT'S FOOLISH. BUT I'D LIKE MY SHADE TO DO IT.
I WOULD SAY: YOU CANNOT IMAGINE. YOUR EXPERIENCE IS A THOUSAND TIMES MORE LIMITED THAN MINE.
YOU ARE NO BETTER THAN I AM, UNTIL YOU HAVE FACED THE THINGS THAT I HAVE.
AND THIS IS SO IMPORTANT, BECAUSE THERE WILL BE MORE WARS.
AND THIS WILL HAPPEN AGAIN.

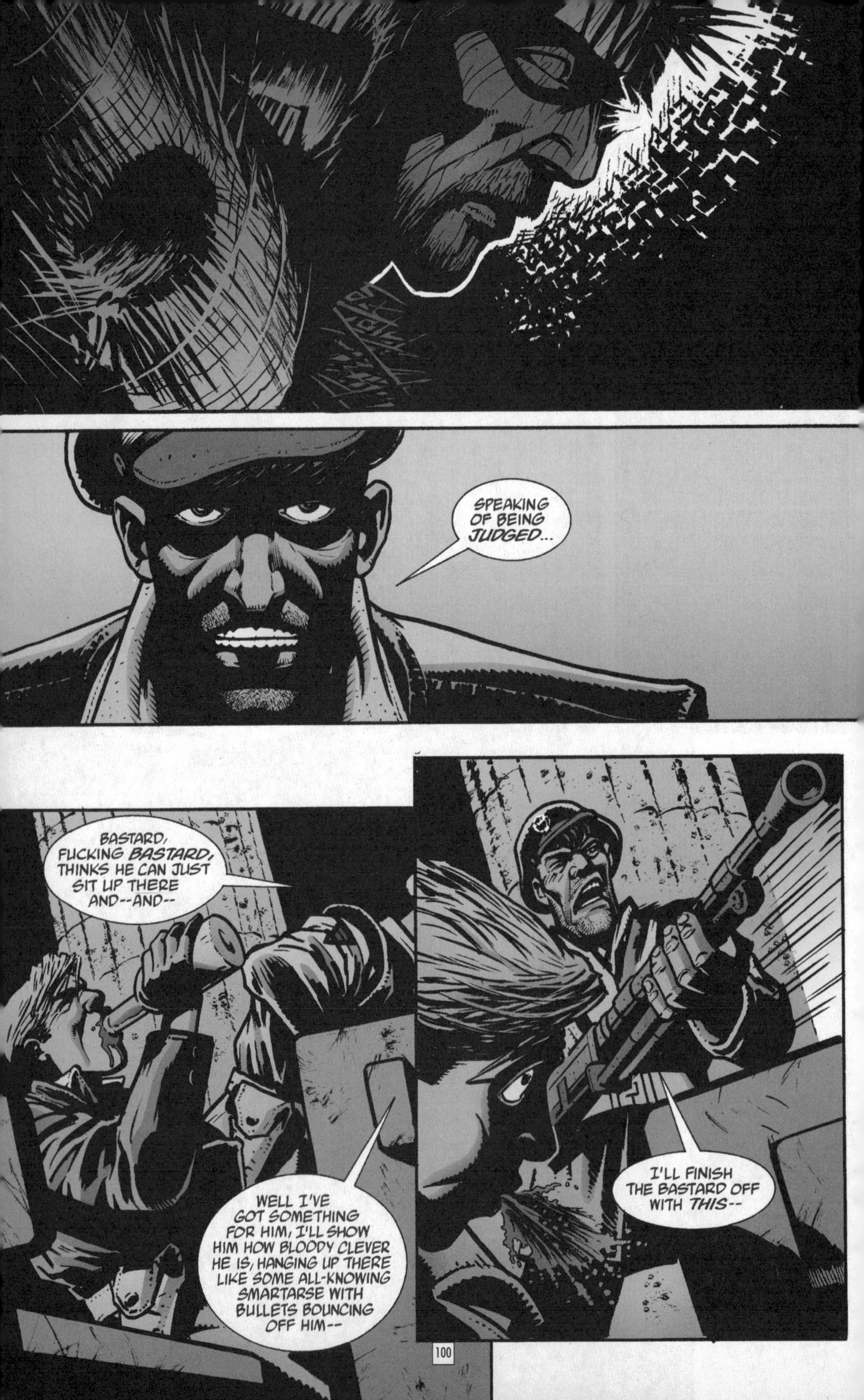
SPEAKING OF BEING JUDGED...
BASTARD, FUCKING BASTARD, THINKS HE CAN JUST SIT UP THERE AND--AND--
WELL I'VE GOT SOMETHING FOR HIM, I'LL SHOW HIM HOW BLOODY CLEVER HE IS, HANGING UP THERE LIKE SOME ALL-KNOWING SMARTARSE WITH BULLETS BOUNCING OFF HIM--
I'LL FINISH THE BASTARD OFF WITH THIS--

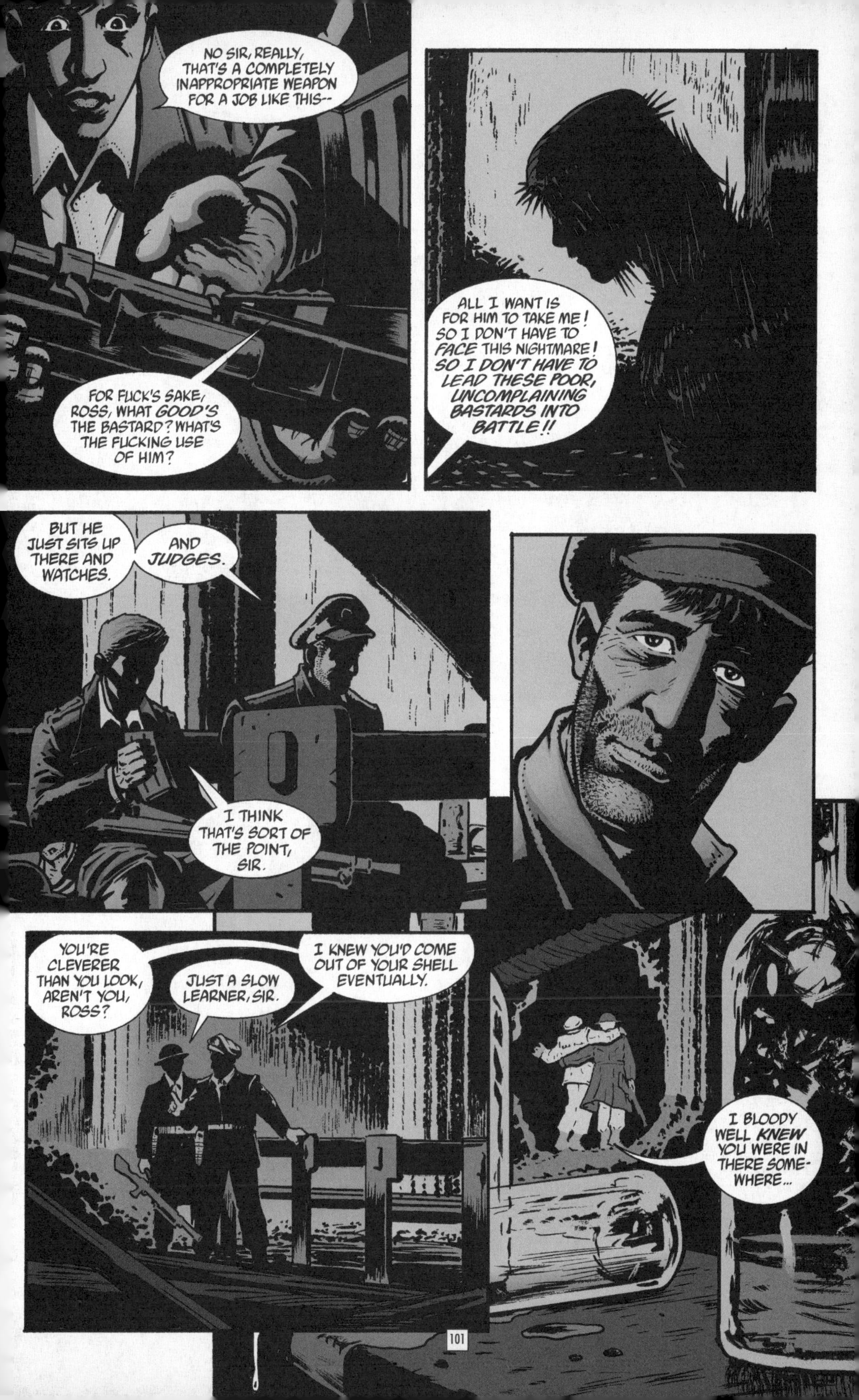
NO SIR, REALLY, THAT'S A COMPLETELY INAPPROPRIATE WEAPON FOR A JOB LIKE THIS--
FOR FUCK'S SAKE, ROSS, WHAT GOOD'S THE BASTARD? WHAT'S THE FUCKING USE OF HIM?
ALL I WANT IS FOR HIM TO TAKE ME! SO I DON'T HAVE TO FACE THIS NIGHTMARE! SO I DON'T HAVE TO LEAD THESE POOR, UNCOMPLAINING BASTARDS INTO BATTLE!!
BUT HE JUST SITS UP THERE AND WATCHES.
AND JUDGES.
I THINK THAT'S SORT OF THE POINT, SIR.
YOU'RE CLEVERER THAN YOU LOOK, AREN'T YOU, ROSS?
JUST A SLOW LEARNER, SIR.
I KNEW YOU'D COME OUT OF YOUR SHELL EVENTUALLY.
I BLOODY WELL KNEW YOU WERE IN THERE SOME-WHERE...

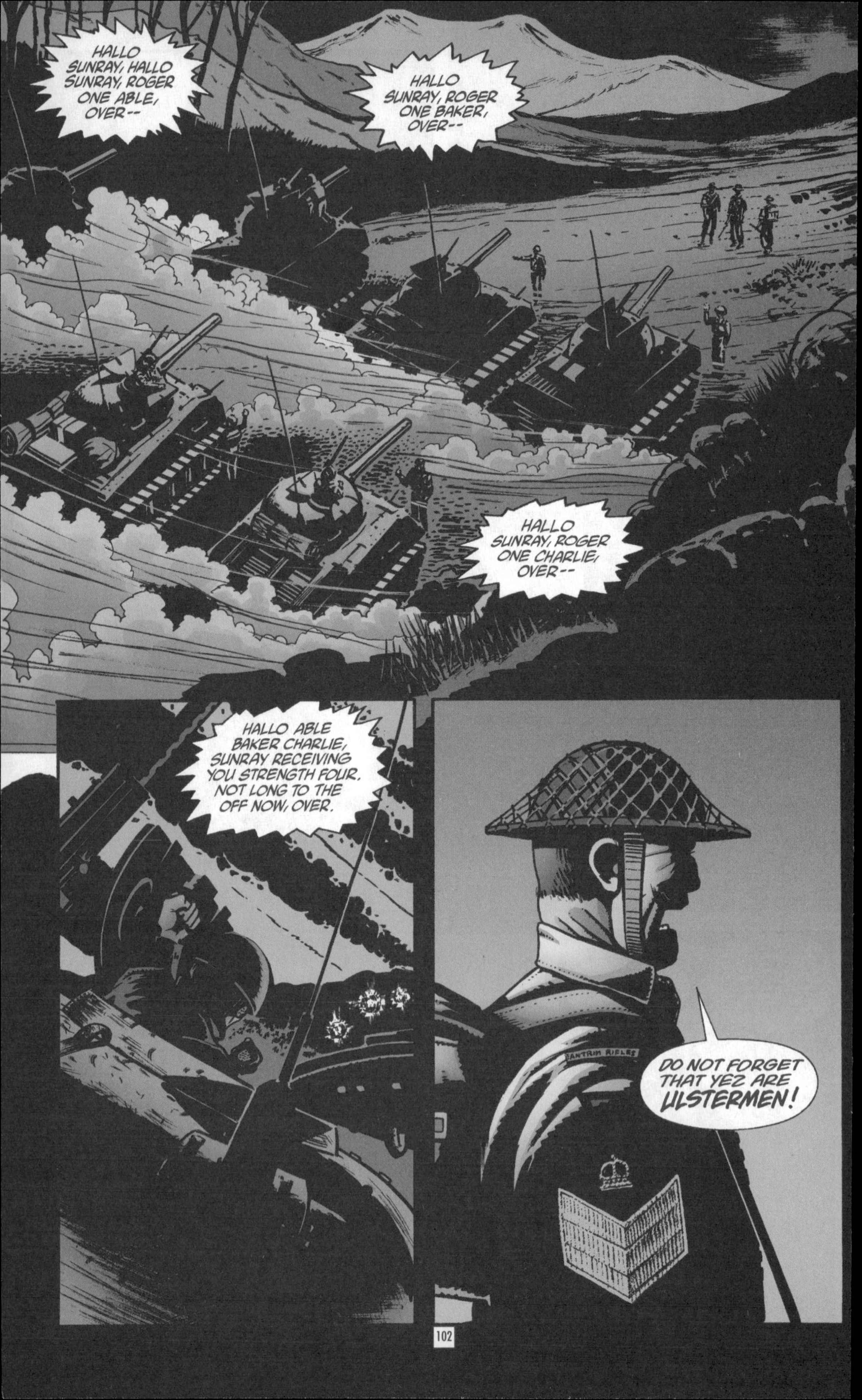
HALLO SUNRAY, HALLO SUNRAY, ROGER ONE ABLE, OVER--
HALLO SUNRAY, ROGER ONE BAKER, OVER--
HALLO SUNRAY, ROGER ONE CHARLIE, OVER--
HALLO ABLE BAKER CHARLIE, SUNRAY RECEIVING YOU STRENGTH FOUR. NOT LONG TO THE OFF NOW, OVER.
ANTRIM RIFLES
DO NOT FORGET THAT YEZ ARE ULSTERMEN!

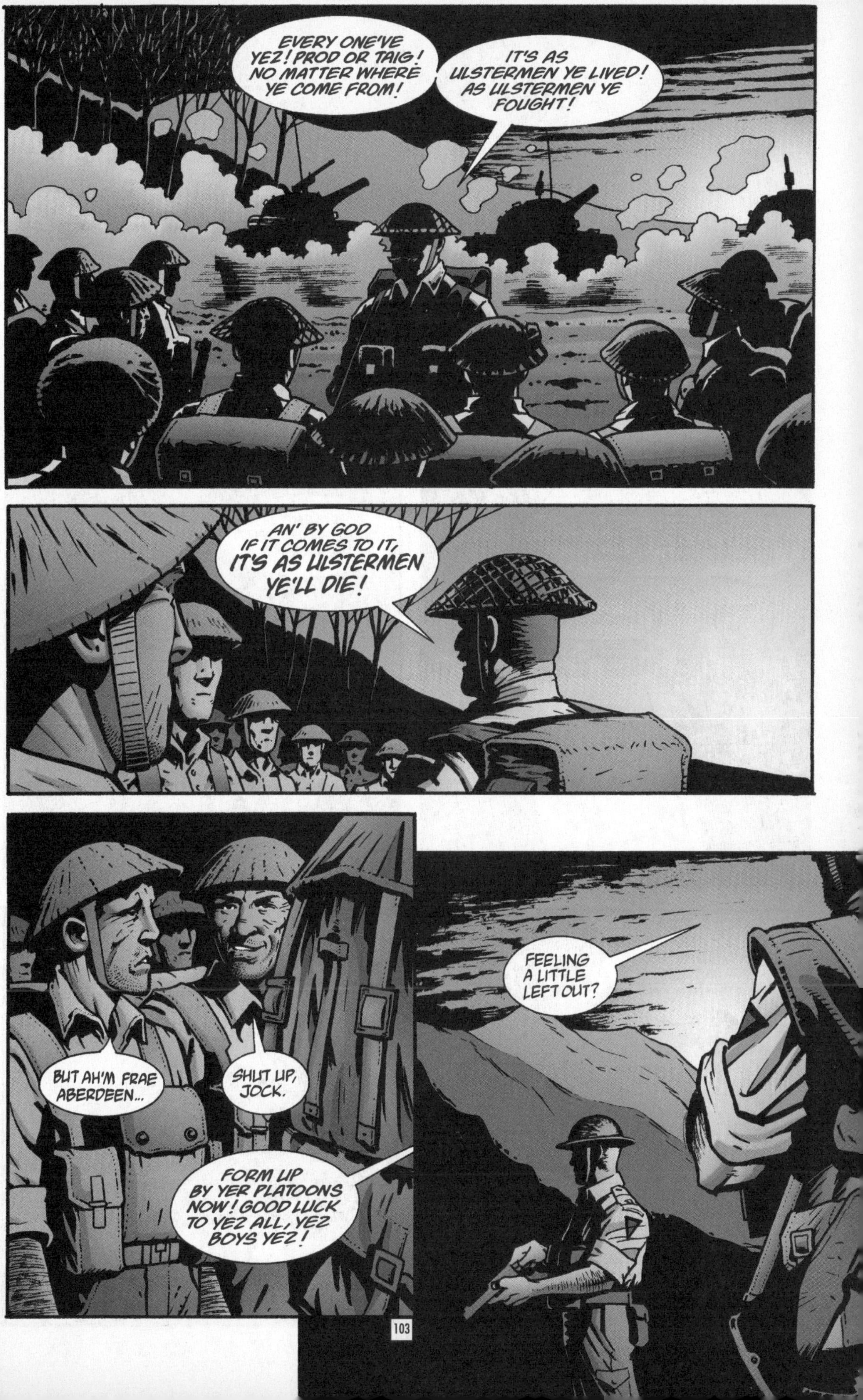

EVERY ONE'VE YEZ! PROD OR TAIG! NO MATTER WHERE YE COME FROM!
IT'S AS ULSTERMEN YE LIVED! AS ULSTERMEN YE FOUGHT!
AN' BY GOD IF IT COMES TO IT, IT'S AS ULSTERMEN YE'LL DIE!
BUT AH'M FRAE ABERDEEN...
SHUT UP, JOCK.
FORM UP BY YER PLATOONS NOW! GOOD LUCK TO YEZ ALL, YEZ BOYS YEZ!
FEELING A LITTLE LEFT OUT?

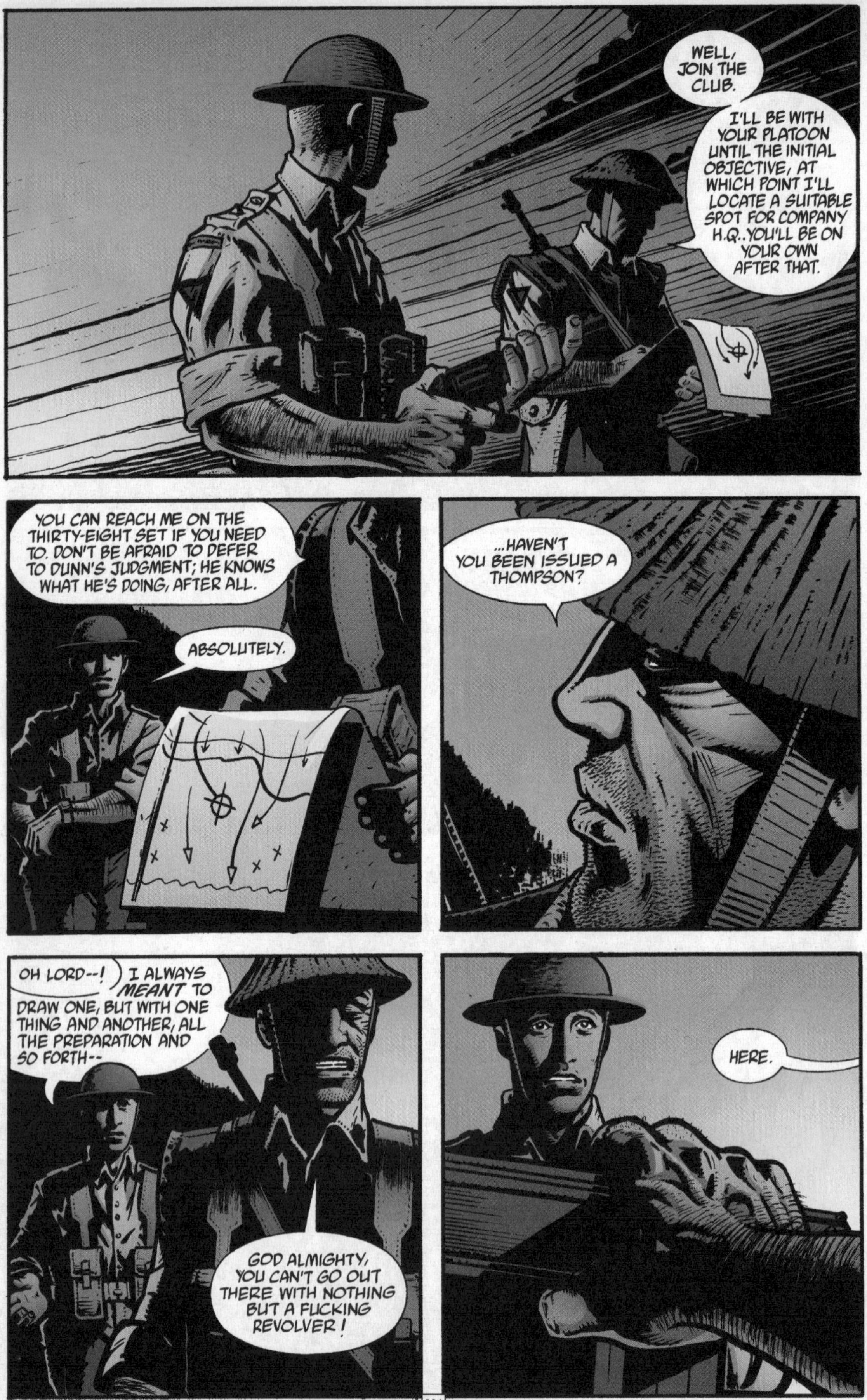

WELL, JOIN THE CLUB.
I'LL BE WITH YOUR PLATOON UNTIL THE INITIAL OBJECTIVE, AT WHICH POINT I'LL LOCATE A SUITABLE SPOT FOR COMPANY H.Q.. YOU'LL BE ON YOUR OWN AFTER THAT.
YOU CAN REACH ME ON THE THIRTY-EIGHT SET IF YOU NEED TO. DON'T BE AFRAID TO DEFER TO DUNN'S JUDGMENT; HE KNOWS WHAT HE'S DOING, AFTER ALL.
ABSOLUTELY.
...HAVEN'T YOU BEEN ISSUED A THOMPSON?
OH LORD--!
I ALWAYS *MEANT* TO DRAW ONE, BUT WITH ONE THING AND ANOTHER, ALL THE PREPARATION AND SO FORTH--
GOD ALMIGHTY, YOU CAN'T GO OUT THERE WITH NOTHING BUT A FUCKING REVOLVER!
HERE.

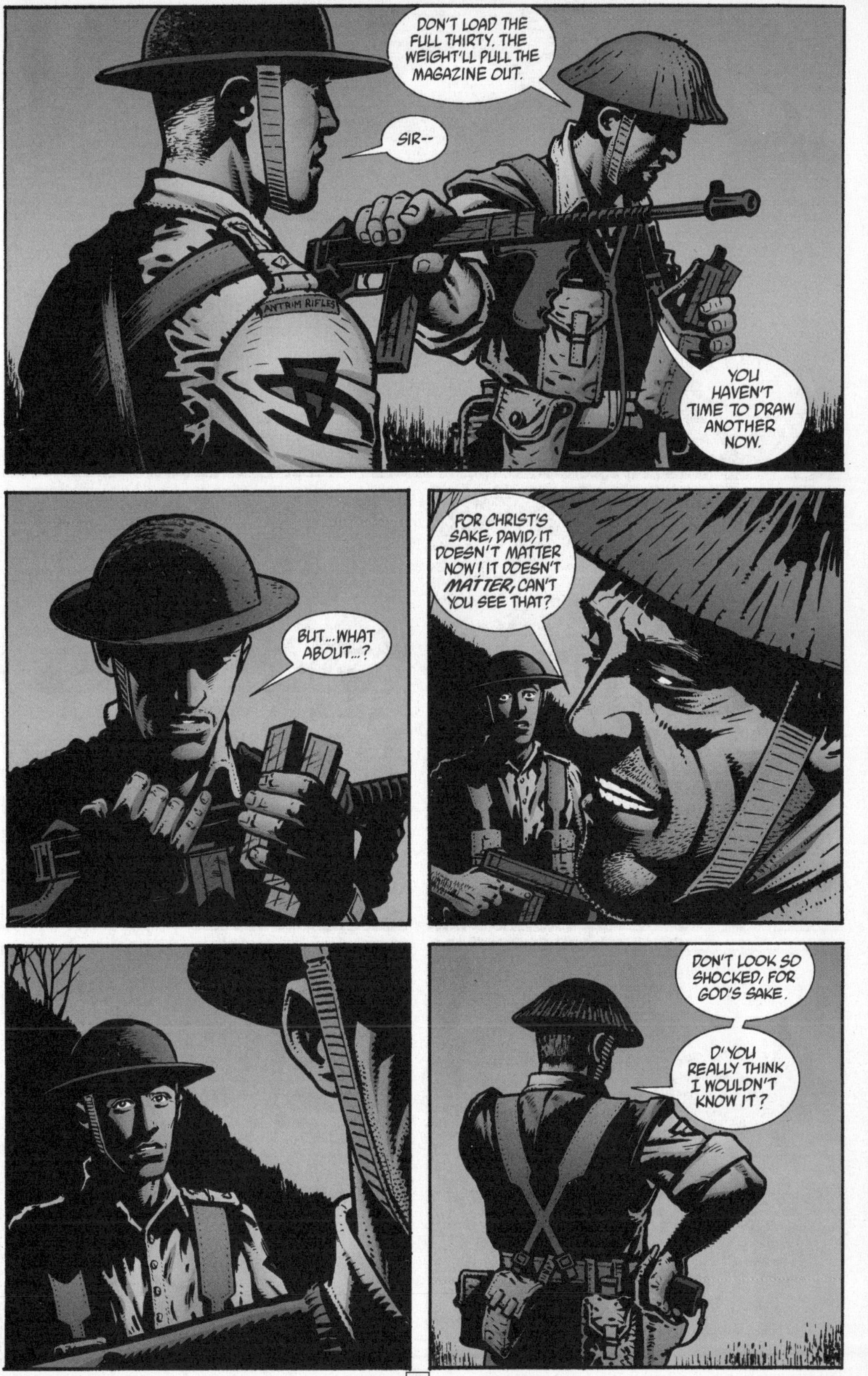
DON'T LOAD THE FULL THIRTY. THE WEIGHT'LL PULL THE MAGAZINE OUT.
SIR--
ANTRIM RIFLES
YOU HAVEN'T TIME TO DRAW ANOTHER NOW.
BUT...WHAT ABOUT...?
FOR CHRIST'S SAKE, DAVID, IT DOESN'T MATTER NOW! IT DOESN'T *MATTER*, CAN'T YOU SEE THAT?
DON'T LOOK SO SHOCKED, FOR GOD'S SAKE.
D'YOU REALLY THINK I WOULDN'T KNOW IT?

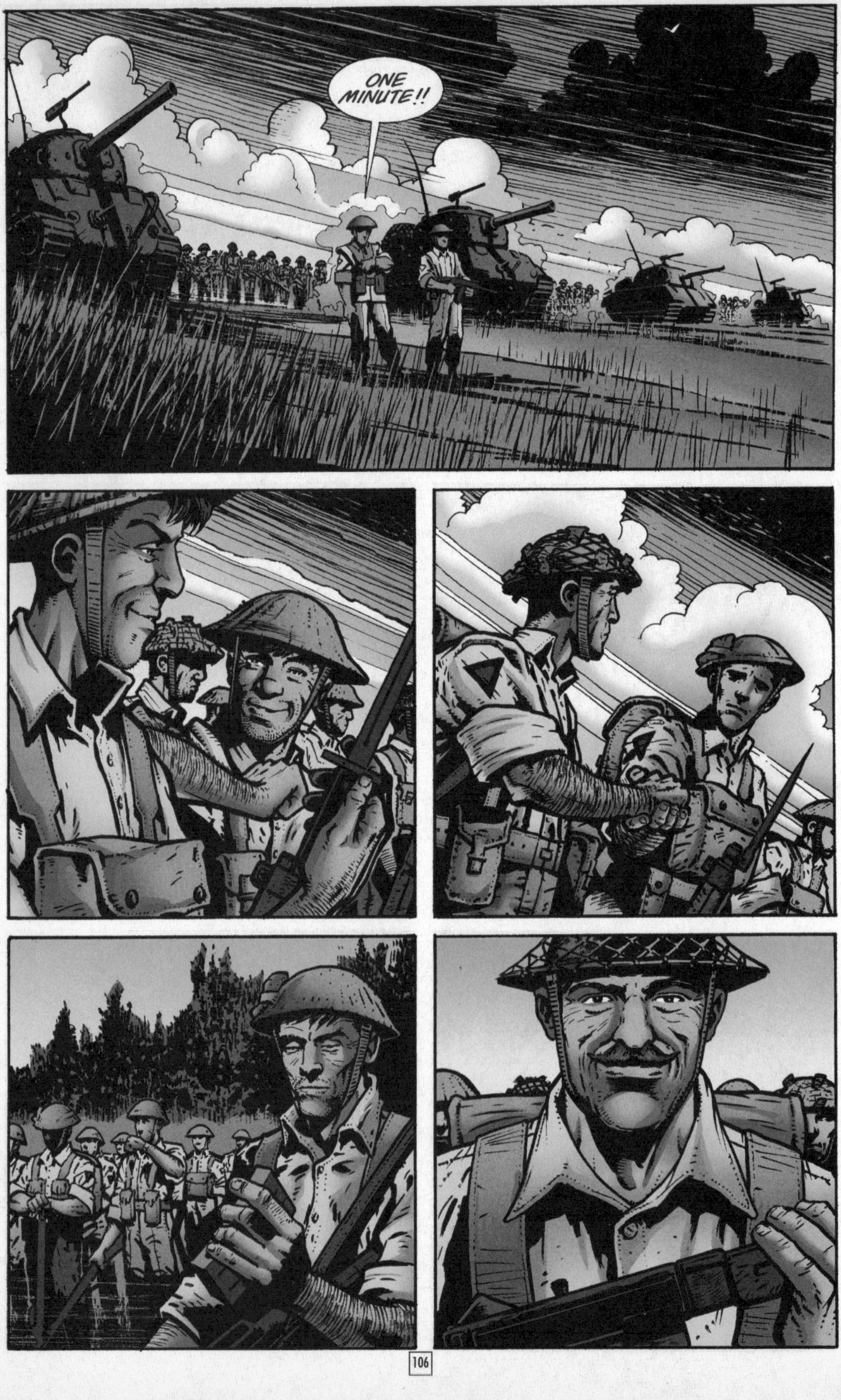
ONE MINUTE!!

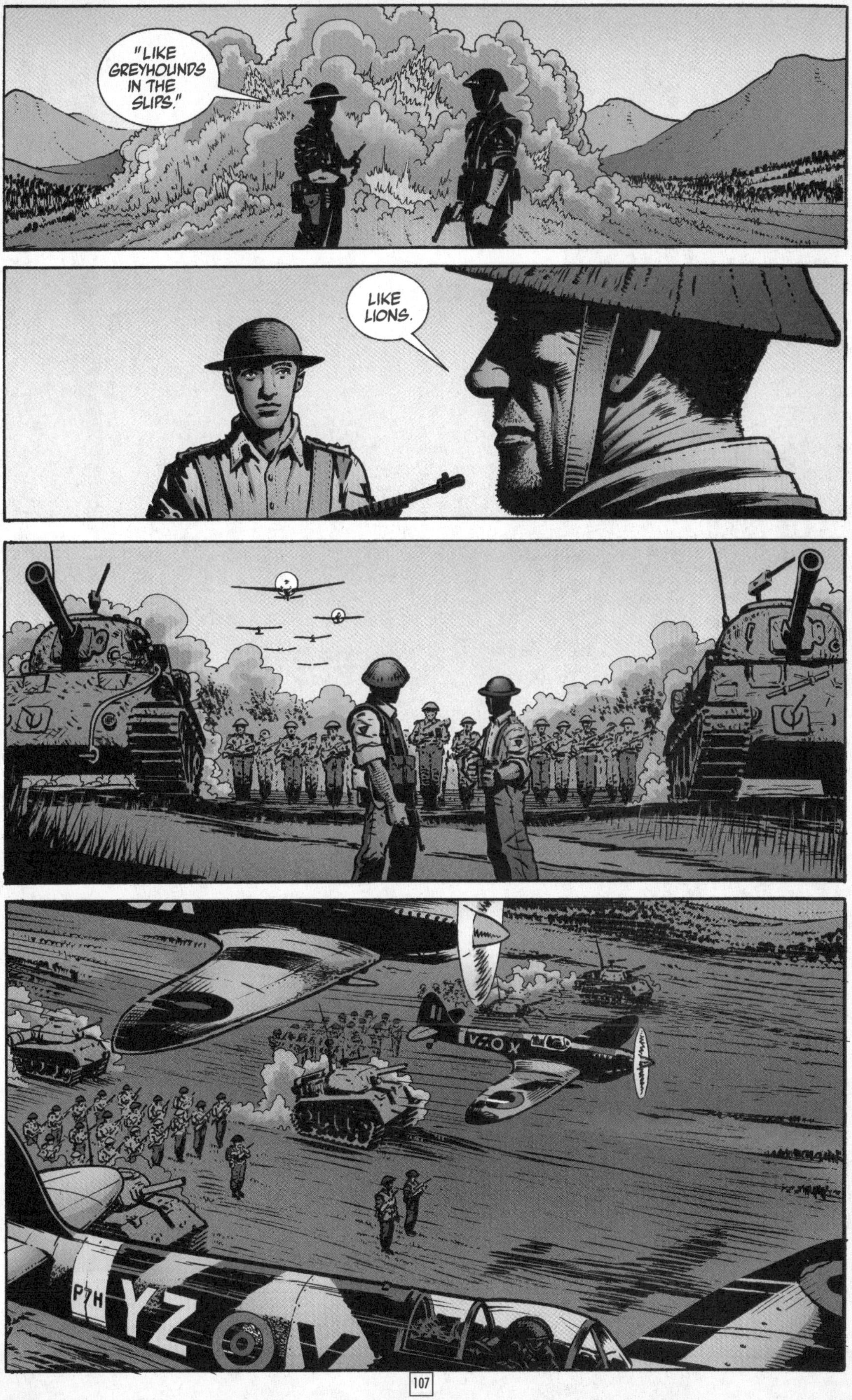
"LIKE GREYHOUNDS IN THE SLIPS."
LIKE LIONS.
P7H YZ

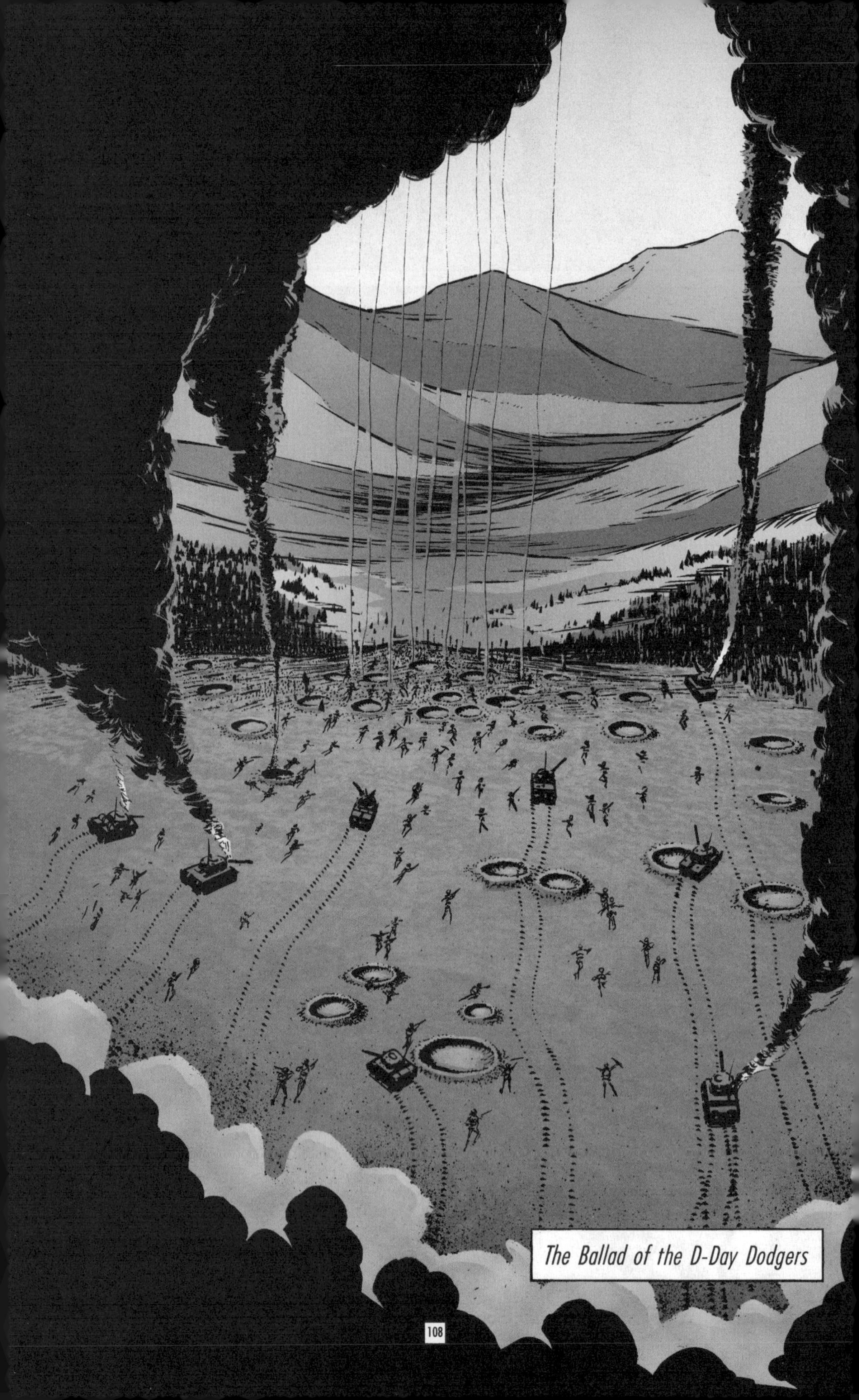
The Ballad of the D-Day Dodgers

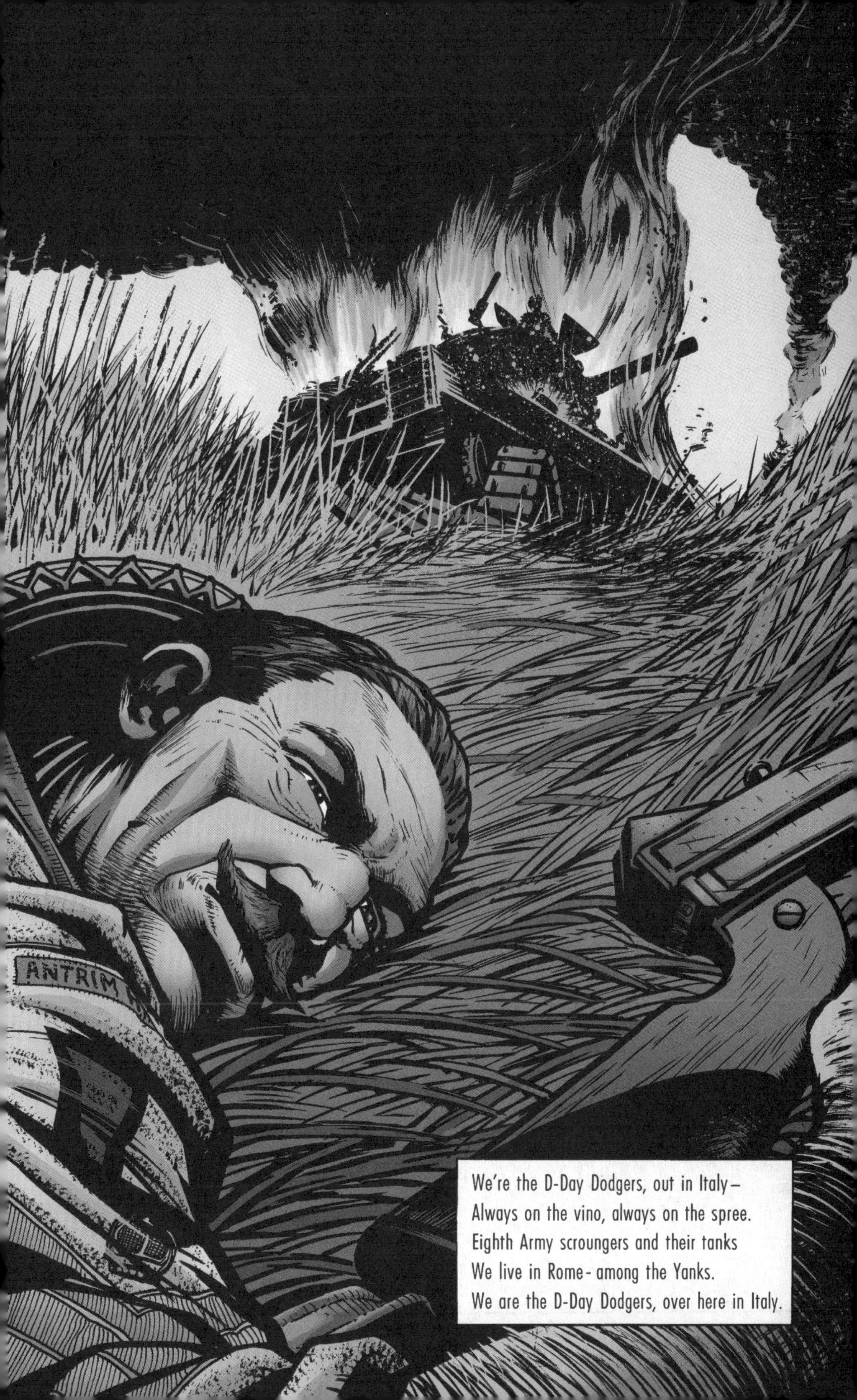
ANTRIM
We're the D-Day Dodgers, out in Italy–
Always on the vino, always on the spree.
Eighth Army scroungers and their tanks
We live in Rome- among the Yanks.
We are the D-Day Dodgers, over here in Italy.

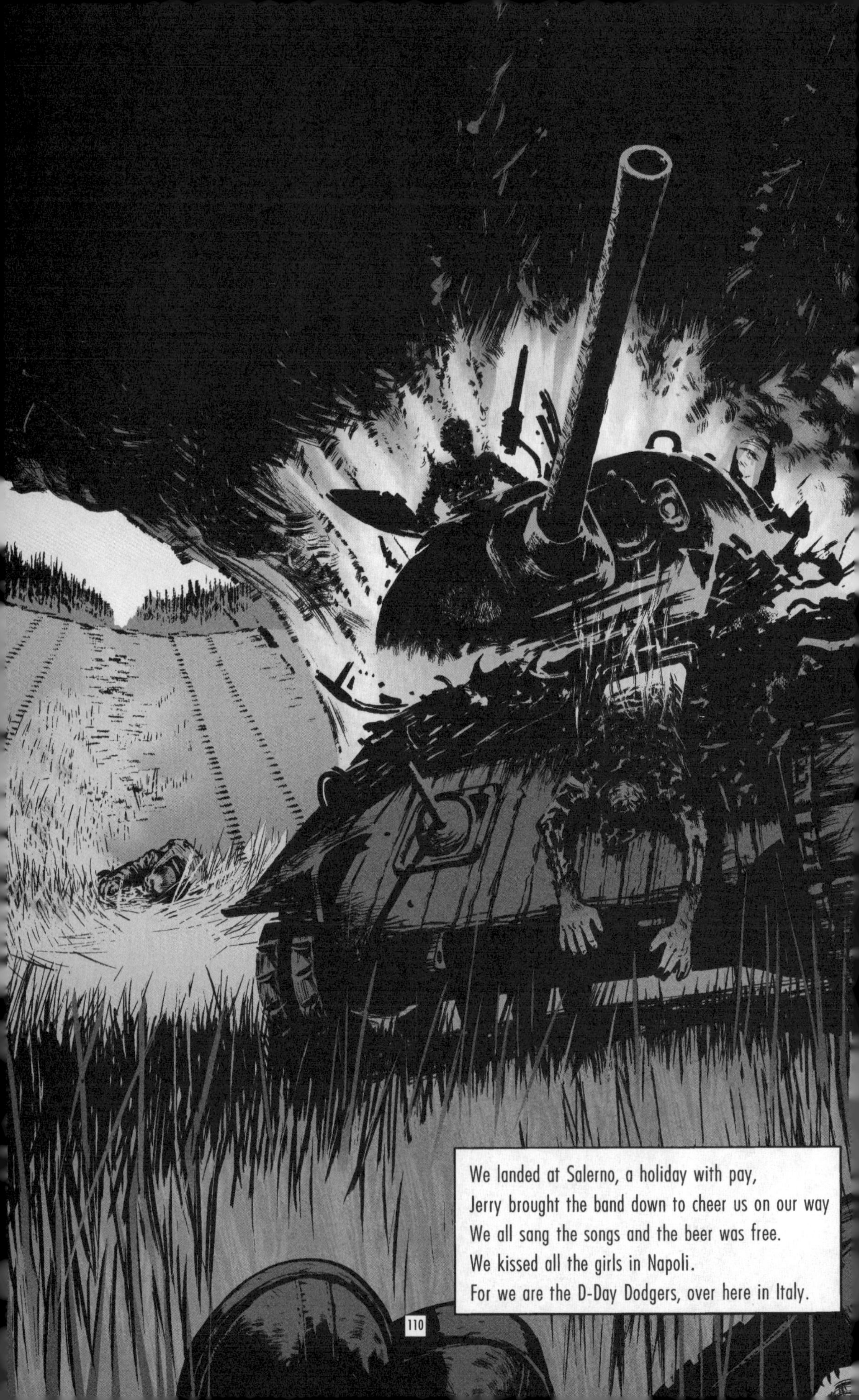
We landed at Salerno, a holiday with pay,
Jerry brought the band down to cheer us on our way
We all sang the songs and the beer was free.
We kissed all the girls in Napoli.
For we are the D-Day Dodgers, over here in Italy.

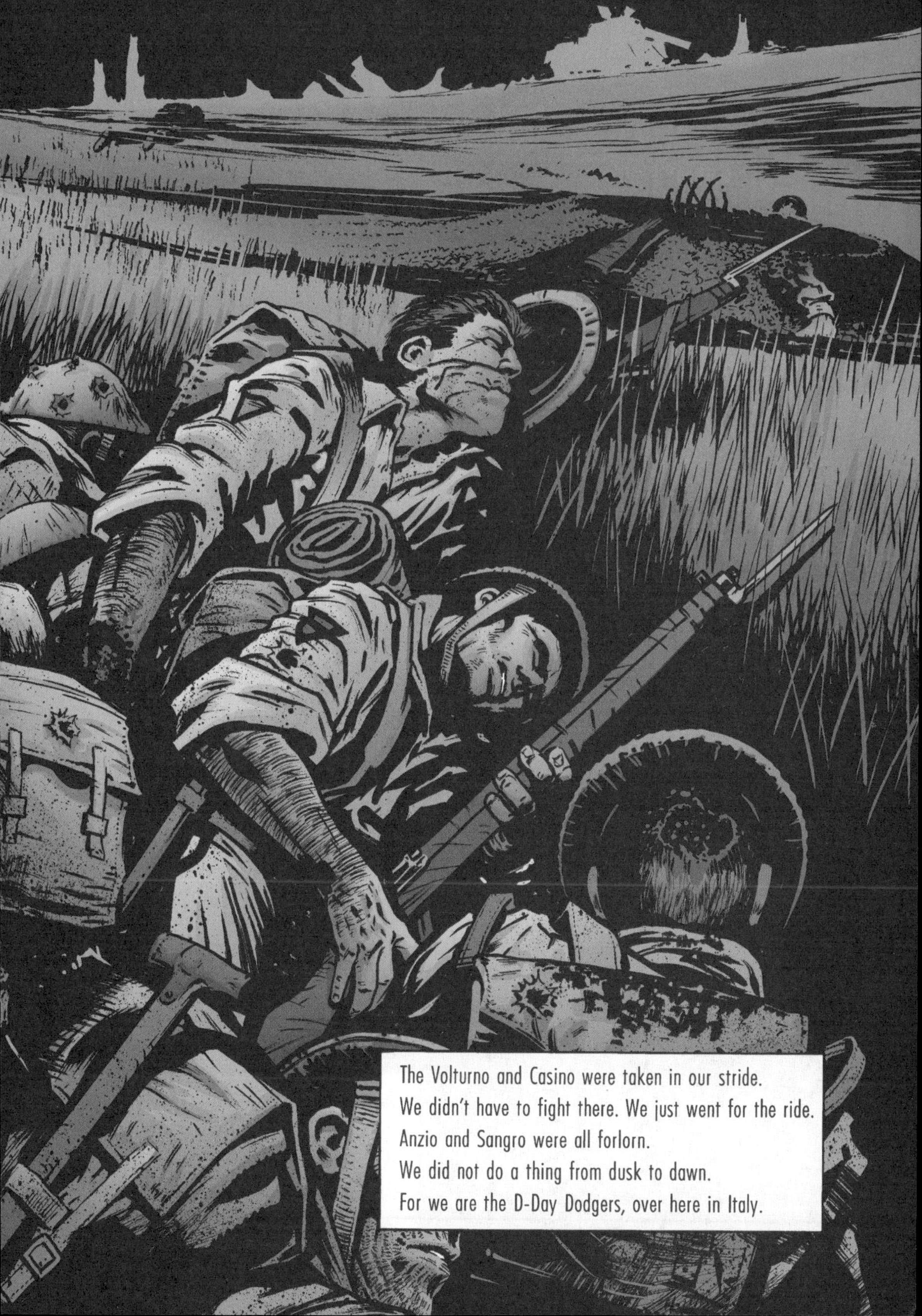
The Volturno and Casino were taken in our stride.
We didn't have to fight there. We just went for the ride.
Anzio and Sangro were all forlorn.
We did not do a thing from dusk to dawn.
For we are the D-Day Dodgers, over here in Italy.

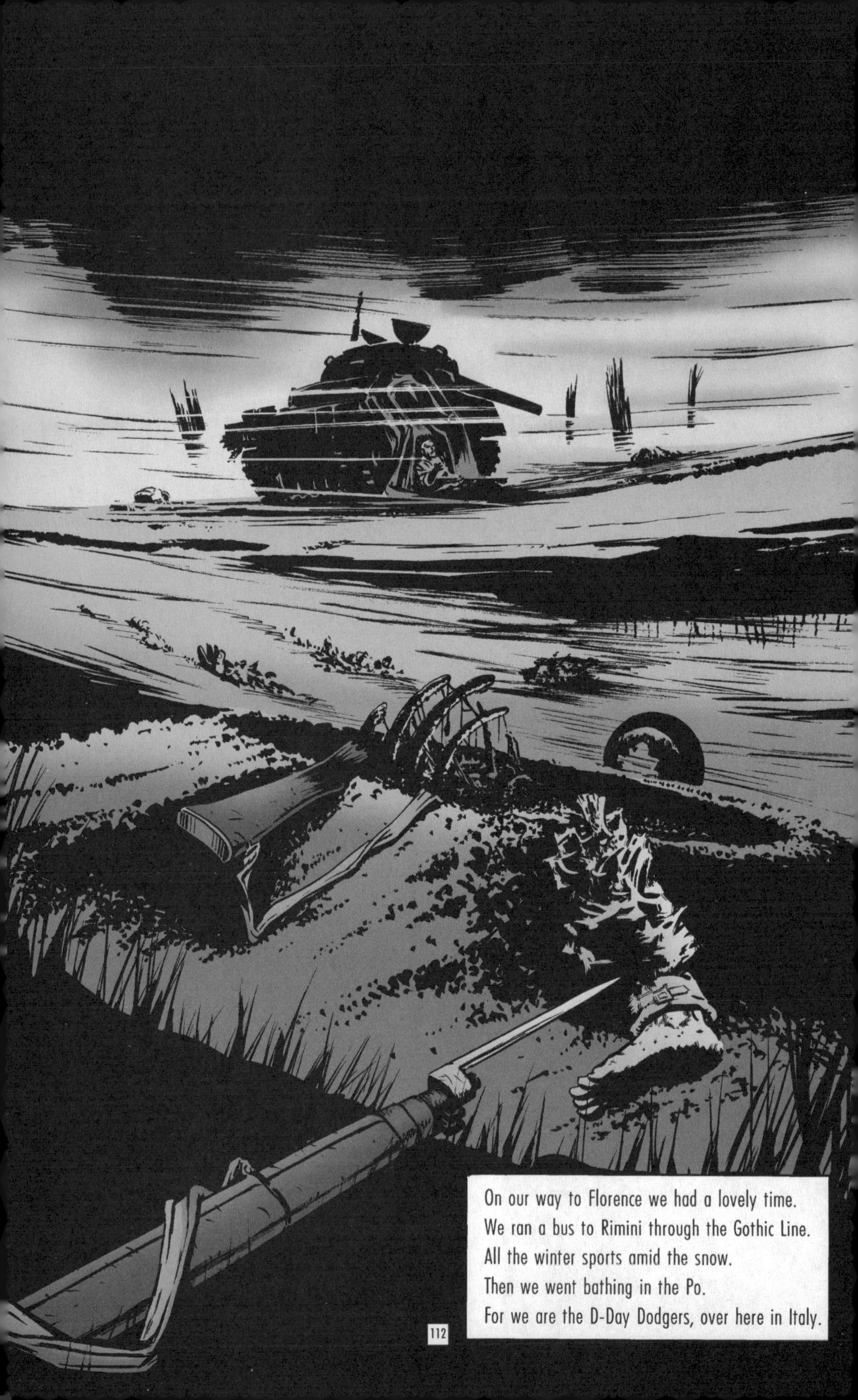
On our way to Florence we had a lovely time.
We ran a bus to Rimini through the Gothic Line.
All the winter sports amid the snow.
Then we went bathing in the Po.
For we are the D-Day Dodgers, over here in Italy.

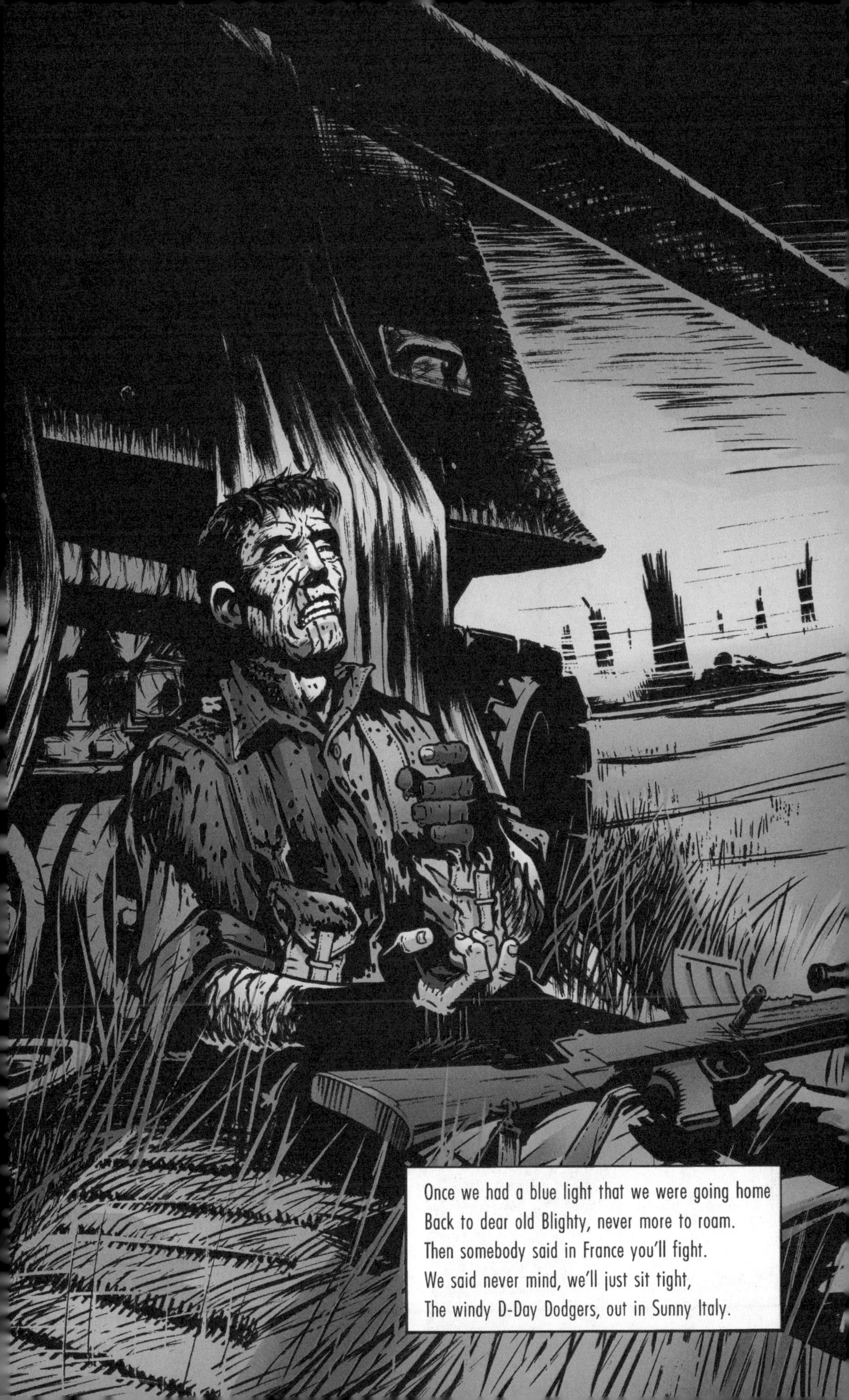
Once we had a blue light that we were going home
Back to dear old Blighty, never more to roam.
Then somebody said in France you'll fight.
We said never mind, we'll just sit tight,
The windy D-Day Dodgers, out in Sunny Italy.

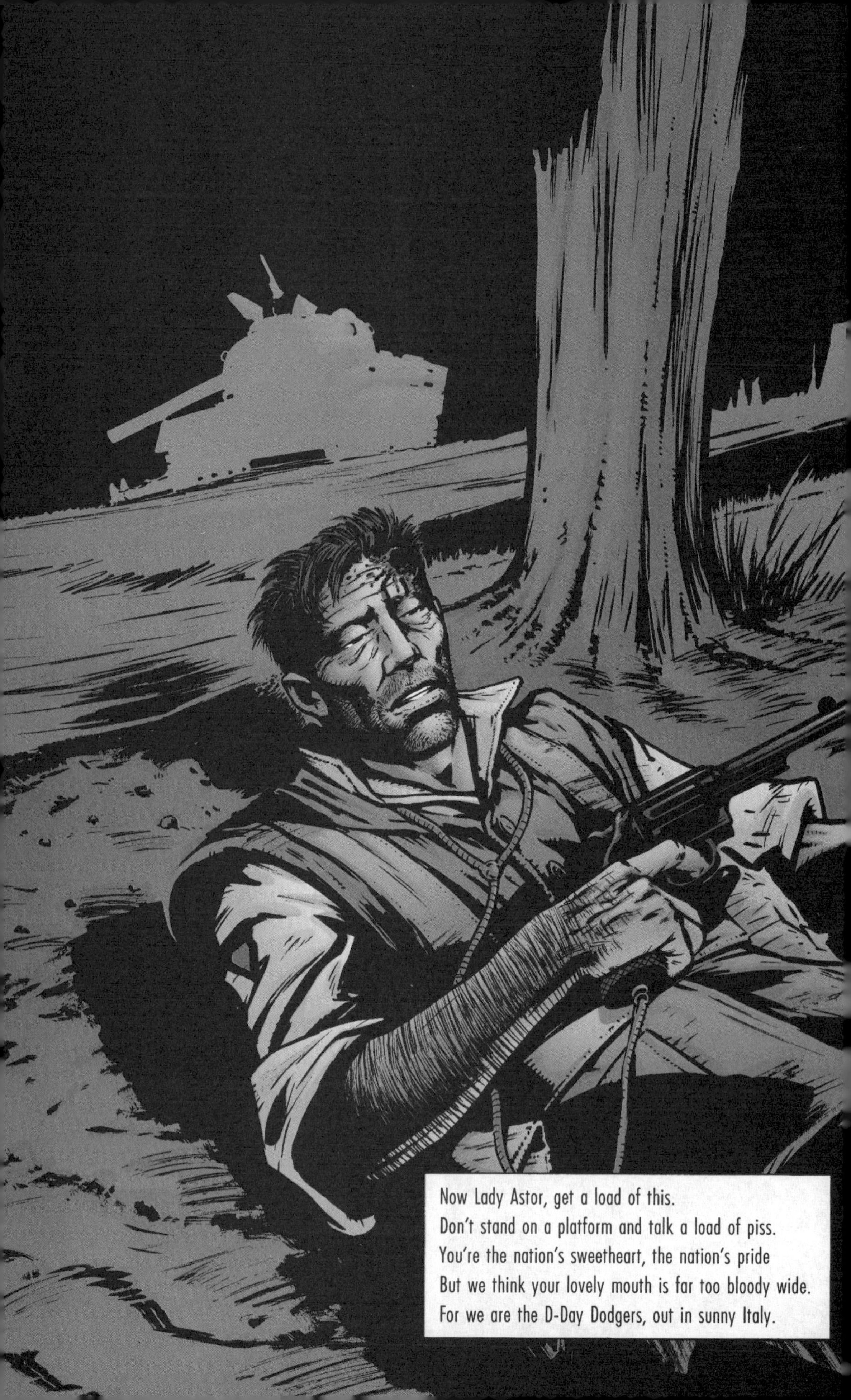
Now Lady Astor, get a load of this.
Don't stand on a platform and talk a load of piss.
You're the nation's sweetheart, the nation's pride
But we think your lovely mouth is far too bloody wide.
For we are the D-Day Dodgers, out in sunny Italy.

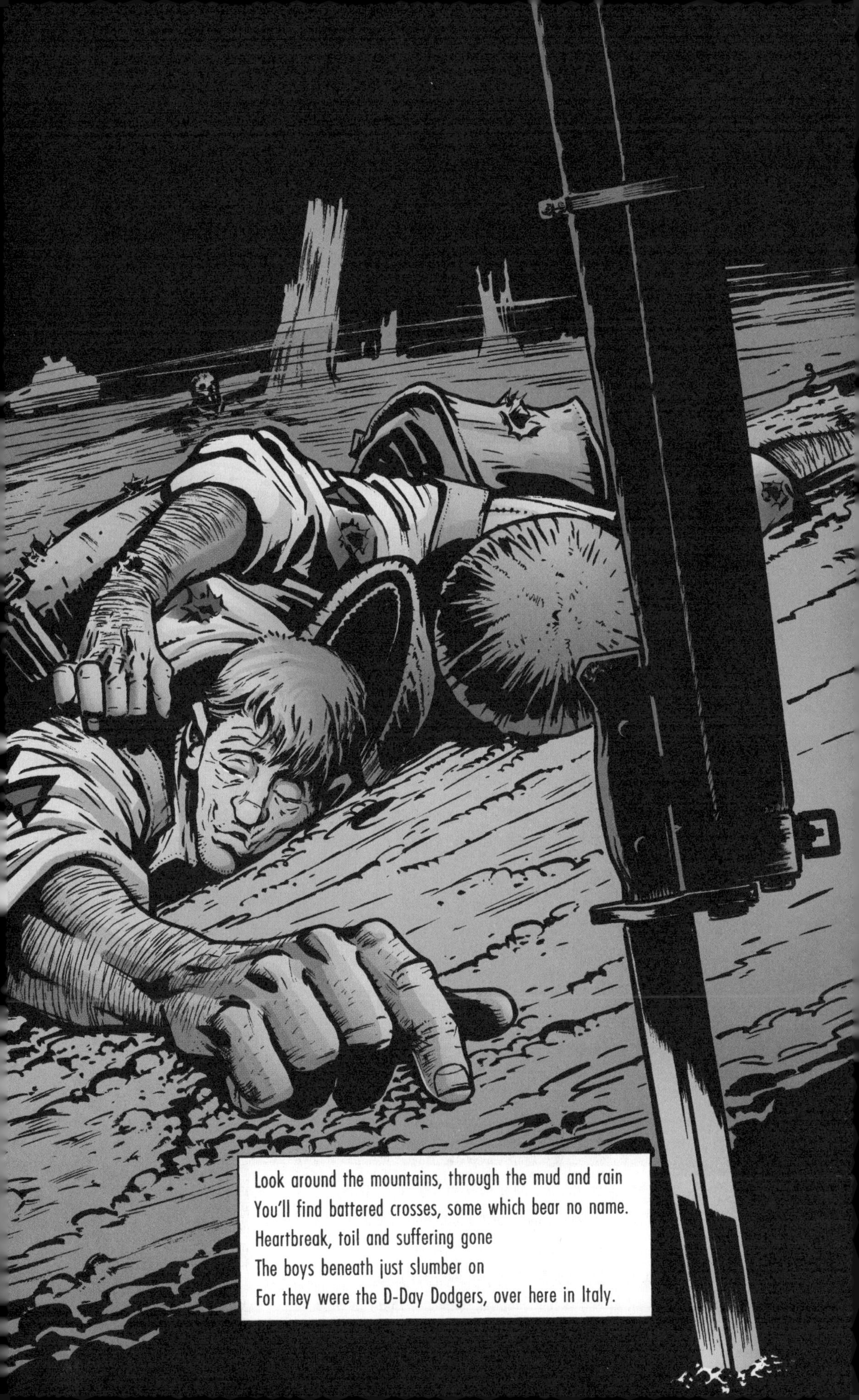
Look around the mountains, through the mud and rain
You'll find battered crosses, some which bear no name.
Heartbreak, toil and suffering gone
The boys beneath just slumber on
For they were the D-Day Dodgers, over here in Italy.

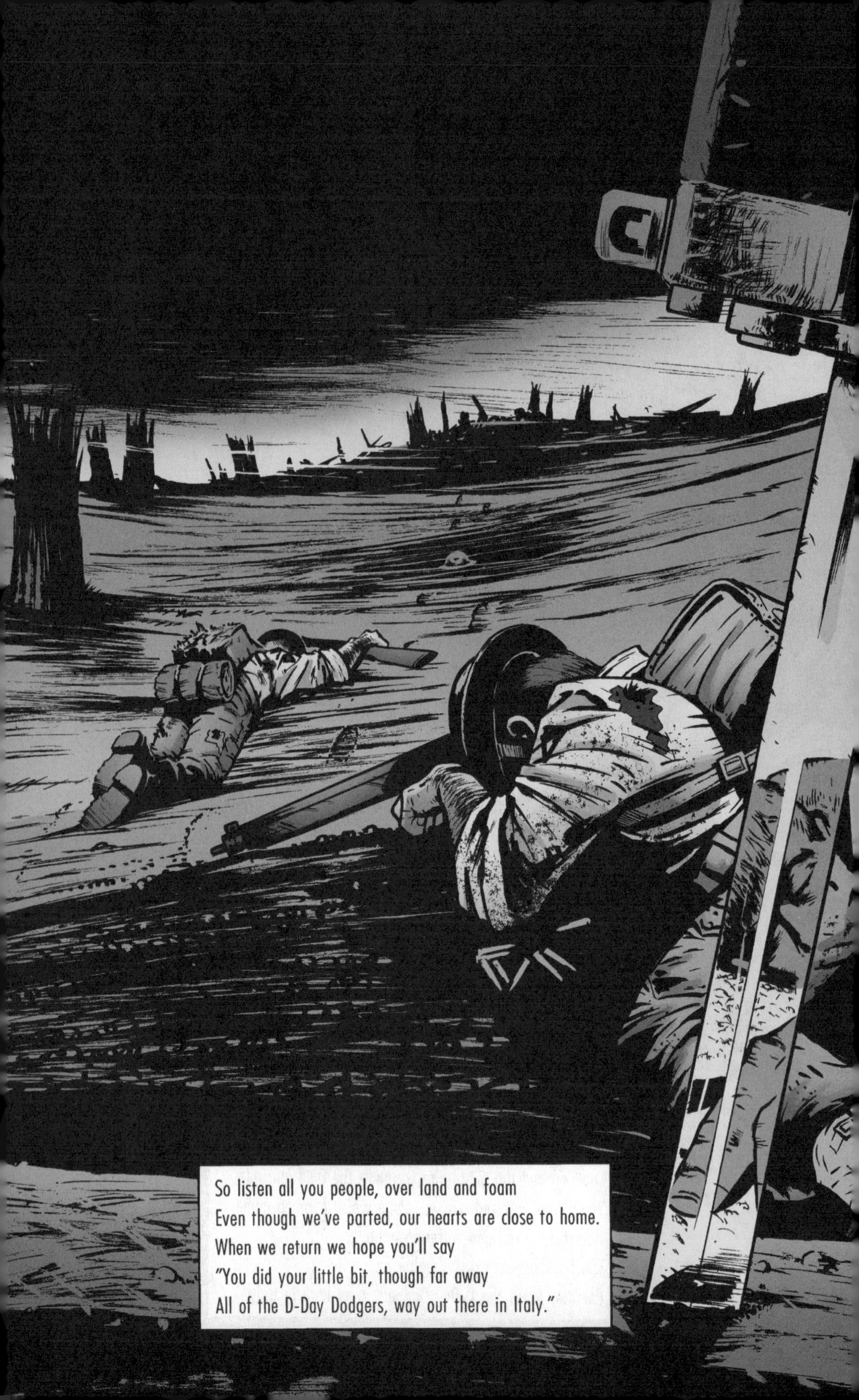
So listen all you people, over land and foam
Even though we've parted, our hearts are close to home.
When we return we hope you'll say
"You did your little bit, though far away
All of the D-Day Dodgers, way out there in Italy."

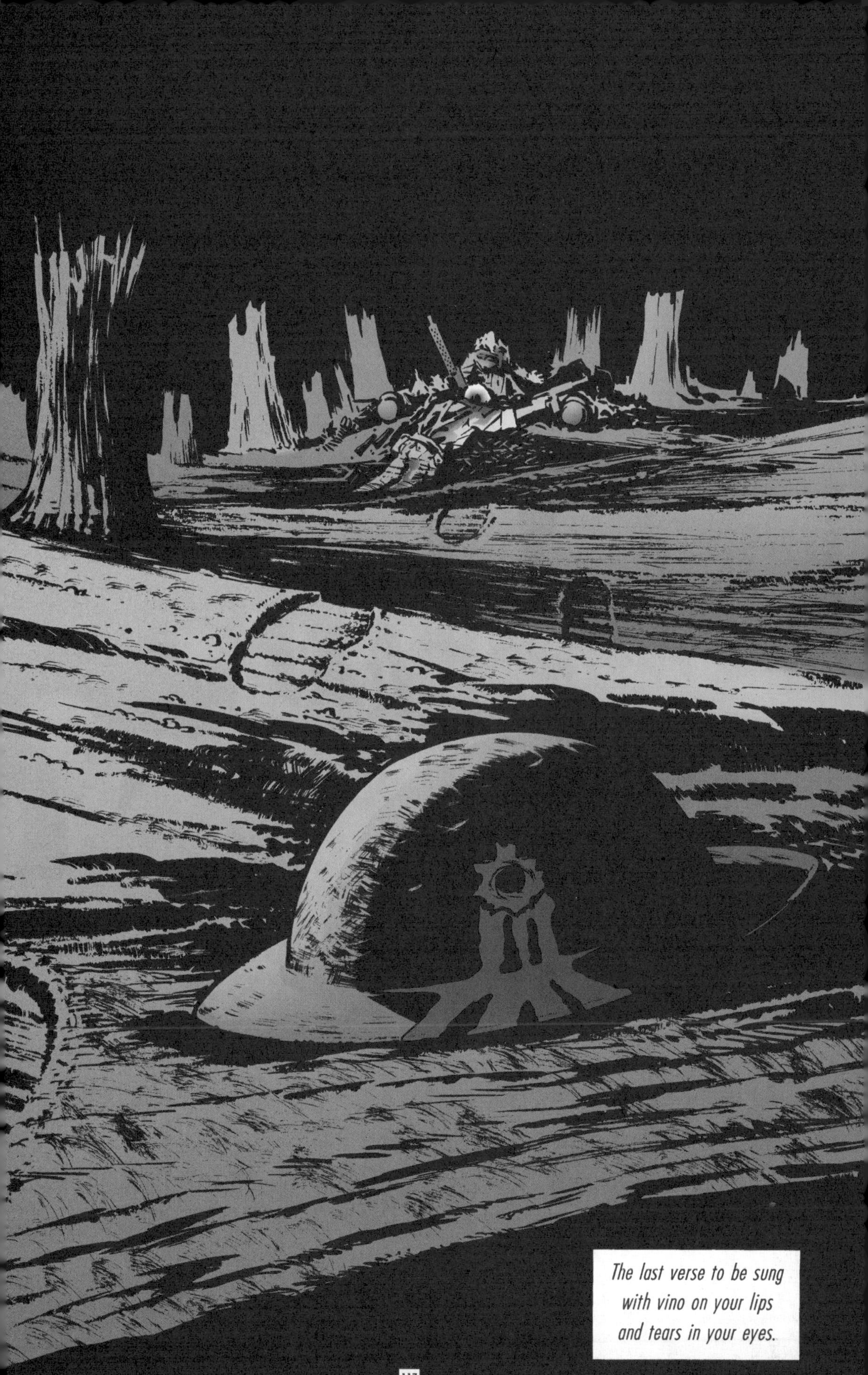
The last verse to be sung with vino on your lips and tears in your eyes.

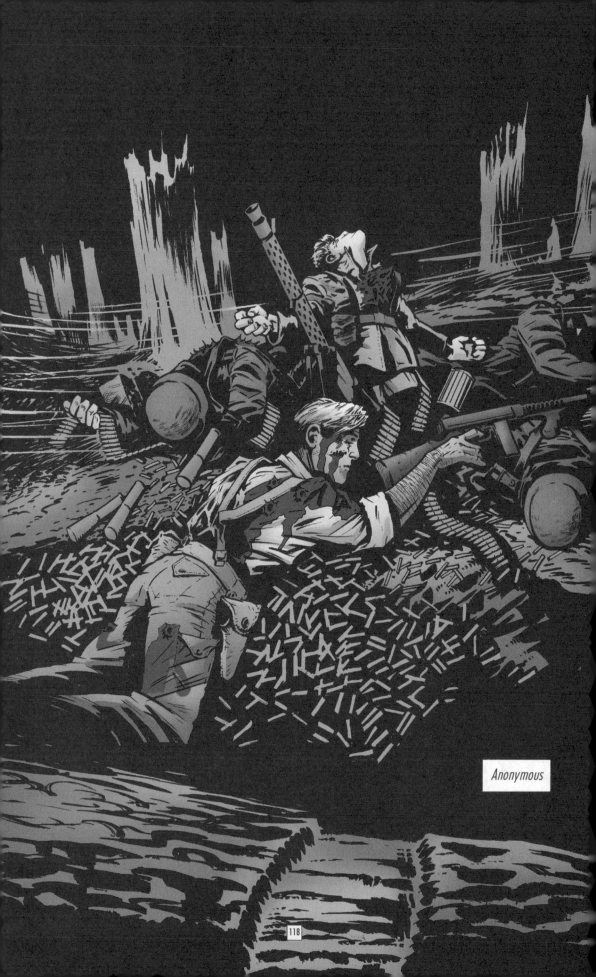

Anonymous

Exactly who wrote *The Ballad of the D-Day Dodgers* remains a mystery to this day.

After the war, Lady Astor claimed never to have made the speech in question.

Almost one hundred thousand Allied soldiers were killed or wounded in the Italian campaign.

Their comrades were still on Italian soil when the war was won, on May the seventh, 1945.

"I DON'T MIND THE WAR, BUT I HATE THE FUCKING ARMY"

WAR STORY

SCREAMING·EAGLES

Most days the old soldier sat on his porch and drank cheap beer, and watched his children and grandchildren play in the sun. He bought the paper only rarely, laughed at a President caught with his pants down, read that stress could be a killer and smiled in quiet wonder.

Other days...

He remembered a guy got hit so hard the brains came out the mouth, the kick of the Thompson in his shoulder, the taste of soil as Spandau answered B.A.R. ... the SLAM-CRASH! of the eighty-eights on the Tigers, an idiot from Kansas who almost got the Medal of Honor, that rising whistle just before the whole world ended ... and how it felt to rake a blond boy with .45 tracers, opening him from crotch to throat, pumping *light* through him 'til at last the shock left his eyes and he was down.

Sometimes the old soldier's children and grandchildren tried their luck, although they knew he'd never had that much to say. *You don't need to know those things,* he thought, *You never will. If any good came out of what I did, that would be it.* But still they came to him, and still they peered, and still they asked.

"What was it like?"

And "How did you do it?"

And "What was it got you through?"

SCREAMING EAGLES

Garth Ennis, writer **Dave Gibbons**, artist

Pamela Rambo, colorist **Clem Robins**, letterer
Heroic Age, separations **John Van Fleet**, cover artist
Tony Bedard & **Will Dennis**, editors

Special thanks to **Axel Alonso**

Cover photo courtesy of
National Archives, photo no, 111-C-681

YOU'RE IN MY LIGHT, SERGEANT.

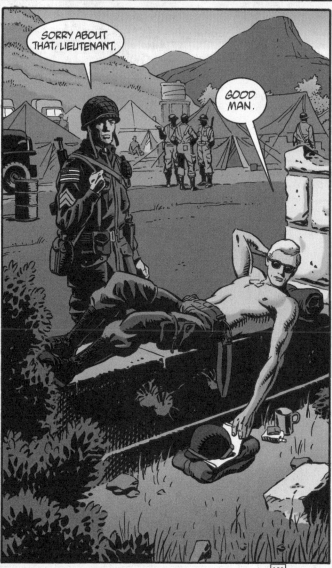

SORRY ABOUT THAT, LIEUTENANT.

GOOD MAN.

THERE'S A COUNTRY HOUSE OF SOME KIND UP NEAR THIS LITTLE PLACE CALLED GRAFALI. GENERAL BLEDDING'S DUE HERE NEXT WEEK; I THOUGHT IT MIGHT MAKE A GOOD HEADQUARTERS FOR HIM AND HIS STAFF.

GO CHECK IT OUT, WILL YOU?

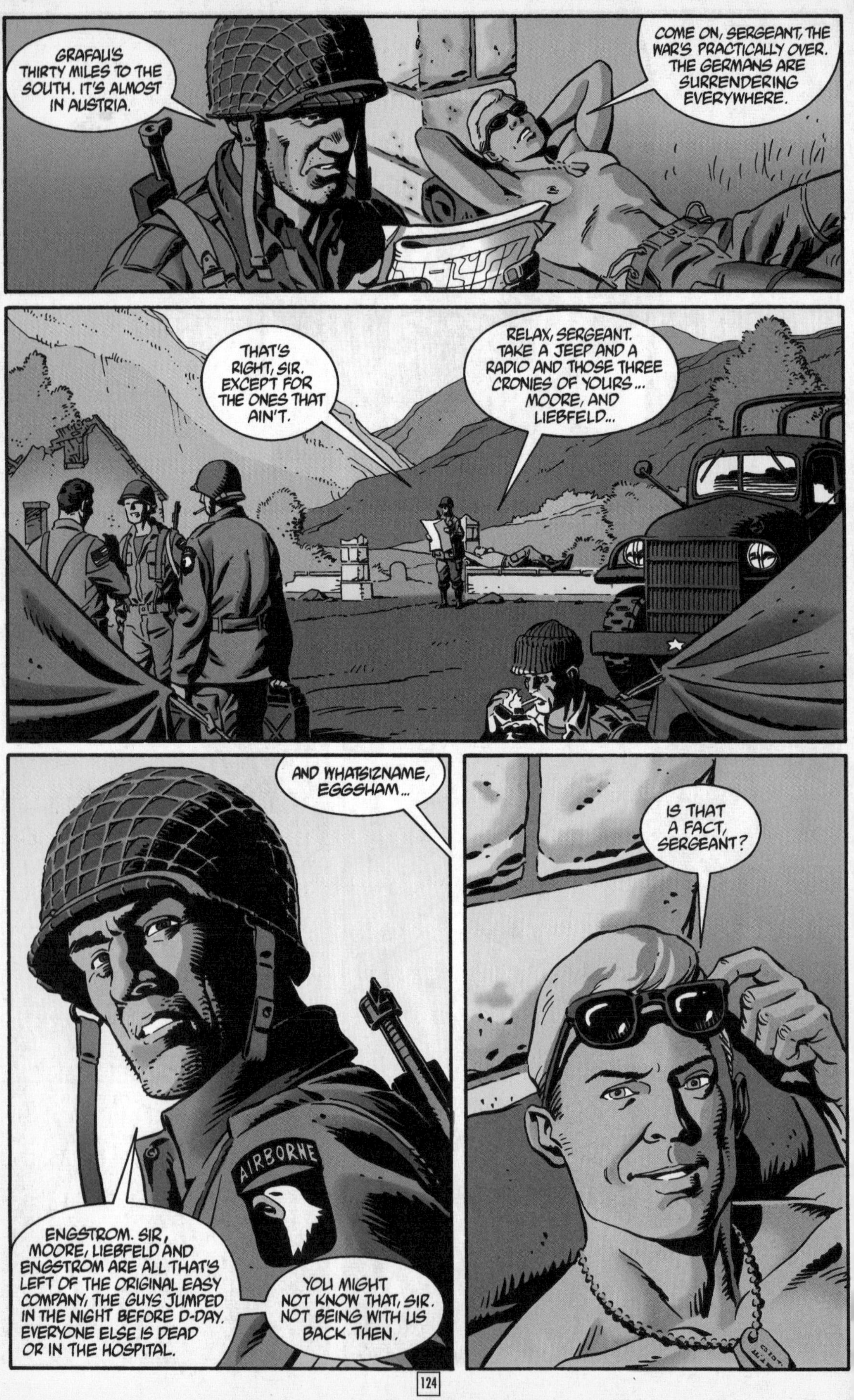
GRAFAU'S THIRTY MILES TO THE SOUTH. IT'S ALMOST IN AUSTRIA.
COME ON, SERGEANT, THE WAR'S PRACTICALLY OVER. THE GERMANS ARE SURRENDERING EVERYWHERE.
THAT'S RIGHT, SIR. EXCEPT FOR THE ONES THAT AIN'T.
RELAX, SERGEANT. TAKE A JEEP AND A RADIO AND THOSE THREE CRONIES OF YOURS... MOORE, AND LIEBFELD...
AND WHATSIZNAME, EGGSHAM...
AIRBORNE
ENGSTROM. SIR, MOORE, LIEBFELD AND ENGSTROM ARE ALL THAT'S LEFT OF THE ORIGINAL EASY COMPANY, THE GUYS JUMPED IN THE NIGHT BEFORE D-DAY. EVERYONE ELSE IS DEAD OR IN THE HOSPITAL.
YOU MIGHT NOT KNOW THAT, SIR. NOT BEING WITH US BACK THEN.
IS THAT A FACT, SERGEANT?

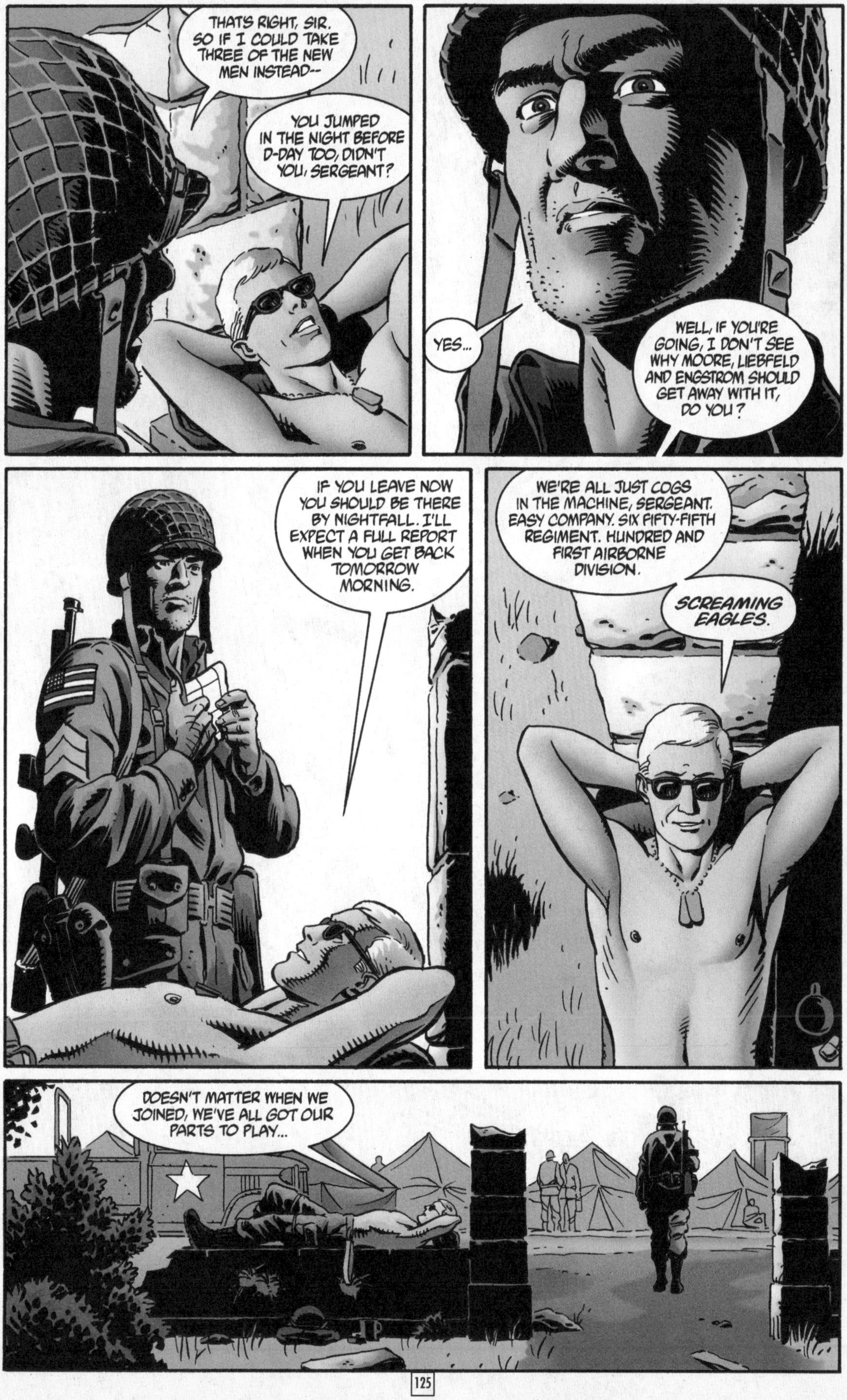
THAT'S RIGHT, SIR. SO IF I COULD TAKE THREE OF THE NEW MEN INSTEAD--
YOU JUMPED IN THE NIGHT BEFORE D-DAY TOO, DIDN'T YOU, SERGEANT?
YES...
WELL, IF YOU'RE GOING, I DON'T SEE WHY MOORE, LIEBFELD AND ENGSTROM SHOULD GET AWAY WITH IT, DO YOU?
IF YOU LEAVE NOW YOU SHOULD BE THERE BY NIGHTFALL. I'LL EXPECT A FULL REPORT WHEN YOU GET BACK TOMORROW MORNING.
WE'RE ALL JUST COGS IN THE MACHINE, SERGEANT. EASY COMPANY. SIX FIFTY-FIFTH REGIMENT. HUNDRED AND FIRST AIRBORNE DIVISION.
SCREAMING EAGLES.
DOESN'T MATTER WHEN WE JOINED, WE'VE ALL GOT OUR PARTS TO PLAY...

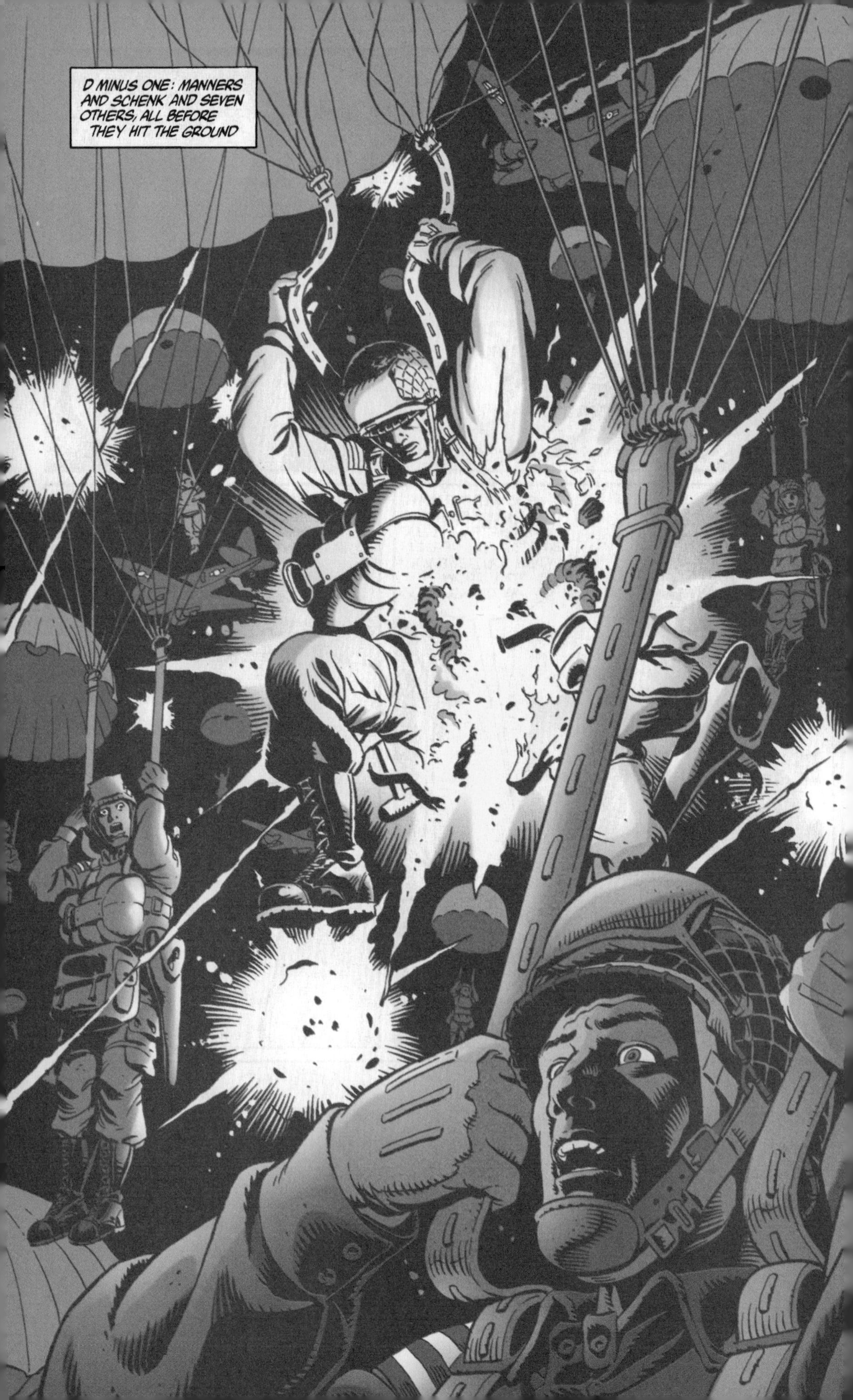
D MINUS ONE: MANNERS AND SCHENK AND SEVEN OTHERS, ALL BEFORE THEY HIT THE GROUND

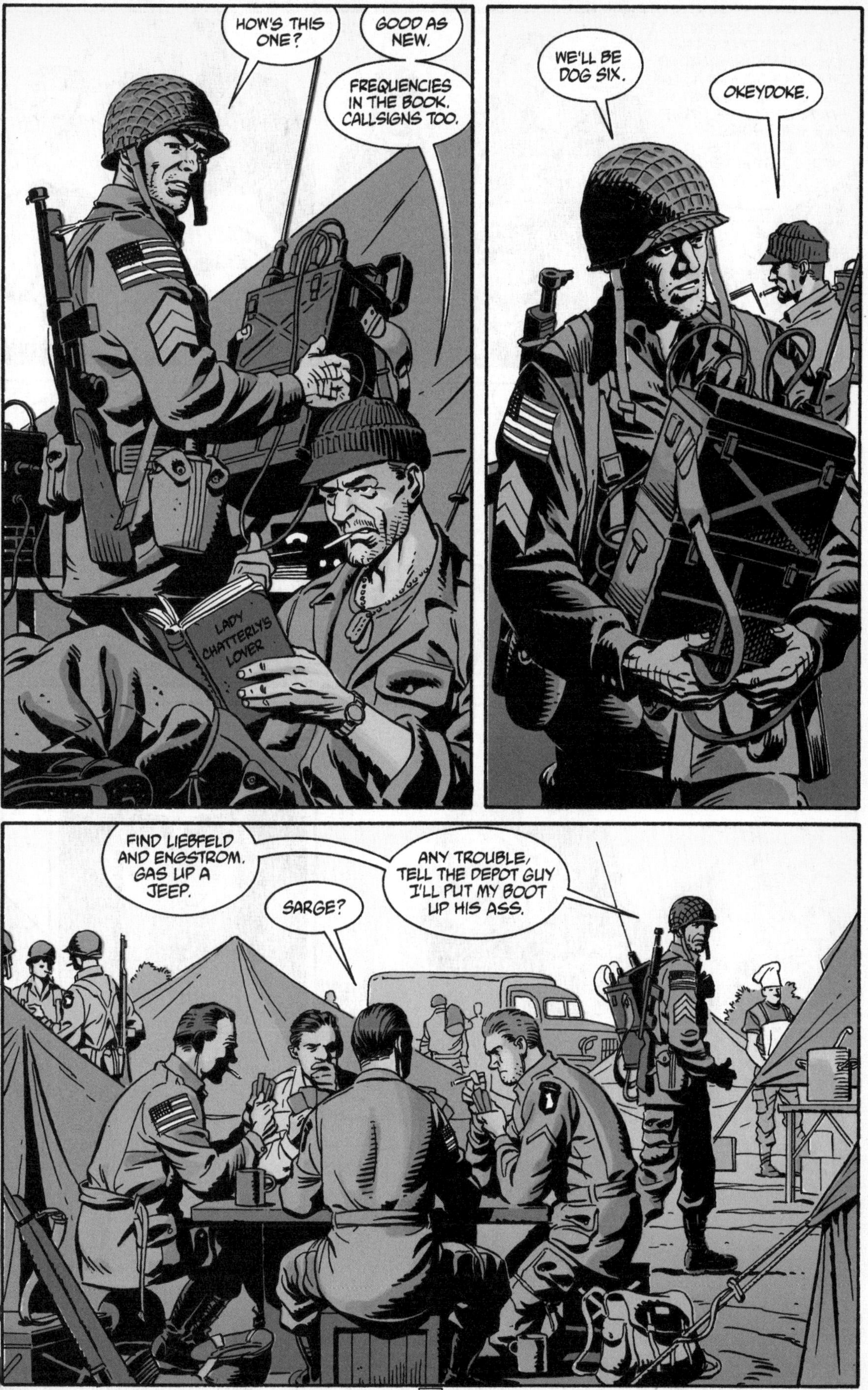
HOW'S THIS ONE?
GOOD AS NEW.
FREQUENCIES IN THE BOOK. CALLSIGNS TOO.
LADY CHATTERLY'S LOVER
WE'LL BE DOG SIX.
OKEYDOKE.
FIND LIEBFELD AND ENGSTROM. GAS UP A JEEP.
SARGE?
ANY TROUBLE, TELL THE DEPOT GUY I'LL PUT MY BOOT UP HIS ASS.

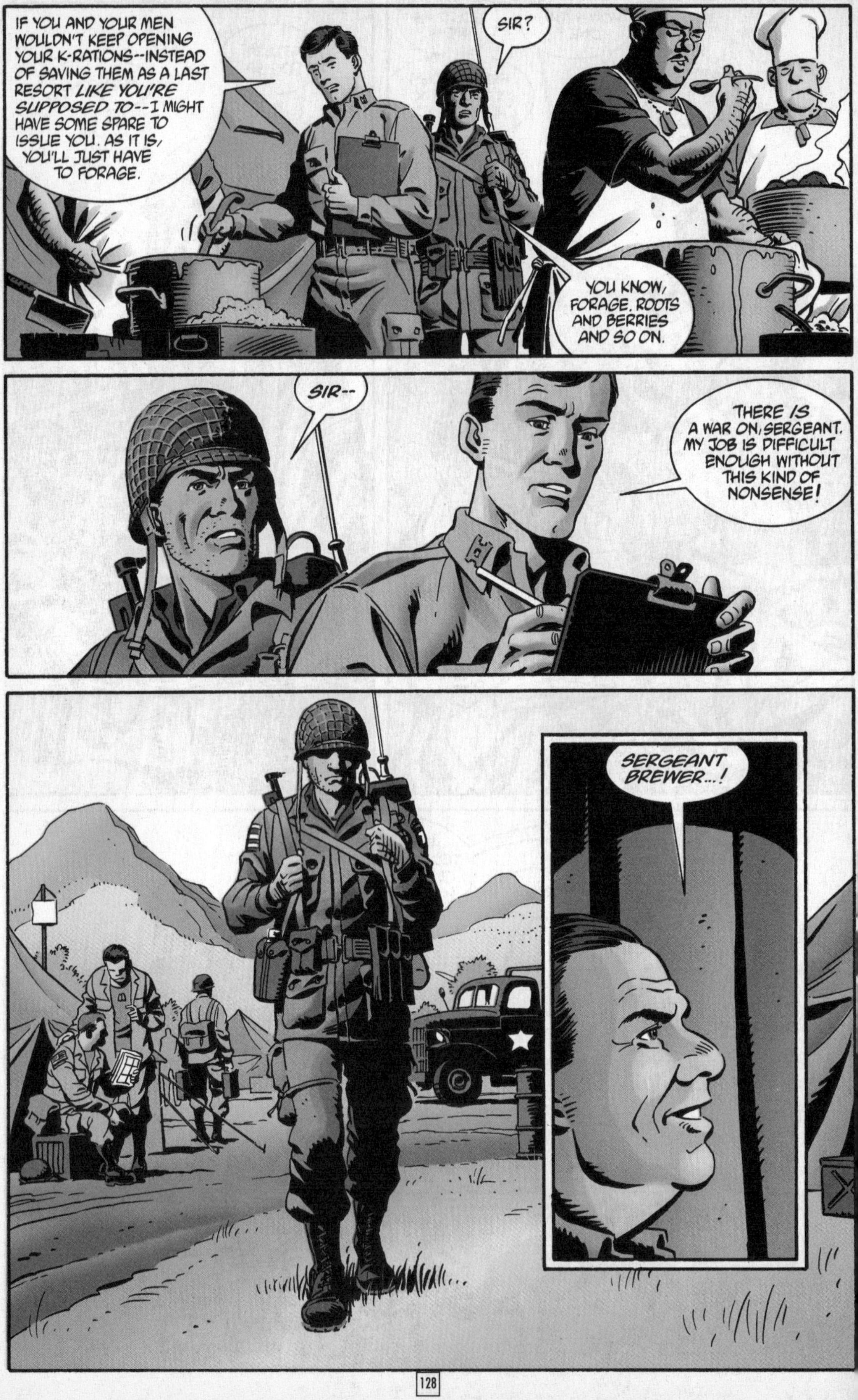
IF YOU AND YOUR MEN WOULDN'T KEEP OPENING YOUR K-RATIONS--INSTEAD OF SAVING THEM AS A LAST RESORT *LIKE YOU'RE SUPPOSED TO*--I MIGHT HAVE SOME SPARE TO ISSUE YOU. AS IT IS, YOU'LL JUST HAVE TO FORAGE.
SIR?
YOU KNOW, FORAGE. ROOTS AND BERRIES AND SO ON.
SIR--
THERE *IS* A WAR ON, SERGEANT. MY JOB IS DIFFICULT ENOUGH WITHOUT THIS KIND OF NONSENSE!
SERGEANT BREWER...!

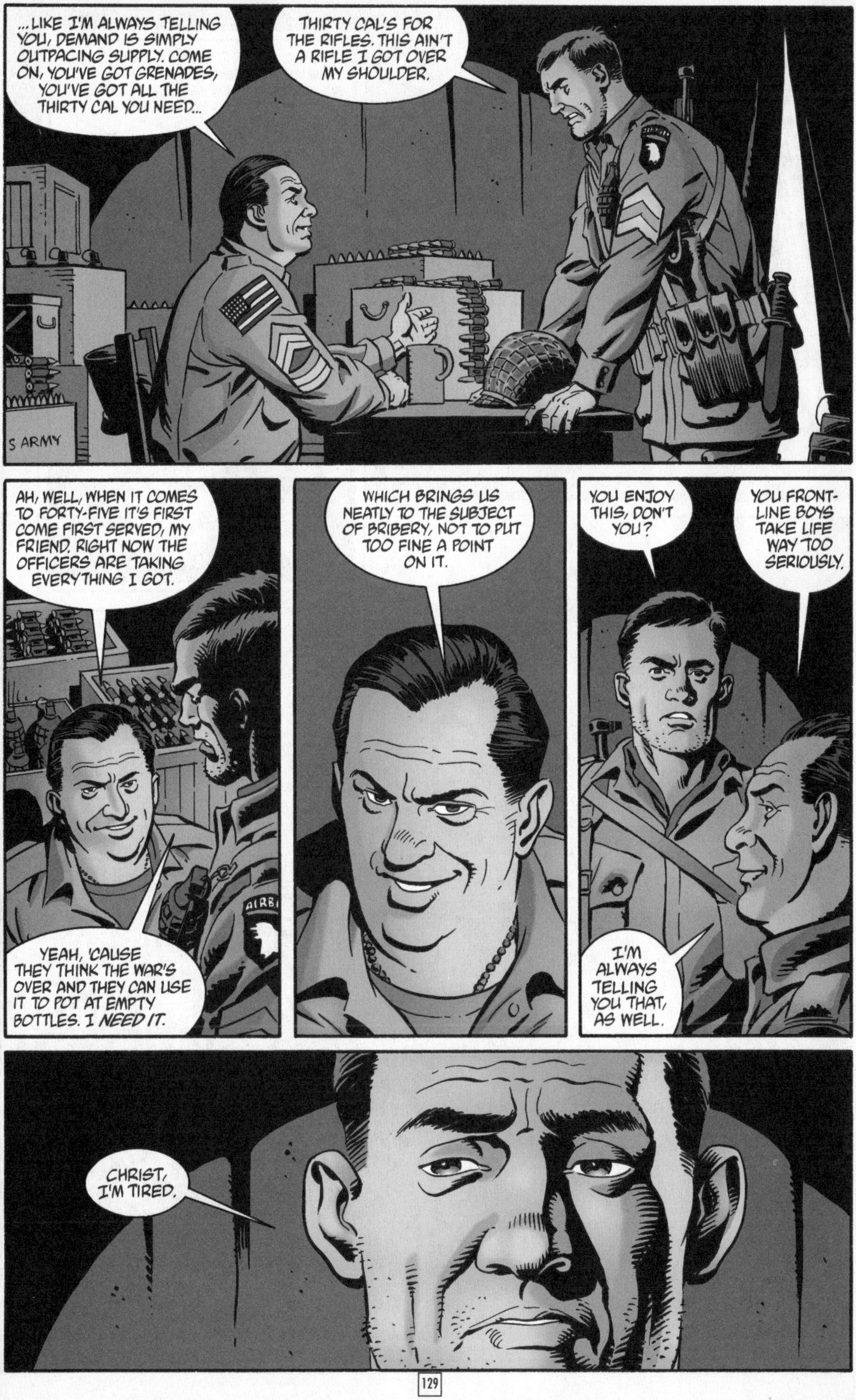
...LIKE I'M ALWAYS TELLING YOU, DEMAND IS SIMPLY OUTPACING SUPPLY. COME ON, YOU'VE GOT GRENADES, YOU'VE GOT ALL THE THIRTY CAL YOU NEED...
THIRTY CAL'S FOR THE RIFLES. THIS AIN'T A RIFLE I GOT OVER MY SHOULDER.
S ARMY
AH, WELL, WHEN IT COMES TO FORTY-FIVE IT'S FIRST COME FIRST SERVED, MY FRIEND. RIGHT NOW THE OFFICERS ARE TAKING EVERYTHING I GOT.
YEAH, 'CAUSE THEY THINK THE WAR'S OVER AND THEY CAN USE IT TO POT AT EMPTY BOTTLES. I *NEED IT*.
WHICH BRINGS US NEATLY TO THE SUBJECT OF BRIBERY, NOT TO PUT TOO FINE A POINT ON IT.
YOU ENJOY THIS, DON'T YOU?
YOU FRONT-LINE BOYS TAKE LIFE WAY TOO SERIOUSLY.
I'M ALWAYS TELLING YOU THAT, AS WELL.
CHRIST, I'M TIRED.

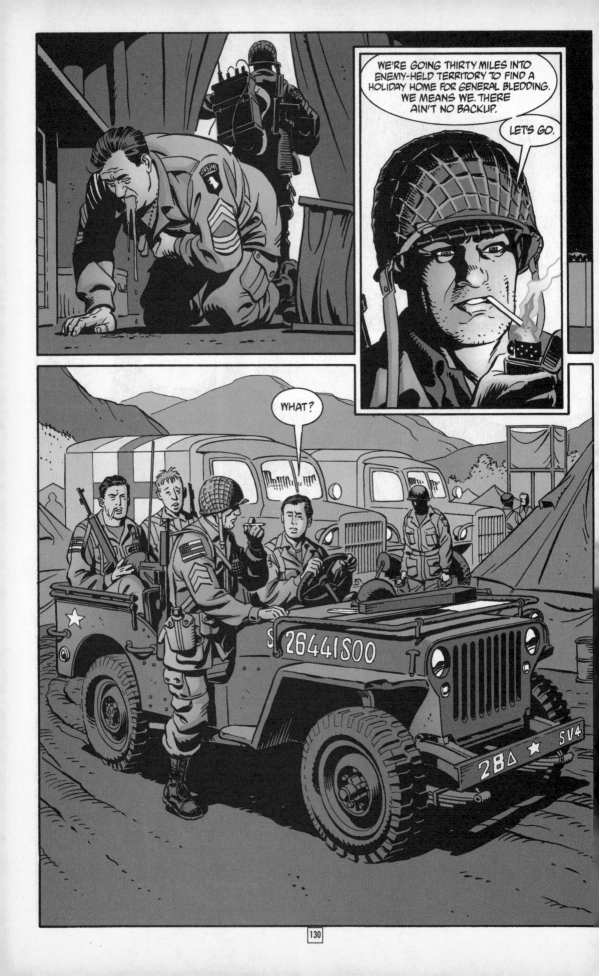

WE'RE GOING THIRTY MILES INTO ENEMY-HELD TERRITORY TO FIND A HOLIDAY HOME FOR GENERAL BLEDDING. WE MEANS WE. THERE AIN'T NO BACKUP.

LET'S GO.

WHAT?

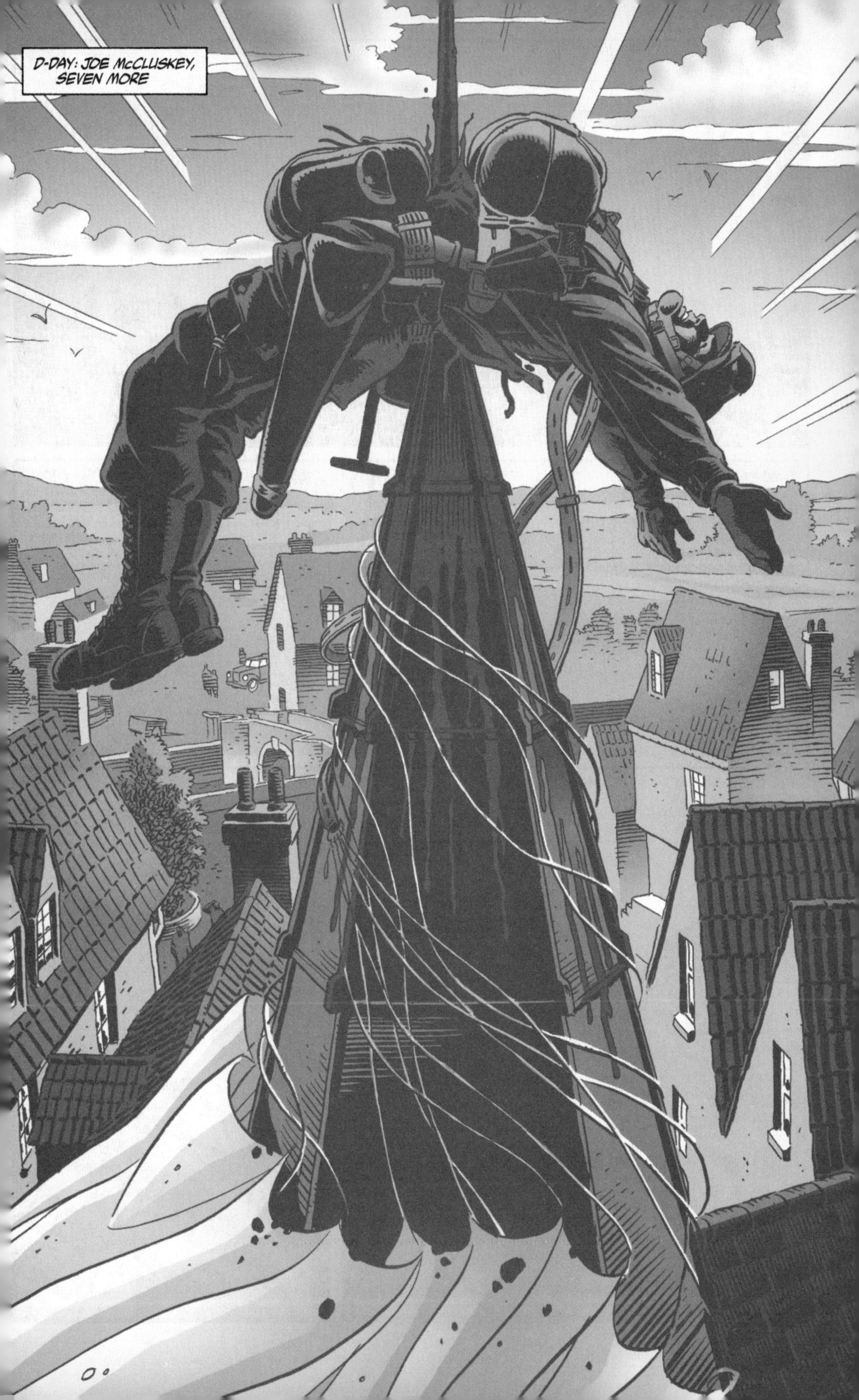
D-DAY: JOE McCLUSKEY, SEVEN MORE

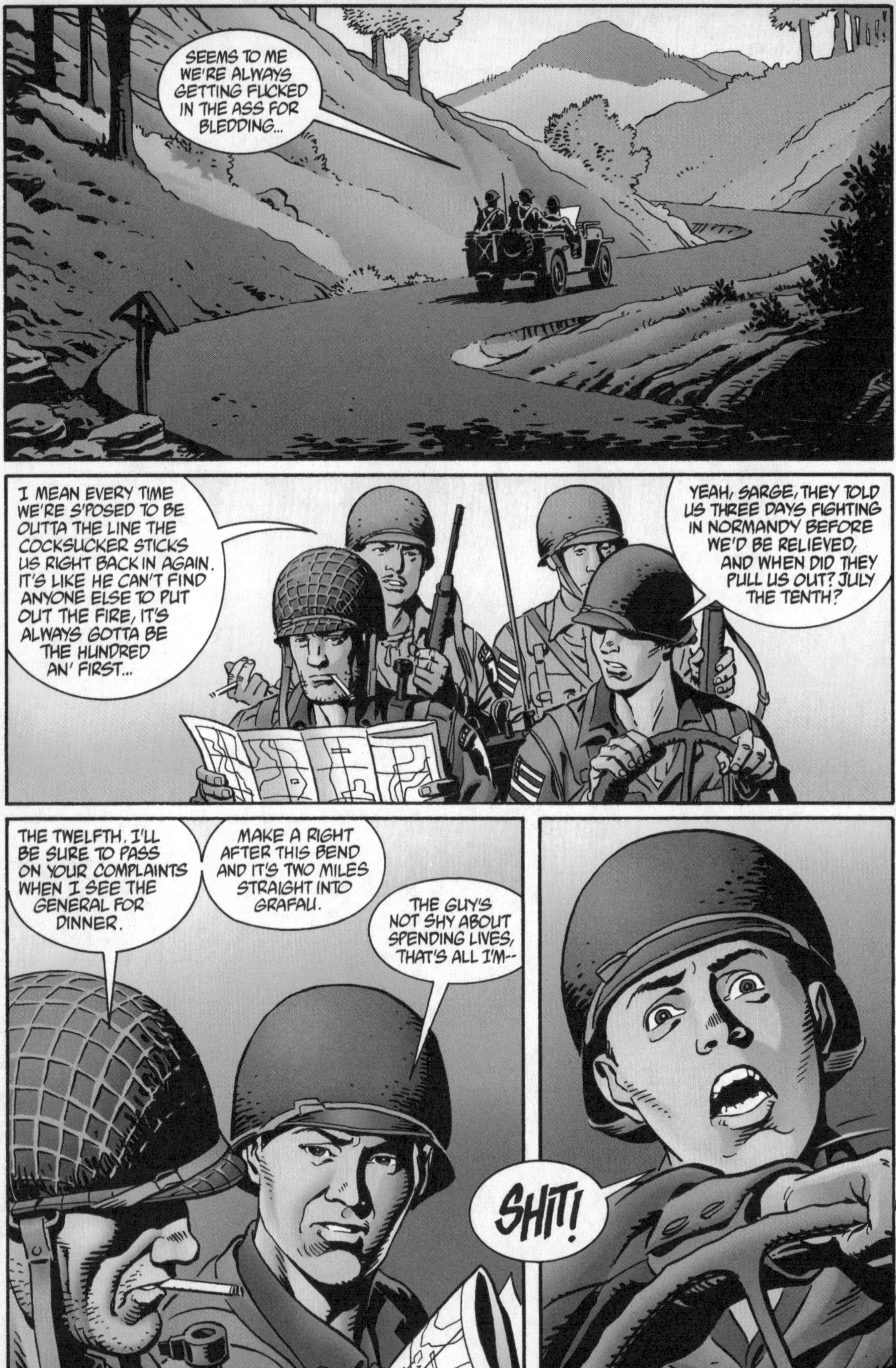
SEEMS TO ME WE'RE ALWAYS GETTING FUCKED IN THE ASS FOR BLEDDING...
I MEAN EVERY TIME WE'RE S'POSED TO BE OUTTA THE LINE THE COCKSUCKER STICKS US RIGHT BACK IN AGAIN. IT'S LIKE HE CAN'T FIND ANYONE ELSE TO PUT OUT THE FIRE, IT'S ALWAYS GOTTA BE THE HUNDRED AN' FIRST...
YEAH, SARGE, THEY TOLD US THREE DAYS FIGHTING IN NORMANDY BEFORE WE'D BE RELIEVED, AND WHEN DID THEY PULL US OUT? JULY THE TENTH?
THE TWELFTH. I'LL BE SURE TO PASS ON YOUR COMPLAINTS WHEN I SEE THE GENERAL FOR DINNER.
MAKE A RIGHT AFTER THIS BEND AND IT'S TWO MILES STRAIGHT INTO GRAFAU.
THE GUY'S NOT SHY ABOUT SPENDING LIVES, THAT'S ALL I'M--
SHIT!

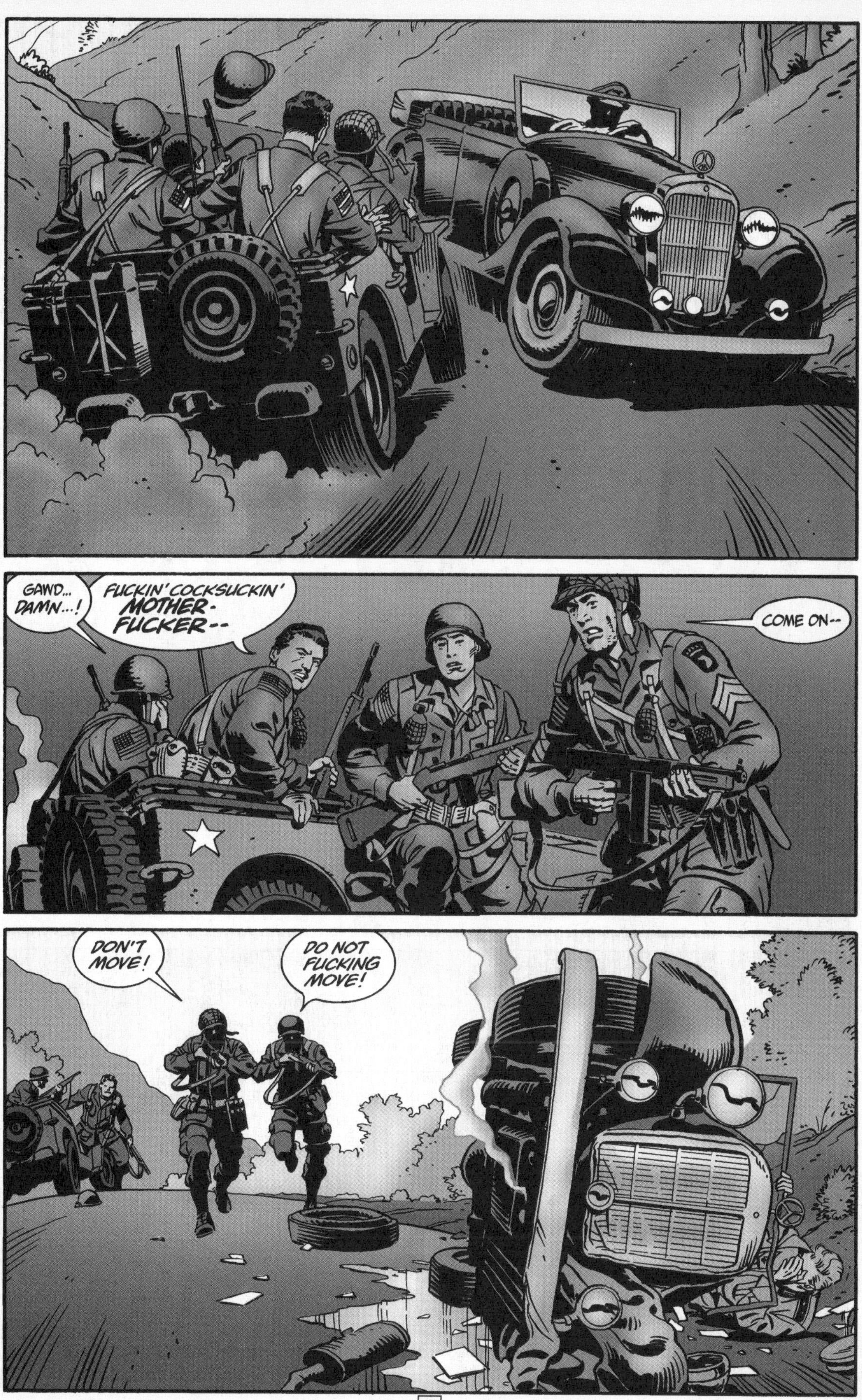
GAWD... DAMN...!
FUCKIN' COCKSUCKIN' MOTHER-FUCKER--
COME ON--
DON'T MOVE!
DO NOT FUCKING MOVE!

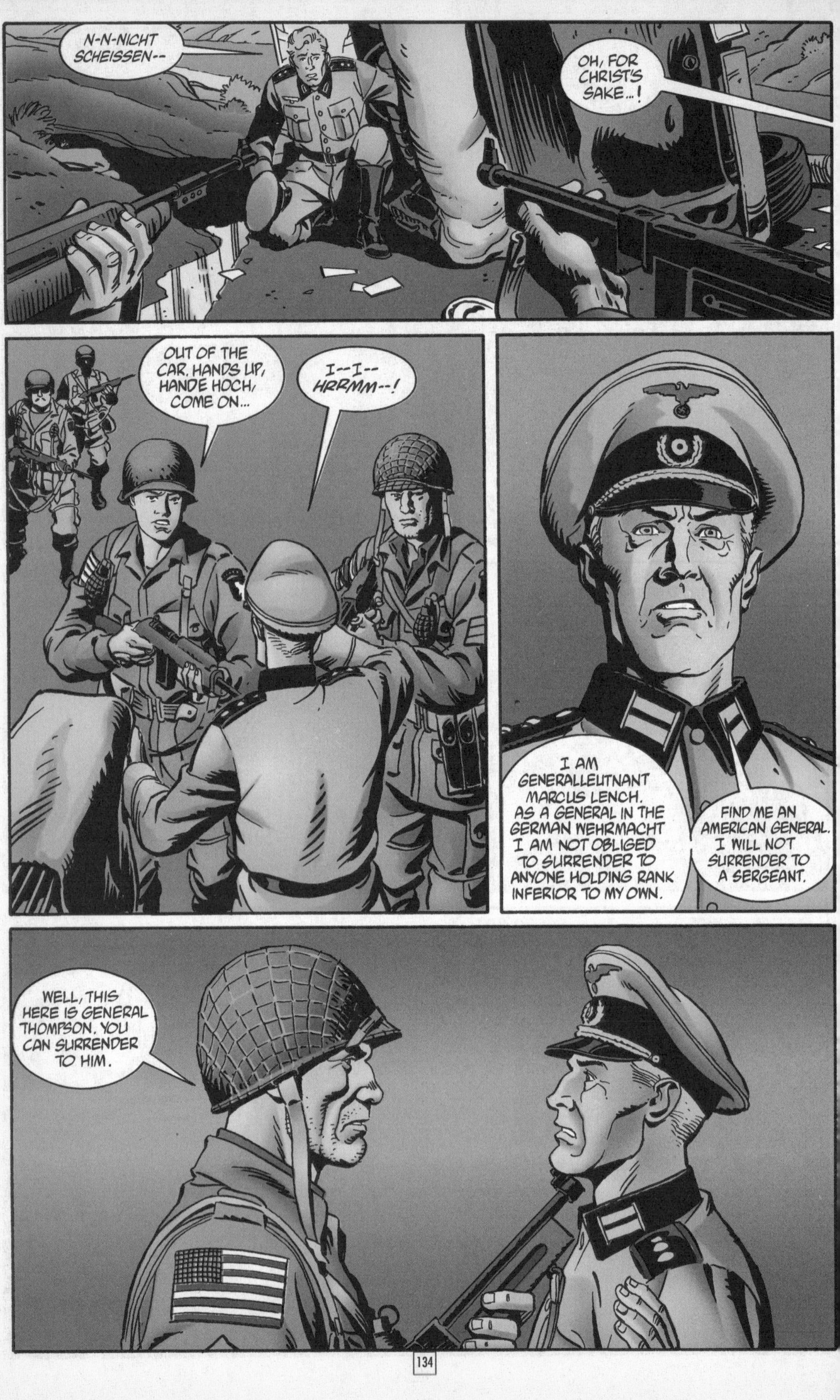
N-N-NICHT SCHEISSEN--
OH, FOR CHRIST'S SAKE...!
OUT OF THE CAR. HANDS UP, HANDE HOCH, COME ON...
I--I-- HRRMM--!
I AM GENERALLEUTNANT MARCUS LENCH. AS A GENERAL IN THE GERMAN WEHRMACHT I AM NOT OBLIGED TO SURRENDER TO ANYONE HOLDING RANK INFERIOR TO MY OWN.
FIND ME AN AMERICAN GENERAL. I WILL NOT SURRENDER TO A SERGEANT.
WELL, THIS HERE IS GENERAL THOMPSON. YOU CAN SURRENDER TO HIM.

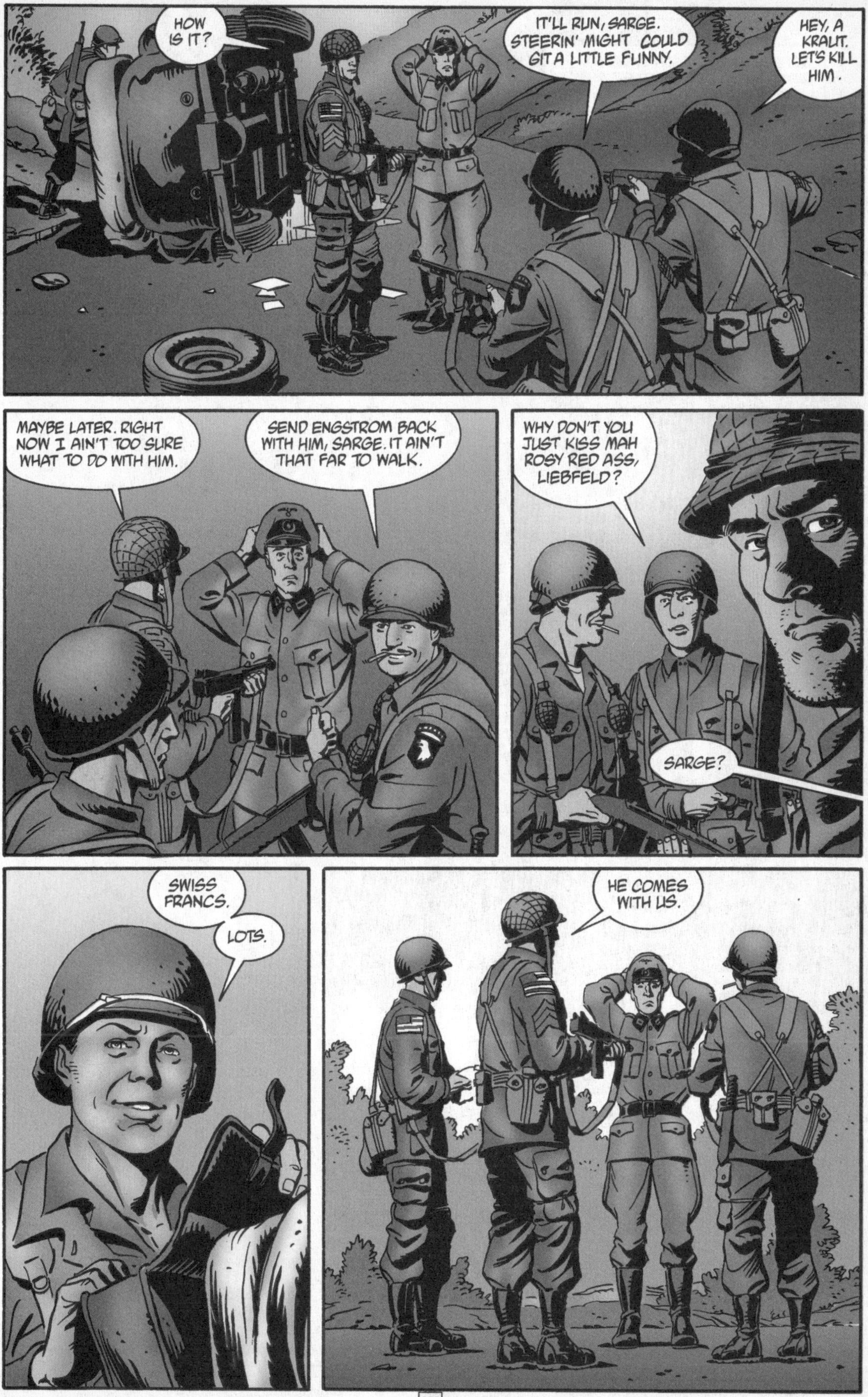
HOW IS IT?
IT'LL RUN, SARGE. STEERIN' MIGHT COULD GIT A LITTLE FUNNY.
HEY, A KRAUT. LET'S KILL HIM.
MAYBE LATER. RIGHT NOW I AIN'T TOO SURE WHAT TO DO WITH HIM.
SEND ENGSTROM BACK WITH HIM, SARGE. IT AIN'T THAT FAR TO WALK.
WHY DON'T YOU JUST KISS MAH ROSY RED ASS, LIEBFELD?
SARGE?
SWISS FRANCS.
LOTS.
HE COMES WITH US.

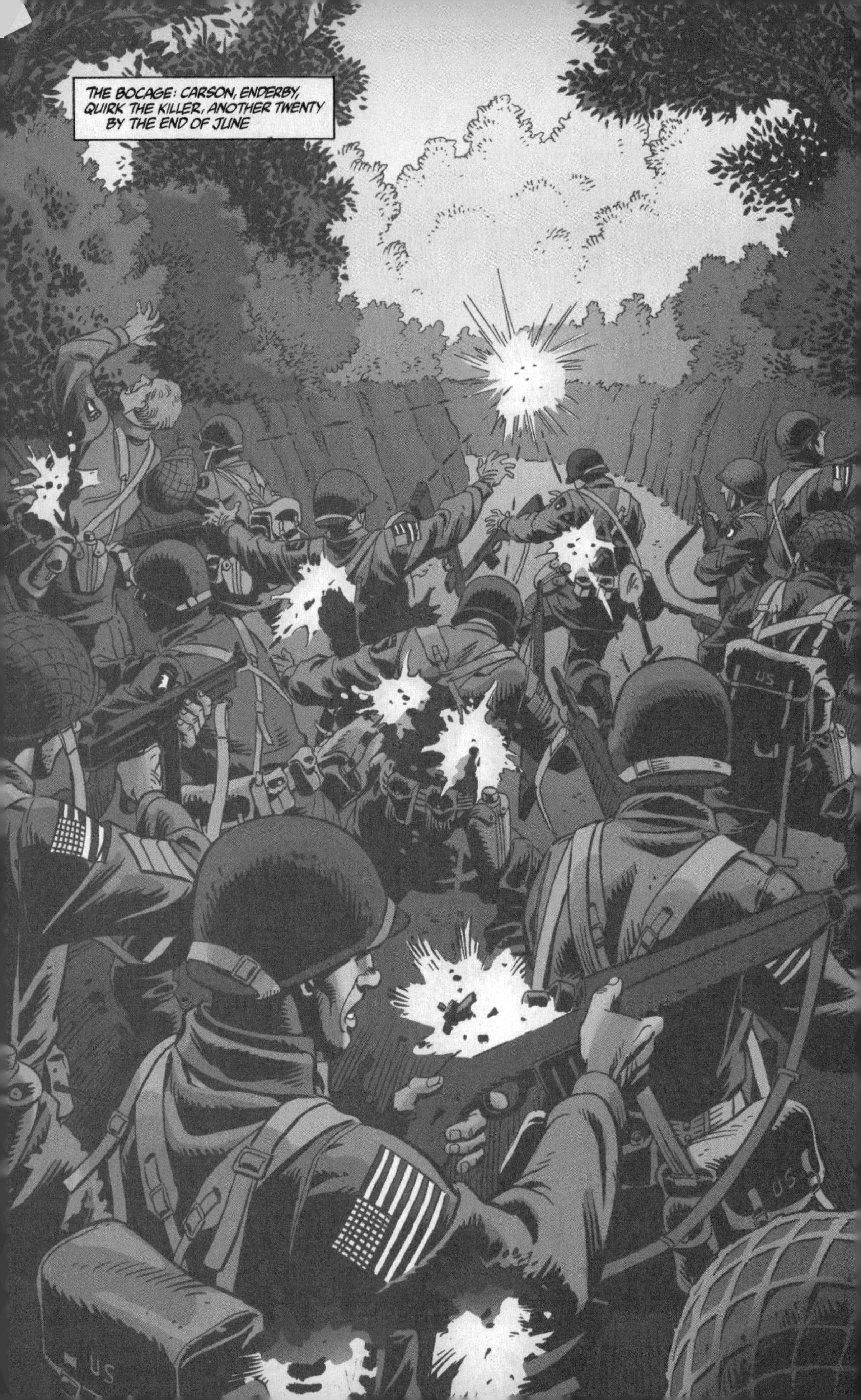
THE BOCAGE: CARSON, ENDERBY, QUIRK THE KILLER, ANOTHER TWENTY BY THE END OF JUNE
US
US
US

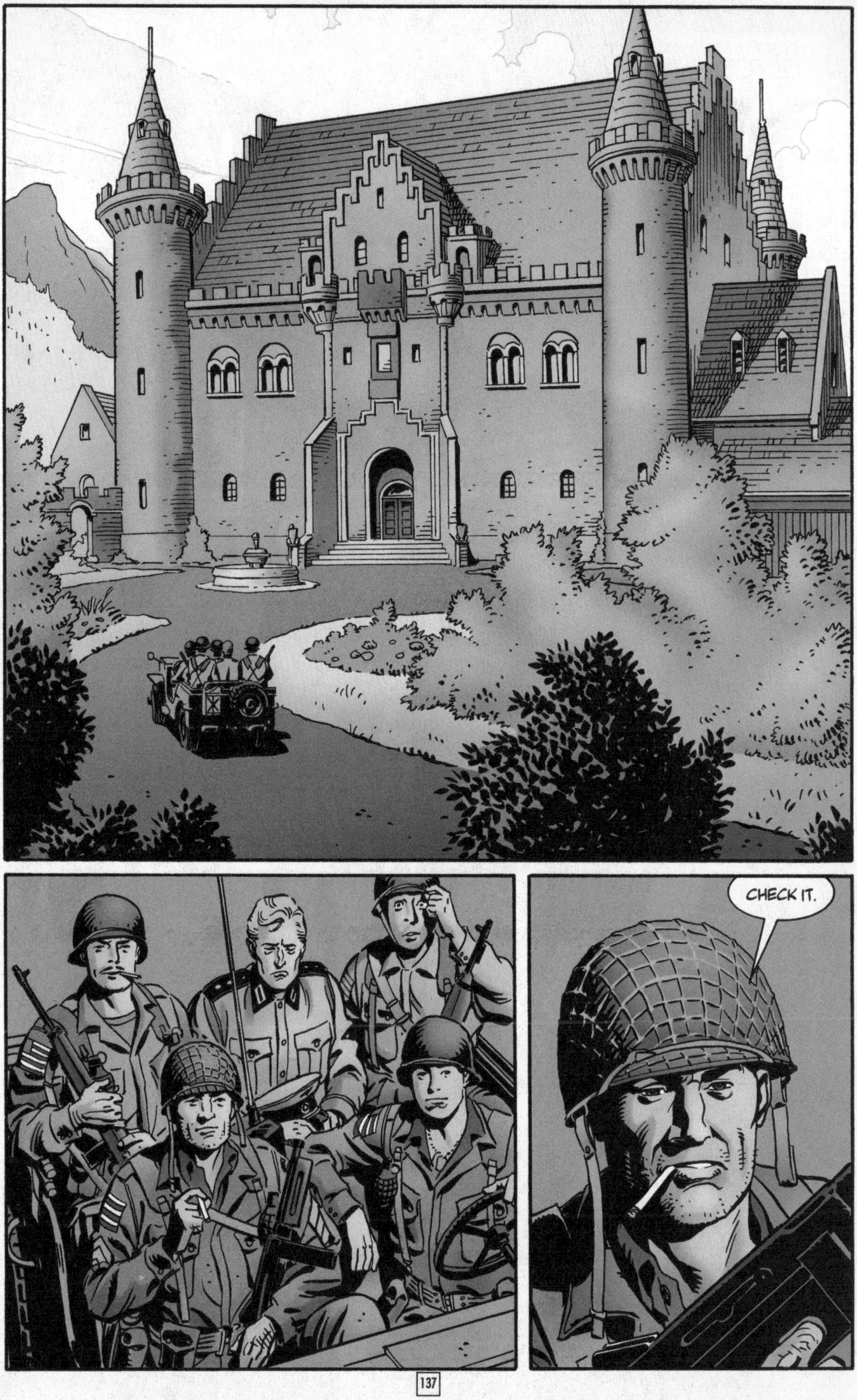
CHECK IT.

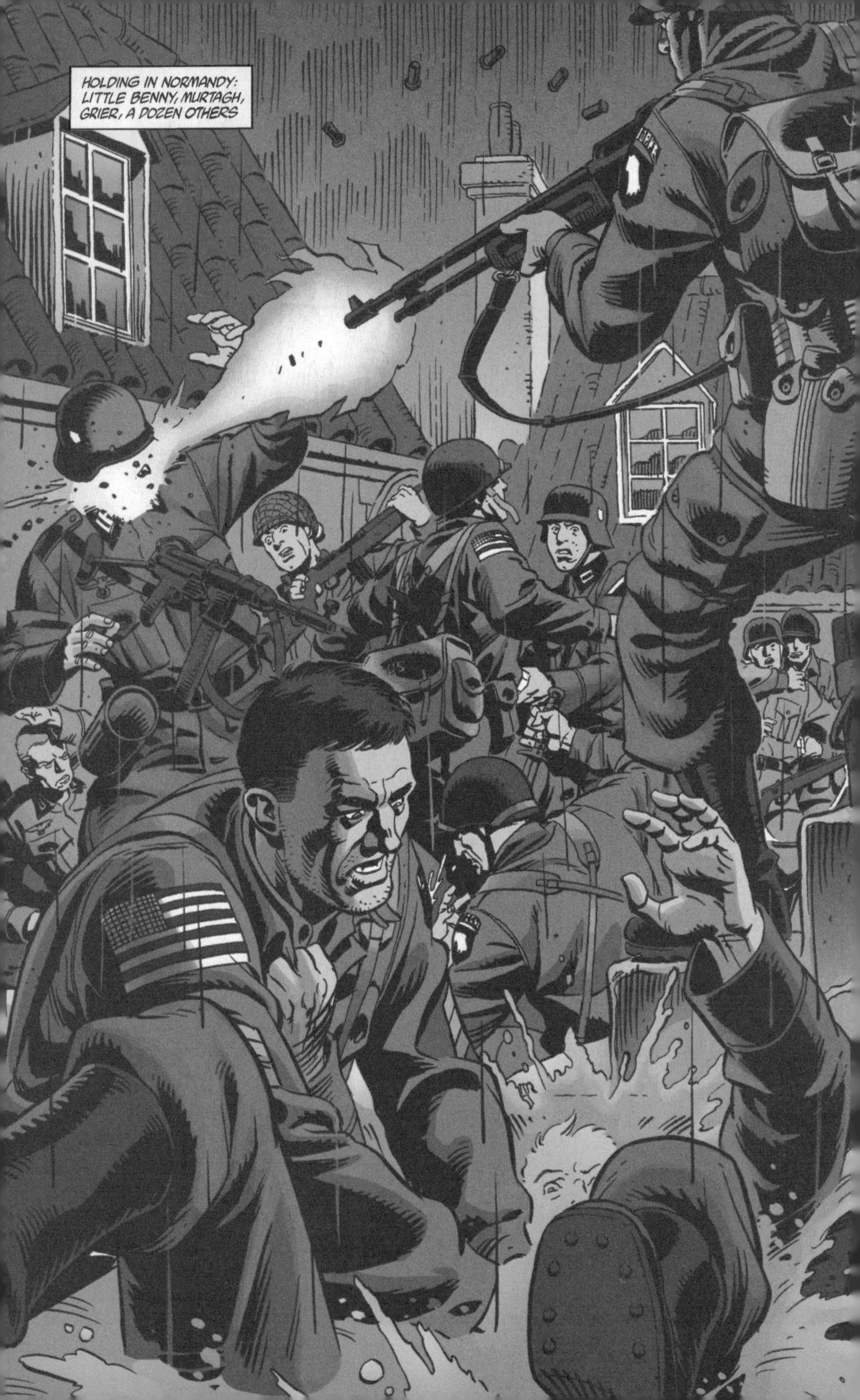
HOLDING IN NORMANDY: LITTLE BENNY, MURTAGH, GRIER, A DOZEN OTHERS

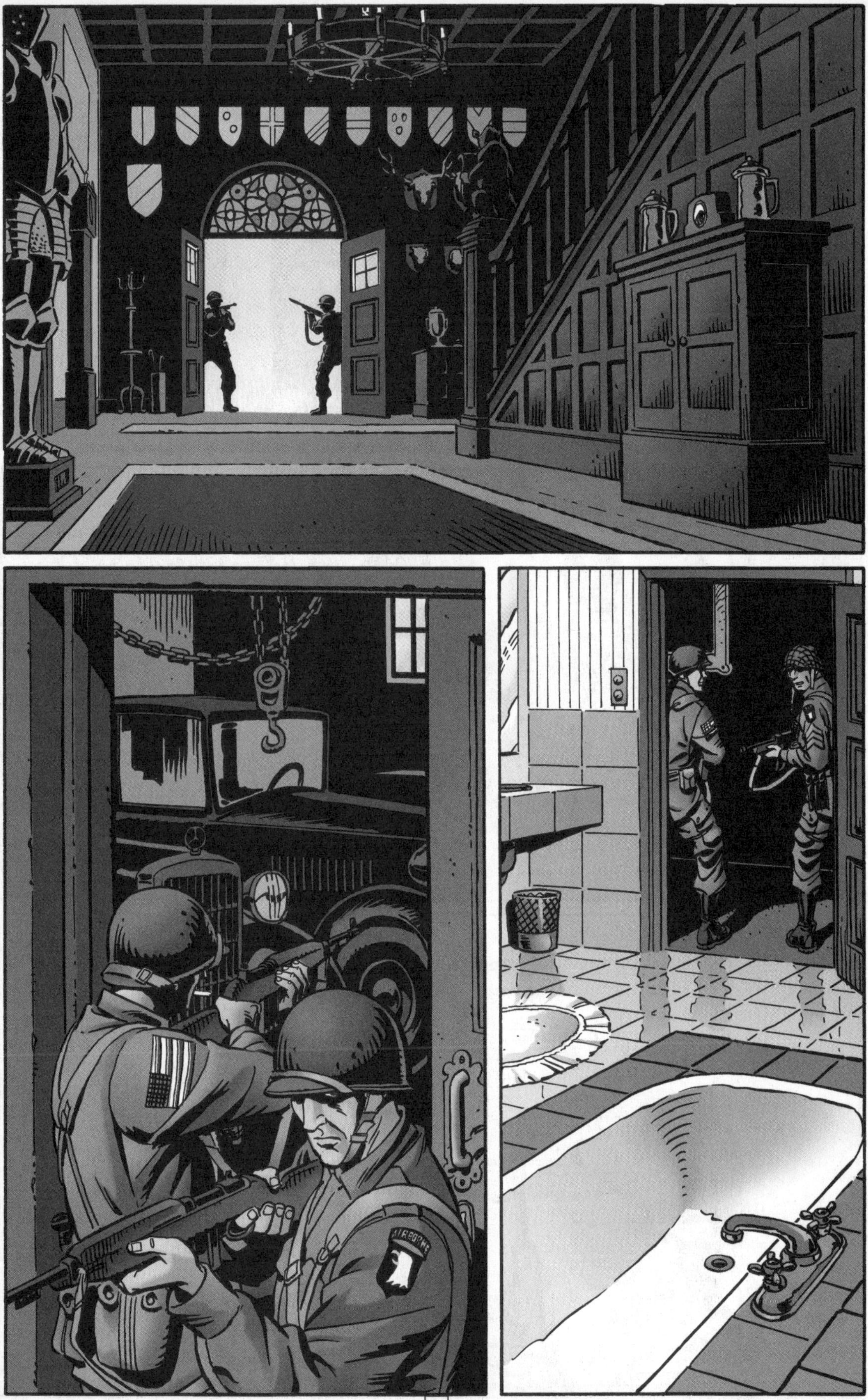

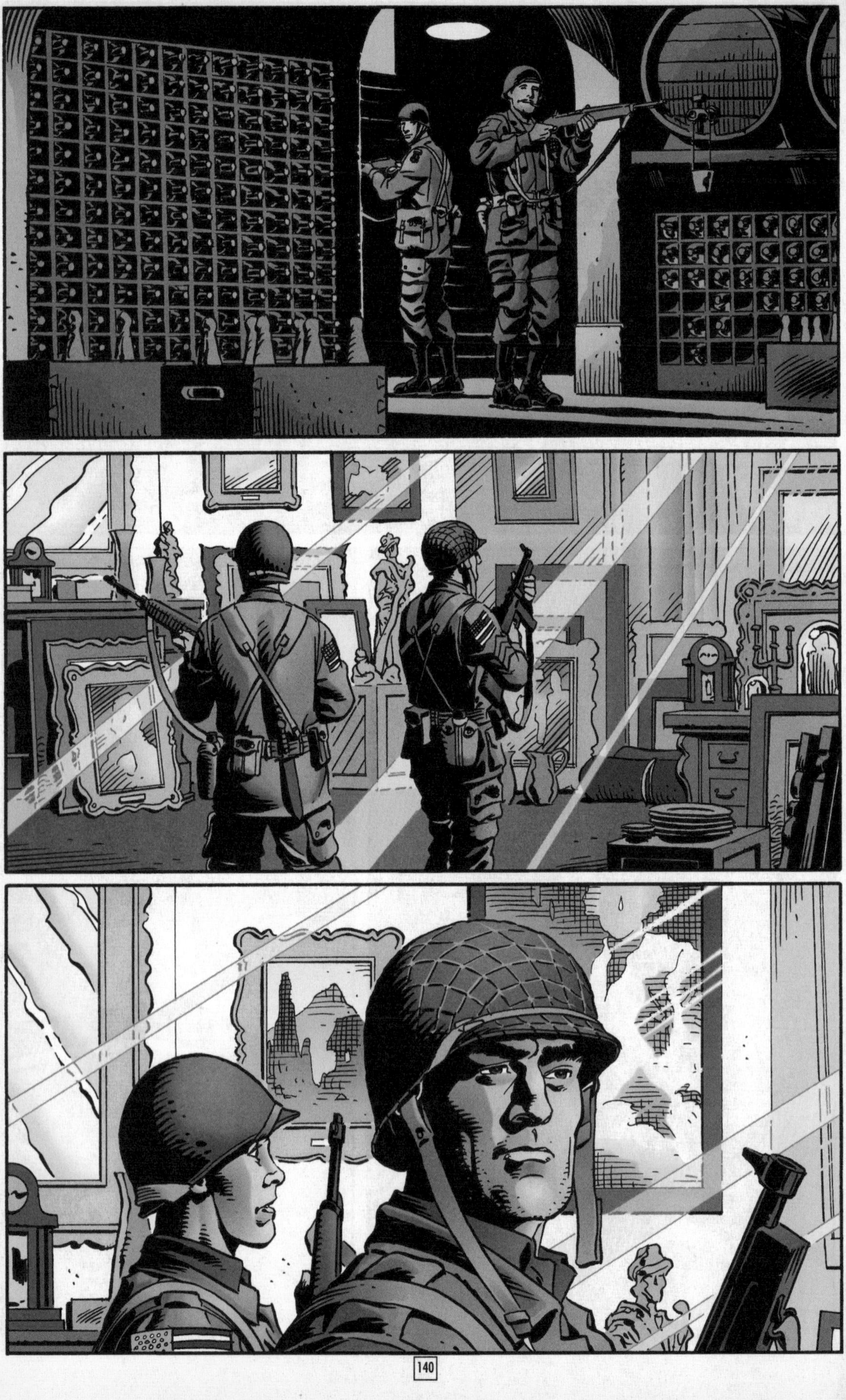

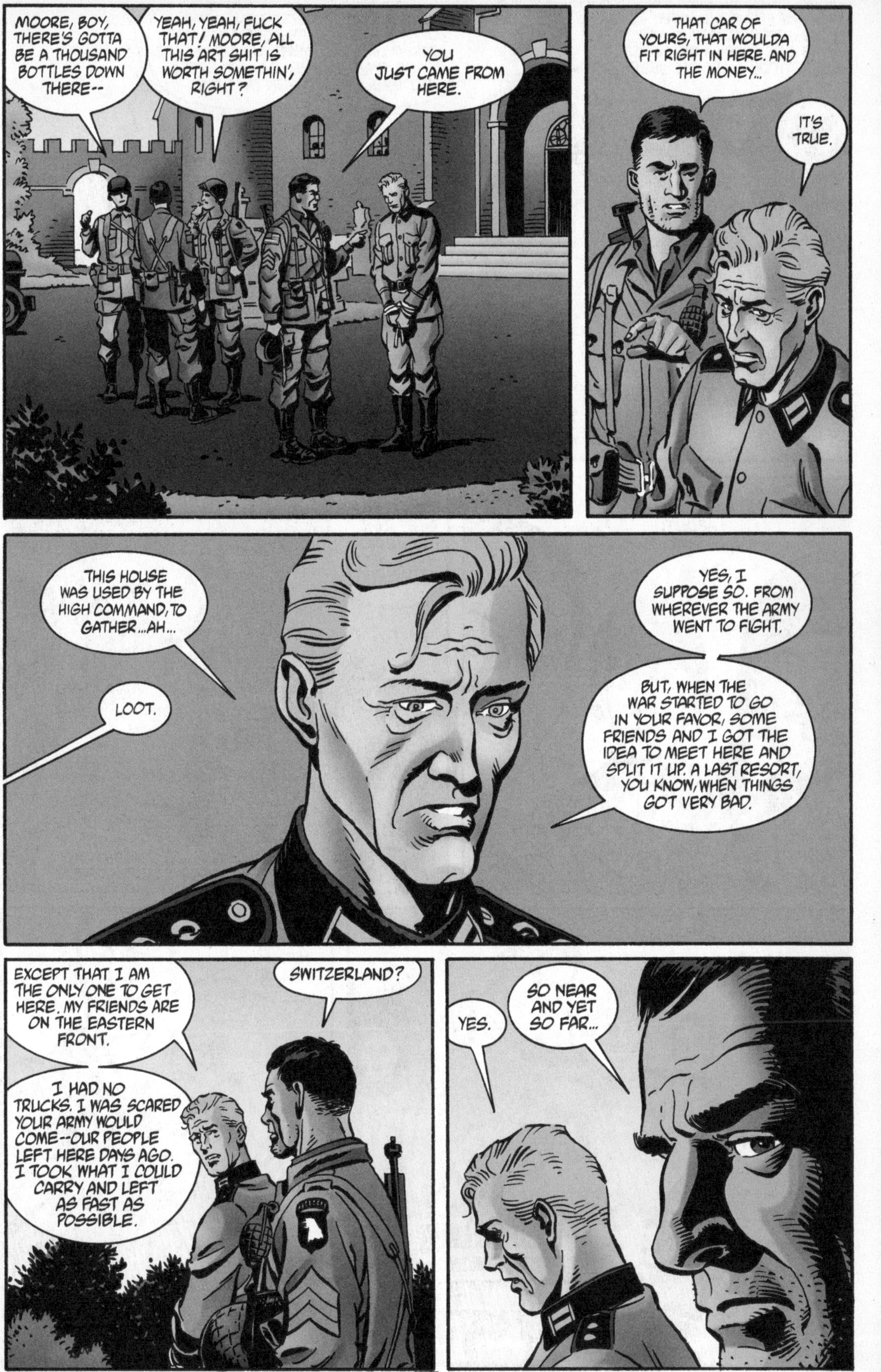
MOORE, BOY, THERE'S GOTTA BE A THOUSAND BOTTLES DOWN THERE--
YEAH, YEAH, FUCK THAT! MOORE, ALL THIS ART SHIT IS WORTH SOMETHIN', RIGHT?
YOU JUST CAME FROM HERE.
THAT CAR OF YOURS, THAT WOULDA FIT RIGHT IN HERE. AND THE MONEY...
IT'S TRUE.
THIS HOUSE WAS USED BY THE HIGH COMMAND, TO GATHER...AH...
LOOT.
YES, I SUPPOSE SO. FROM WHEREVER THE ARMY WENT TO FIGHT.
BUT, WHEN THE WAR STARTED TO GO IN YOUR FAVOR, SOME FRIENDS AND I GOT THE IDEA TO MEET HERE AND SPLIT IT UP. A LAST RESORT, YOU KNOW, WHEN THINGS GOT VERY BAD.
EXCEPT THAT I AM THE ONLY ONE TO GET HERE. MY FRIENDS ARE ON THE EASTERN FRONT.
I HAD NO TRUCKS. I WAS SCARED YOUR ARMY WOULD COME--OUR PEOPLE LEFT HERE DAYS AGO. I TOOK WHAT I COULD CARRY AND LEFT AS FAST AS POSSIBLE.
SWITZERLAND?
YES.
SO NEAR AND YET SO FAR...

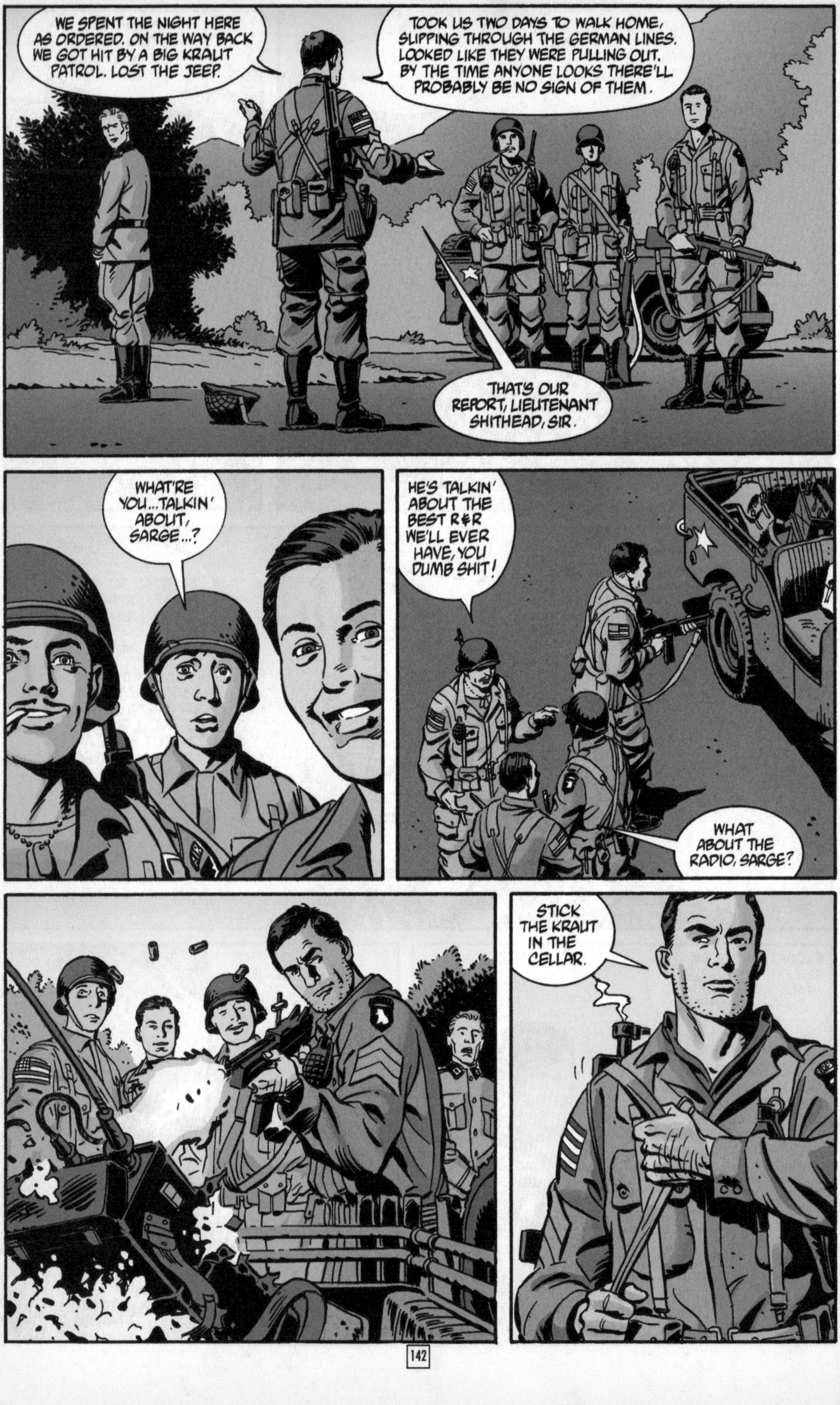
WE SPENT THE NIGHT HERE AS ORDERED. ON THE WAY BACK WE GOT HIT BY A BIG KRAUT PATROL. LOST THE JEEP.
TOOK US TWO DAYS TO WALK HOME, SLIPPING THROUGH THE GERMAN LINES. LOOKED LIKE THEY WERE PULLING OUT. BY THE TIME ANYONE LOOKS THERE'LL PROBABLY BE NO SIGN OF THEM.
THAT'S OUR REPORT, LIEUTENANT SHITHEAD, SIR.
WHAT'RE YOU...TALKIN' ABOUT, SARGE...?
HE'S TALKIN' ABOUT THE BEST R&R WE'LL EVER HAVE, YOU DUMB SHIT!
WHAT ABOUT THE RADIO, SARGE?
STICK THE KRAUT IN THE CELLAR.

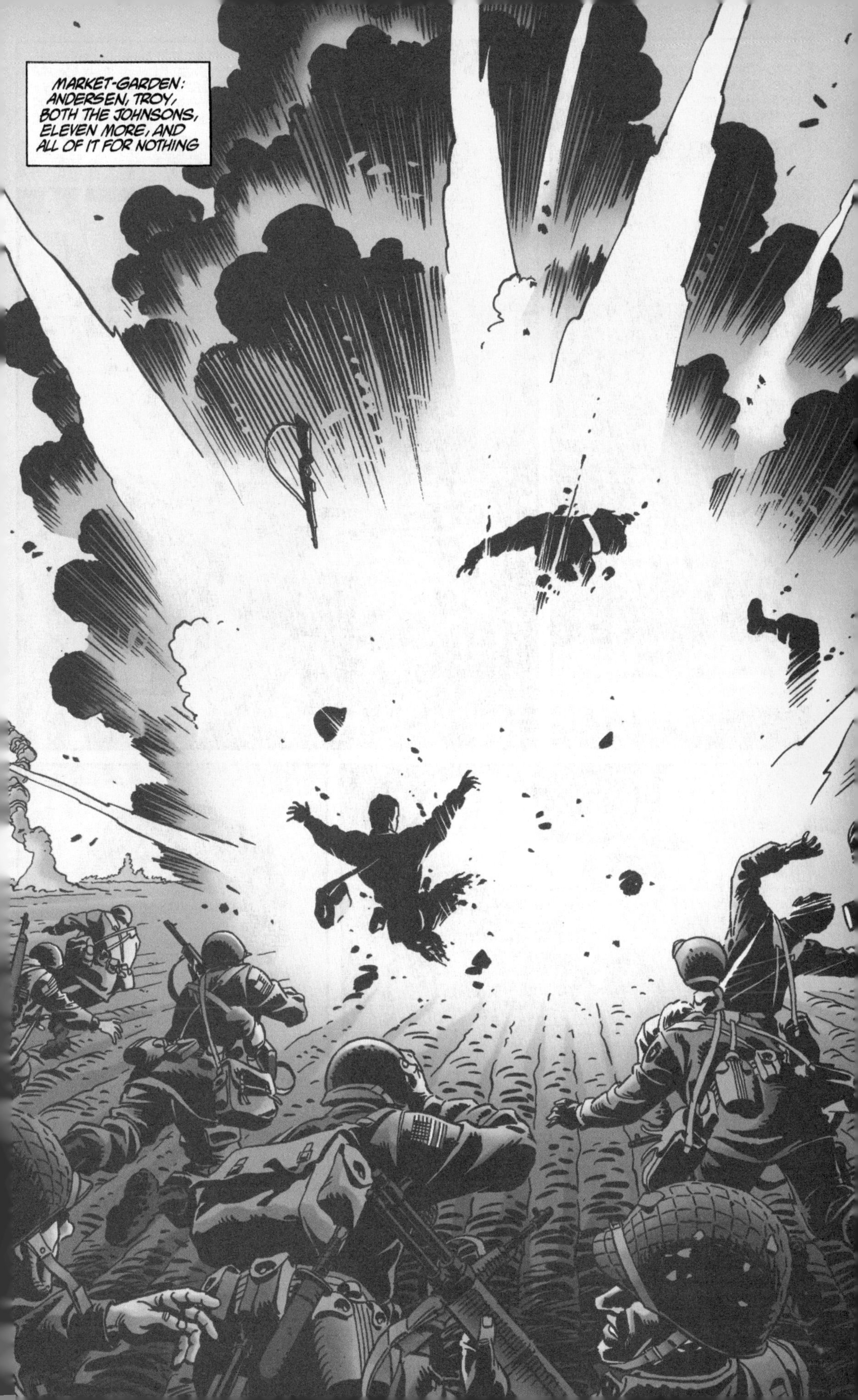
MARKET-GARDEN: ANDERSEN, TROY, BOTH THE JOHNSONS, ELEVEN MORE, AND ALL OF IT FOR NOTHING

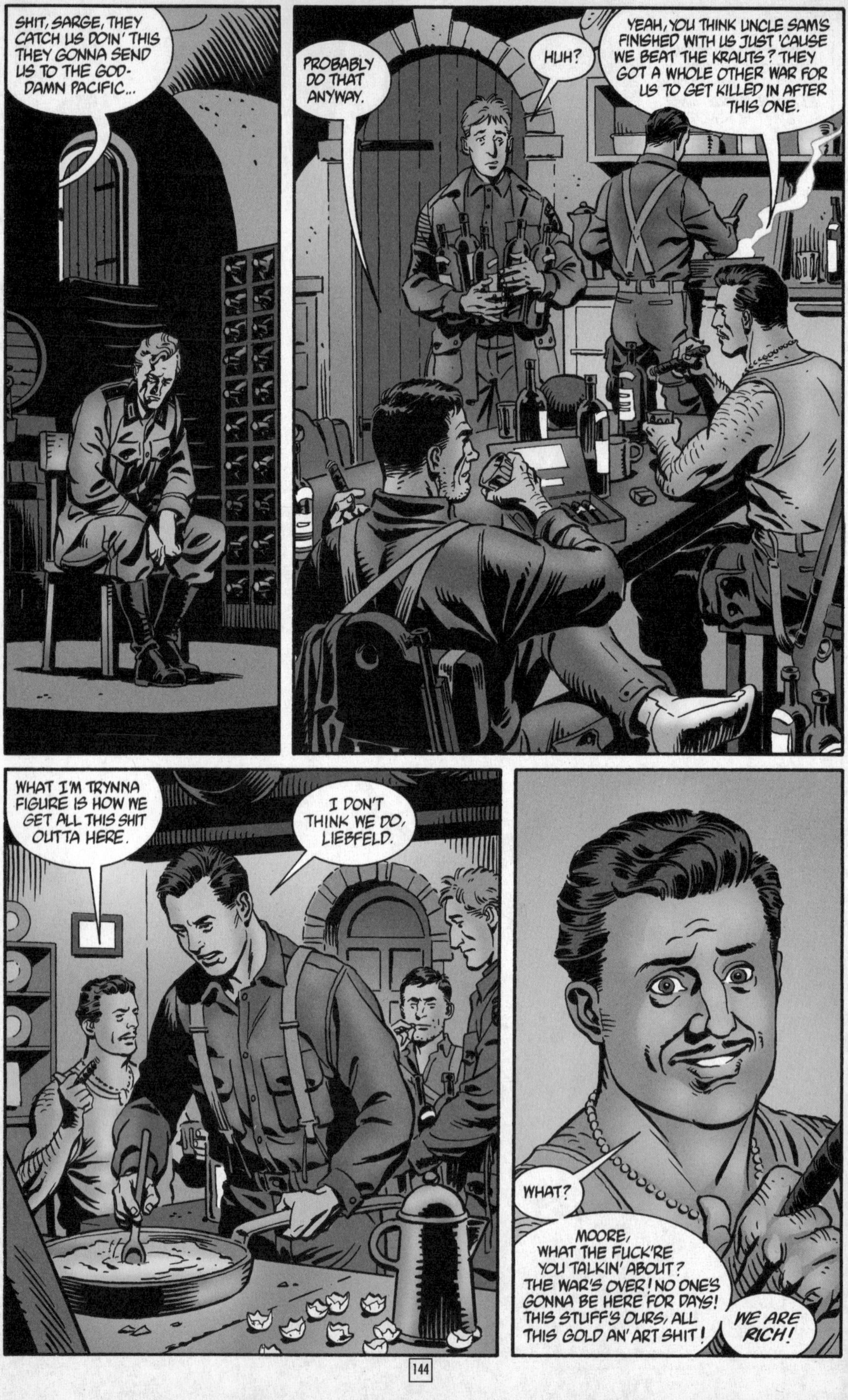

SHIT, SARGE, THEY CATCH US DOIN' THIS THEY GONNA SEND US TO THE GOD-DAMN PACIFIC...
PROBABLY DO THAT ANYWAY.
HUH?
YEAH, YOU THINK UNCLE SAM'S FINISHED WITH US JUST 'CAUSE WE BEAT THE KRAUTS? THEY GOT A WHOLE OTHER WAR FOR US TO GET KILLED IN AFTER THIS ONE.
WHAT I'M TRYNNA FIGURE IS HOW WE GET ALL THIS SHIT OUTTA HERE.
I DON'T THINK WE DO, LIEBFELD.
WHAT?
MOORE, WHAT THE FUCK'RE YOU TALKIN' ABOUT? THE WAR'S OVER! NO ONE'S GONNA BE HERE FOR DAYS! THIS STUFF'S OURS, ALL THIS GOLD AN' ART SHIT!
WE ARE RICH!

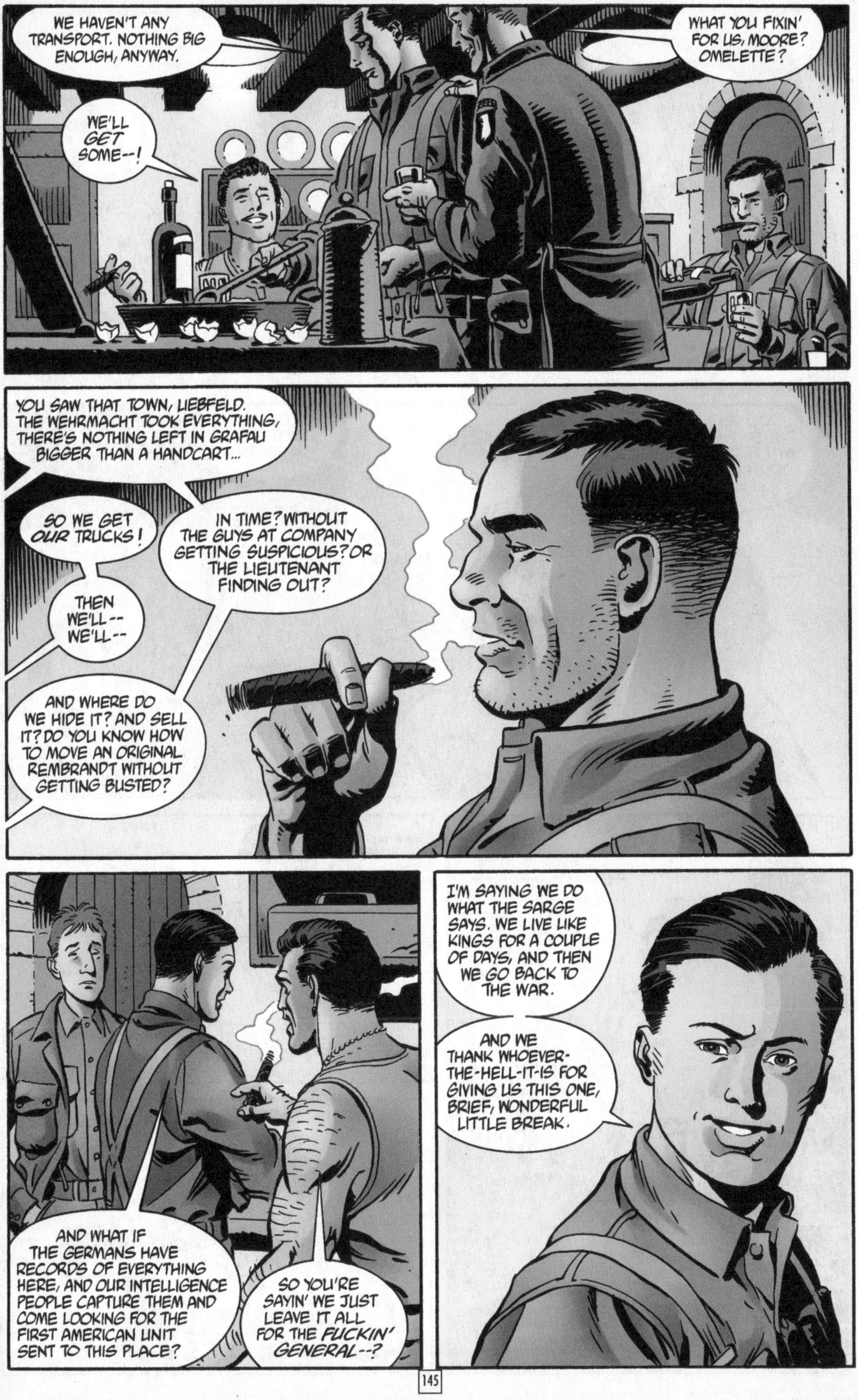
WE HAVEN'T ANY TRANSPORT. NOTHING BIG ENOUGH, ANYWAY.
WHAT YOU FIXIN' FOR US, MOORE? OMELETTE?
WE'LL GET SOME--!
YOU SAW THAT TOWN, LIEBFELD. THE WEHRMACHT TOOK EVERYTHING, THERE'S NOTHING LEFT IN GRAFAU BIGGER THAN A HANDCART...
SO WE GET OUR TRUCKS!
IN TIME? WITHOUT THE GUYS AT COMPANY GETTING SUSPICIOUS? OR THE LIEUTENANT FINDING OUT?
THEN WE'LL-- WE'LL--
AND WHERE DO WE HIDE IT? AND SELL IT? DO YOU KNOW HOW TO MOVE AN ORIGINAL REMBRANDT WITHOUT GETTING BUSTED?
AND WHAT IF THE GERMANS HAVE RECORDS OF EVERYTHING HERE, AND OUR INTELLIGENCE PEOPLE CAPTURE THEM AND COME LOOKING FOR THE FIRST AMERICAN UNIT SENT TO THIS PLACE?
SO YOU'RE SAYIN' WE JUST LEAVE IT ALL FOR THE FUCKIN' GENERAL--?
I'M SAYING WE DO WHAT THE SARGE SAYS. WE LIVE LIKE KINGS FOR A COUPLE OF DAYS, AND THEN WE GO BACK TO THE WAR.
AND WE THANK WHOEVER-THE-HELL-IT-IS FOR GIVING US THIS ONE, BRIEF, WONDERFUL LITTLE BREAK.

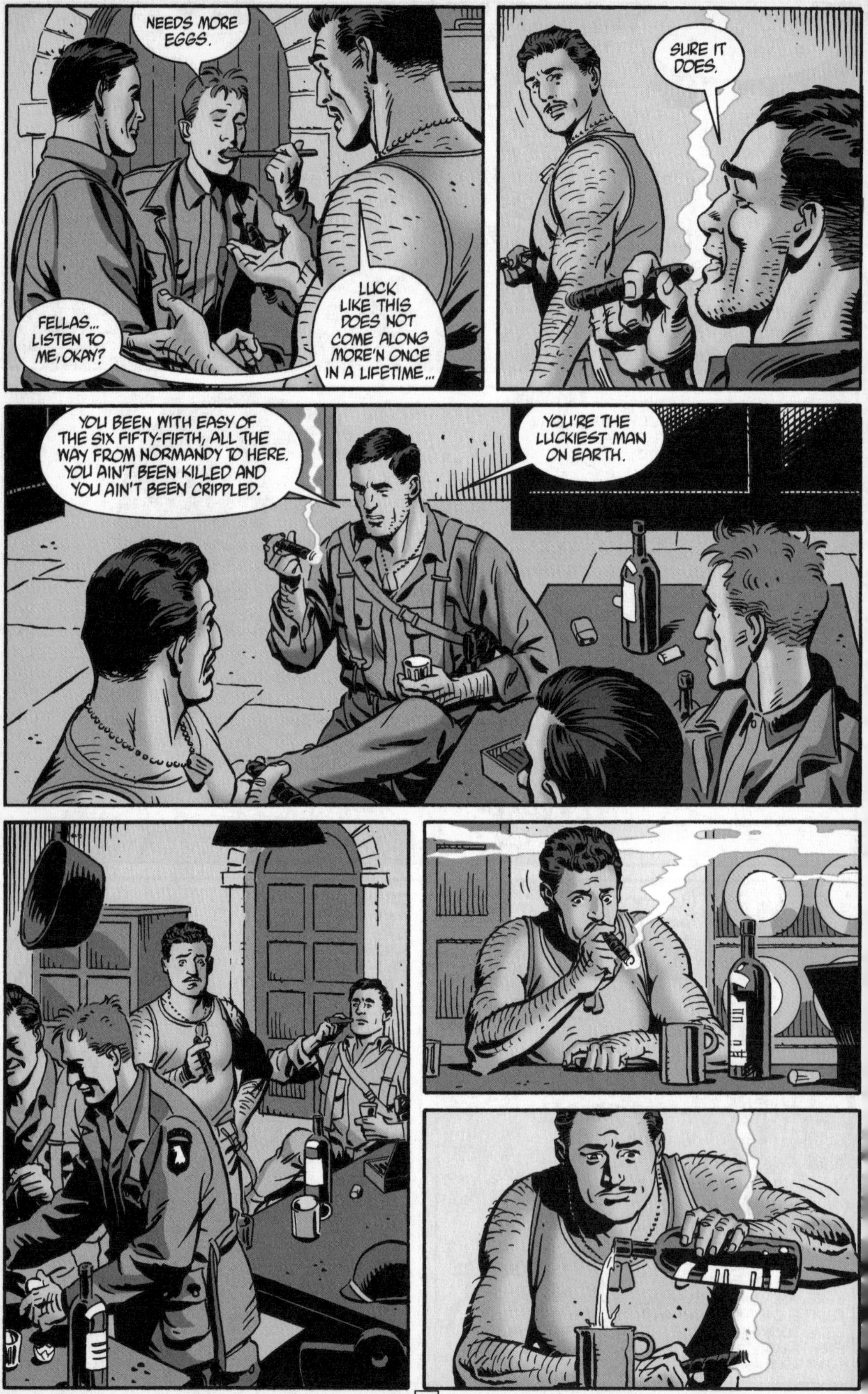
NEEDS MORE EGGS.
FELLAS... LISTEN TO ME, OKAY?
LUCK LIKE THIS DOES NOT COME ALONG MORE'N ONCE IN A LIFETIME...
SURE IT DOES.
YOU BEEN WITH EASY OF THE SIX FIFTY-FIFTH, ALL THE WAY FROM NORMANDY TO HERE. YOU AIN'T BEEN KILLED AND YOU AIN'T BEEN CRIPPLED.
YOU'RE THE LUCKIEST MAN ON EARTH.

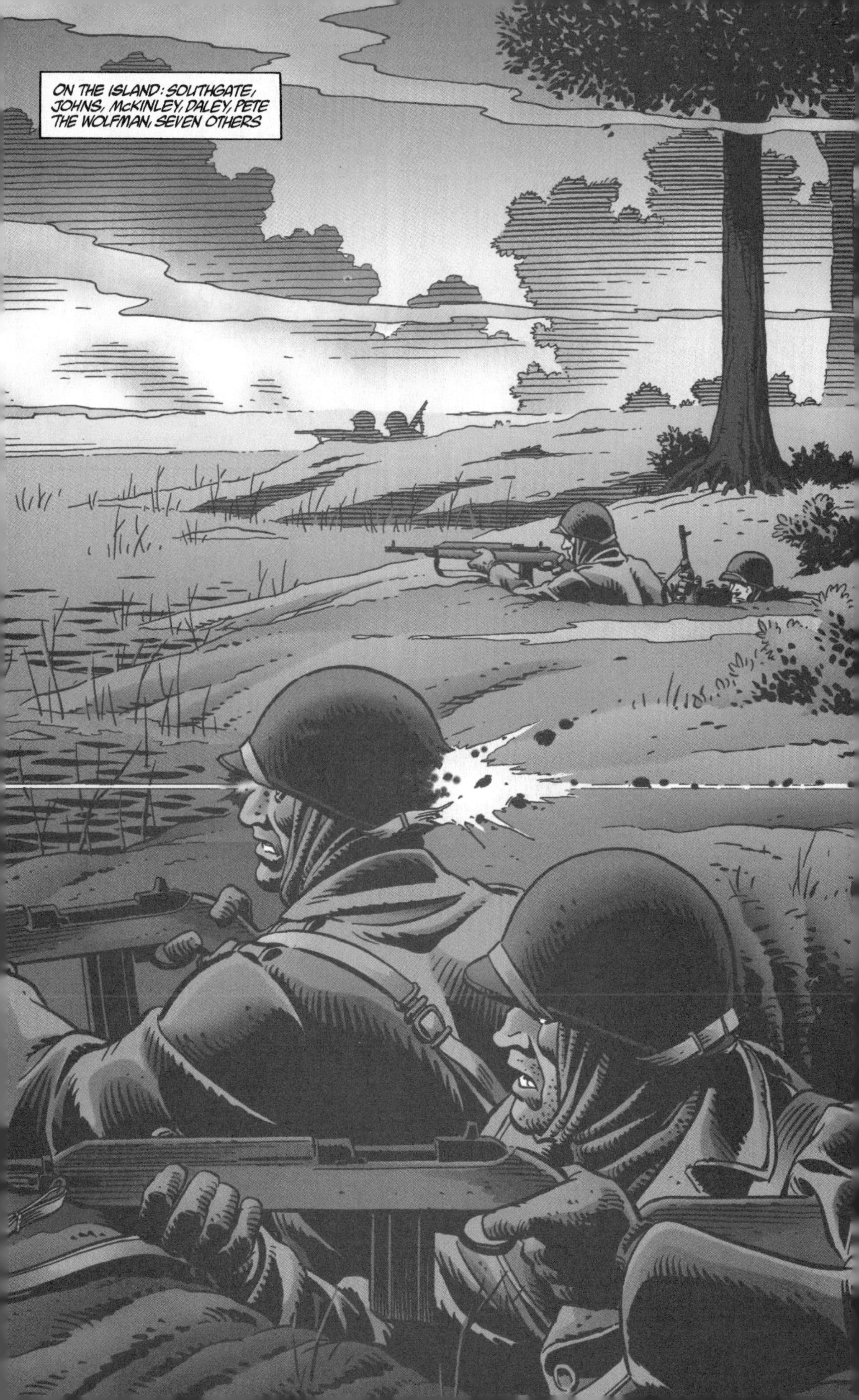
ON THE ISLAND: SOUTHGATE, JOHNS, McKINLEY, DALEY, PETE THE WOLFMAN, SEVEN OTHERS

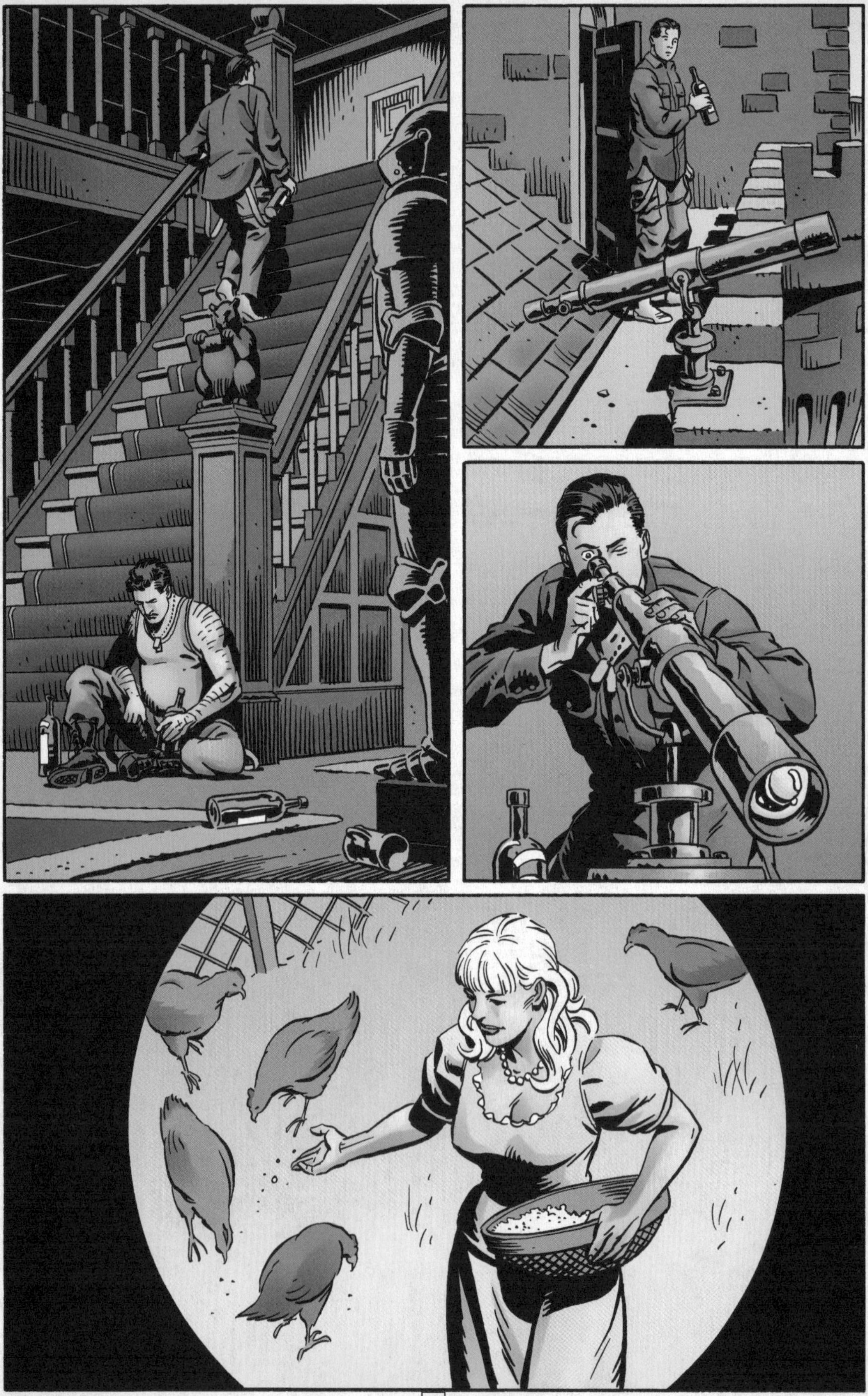

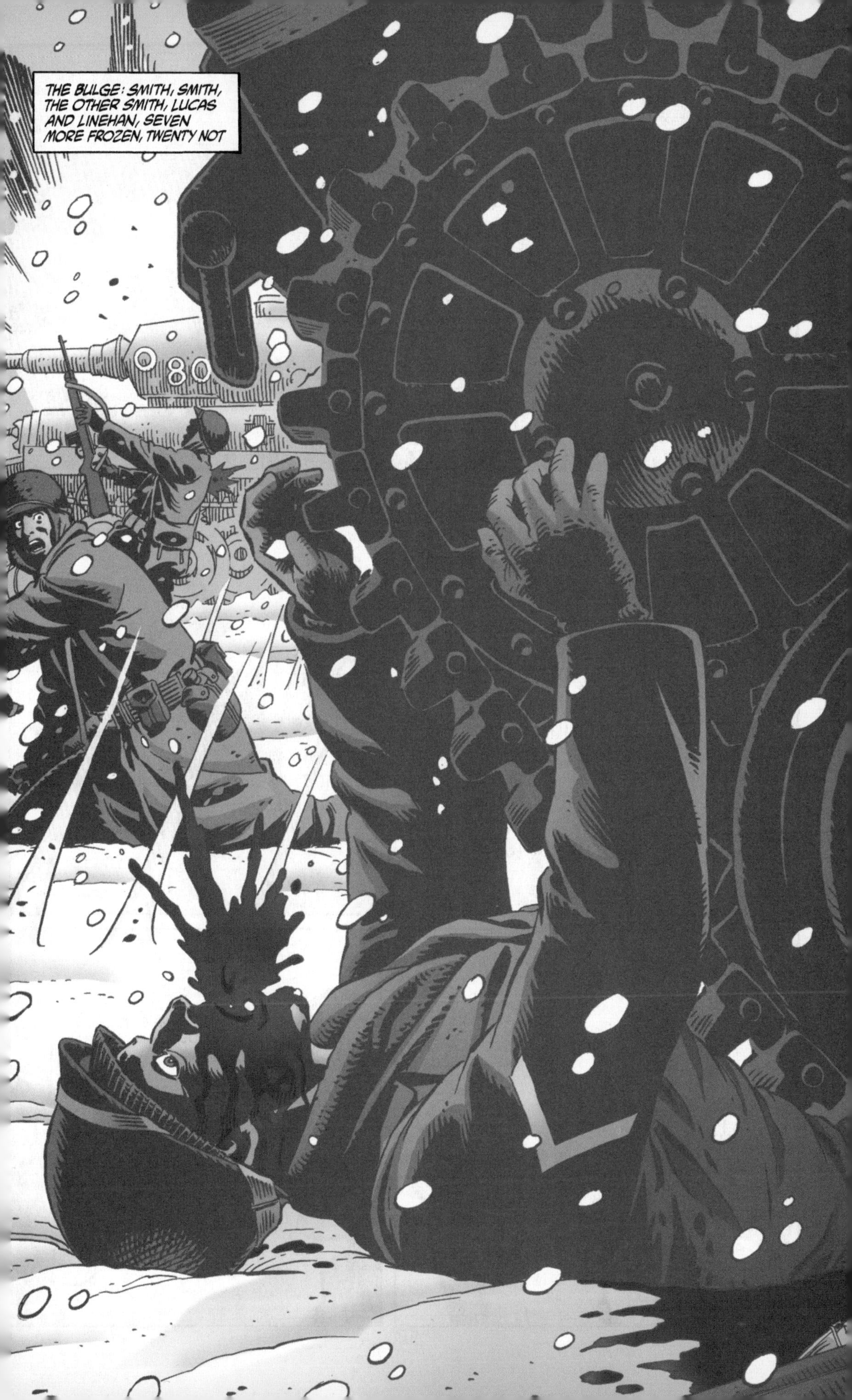
THE BULGE: SMITH, SMITH, THE OTHER SMITH, LUCAS AND LINEHAN, SEVEN MORE FROZEN, TWENTY NOT
80

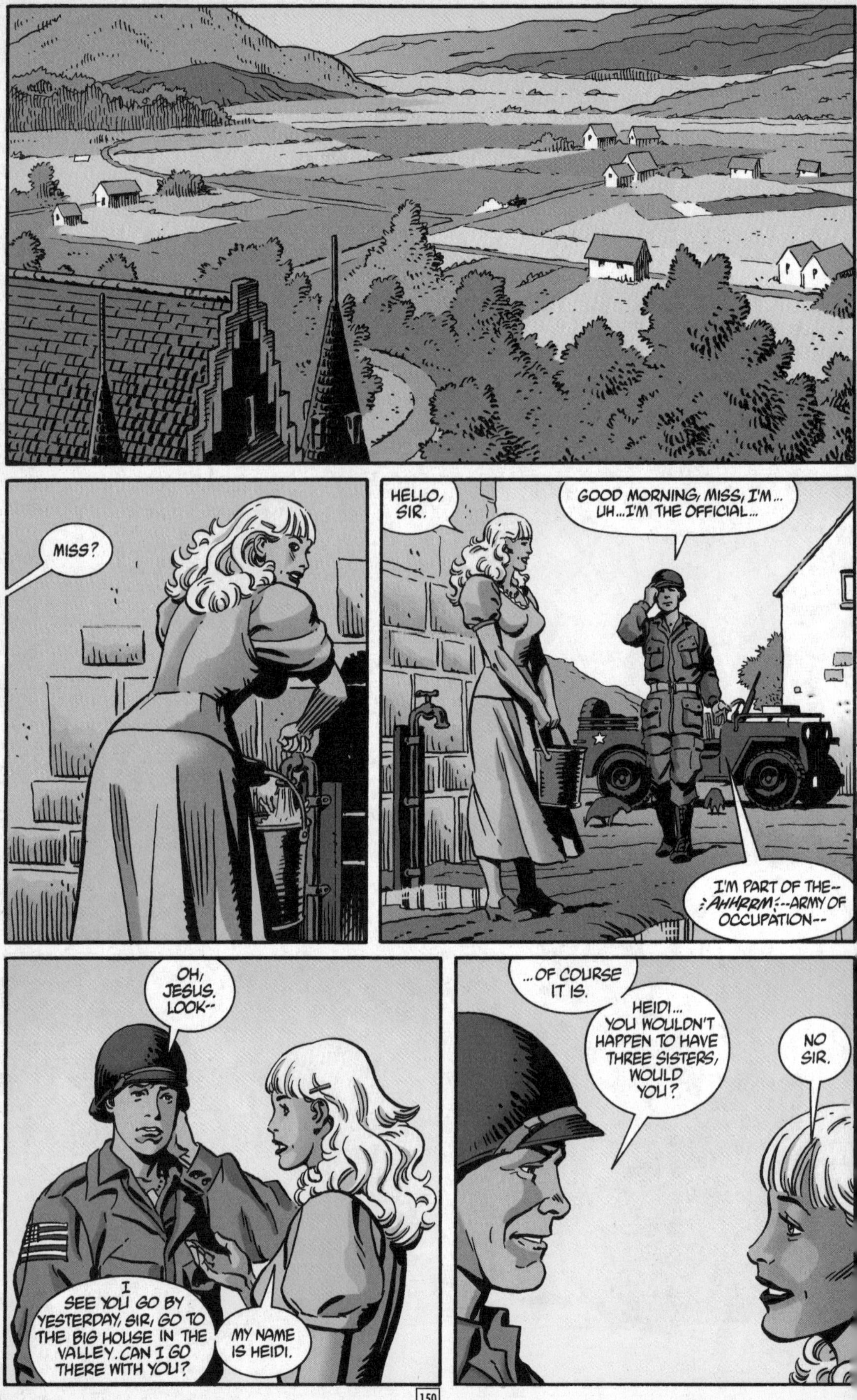
MISS?
HELLO, SIR.
GOOD MORNING, MISS, I'M... UH...I'M THE OFFICIAL...
I'M PART OF THE-- AHHRRM--ARMY OF OCCUPATION--
OH, JESUS. LOOK--
I SEE YOU GO BY YESTERDAY, SIR, GO TO THE BIG HOUSE IN THE VALLEY. CAN I GO THERE WITH YOU?
MY NAME IS HEIDI.
...OF COURSE IT IS.
HEIDI... YOU WOULDN'T HAPPEN TO HAVE THREE SISTERS, WOULD YOU?
NO SIR.

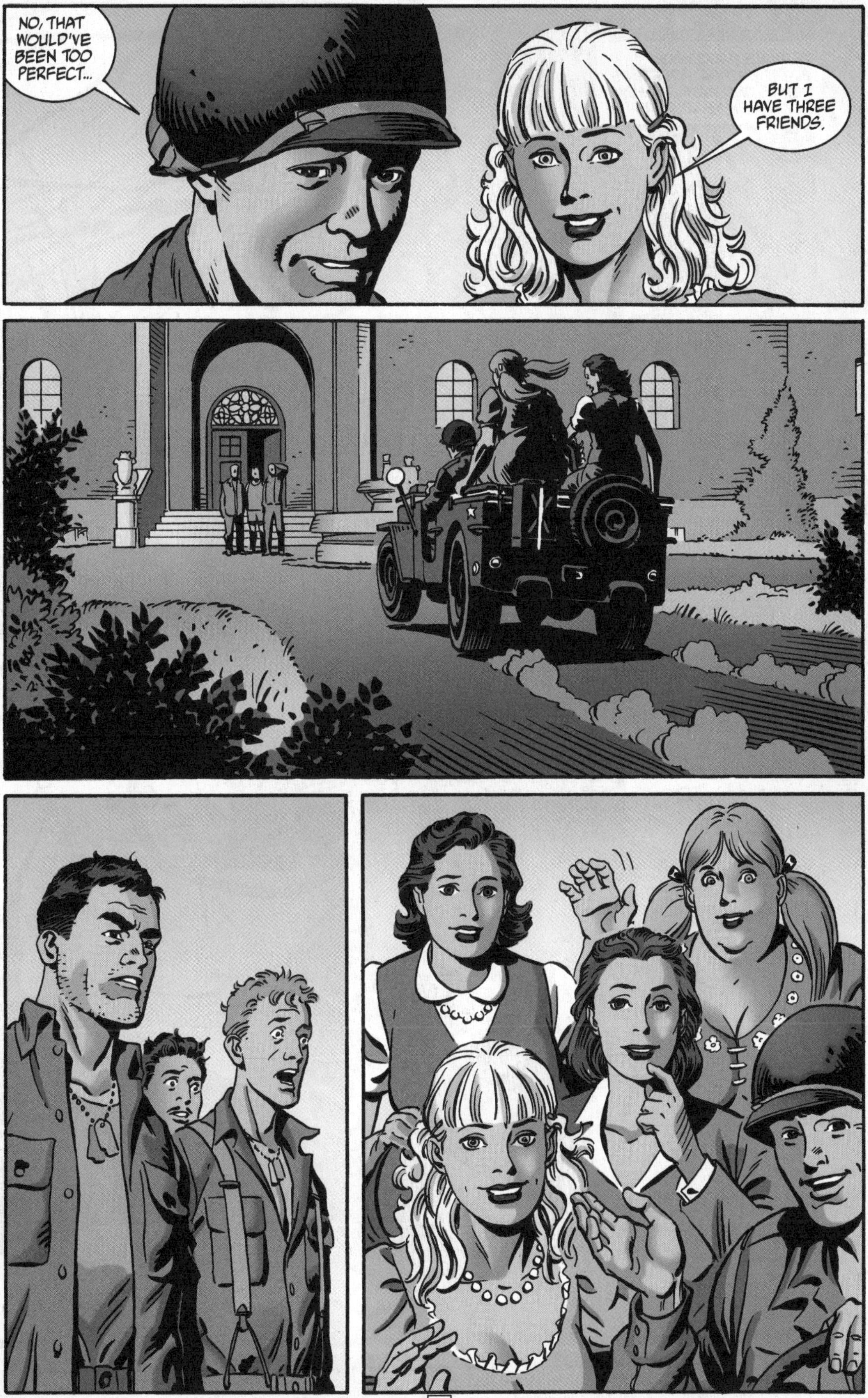
NO, THAT WOULD'VE BEEN TOO PERFECT...
BUT I HAVE THREE FRIENDS.

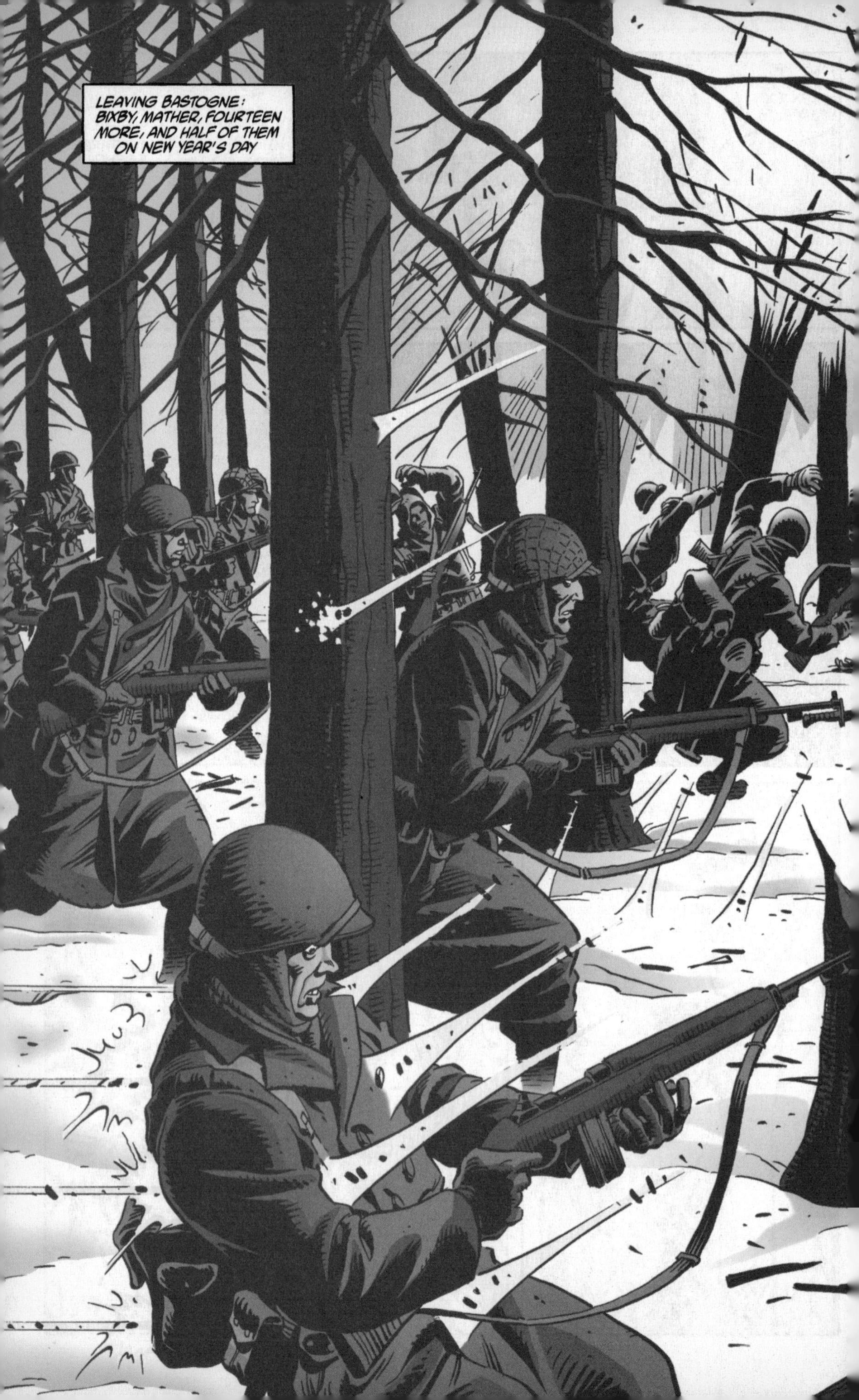
LEAVING BASTOGNE: BIXBY, MATHER, FOURTEEN MORE, AND HALF OF THEM ON NEW YEAR'S DAY

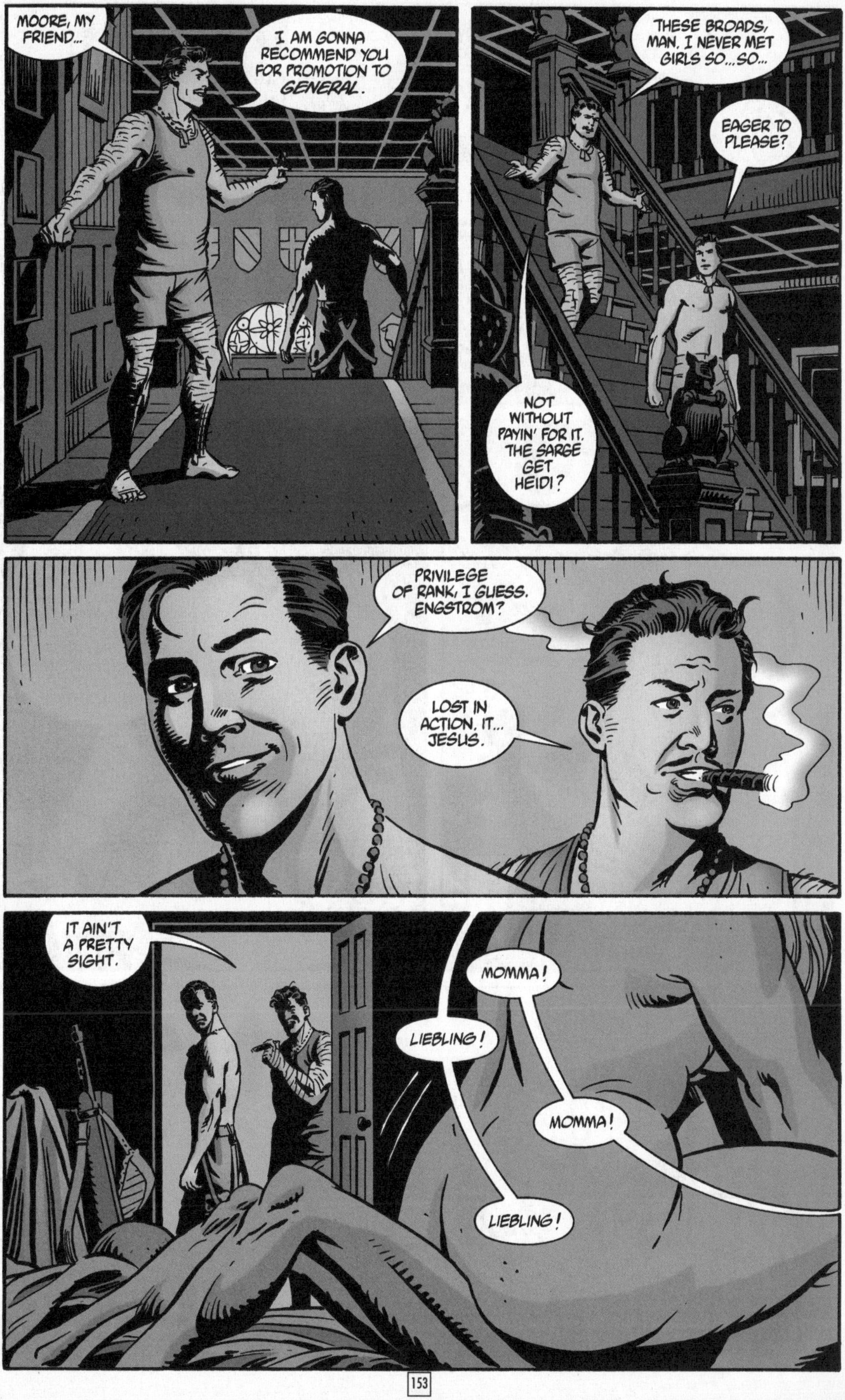
MOORE, MY FRIEND...
I AM GONNA RECOMMEND YOU FOR PROMOTION TO GENERAL.
THESE BROADS, MAN, I NEVER MET GIRLS SO...SO...
EAGER TO PLEASE?
NOT WITHOUT PAYIN' FOR IT. THE SARGE GET HEIDI?
PRIVILEGE OF RANK, I GUESS. ENGSTROM?
LOST IN ACTION. IT... JESUS.
IT AIN'T A PRETTY SIGHT.
MOMMA!
LIEBLING!
MOMMA!
LIEBLING!

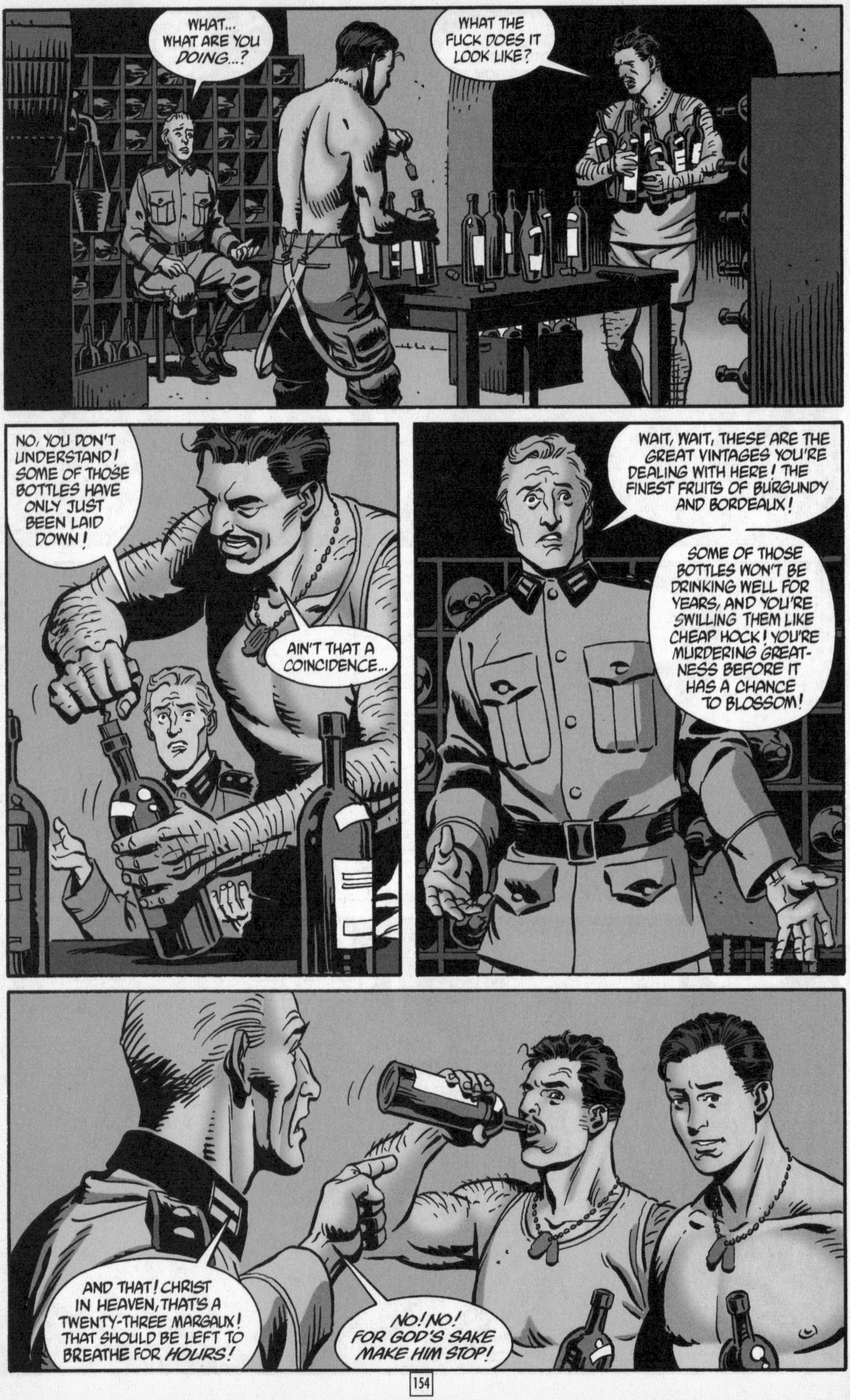
WHAT... WHAT ARE YOU *DOING*...?
WHAT THE FUCK DOES IT LOOK LIKE?
NO, YOU DON'T UNDERSTAND! SOME OF THOSE BOTTLES HAVE ONLY JUST BEEN LAID DOWN!
AIN'T THAT A COINCIDENCE...
WAIT, WAIT, THESE ARE THE GREAT VINTAGES YOU'RE DEALING WITH HERE! THE FINEST FRUITS OF BURGUNDY AND BORDEAUX!
SOME OF THOSE BOTTLES WON'T BE DRINKING WELL FOR YEARS, AND YOU'RE SWILLING THEM LIKE CHEAP HOCK! YOU'RE MURDERING GREATNESS BEFORE IT HAS A CHANCE TO BLOSSOM!
AND THAT! CHRIST IN HEAVEN, THAT'S A TWENTY-THREE MARGAUX! THAT SHOULD BE LEFT TO BREATHE FOR *HOURS*!
NO! NO! FOR GOD'S SAKE MAKE HIM STOP!

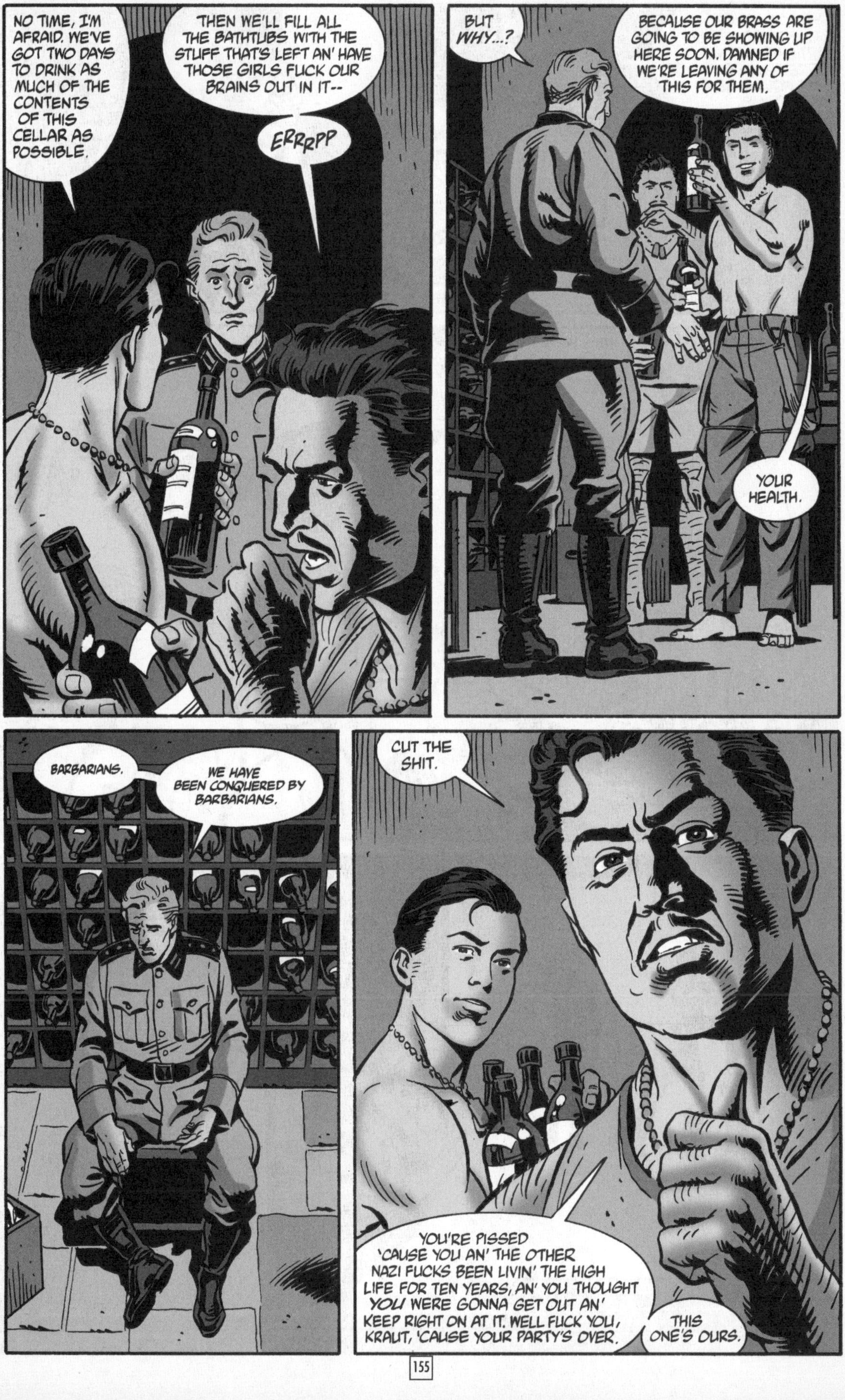

NO TIME, I'M AFRAID. WE'VE GOT TWO DAYS TO DRINK AS MUCH OF THE CONTENTS OF THIS CELLAR AS POSSIBLE.
THEN WE'LL FILL ALL THE BATHTUBS WITH THE STUFF THAT'S LEFT AN' HAVE THOSE GIRLS FUCK OUR BRAINS OUT IN IT--
ERRRPP
BUT WHY...?
BECAUSE OUR BRASS ARE GOING TO BE SHOWING UP HERE SOON. DAMNED IF WE'RE LEAVING ANY OF THIS FOR THEM.
YOUR HEALTH.
BARBARIANS.
WE HAVE BEEN CONQUERED BY BARBARIANS.
CUT THE SHIT.
YOU'RE PISSED 'CAUSE YOU AN' THE OTHER NAZI FUCKS BEEN LIVIN' THE HIGH LIFE FOR TEN YEARS, AN' YOU THOUGHT YOU WERE GONNA GET OUT AN' KEEP RIGHT ON AT IT. WELL FUCK YOU, KRAUT, 'CAUSE YOUR PARTY'S OVER.
THIS ONE'S OURS.

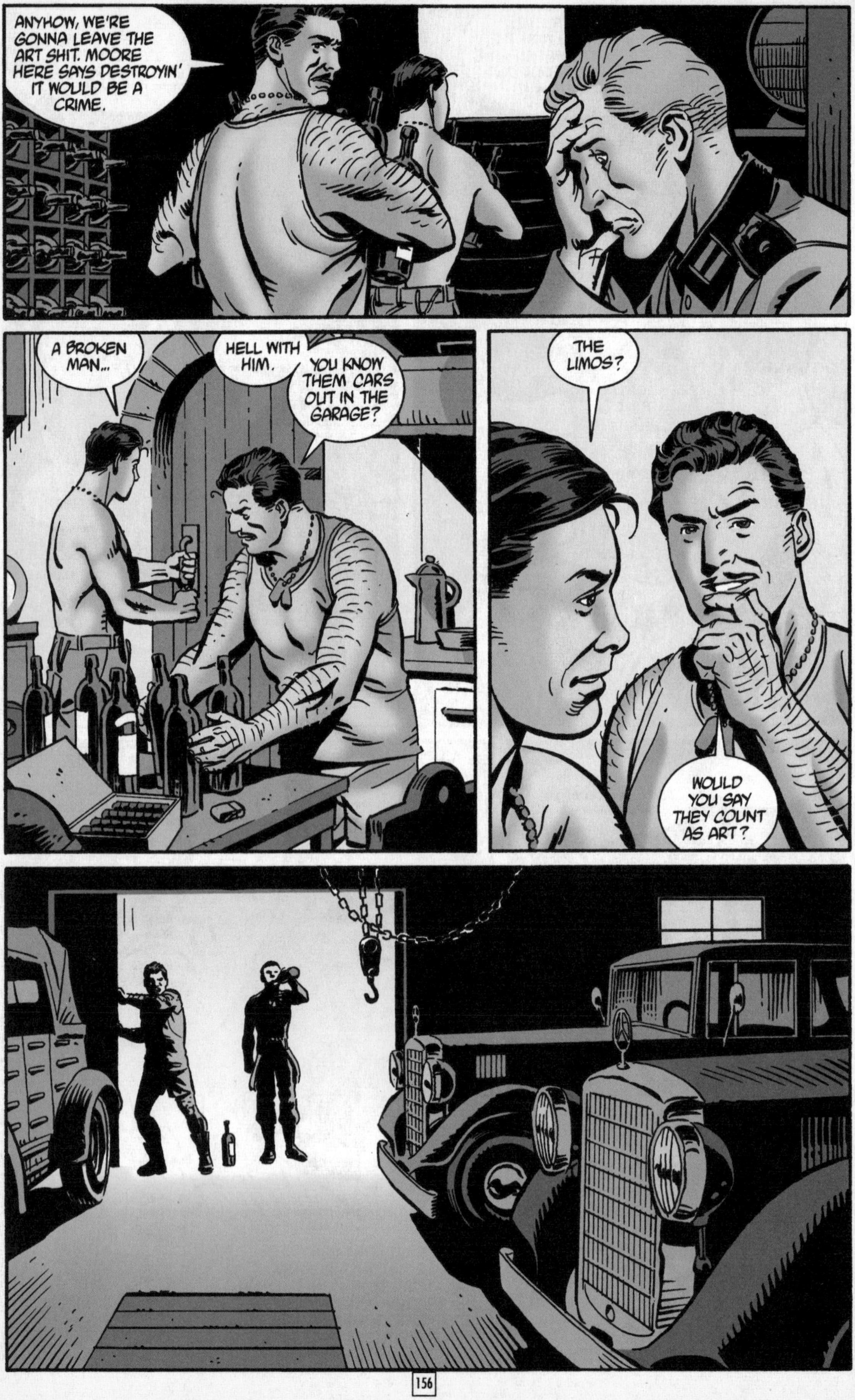

ANYHOW, WE'RE GONNA LEAVE THE ART SHIT. MOORE HERE SAYS DESTROYIN' IT WOULD BE A CRIME.
A BROKEN MAN...
HELL WITH HIM.
YOU KNOW THEM CARS OUT IN THE GARAGE?
THE LIMOS?
WOULD YOU SAY THEY COUNT AS ART?

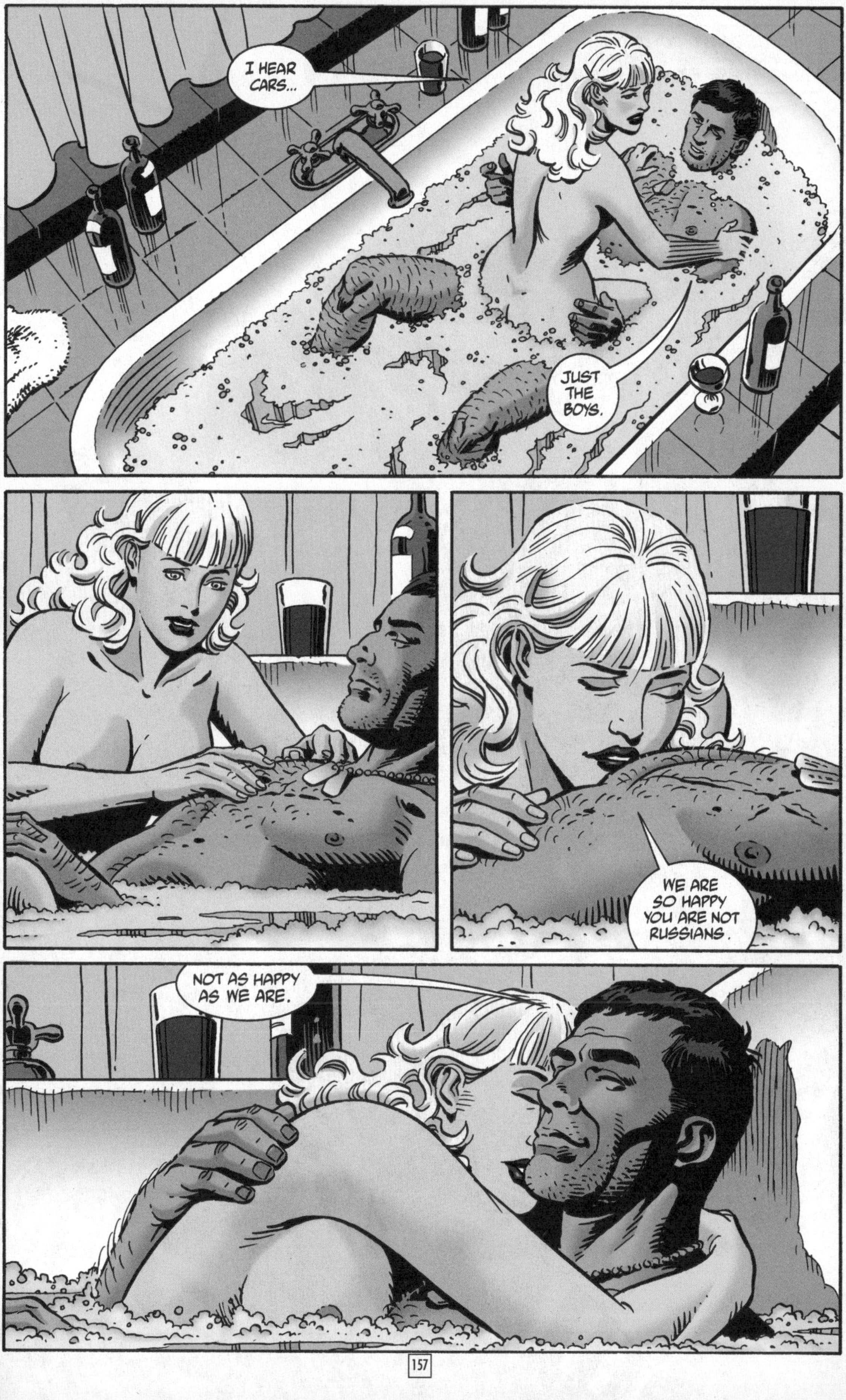
I HEAR CARS...
JUST THE BOYS.
WE ARE SO HAPPY YOU ARE NOT RUSSIANS.
NOT AS HAPPY AS WE ARE.

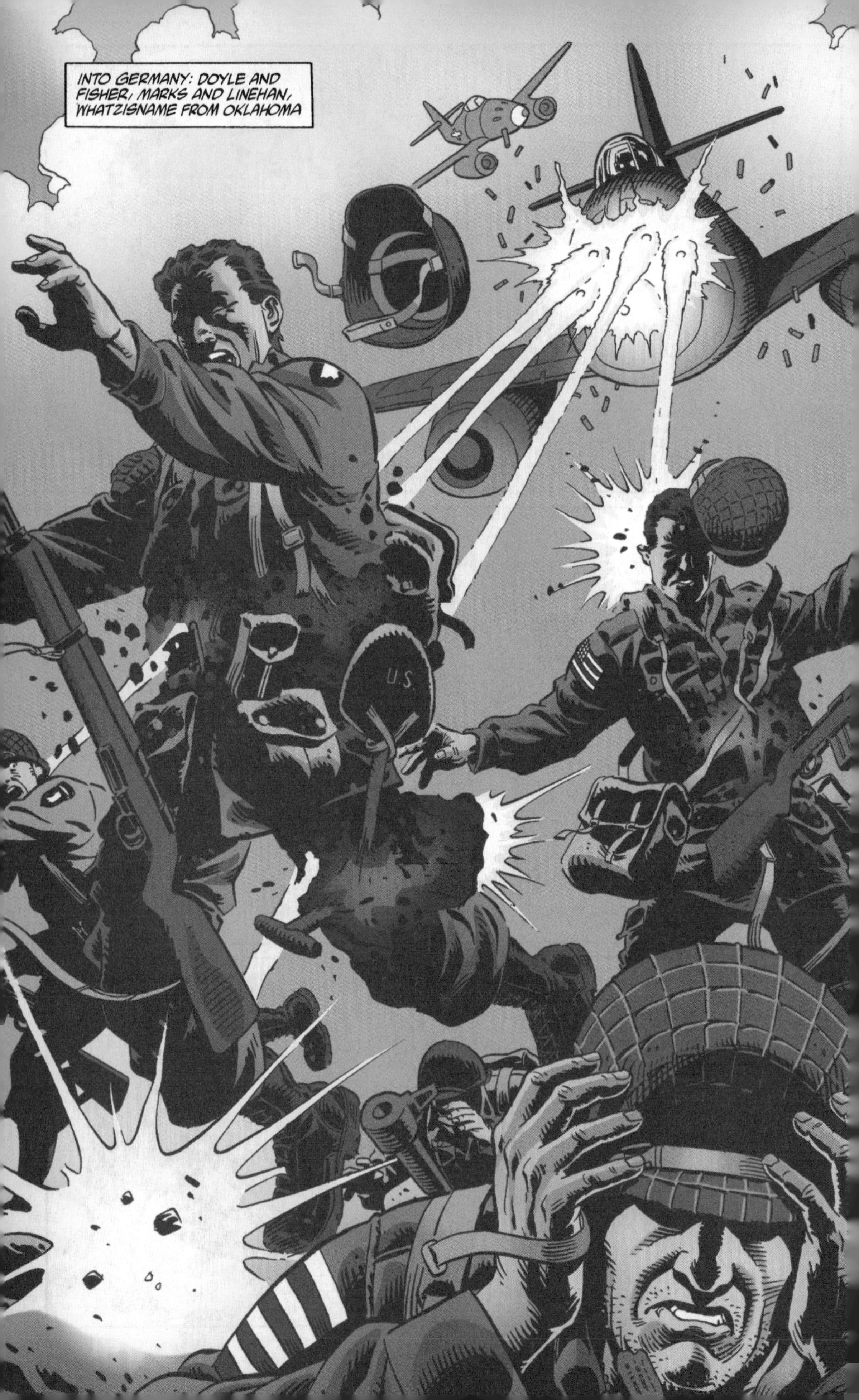
INTO GERMANY: DOYLE AND FISHER, MARKS AND LINEHAN, WHATZISNAME FROM OKLAHOMA
U.S.

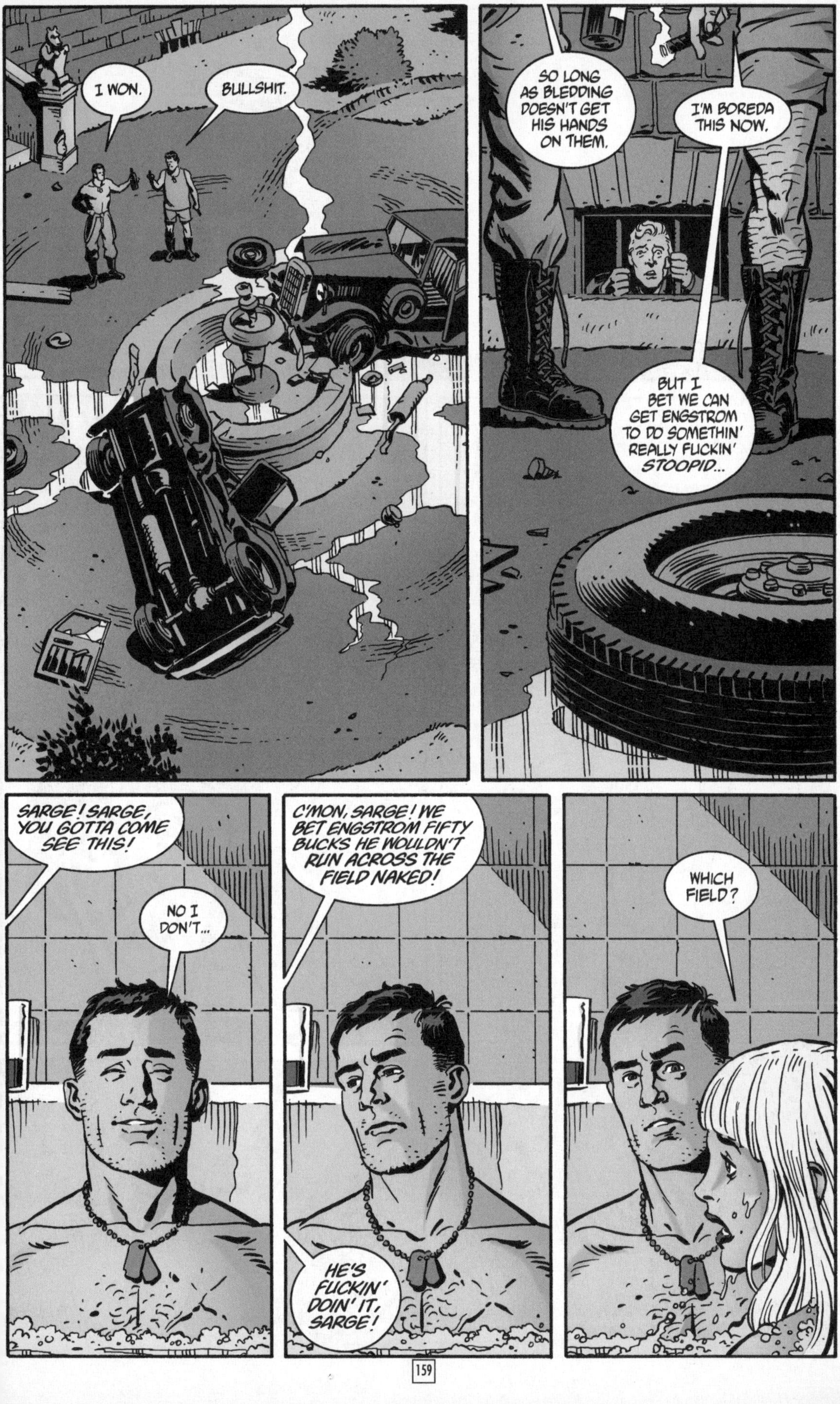
I WON.
BULLSHIT.
SO LONG AS BLEDDING DOESN'T GET HIS HANDS ON THEM.
I'M BOREDA THIS NOW.
BUT I BET WE CAN GET ENGSTROM TO DO SOMETHIN' REALLY FUCKIN' STOOPID...
SARGE! SARGE, YOU GOTTA COME SEE THIS!
NO I DON'T...
C'MON, SARGE! WE BET ENGSTROM FIFTY BUCKS HE WOULDN'T RUN ACROSS THE FIELD NAKED!
HE'S FUCKIN' DOIN' IT, SARGE!
WHICH FIELD?

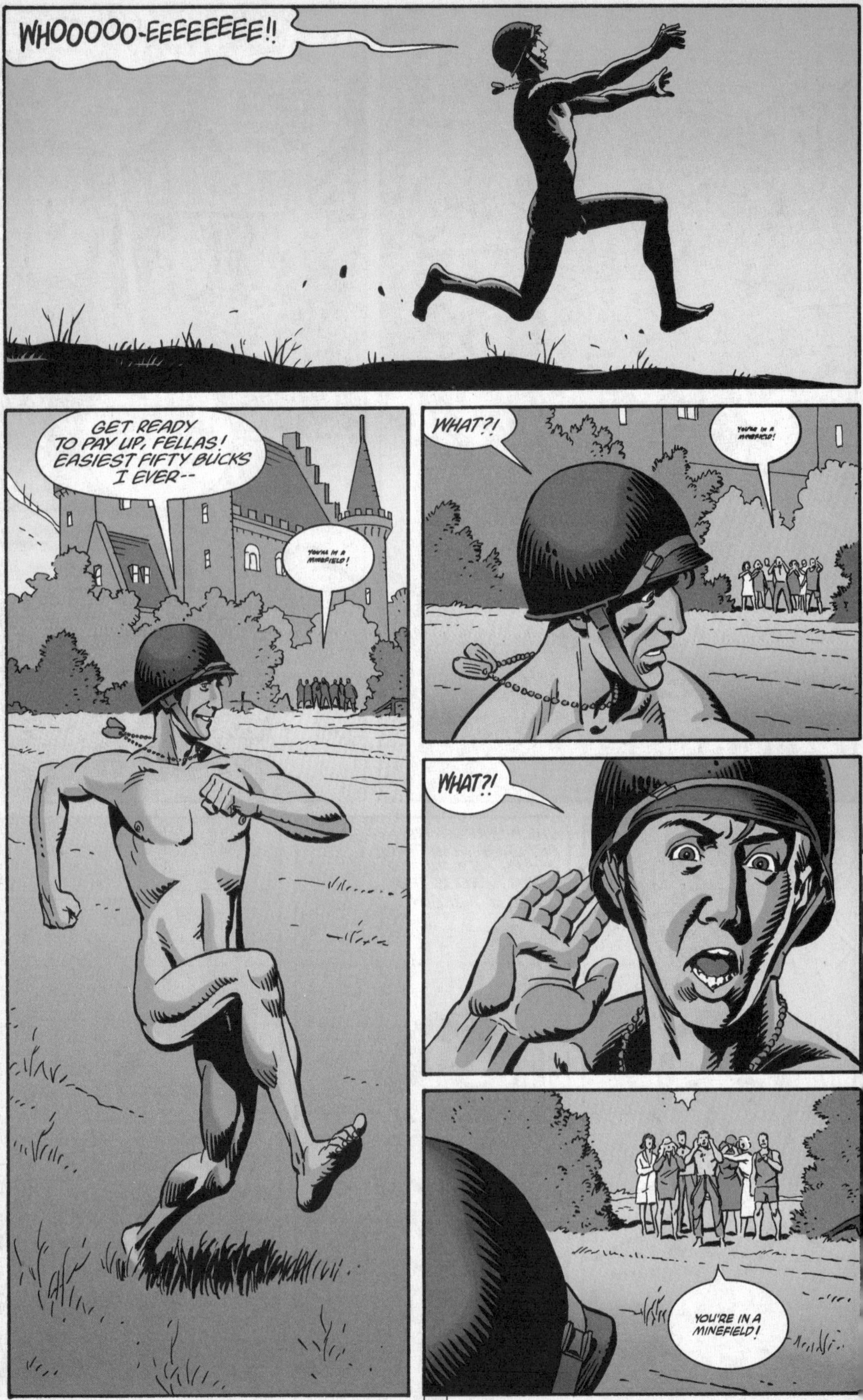
WHOOOOO-EEEEEEEE!!
GET READY TO PAY UP, FELLAS! EASIEST FIFTY BUCKS I EVER--
WHAT?!
WHAT?!
YOU'RE IN A MINEFIELD!

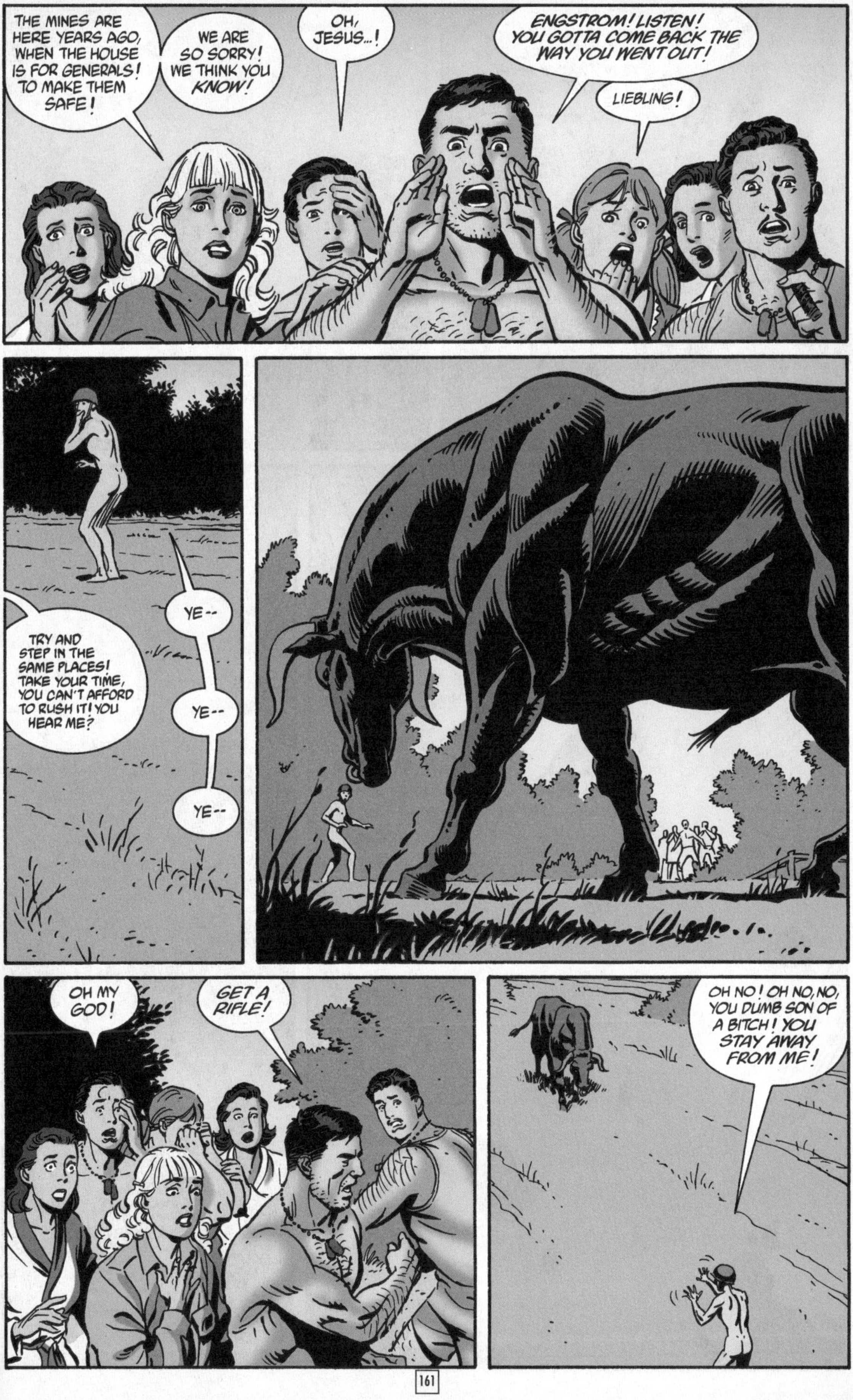
THE MINES ARE HERE YEARS AGO, WHEN THE HOUSE IS FOR GENERALS! TO MAKE THEM SAFE!
WE ARE SO SORRY! WE THINK YOU KNOW!
OH, JESUS...!
ENGSTROM! LISTEN! YOU GOTTA COME BACK THE WAY YOU WENT OUT!
LIEBLING!
YE--
TRY AND STEP IN THE SAME PLACES! TAKE YOUR TIME, YOU CAN'T AFFORD TO RUSH IT! YOU HEAR ME?
YE--
YE--
OH MY GOD!
GET A RIFLE!
OH NO! OH NO, NO, YOU DUMB SON OF A BITCH! YOU STAY AWAY FROM ME!

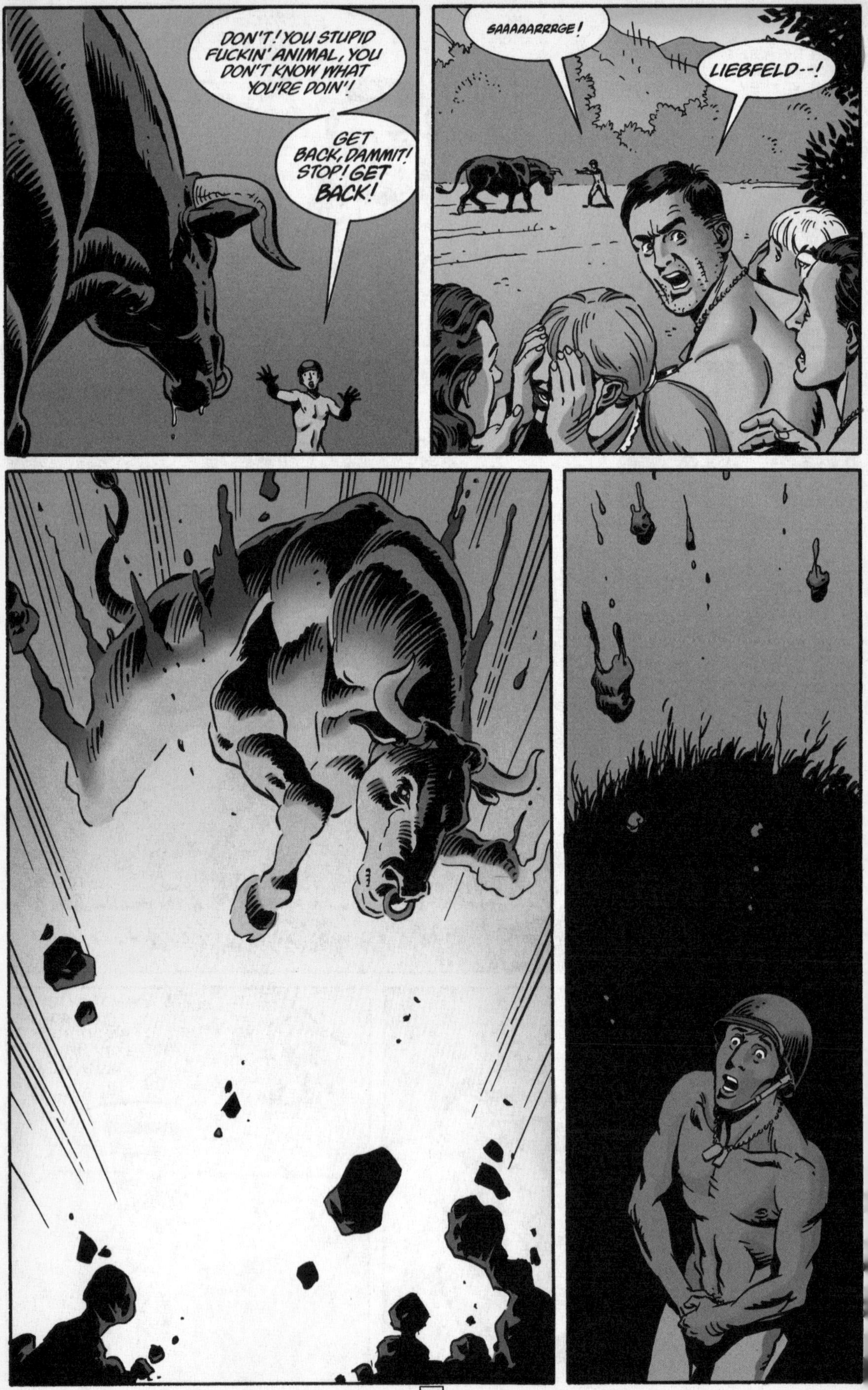
DON'T! YOU STUPID FUCKIN' ANIMAL, YOU DON'T KNOW WHAT YOU'RE DOIN'!
GET BACK, DAMMIT! STOP! GET BACK!
SAAAAAARRRGE!
LIEBFELD--!

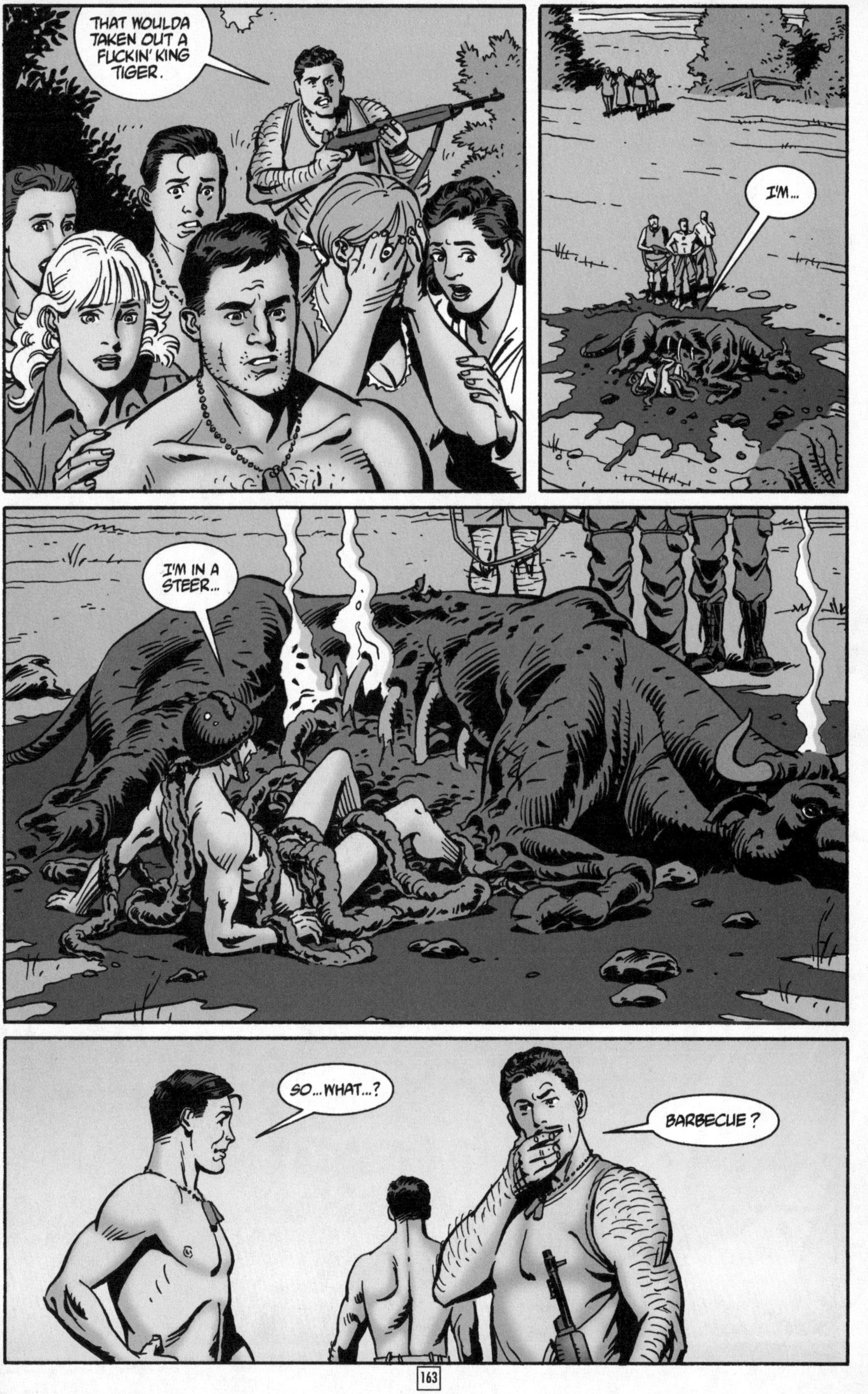
THAT WOULDA TAKEN OUT A FUCKIN' KING TIGER.
I'M...
I'M IN A STEER...
SO...WHAT...?
BARBECUE?

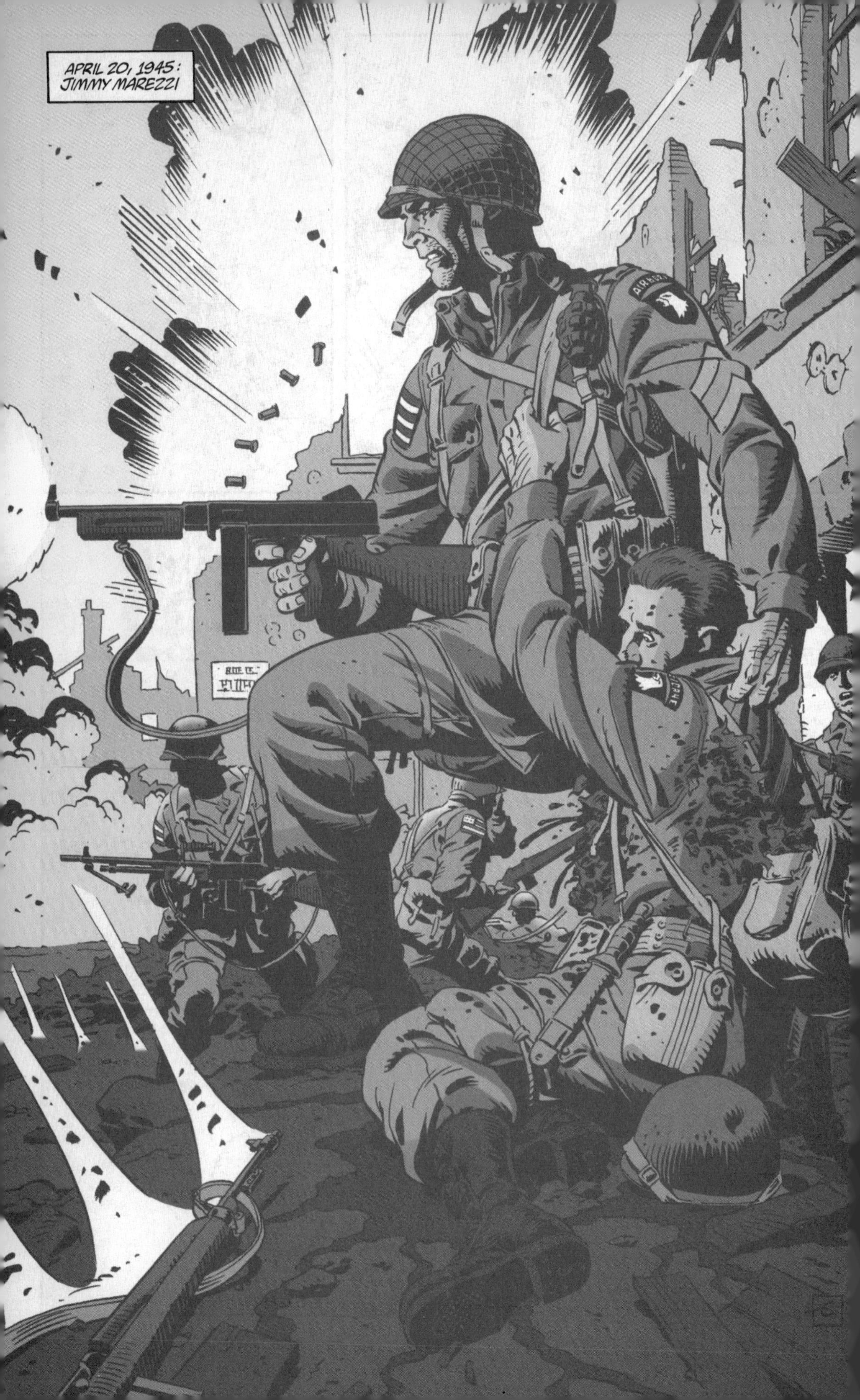
APRIL 20, 1945:
JIMMY MAREZZI

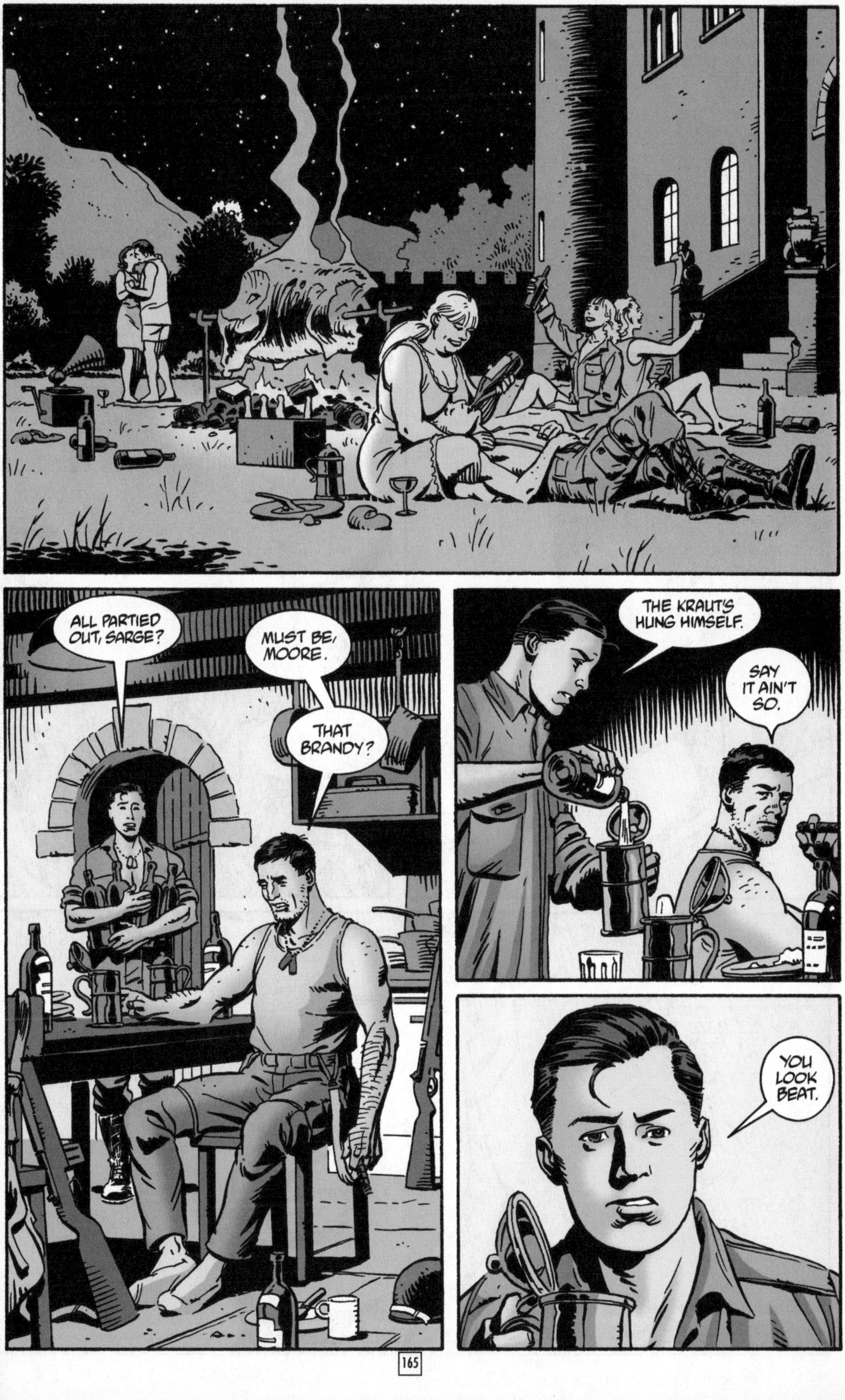
ALL PARTIED OUT, SARGE?
MUST BE, MOORE.
THAT BRANDY?
THE KRAUT'S HUNG HIMSELF.
SAY IT AIN'T SO.
YOU LOOK BEAT.

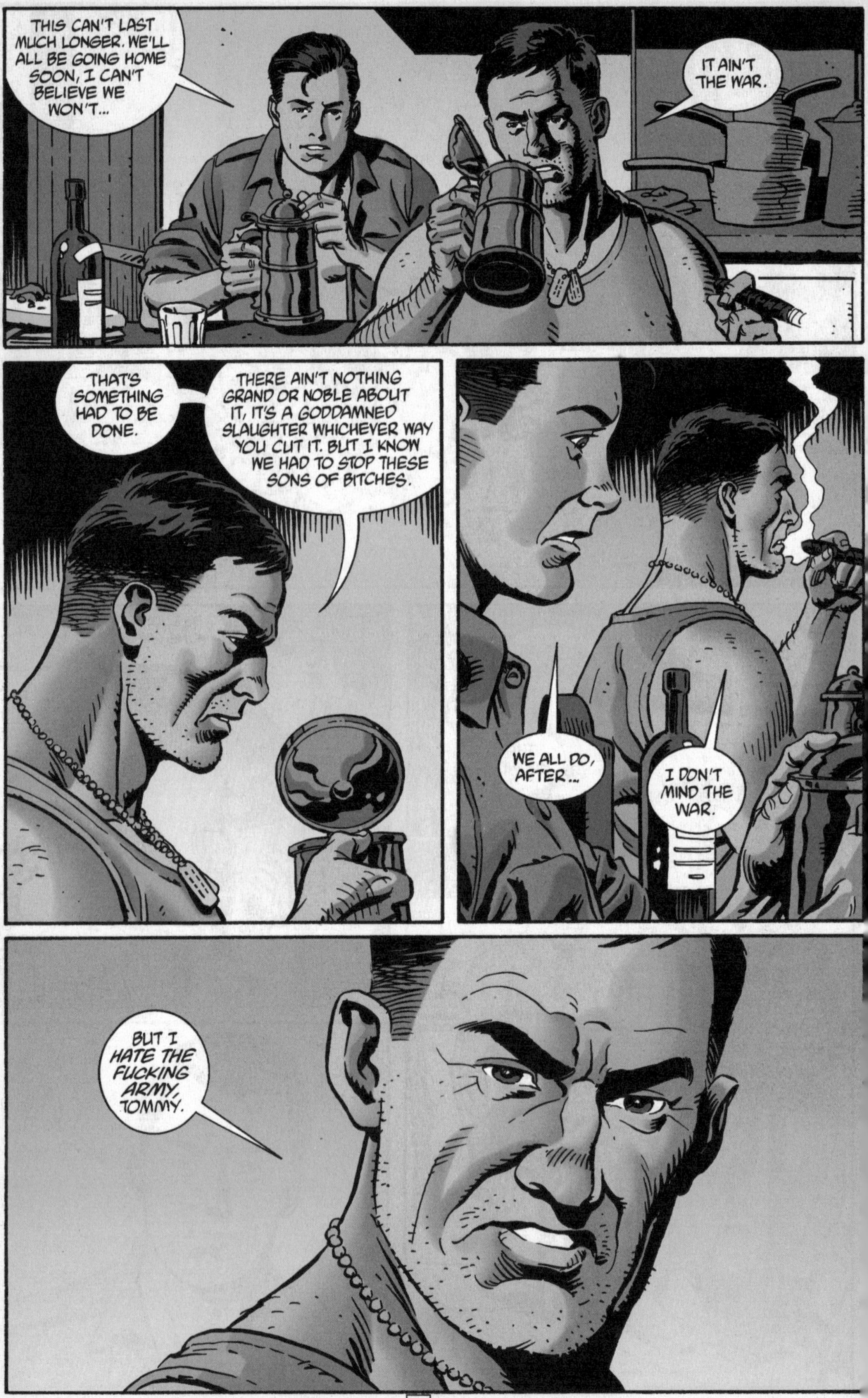
THIS CAN'T LAST MUCH LONGER. WE'LL ALL BE GOING HOME SOON, I CAN'T BELIEVE WE WON'T...
IT AIN'T THE WAR.
THAT'S SOMETHING HAD TO BE DONE.
THERE AIN'T NOTHING GRAND OR NOBLE ABOUT IT, IT'S A GODDAMNED SLAUGHTER WHICHEVER WAY YOU CUT IT. BUT I KNOW WE HAD TO STOP THESE SONS OF BITCHES.
WE ALL DO, AFTER...
I DON'T MIND THE WAR.
BUT I HATE THE FUCKING ARMY, TOMMY.

I HATE THE STUPID REGULATIONS THEY HAVE FOR US. I HATE ALL THE LITTLE DICTATORS AN' THE CHICKENSHIT WE HAVE TO PUT UP WITH. I HATE THE WAY NO ONE KNOWS WHAT THEY'RE SUPPOSED TO BE DOIN', AN' SO GUYS HAVE TO SUFFER BECAUSE OF IT.

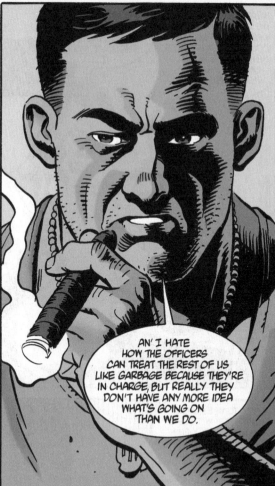

AN' I HATE HOW THE OFFICERS CAN TREAT THE REST OF US LIKE GARBAGE BECAUSE THEY'RE IN CHARGE, BUT REALLY THEY DON'T HAVE ANY MORE IDEA WHAT'S GOING ON THAN WE DO.

LOOK AT THAT PRICK SENT US HERE. YOU THINK HE KNEW HE WAS DOING US A FAVOR? HE WAS USING US SO HE COULD KISS THE GENERAL'S ASS.

AND BLEDDING--IT'S LIKE LIEBFELD SAID, HOW COME WE KEEP GETTING STUCK BACK IN THE LINE? IF HE'S CLEVER ENOUGH TO BE IN CHARGE, WHY DIDN'T HE HAVE RESERVES READY IN CASE OF SOMETHING LIKE THE BULGE? HOW COME WE HAD TO GET PULLED OFF R AN' R WHEN WE ONLY JUST GOT OFF THE ISLAND?

I GUESS HE CAN'T KNOW EVERYTHING...

THEN HE SHOULDN'T BE IN COMMAND. WE'RE TALKING ABOUT GUYS' LIVES HERE.

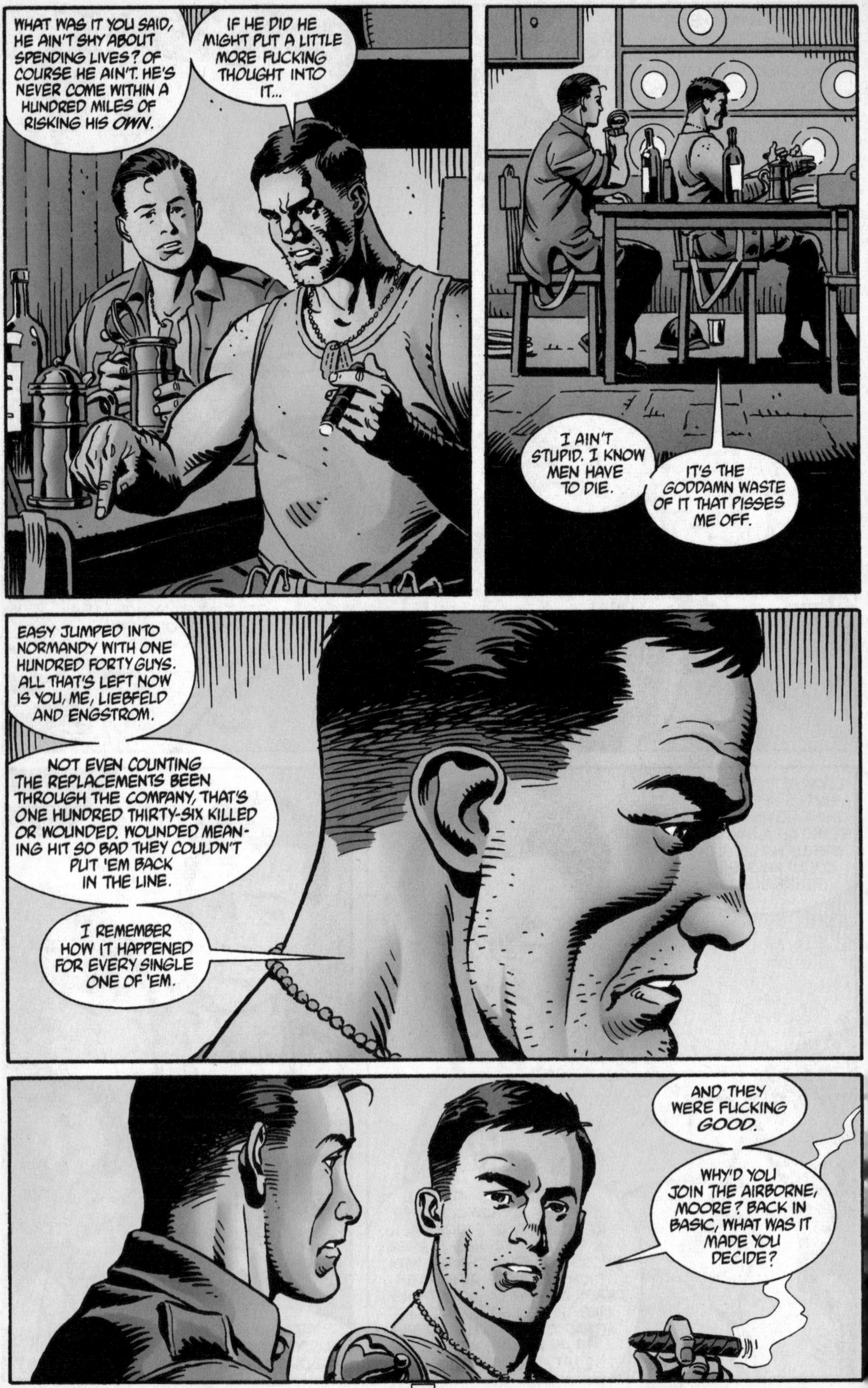
WHAT WAS IT YOU SAID, HE AIN'T SHY ABOUT SPENDING LIVES? OF COURSE HE AIN'T. HE'S NEVER COME WITHIN A HUNDRED MILES OF RISKING HIS *OWN*.
IF HE DID HE MIGHT PUT A LITTLE MORE FUCKING THOUGHT INTO IT...
I AIN'T STUPID. I KNOW MEN HAVE TO DIE.
IT'S THE GODDAMN WASTE OF IT THAT PISSES ME OFF.
EASY JUMPED INTO NORMANDY WITH ONE HUNDRED FORTY GUYS. ALL THAT'S LEFT NOW IS YOU, ME, LIEBFELD AND ENGSTROM.
NOT EVEN COUNTING THE REPLACEMENTS BEEN THROUGH THE COMPANY, THAT'S ONE HUNDRED THIRTY-SIX KILLED OR WOUNDED. WOUNDED MEANING HIT SO BAD THEY COULDN'T PUT 'EM BACK IN THE LINE.
I REMEMBER HOW IT HAPPENED FOR EVERY SINGLE ONE OF 'EM.
AND THEY WERE FUCKING *GOOD*.
WHY'D YOU JOIN THE AIRBORNE, MOORE? BACK IN BASIC, WHAT WAS IT MADE YOU DECIDE?

I GUESS I WANTED TO BE WITH THE BEST. IF I HAD TO GO INTO COMBAT, I WANTED TO HAVE GUYS AROUND ME I COULD DEPEND ON.

YOU'RE EDUCATED, MOORE, BUT THAT DON'T MEAN YOU'RE STUPID.

YOU REMEMBER THE KINDA ASS-HOLES YOU USED TO SEE AT THE DEPOTS? THEY'D GET YOU KILLED IN THE FIRST FIVE GODDAMN MINUTES.

THAT'S WHY I HATE THAT WE LOST SO MANY GUYS IN EASY.

'CAUSE THEY WERE THE EXACT OPPOSITE.

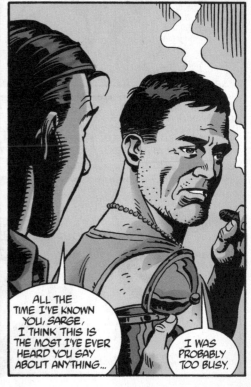

ALL THE TIME I'VE KNOWN YOU, SARGE, I THINK THIS IS THE MOST I'VE EVER HEARD YOU SAY ABOUT ANYTHING...

I WAS PROBABLY TOO BUSY.

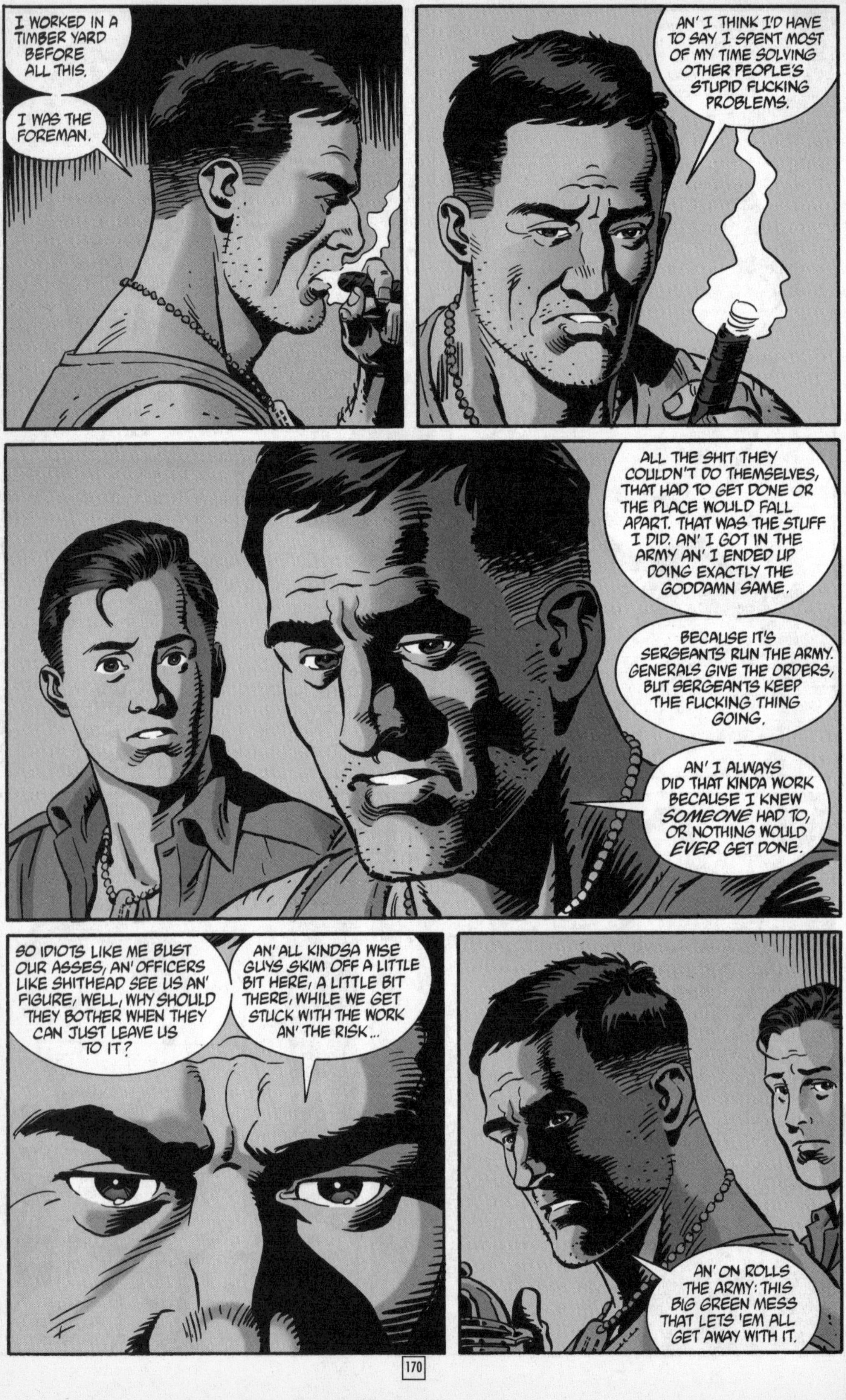
I WORKED IN A TIMBER YARD BEFORE ALL THIS.
I WAS THE FOREMAN.
AN' I THINK I'D HAVE TO SAY I SPENT MOST OF MY TIME SOLVING OTHER PEOPLE'S STUPID FUCKING PROBLEMS.
ALL THE SHIT THEY COULDN'T DO THEMSELVES, THAT HAD TO GET DONE OR THE PLACE WOULD FALL APART. THAT WAS THE STUFF I DID. AN' I GOT IN THE ARMY AN' I ENDED UP DOING EXACTLY THE GODDAMN SAME.
BECAUSE IT'S SERGEANTS RUN THE ARMY. GENERALS GIVE THE ORDERS, BUT SERGEANTS KEEP THE FUCKING THING GOING.
AN' I ALWAYS DID THAT KINDA WORK BECAUSE I KNEW *SOMEONE* HAD TO, OR NOTHING WOULD *EVER* GET DONE.
SO IDIOTS LIKE ME BUST OUR ASSES, AN' OFFICERS LIKE SHITHEAD SEE US AN' FIGURE, WELL, WHY SHOULD THEY BOTHER WHEN THEY CAN JUST LEAVE US TO IT?
AN' ALL KINDSA WISE GUYS SKIM OFF A LITTLE BIT HERE, A LITTLE BIT THERE, WHILE WE GET STUCK WITH THE WORK AN' THE RISK...
AN' ON ROLLS THE ARMY: THIS BIG GREEN MESS THAT LETS 'EM ALL GET AWAY WITH IT.

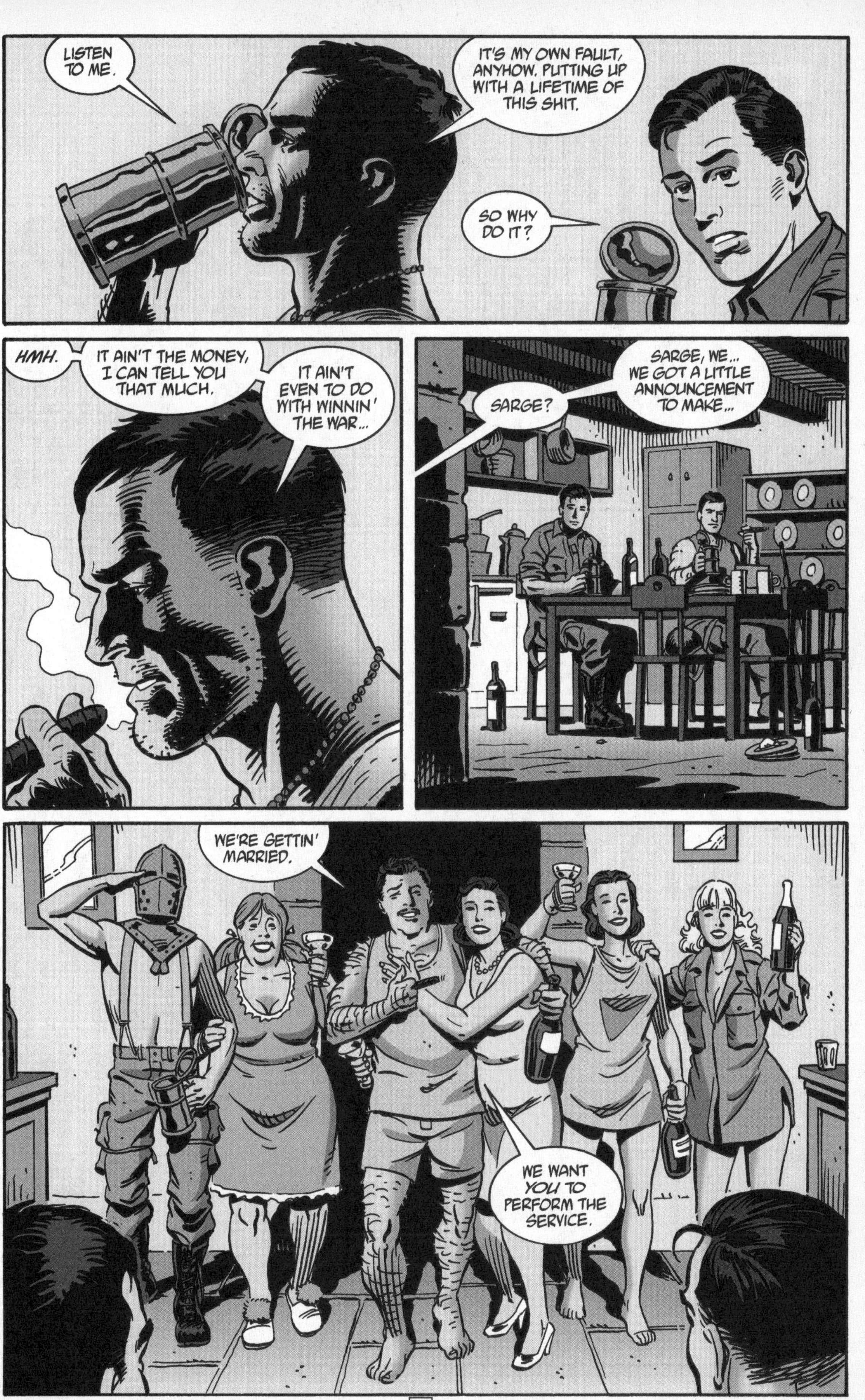
LISTEN TO ME.
IT'S MY OWN FAULT, ANYHOW. PUTTING UP WITH A LIFETIME OF THIS SHIT.
SO WHY DO IT?
HMH.
IT AIN'T THE MONEY, I CAN TELL YOU THAT MUCH.
IT AIN'T EVEN TO DO WITH WINNIN' THE WAR...
SARGE?
SARGE, WE... WE GOT A LITTLE ANNOUNCEMENT TO MAKE...
WE'RE GETTIN' MARRIED.
WE WANT *YOU* TO PERFORM THE SERVICE.

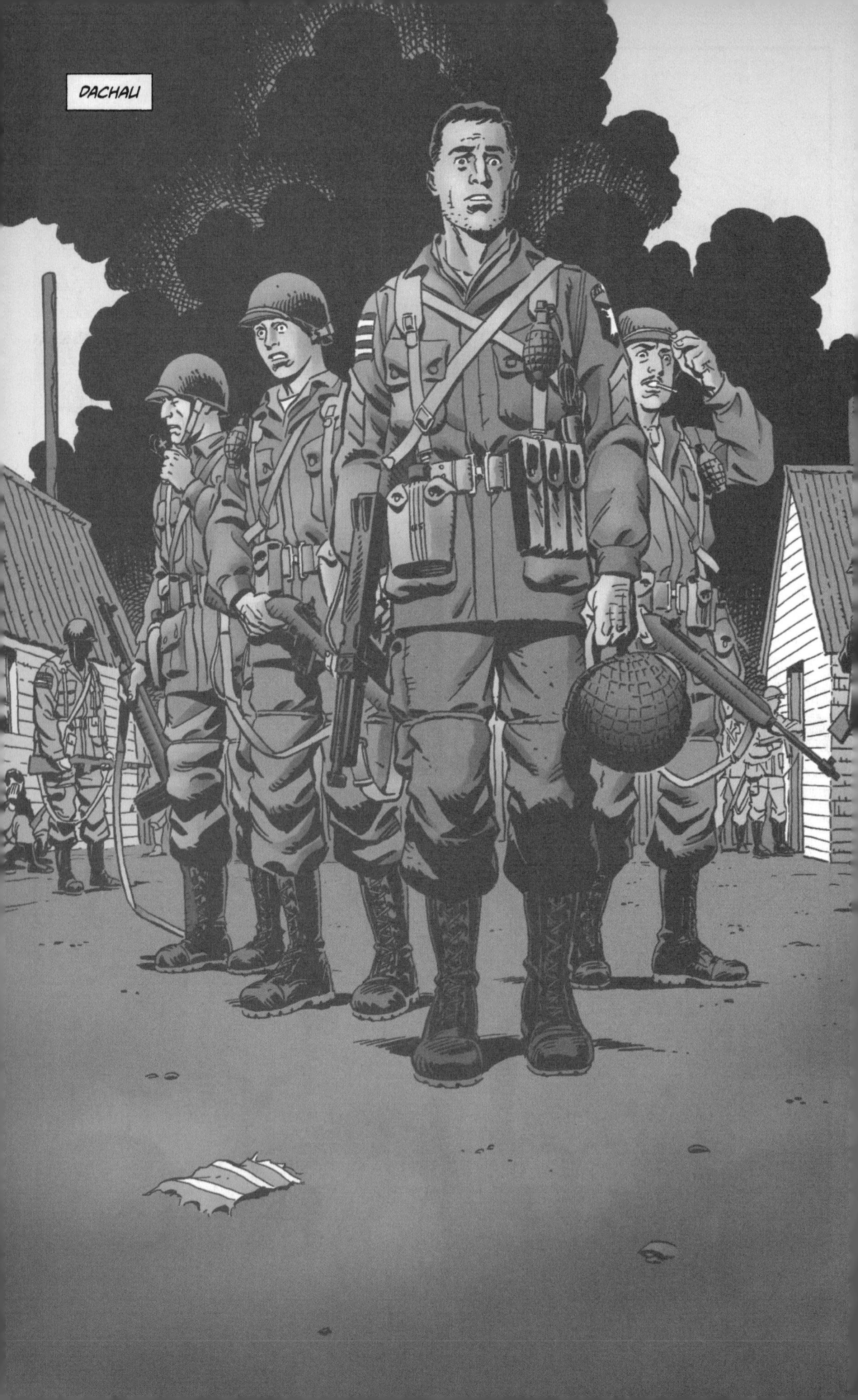
DACHAU

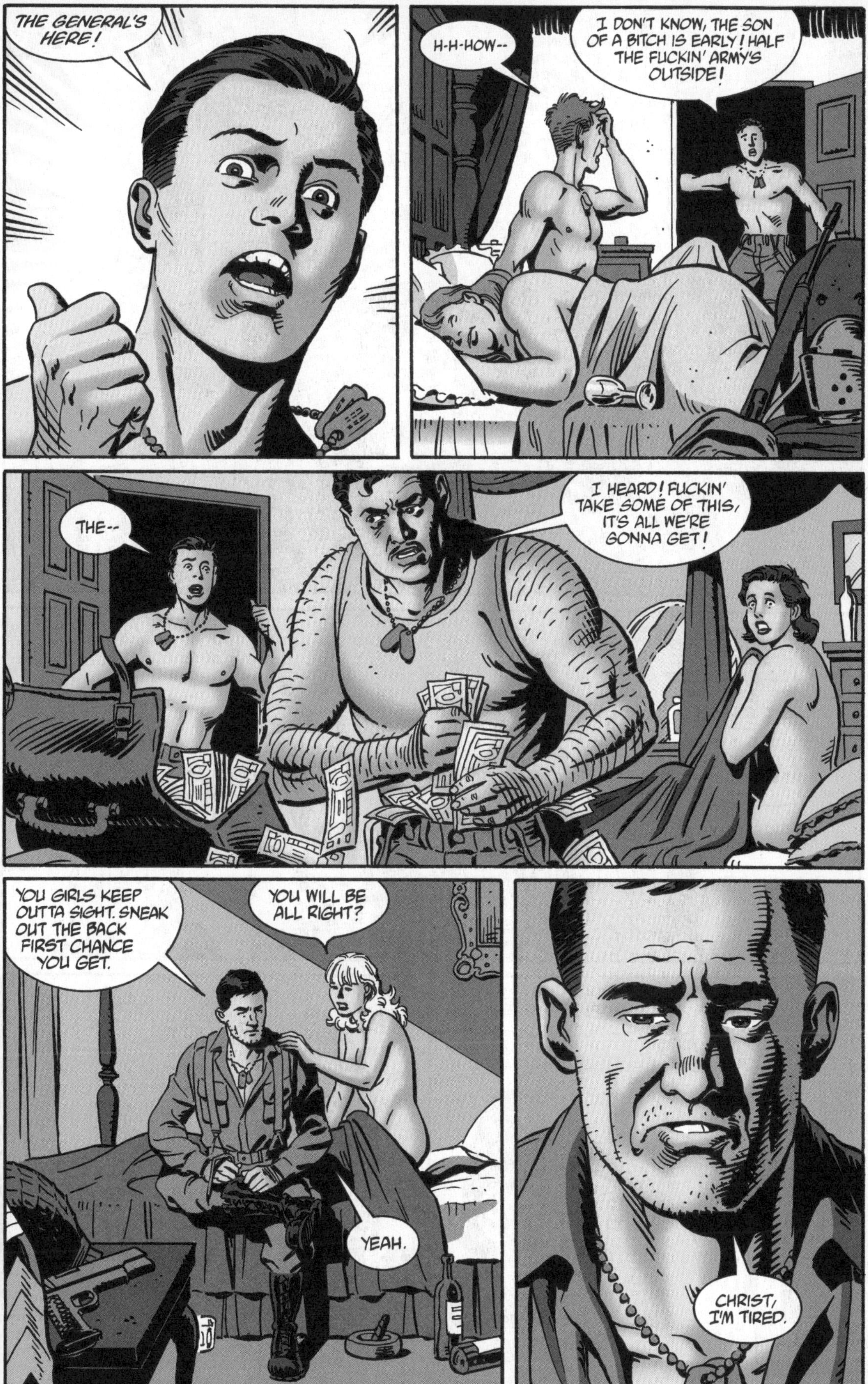
THE GENERAL'S HERE!
H-H-HOW--
I DON'T KNOW, THE SON OF A BITCH IS EARLY! HALF THE FUCKIN' ARMY'S OUTSIDE!
THE--
I HEARD! FUCKIN' TAKE SOME OF THIS, IT'S ALL WE'RE GONNA GET!
YOU GIRLS KEEP OUTTA SIGHT. SNEAK OUT THE BACK FIRST CHANCE YOU GET.
YOU WILL BE ALL RIGHT?
YEAH.
CHRIST, I'M TIRED.

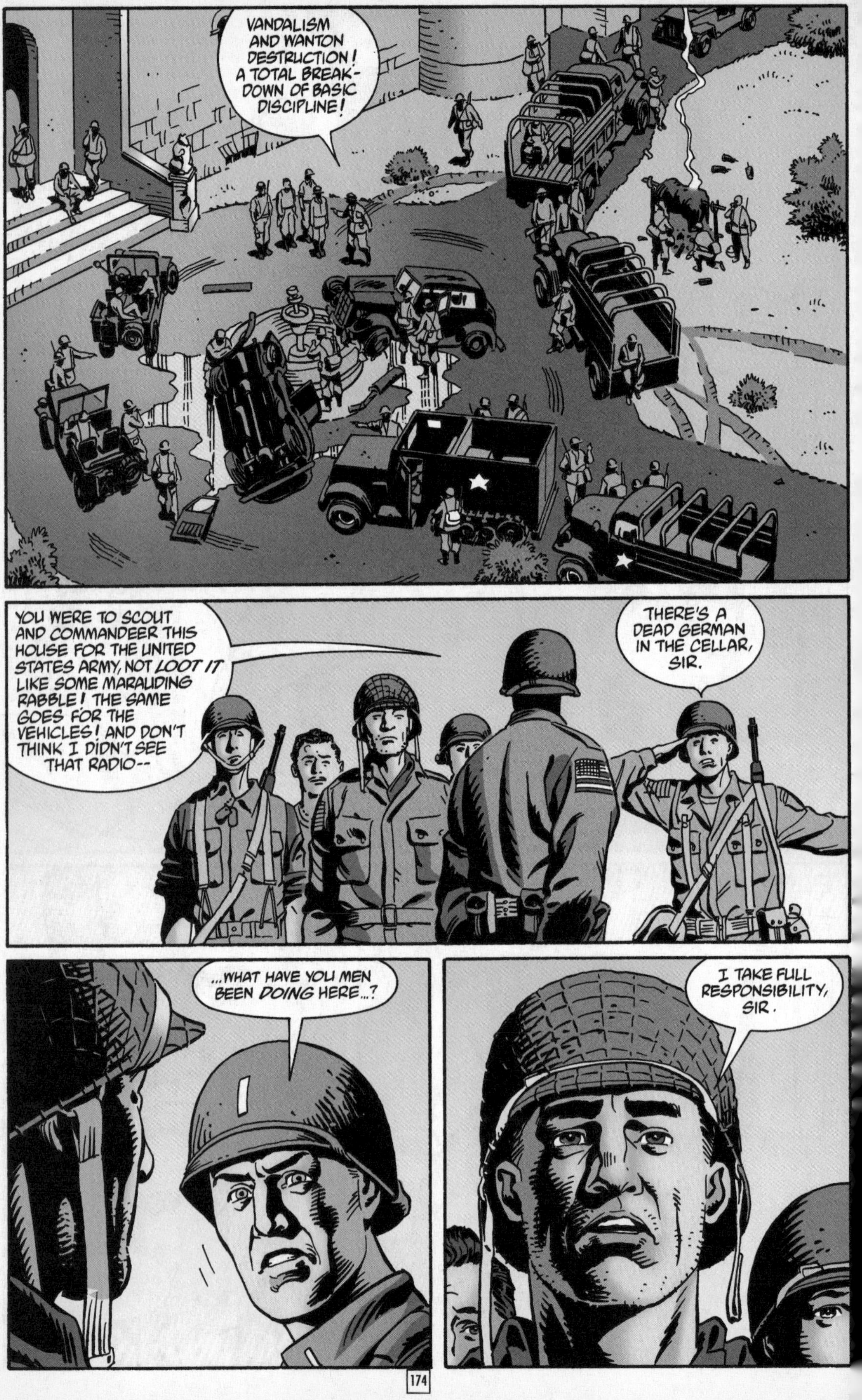
VANDALISM AND WANTON DESTRUCTION! A TOTAL BREAK-DOWN OF BASIC DISCIPLINE!
YOU WERE TO SCOUT AND COMMANDEER THIS HOUSE FOR THE UNITED STATES ARMY, NOT *LOOT IT* LIKE SOME MARAUDING RABBLE! THE SAME GOES FOR THE VEHICLES! AND DON'T THINK I DIDN'T SEE THAT RADIO--
THERE'S A DEAD GERMAN IN THE CELLAR, SIR.
...WHAT HAVE YOU MEN BEEN *DOING* HERE...?
I TAKE FULL RESPONSIBILITY, SIR.

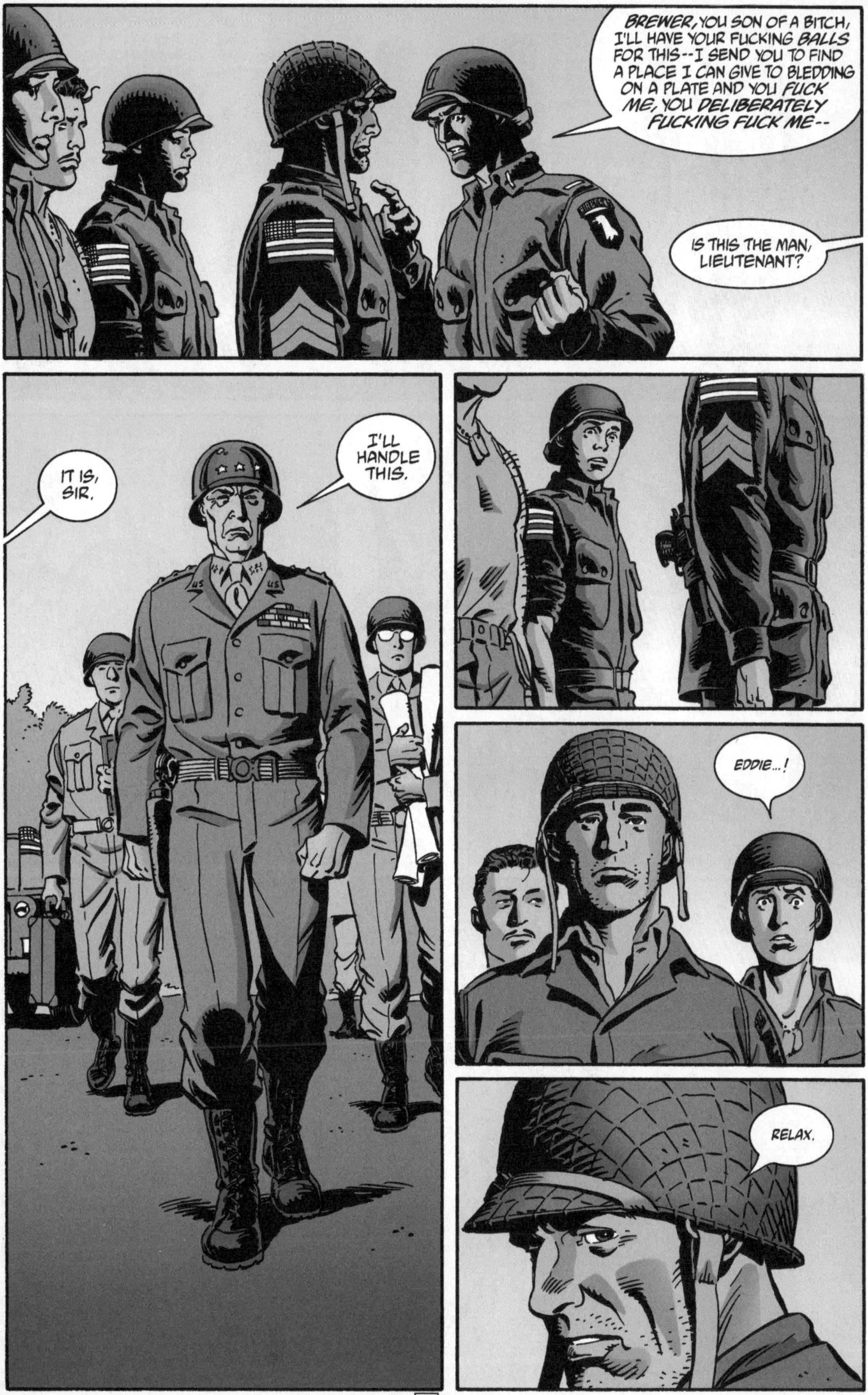
BREWER, YOU SON OF A BITCH, I'LL HAVE YOUR FUCKING BALLS FOR THIS--I SEND YOU TO FIND A PLACE I CAN GIVE TO BLEDDING ON A PLATE AND YOU FUCK ME, YOU DELIBERATELY FUCKING FUCK ME--
IS THIS THE MAN, LIEUTENANT?
IT IS, SIR.
I'LL HANDLE THIS.
EDDIE...!
RELAX.

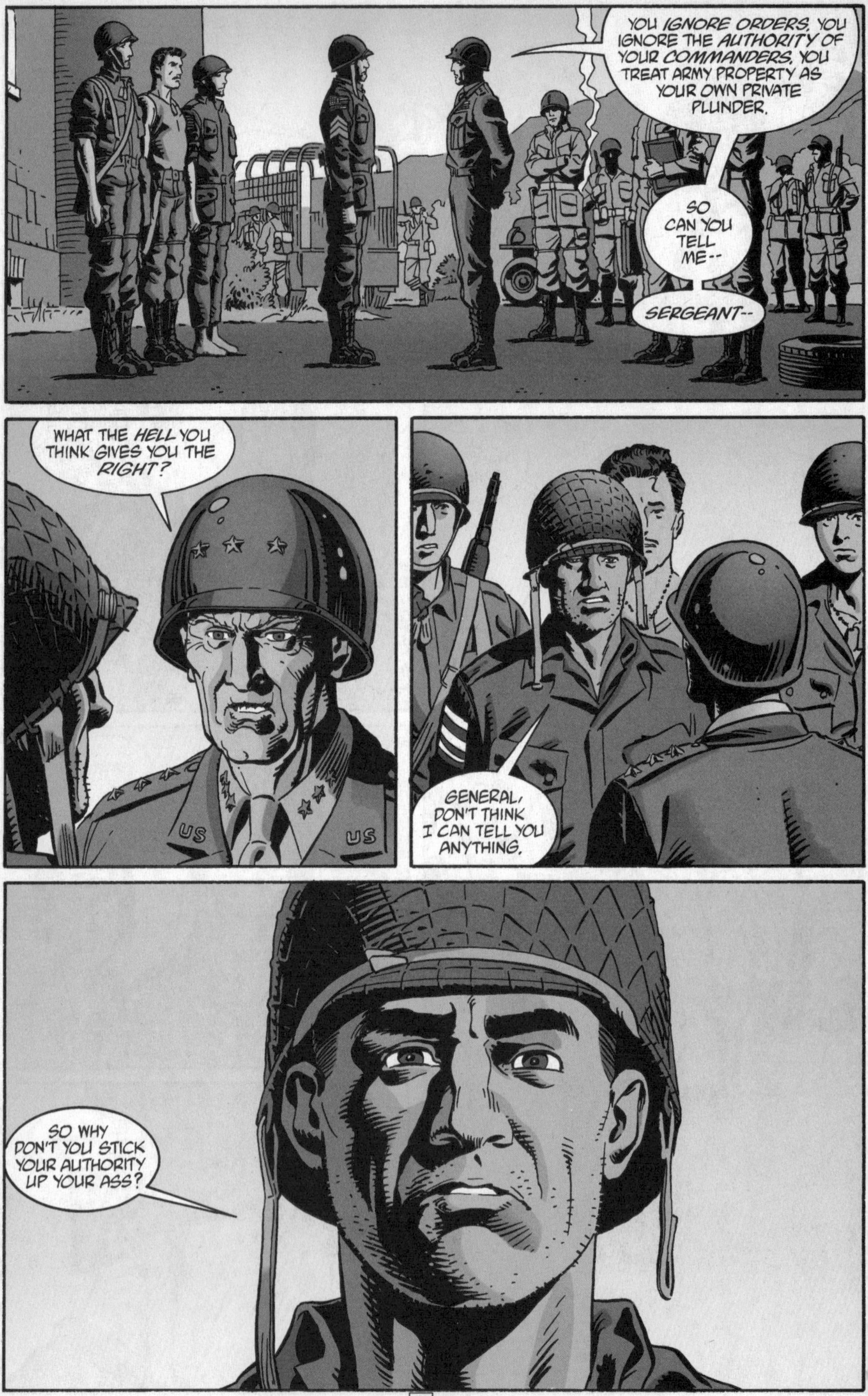
YOU IGNORE ORDERS, YOU IGNORE THE AUTHORITY OF YOUR COMMANDERS, YOU TREAT ARMY PROPERTY AS YOUR OWN PRIVATE PLUNDER.
SO CAN YOU TELL ME--
SERGEANT--
WHAT THE HELL YOU THINK GIVES YOU THE RIGHT?
US
US
GENERAL, DON'T THINK I CAN TELL YOU ANYTHING.
SO WHY DON'T YOU STICK YOUR AUTHORITY UP YOUR ASS?

Sometimes the old soldier's children and grandchildren tried their luck, and came to him, and peered and asked their questions.

"What was it like?"

And "How did you do it?"

And "What was it got you through?"

And the old soldier smiled and just said, "It was easy."

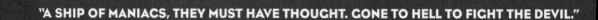
"A SHIP OF MANIACS, THEY MUST HAVE THOUGHT. GONE TO HELL TO FIGHT THE DEVIL."

WAR
STORY

NIGHTINGALE

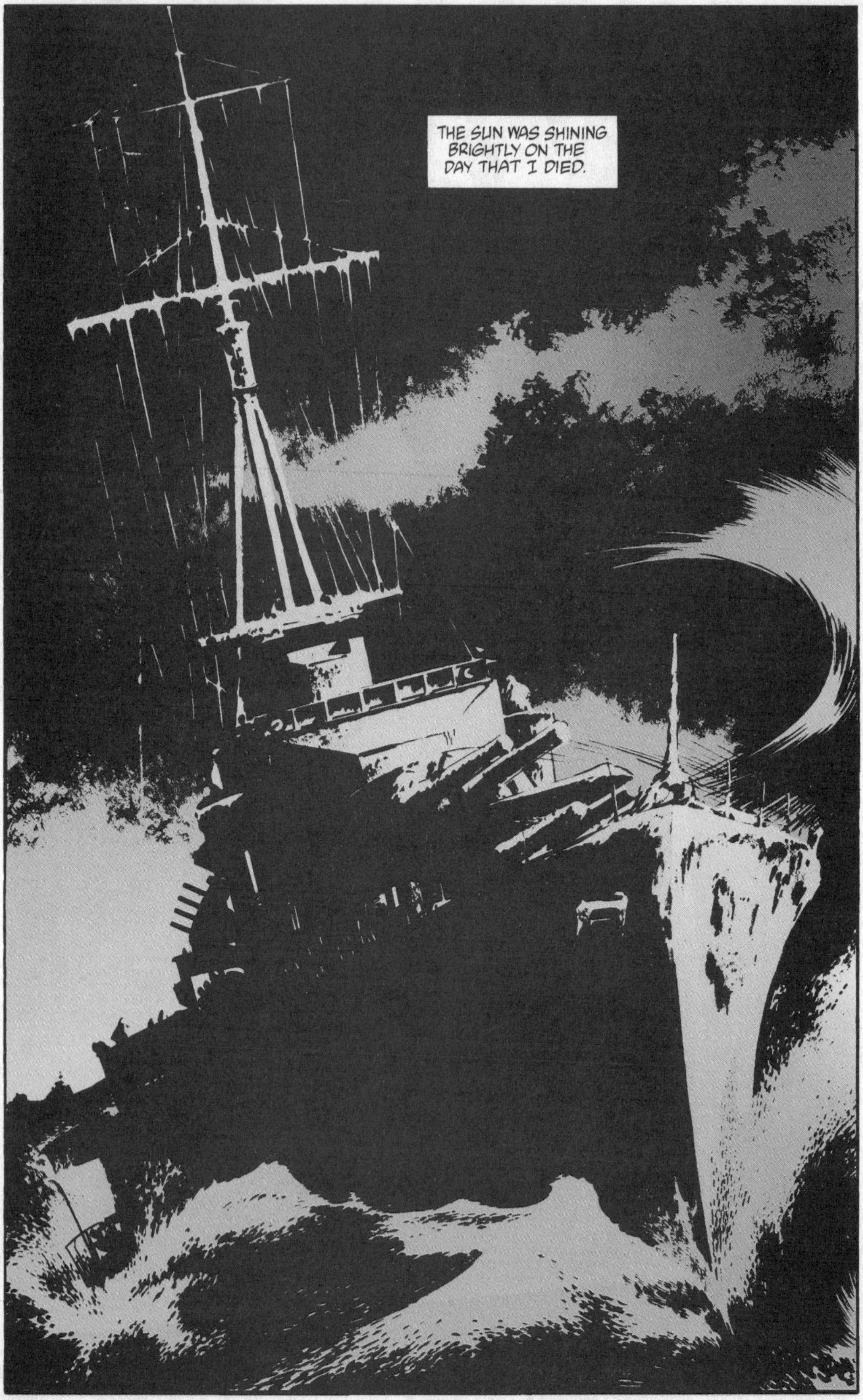
THE SUN WAS SHINING BRIGHTLY ON THE DAY THAT I DIED.

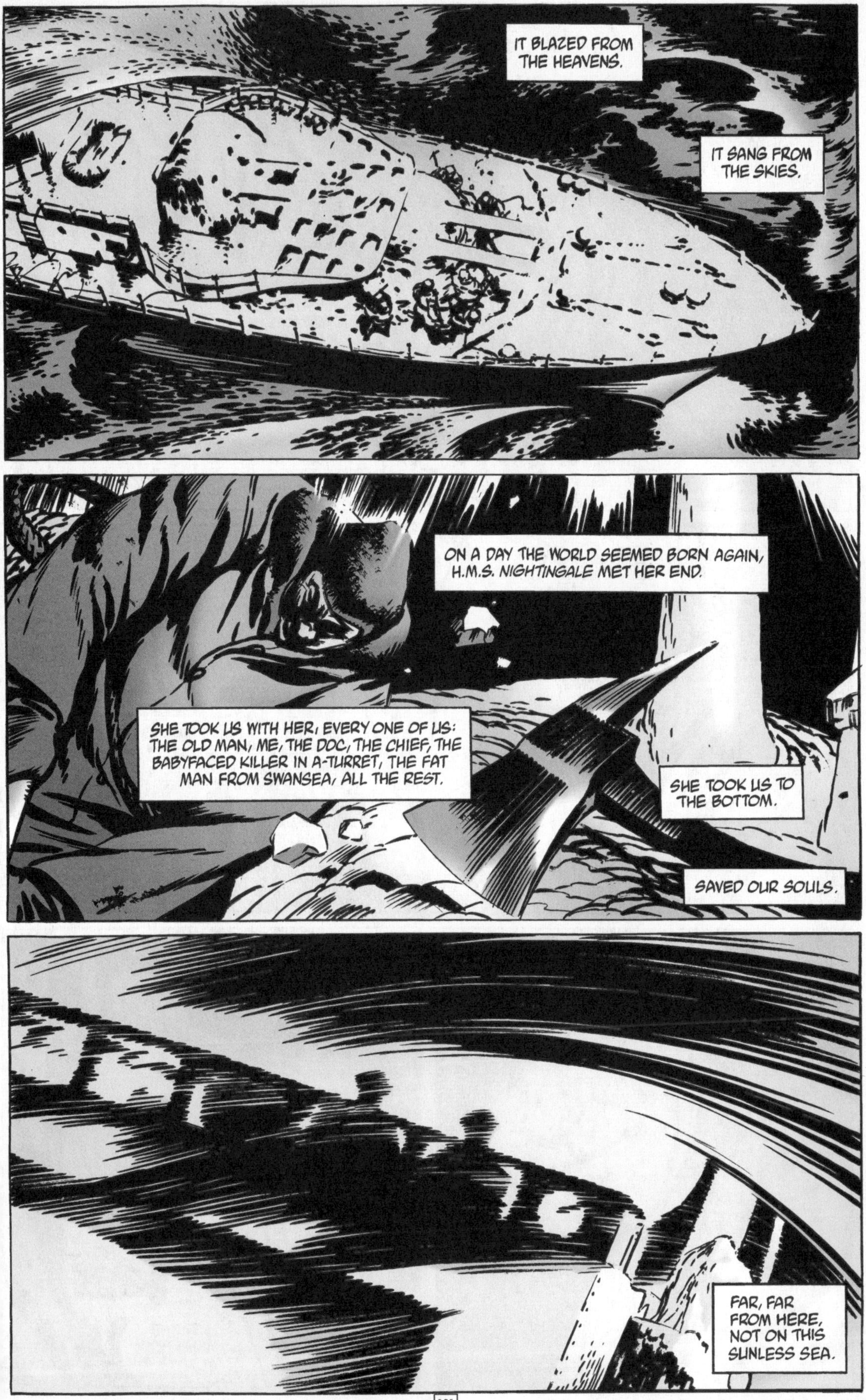
IT BLAZED FROM THE HEAVENS.
IT SANG FROM THE SKIES.
ON A DAY THE WORLD SEEMED BORN AGAIN, H.M.S. NIGHTINGALE MET HER END.
SHE TOOK US WITH HER, EVERY ONE OF US: THE OLD MAN, ME, THE DOC, THE CHIEF, THE BABYFACED KILLER IN A-TURRET, THE FAT MAN FROM SWANSEA, ALL THE REST.
SHE TOOK US TO THE BOTTOM.
SAVED OUR SOULS.
FAR, FAR FROM HERE, NOT ON THIS SUNLESS SEA.

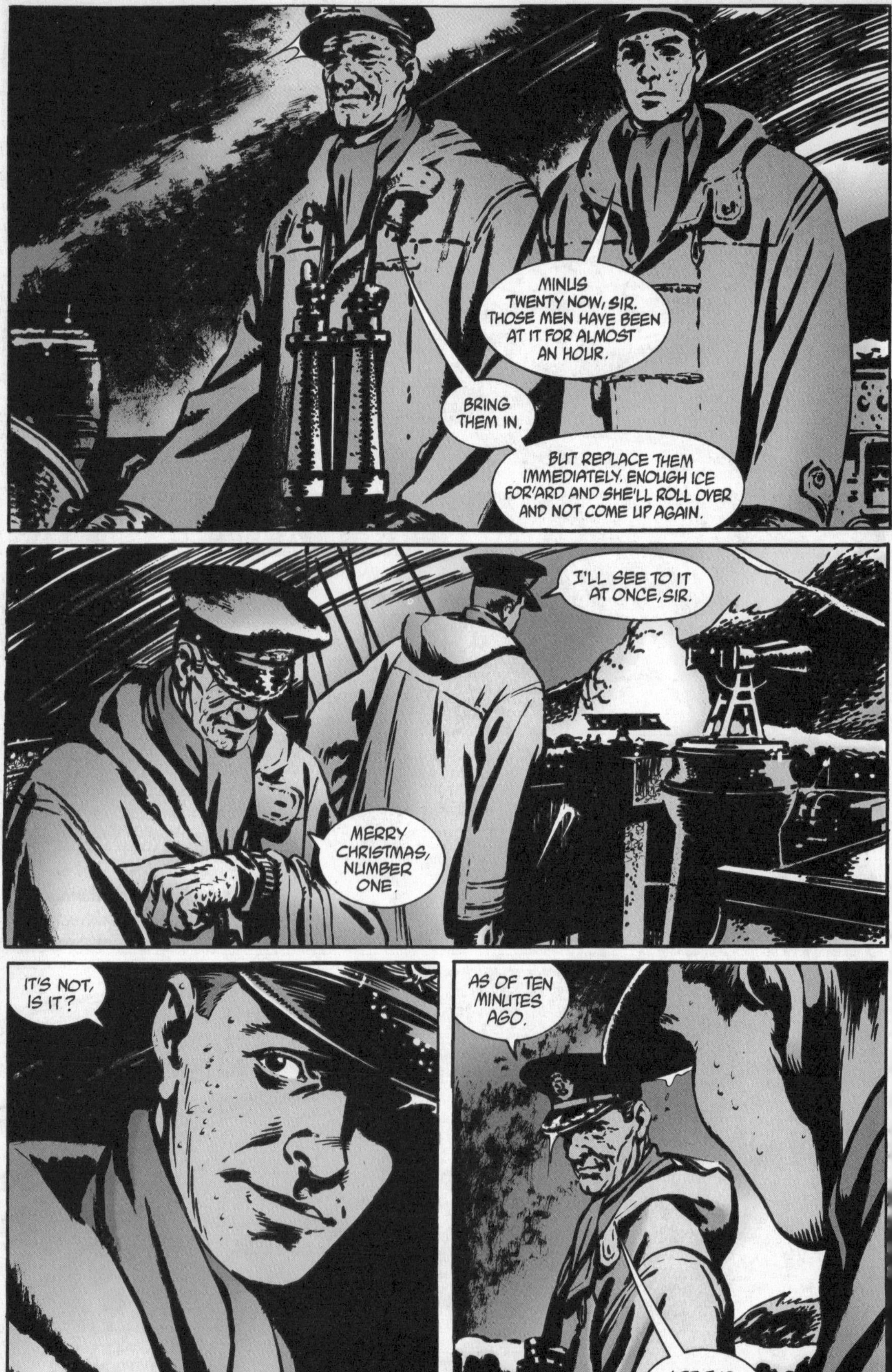
MINUS TWENTY NOW, SIR. THOSE MEN HAVE BEEN AT IT FOR ALMOST AN HOUR.
BRING THEM IN.
BUT REPLACE THEM IMMEDIATELY. ENOUGH ICE FOR'ARD AND SHE'LL ROLL OVER AND NOT COME UP AGAIN.
I'LL SEE TO IT AT ONCE, SIR.
MERRY CHRISTMAS, NUMBER ONE.
IT'S NOT, IS IT?
AS OF TEN MINUTES AGO.
LET THE MEN KNOW, WILL YOU?

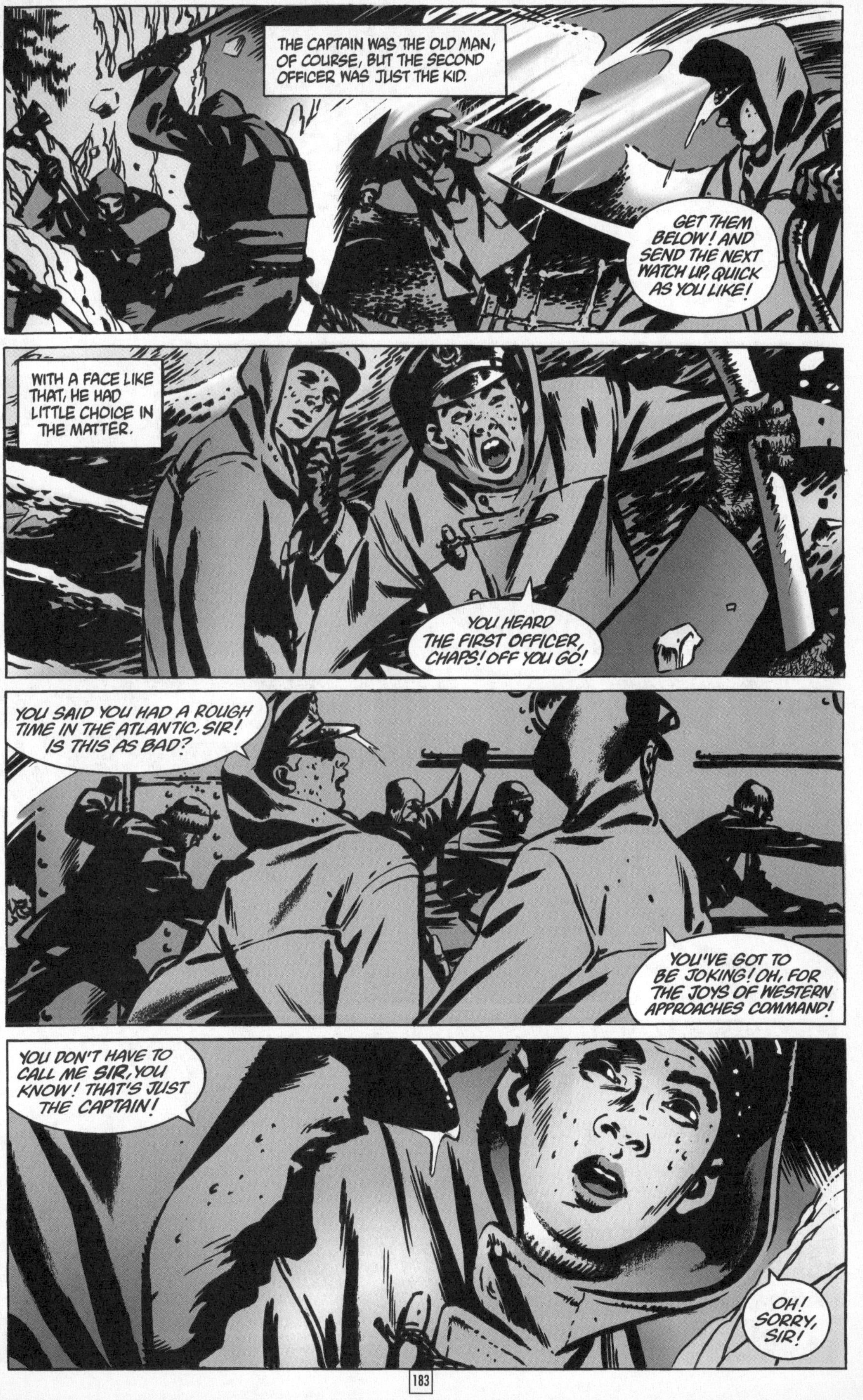

THE CAPTAIN WAS THE OLD MAN, OF COURSE, BUT THE SECOND OFFICER WAS JUST THE KID.
GET THEM BELOW! AND SEND THE NEXT WATCH UP, QUICK AS YOU LIKE!
WITH A FACE LIKE THAT, HE HAD LITTLE CHOICE IN THE MATTER.
YOU HEARD THE FIRST OFFICER, CHAPS! OFF YOU GO!
YOU SAID YOU HAD A ROUGH TIME IN THE ATLANTIC, SIR! IS THIS AS BAD?
YOU'VE GOT TO BE JOKING! OH, FOR THE JOYS OF WESTERN APPROACHES COMMAND!
YOU DON'T HAVE TO CALL ME SIR, YOU KNOW! THAT'S JUST THE CAPTAIN!
OH! SORRY, SIR!

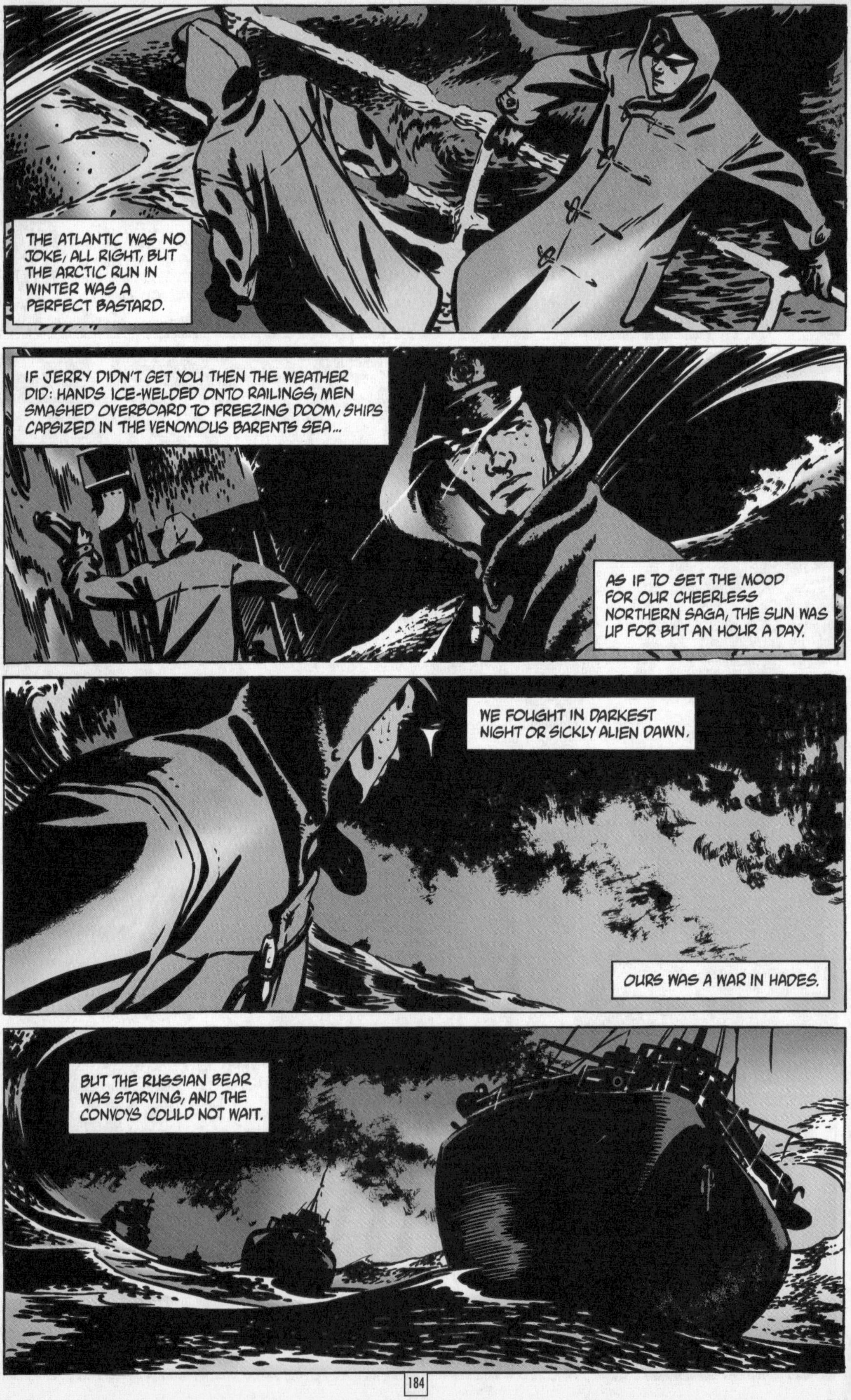
THE ATLANTIC WAS NO JOKE, ALL RIGHT, BUT THE ARCTIC RUN IN WINTER WAS A PERFECT BASTARD.
IF JERRY DIDN'T GET YOU THEN THE WEATHER DID: HANDS ICE-WELDED ONTO RAILINGS, MEN SMASHED OVERBOARD TO FREEZING DOOM, SHIPS CAPSIZED IN THE VENOMOUS BARENTS SEA...
AS IF TO SET THE MOOD FOR OUR CHEERLESS NORTHERN SAGA, THE SUN WAS UP FOR BUT AN HOUR A DAY.
WE FOUGHT IN DARKEST NIGHT OR SICKLY ALIEN DAWN.
OURS WAS A WAR IN HADES.
BUT THE RUSSIAN BEAR WAS STARVING, AND THE CONVOYS COULD NOT WAIT.

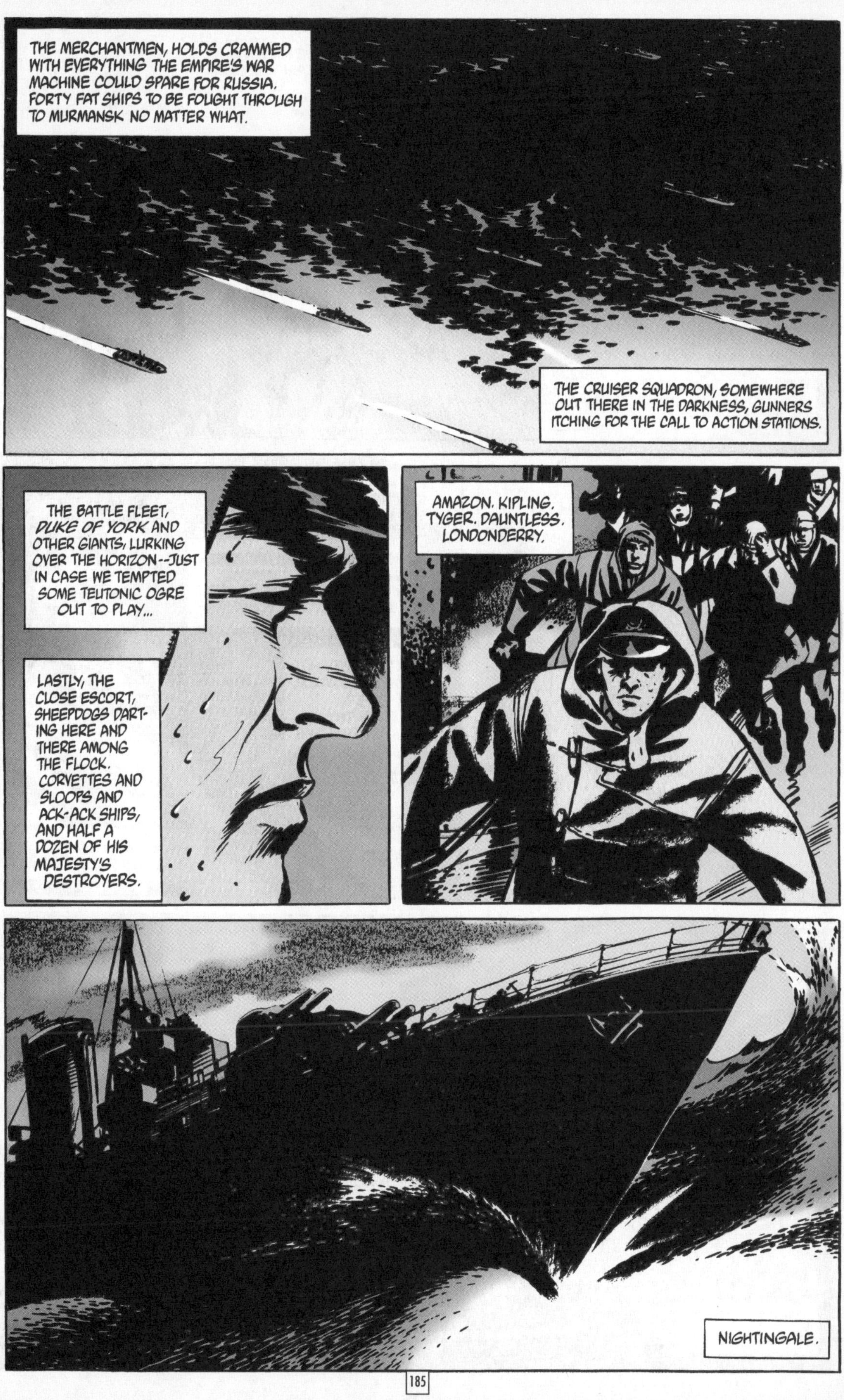
THE MERCHANTMEN, HOLDS CRAMMED WITH EVERYTHING THE EMPIRE'S WAR MACHINE COULD SPARE FOR RUSSIA. FORTY FAT SHIPS TO BE FOUGHT THROUGH TO MURMANSK NO MATTER WHAT.
THE CRUISER SQUADRON, SOMEWHERE OUT THERE IN THE DARKNESS, GUNNERS ITCHING FOR THE CALL TO ACTION STATIONS.
THE BATTLE FLEET, *DUKE OF YORK* AND OTHER GIANTS, LURKING OVER THE HORIZON--JUST IN CASE WE TEMPTED SOME TEUTONIC OGRE OUT TO PLAY...
LASTLY, THE CLOSE ESCORT, SHEEPDOGS DARTING HERE AND THERE AMONG THE FLOCK. CORVETTES AND SLOOPS AND ACK-ACK SHIPS, AND HALF A DOZEN OF HIS MAJESTY'S DESTROYERS.
AMAZON. KIPLING. TYGER. DAUNTLESS. LONDONDERRY.
NIGHTINGALE.

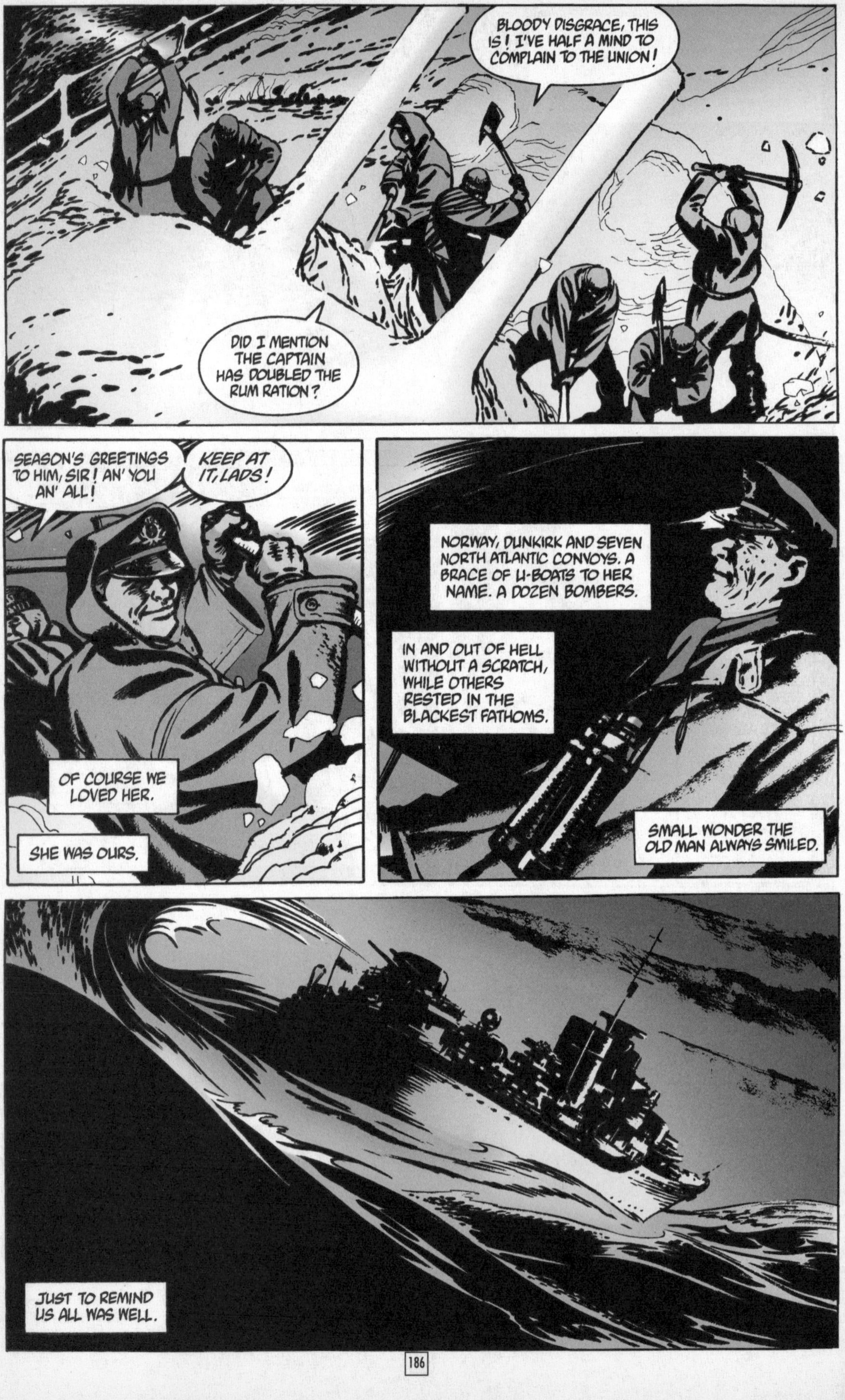
BLOODY DISGRACE, THIS IS! I'VE HALF A MIND TO COMPLAIN TO THE UNION!
DID I MENTION THE CAPTAIN HAS DOUBLED THE RUM RATION?
SEASON'S GREETINGS TO HIM, SIR! AN' YOU AN' ALL!
KEEP AT IT, LADS!
OF COURSE WE LOVED HER.
SHE WAS OURS.
NORWAY, DUNKIRK AND SEVEN NORTH ATLANTIC CONVOYS. A BRACE OF U-BOATS TO HER NAME. A DOZEN BOMBERS.
IN AND OUT OF HELL WITHOUT A SCRATCH, WHILE OTHERS RESTED IN THE BLACKEST FATHOMS.
SMALL WONDER THE OLD MAN ALWAYS SMILED.
JUST TO REMIND US ALL WAS WELL.

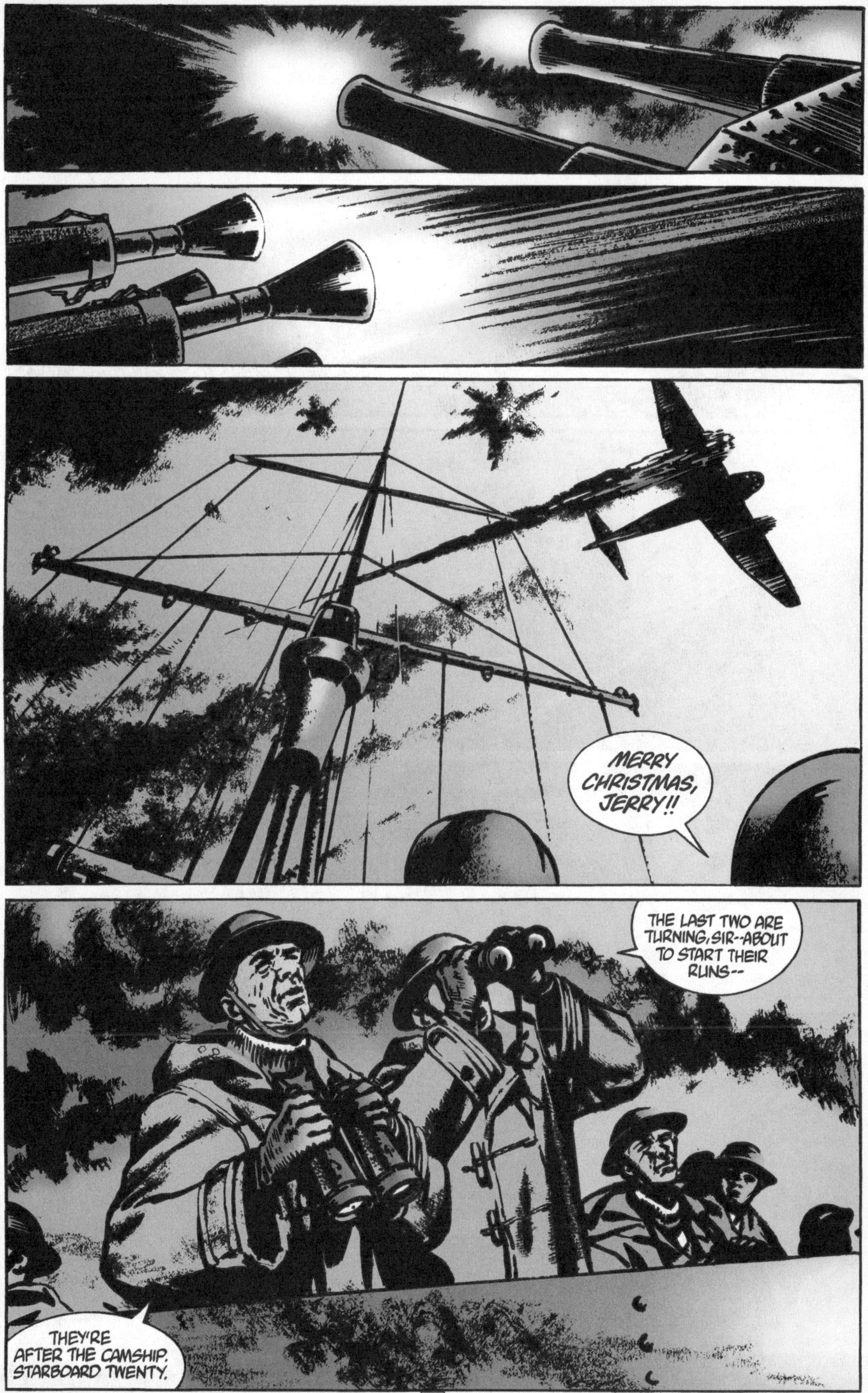
MERRY CHRISTMAS, JERRY!!
THE LAST TWO ARE TURNING, SIR--ABOUT TO START THEIR RUNS--
THEY'RE AFTER THE CAMSHIP. STARBOARD TWENTY.

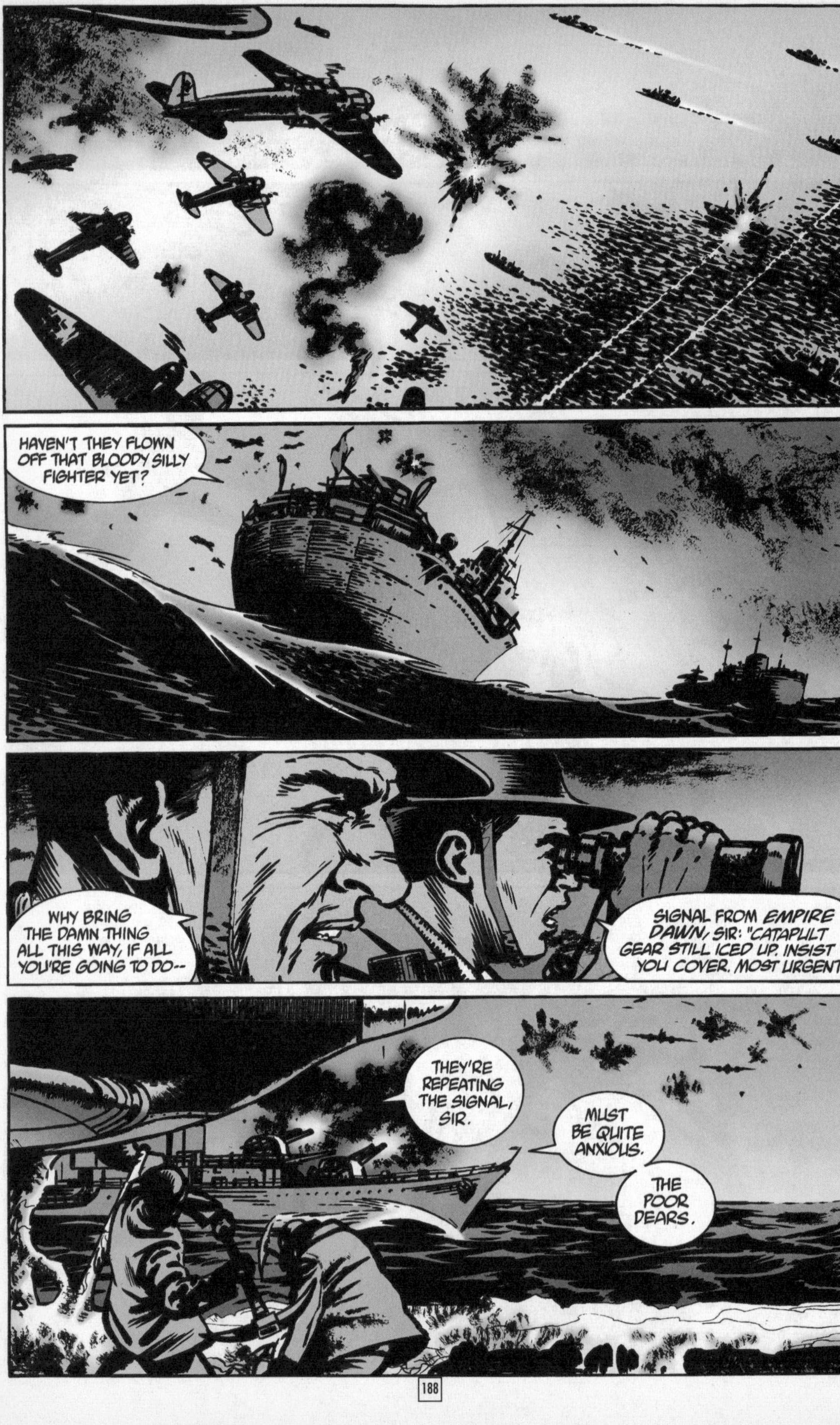
HAVEN'T THEY FLOWN OFF THAT BLOODY SILLY FIGHTER YET?
WHY BRING THE DAMN THING ALL THIS WAY, IF ALL YOU'RE GOING TO DO--
SIGNAL FROM *EMPIRE DAWN*, SIR: "CATAPULT GEAR STILL ICED UP. INSIST YOU COVER. MOST URGENT."
THEY'RE REPEATING THE SIGNAL, SIR.
MUST BE QUITE ANXIOUS.
THE POOR DEARS.

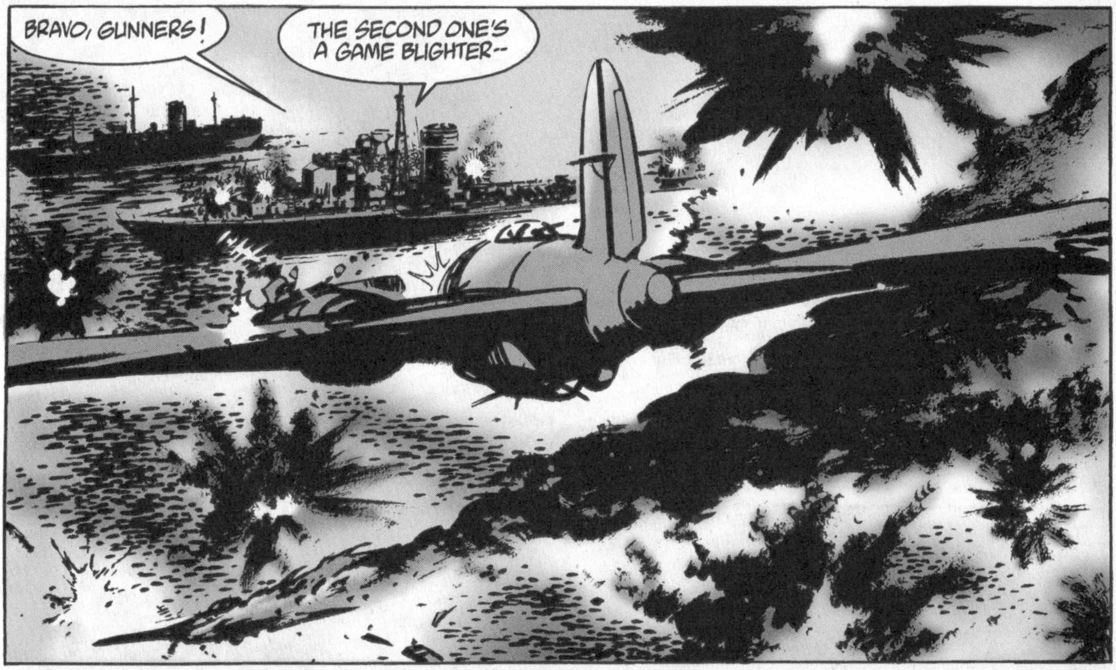
BRAVO, GUNNERS!
THE SECOND ONE'S A GAME BLIGHTER--

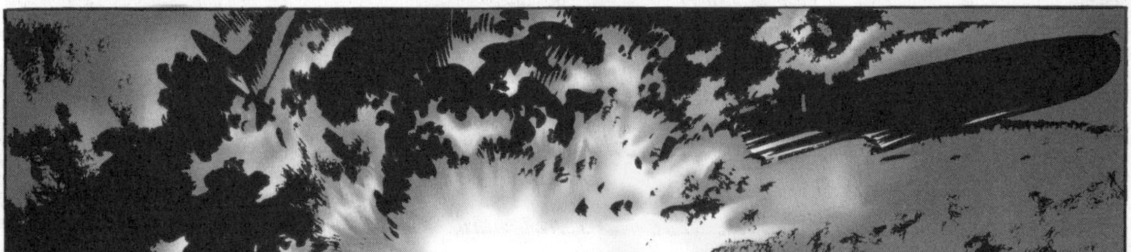

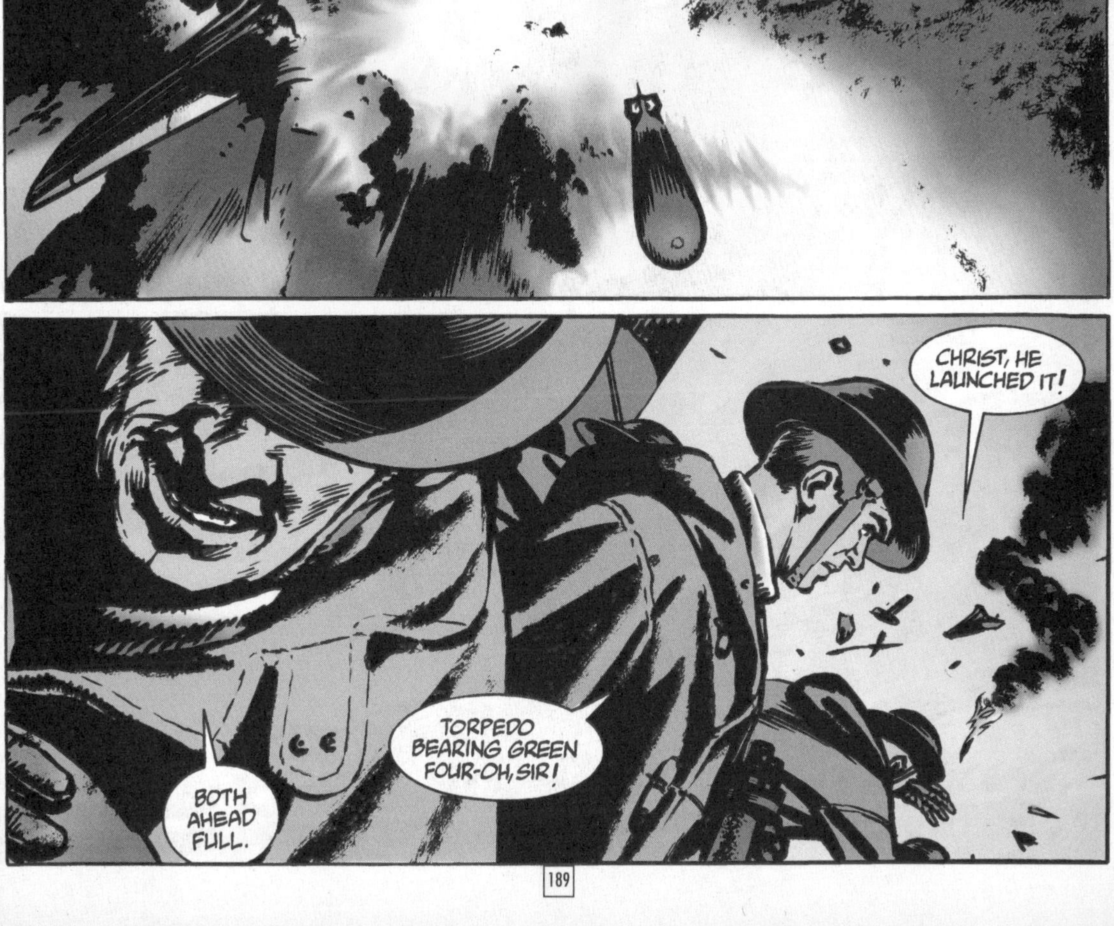
CHRIST, HE LAUNCHED IT!
TORPEDO BEARING GREEN FOUR-OH, SIR!
BOTH AHEAD FULL.

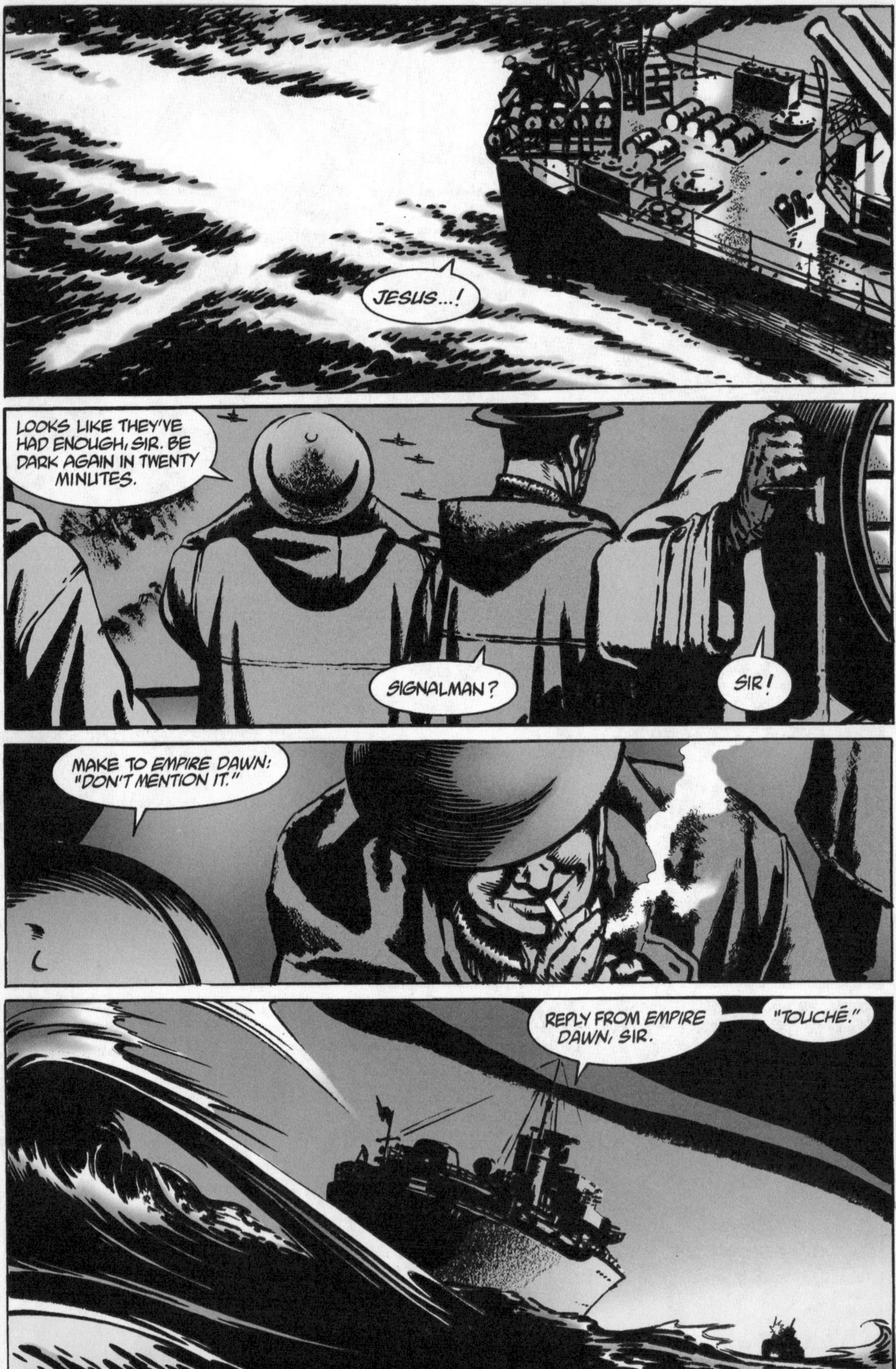
JESUS...!
LOOKS LIKE THEY'VE HAD ENOUGH, SIR. BE DARK AGAIN IN TWENTY MINUTES.
SIGNALMAN?
SIR!
MAKE TO EMPIRE DAWN: "DON'T MENTION IT."
REPLY FROM EMPIRE DAWN, SIR.
"TOUCHÉ."

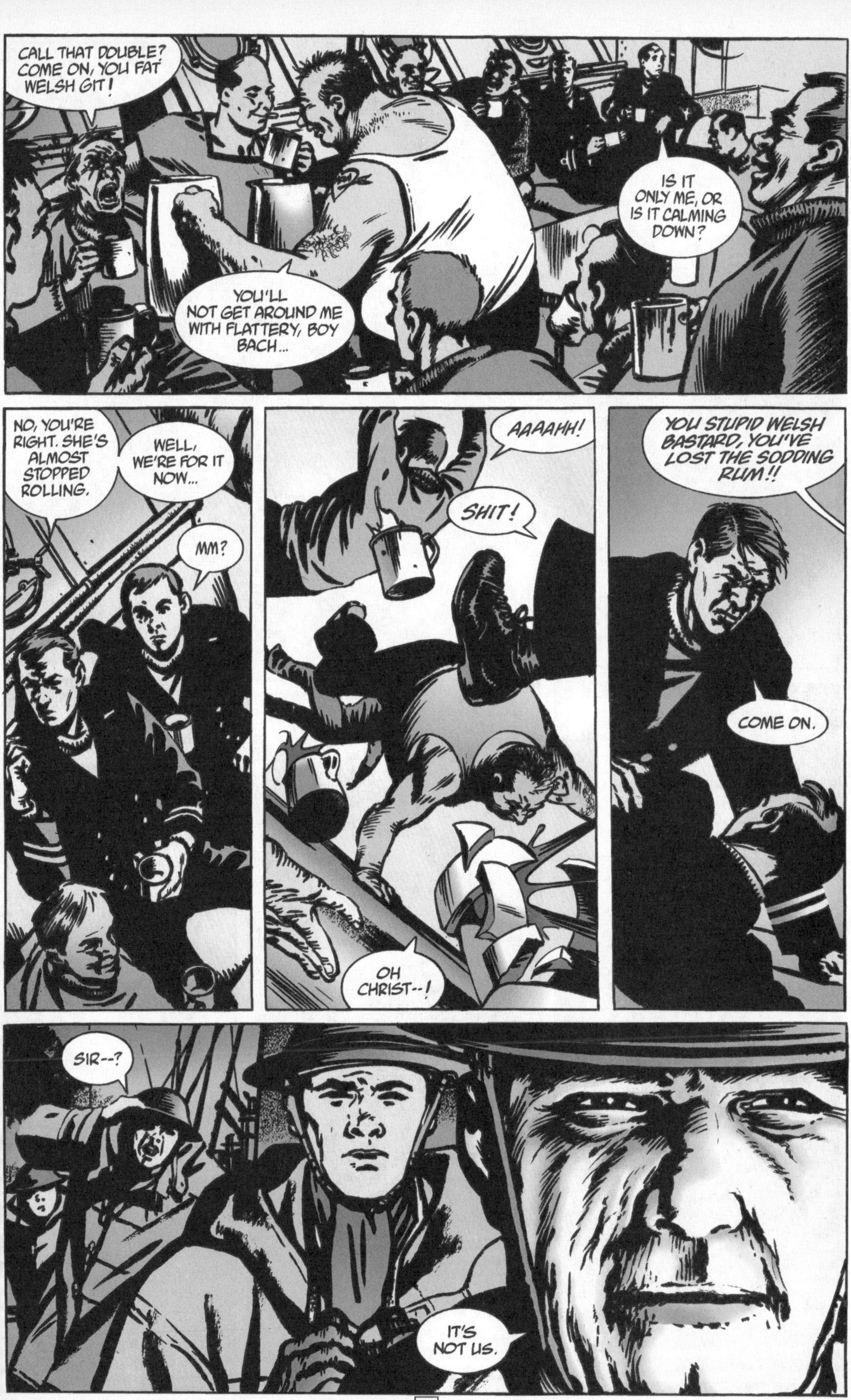
CALL THAT DOUBLE? COME ON, YOU FAT WELSH GIT!
IS IT ONLY ME, OR IS IT CALMING DOWN?
YOU'LL NOT GET AROUND ME WITH FLATTERY, BOY BACH...
NO, YOU'RE RIGHT. SHE'S ALMOST STOPPED ROLLING.
WELL, WE'RE FOR IT NOW...
MM?
AAAAHH!
SHIT!
OH CHRIST--!
YOU STUPID WELSH BASTARD, YOU'VE LOST THE SODDING RUM!!
COME ON.
SIR--?
IT'S NOT US.

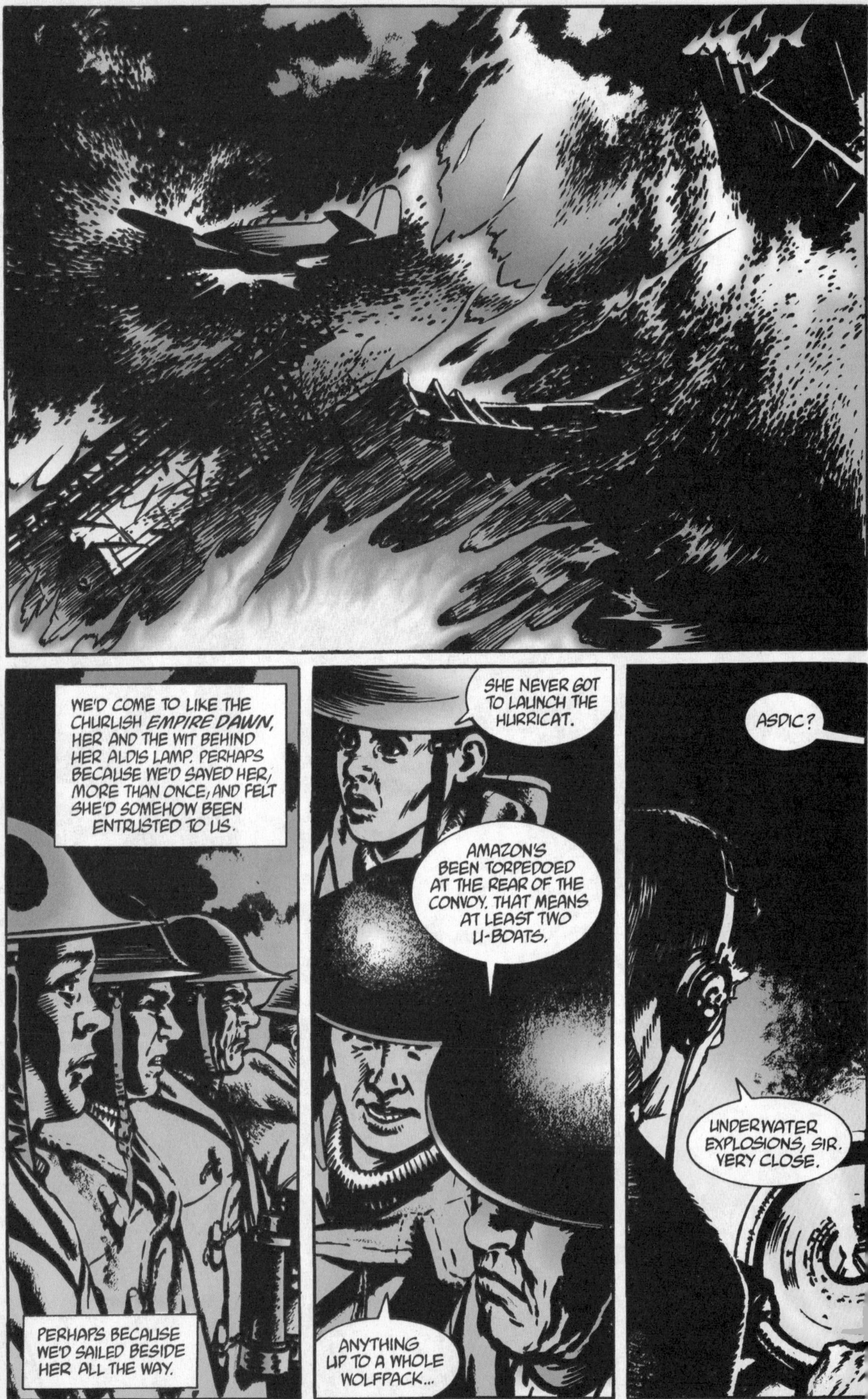
WE'D COME TO LIKE THE CHURLISH *EMPIRE DAWN*, HER AND THE WIT BEHIND HER ALDIS LAMP. PERHAPS BECAUSE WE'D SAVED HER, MORE THAN ONCE, AND FELT SHE'D SOMEHOW BEEN ENTRUSTED TO US.
PERHAPS BECAUSE WE'D SAILED BESIDE HER ALL THE WAY.
SHE NEVER GOT TO LAUNCH THE HURRICAT.
AMAZON'S BEEN TORPEDOED AT THE REAR OF THE CONVOY. THAT MEANS AT LEAST TWO U-BOATS.
ANYTHING UP TO A WHOLE WOLFPACK...
ASDIC?
UNDERWATER EXPLOSIONS, SIR. VERY CLOSE.

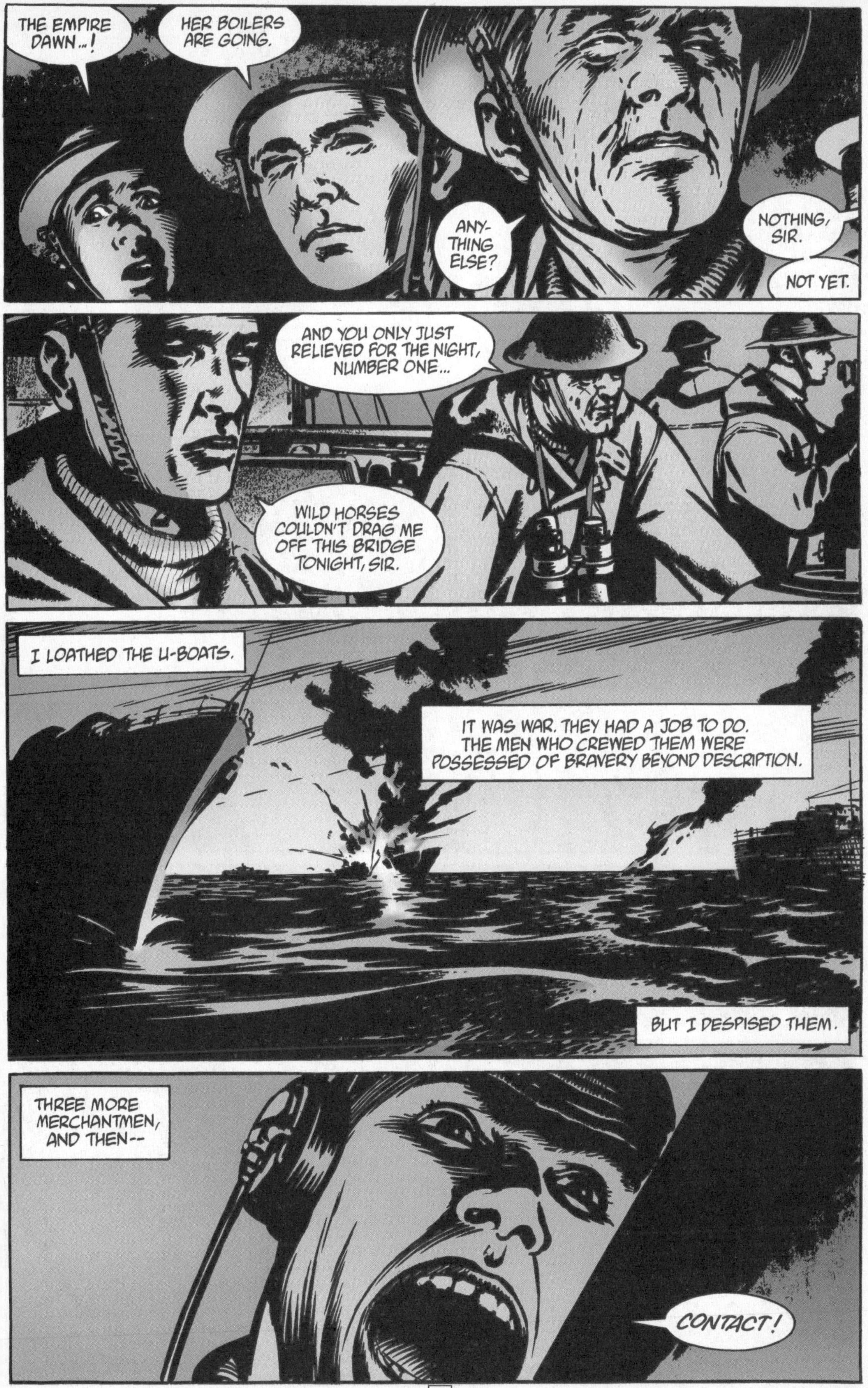
THE EMPIRE DAWN...!
HER BOILERS ARE GOING.
ANY-THING ELSE?
NOTHING, SIR.
NOT YET.
AND YOU ONLY JUST RELIEVED FOR THE NIGHT, NUMBER ONE...
WILD HORSES COULDN'T DRAG ME OFF THIS BRIDGE TONIGHT, SIR.
I LOATHED THE U-BOATS.
IT WAS WAR. THEY HAD A JOB TO DO. THE MEN WHO CREWED THEM WERE POSSESSED OF BRAVERY BEYOND DESCRIPTION.
BUT I DESPISED THEM.
THREE MORE MERCHANTMEN, AND THEN--
CONTACT!

CONTACT BEARING RED FOUR-OH! RANGE THIRTEEN HUNDRED YARDS!
PORT TWENTY! STAND BY DEPTH CHARGE, SHALLOW FUSE!
CONTACT MOVING TO STARBOARD! SPEED FIVE KNOTS! RANGE THIRTEEN HUNDRED YARDS, DECREASING!
BOTH AHEAD FULL!
BOTH AHEAD FULL, SIR--
...RANGE FIVE HUNDRED YARDS, DECREASING! CONTACT NOW DEAD AHEAD!
RANGE FOUR-FIFTY!
FOUR!
...NOW!
FIRE!
FIRE!

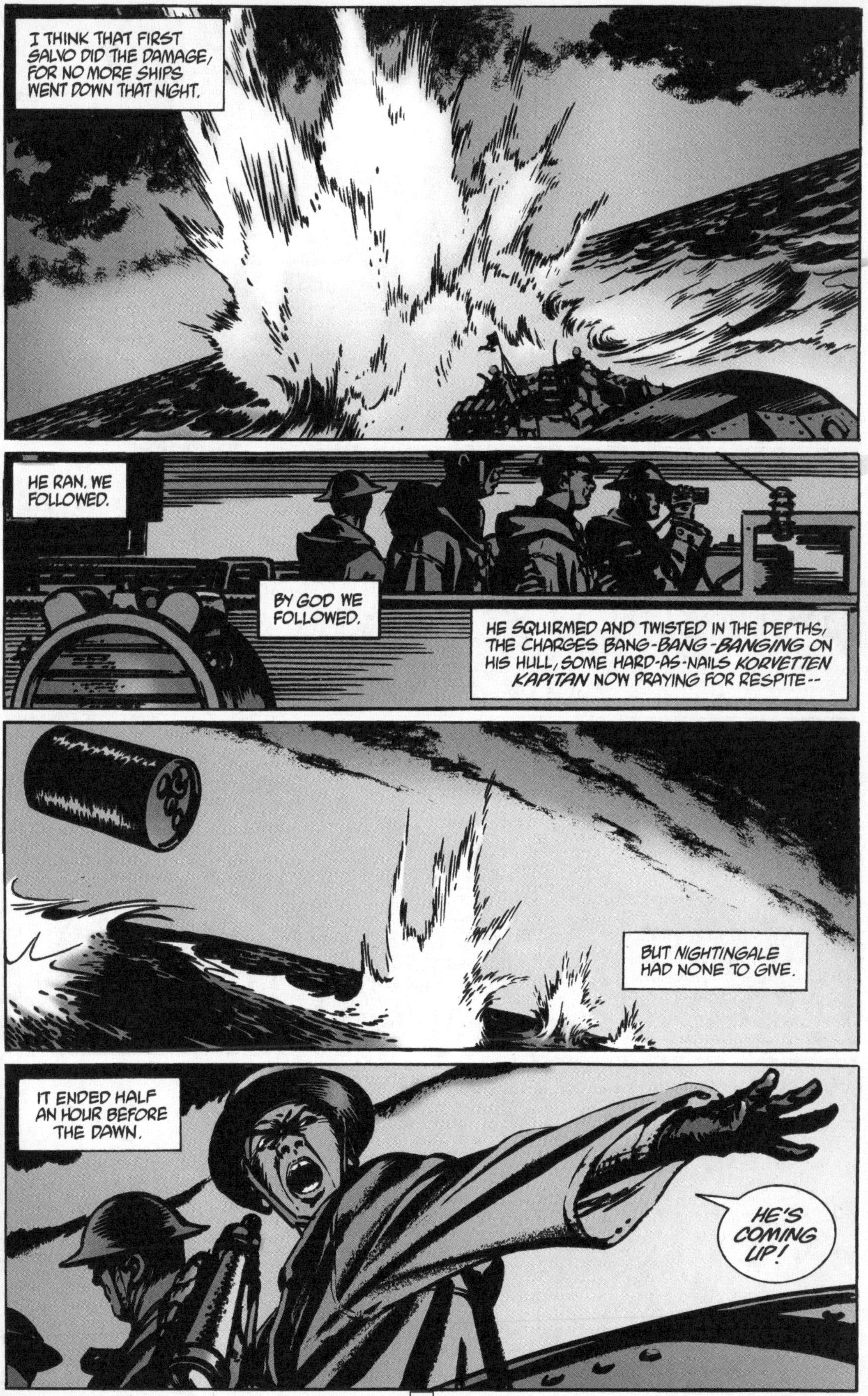
I THINK THAT FIRST SALVO DID THE DAMAGE, FOR NO MORE SHIPS WENT DOWN THAT NIGHT.
HE RAN. WE FOLLOWED.
BY GOD WE FOLLOWED.
HE SQUIRMED AND TWISTED IN THE DEPTHS, THE CHARGES BANG-*BANG*-*BANGING* ON HIS HULL, SOME HARD-AS-NAILS *KORVETTEN KAPITAN* NOW PRAYING FOR RESPITE--
BUT *NIGHTINGALE* HAD NONE TO GIVE.
IT ENDED HALF AN HOUR BEFORE THE DAWN.
HE'S COMING UP!

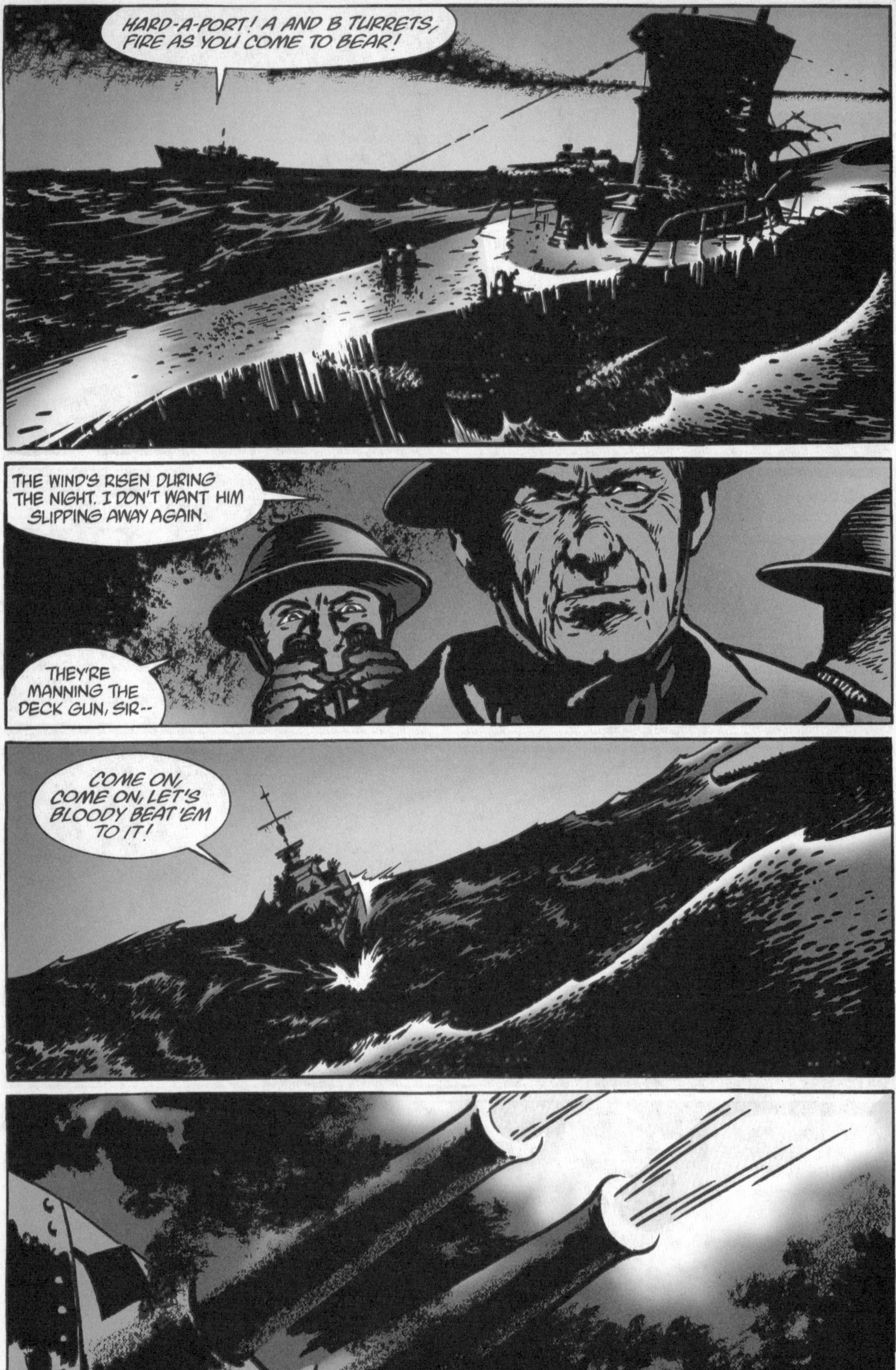
HARD-A-PORT! A AND B TURRETS, FIRE AS YOU COME TO BEAR!
THE WIND'S RISEN DURING THE NIGHT. I DON'T WANT HIM SLIPPING AWAY AGAIN.
THEY'RE MANNING THE DECK GUN, SIR--
COME ON, COME ON, LET'S BLOODY BEAT 'EM TO IT!

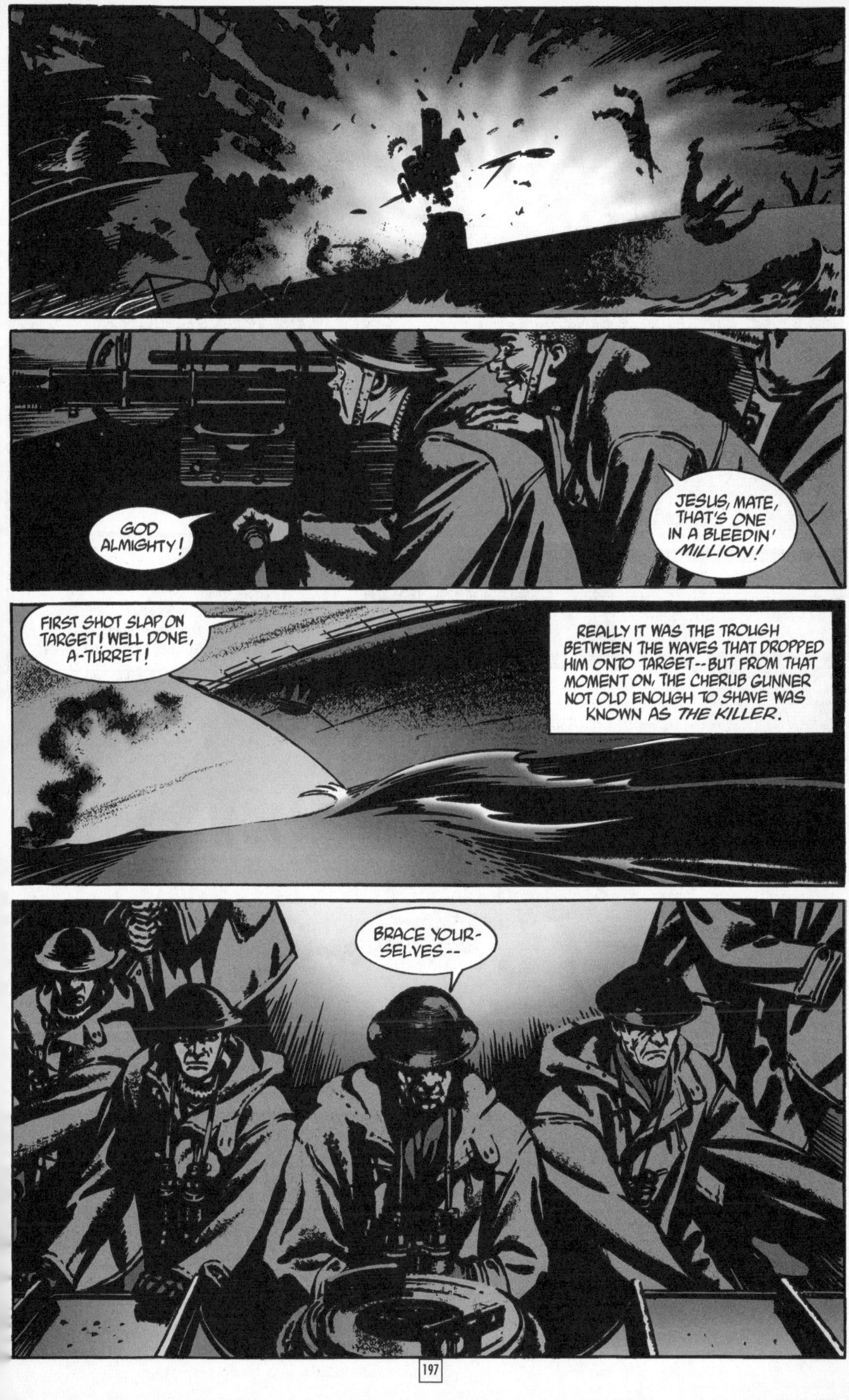
GOD ALMIGHTY!
JESUS, MATE, THAT'S ONE IN A BLEEDIN' MILLION!
FIRST SHOT SLAP ON TARGET! WELL DONE, A-TURRET!
REALLY IT WAS THE TROUGH BETWEEN THE WAVES THAT DROPPED HIM ONTO TARGET--BUT FROM THAT MOMENT ON, THE CHERUB GUNNER NOT OLD ENOUGH TO SHAVE WAS KNOWN AS THE KILLER.
BRACE YOUR-SELVES--

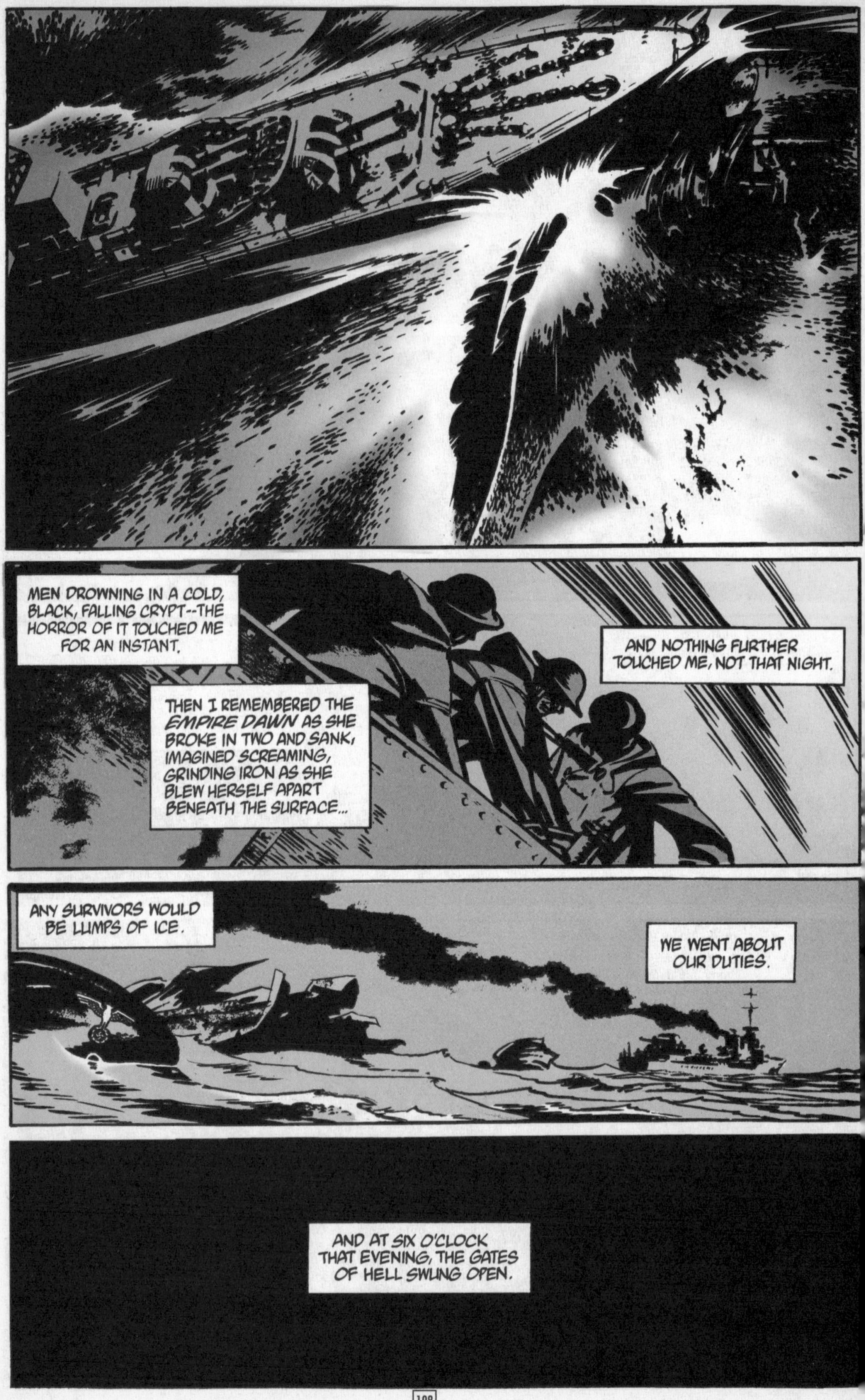
MEN DROWNING IN A COLD, BLACK, FALLING CRYPT--THE HORROR OF IT TOUCHED ME FOR AN INSTANT.
THEN I REMEMBERED THE *EMPIRE DAWN* AS SHE BROKE IN TWO AND SANK, IMAGINED SCREAMING, GRINDING IRON AS SHE BLEW HERSELF APART BENEATH THE SURFACE...
AND NOTHING FURTHER TOUCHED ME, NOT THAT NIGHT.
ANY SURVIVORS WOULD BE LUMPS OF ICE.
WE WENT ABOUT OUR DUTIES.
AND AT SIX O'CLOCK THAT EVENING, THE GATES OF HELL SWUNG OPEN.

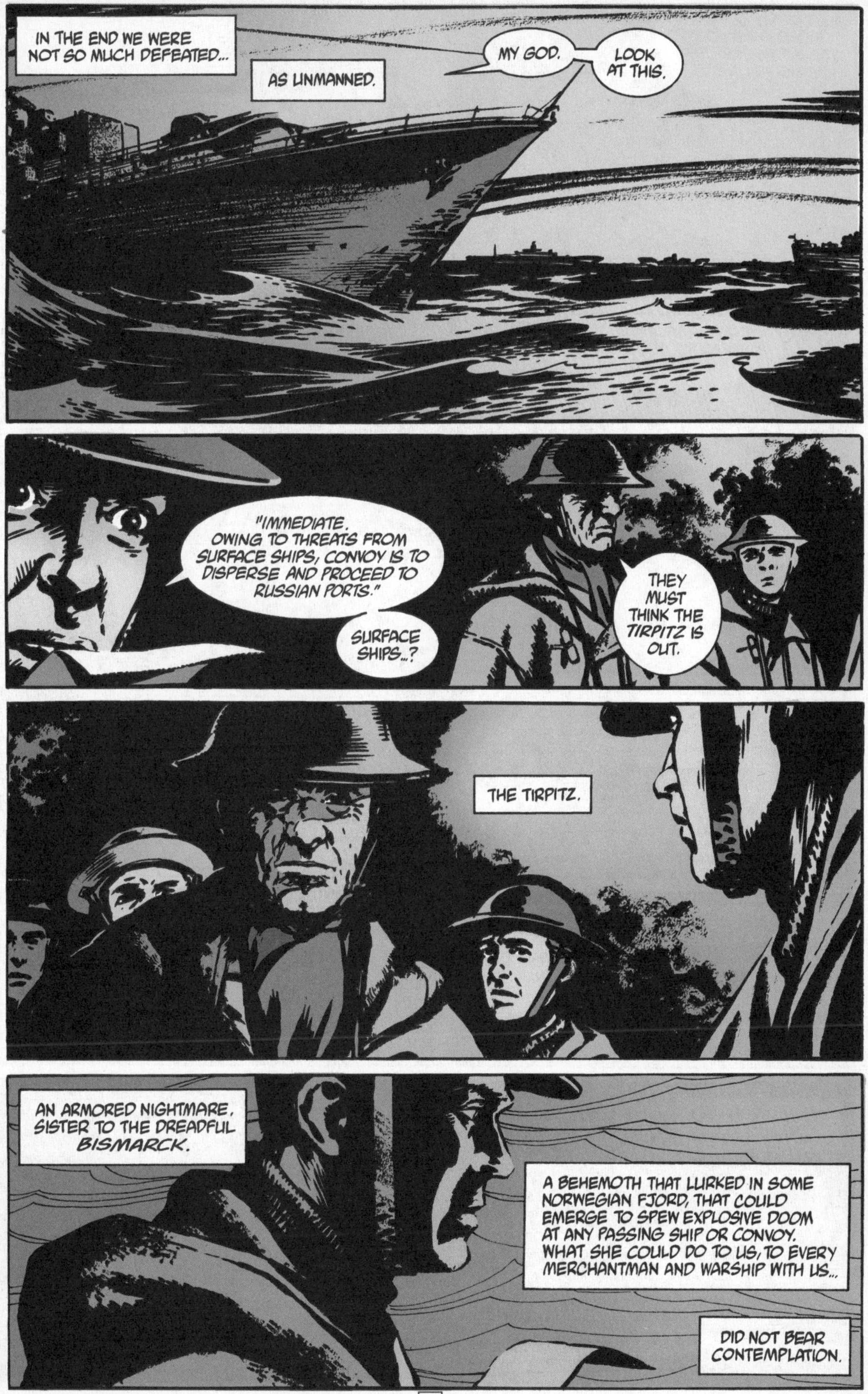

IN THE END WE WERE NOT SO MUCH DEFEATED...
AS UNMANNED.
MY GOD.
LOOK AT THIS.
"IMMEDIATE. OWING TO THREATS FROM SURFACE SHIPS, CONVOY IS TO DISPERSE AND PROCEED TO RUSSIAN PORTS."
SURFACE SHIPS...?
THEY MUST THINK THE *TIRPITZ* IS OUT.
THE TIRPITZ.
AN ARMORED NIGHTMARE, SISTER TO THE DREADFUL *BISMARCK*.
A BEHEMOTH THAT LURKED IN SOME NORWEGIAN FJORD, THAT COULD EMERGE TO SPEW EXPLOSIVE DOOM AT ANY PASSING SHIP OR CONVOY. WHAT SHE COULD DO TO US, TO EVERY MERCHANTMAN AND WARSHIP WITH US...
DID NOT BEAR CONTEMPLATION.

SPLIT UP THE CONVOY? IF THOSE SHIPS GO ON WITHOUT ESCORT THE U-BOATS WILL EAT THEM ALIVE...

WE CAN'T FIGHT THEM PAST THE *TIRPITZ*, SIR. THE BEAST'LL SEND THE LOT TO THE BOTTOM.

BEST TO LEAVE THE JOB TO THE BATTLE FLEET NOW.

THAT'S ASSUMING THE ADMIRALTY'S INTELLIGENCE IS CORRECT.

WELL... THEY MUST KNOW WHAT THEY'RE DOING, BACK IN LONDON, SIR...

INTERESTING THEORY, NUMBER ONE.

FROM THE ADMIRALTY, SIR!

"MOST IMMEDIATE." IT SAID.

"CONVOY IS TO SCATTER."

THAT'S THAT, THEN.

IT WAS ONLY LATER -- WITH THE *NIGHTINGALE* CLOSED UP TO ACTION STATIONS AND THE CONVOY STREWN ACROSS THE MIDNIGHT SEAS BEHIND US -- THAT I REALIZED.

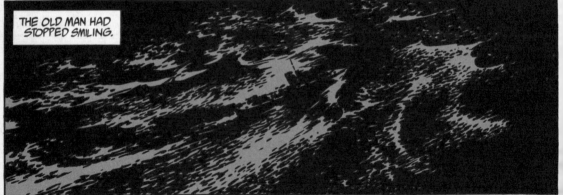

THE OLD MAN HAD STOPPED SMILING.

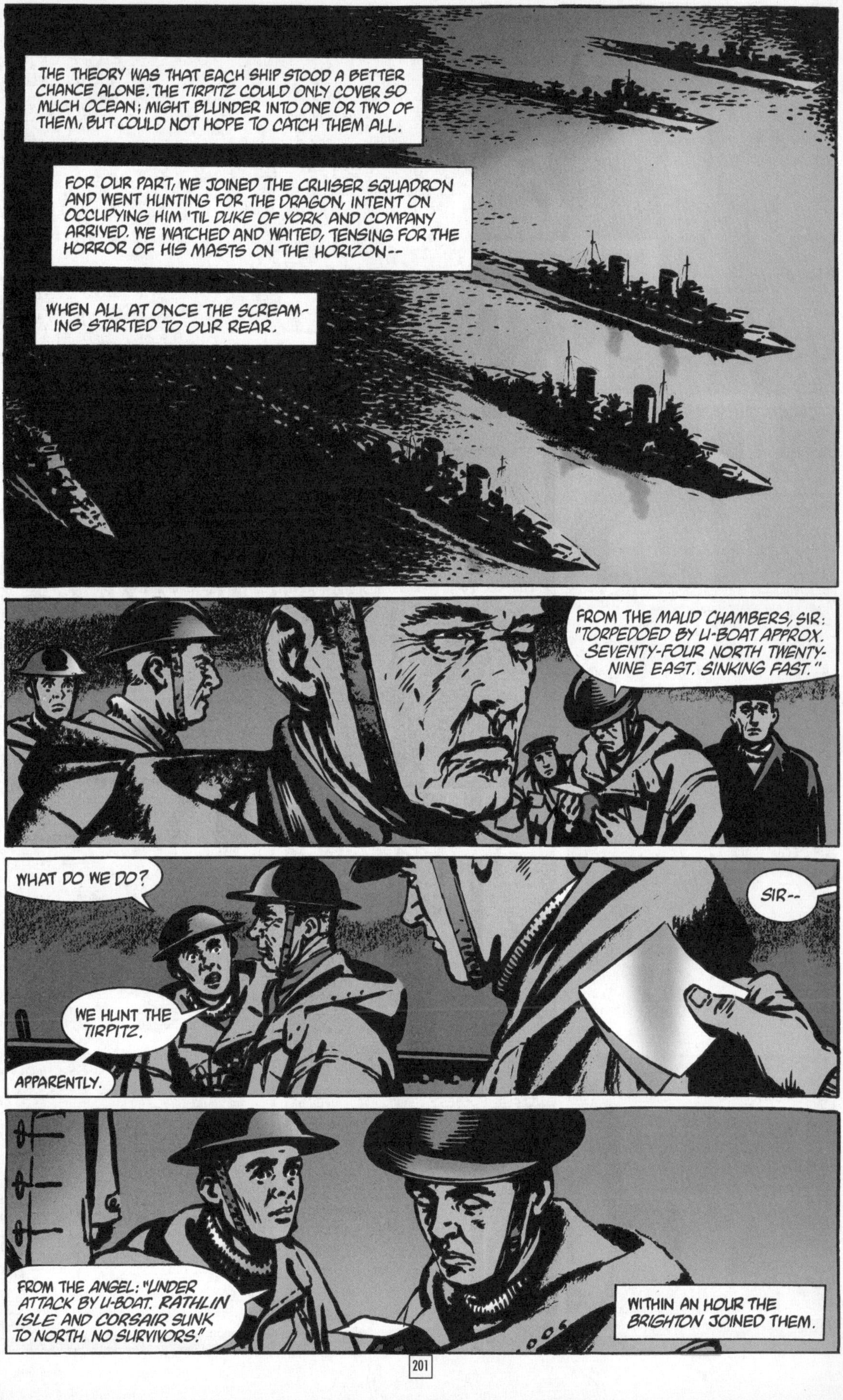
THE THEORY WAS THAT EACH SHIP STOOD A BETTER CHANCE ALONE. THE TIRPITZ COULD ONLY COVER SO MUCH OCEAN; MIGHT BLUNDER INTO ONE OR TWO OF THEM, BUT COULD NOT HOPE TO CATCH THEM ALL.
FOR OUR PART, WE JOINED THE CRUISER SQUADRON AND WENT HUNTING FOR THE DRAGON, INTENT ON OCCUPYING HIM 'TIL DUKE OF YORK AND COMPANY ARRIVED. WE WATCHED AND WAITED, TENSING FOR THE HORROR OF HIS MASTS ON THE HORIZON--
WHEN ALL AT ONCE THE SCREAMING STARTED TO OUR REAR.
FROM THE MAUD CHAMBERS, SIR: "TORPEDOED BY U-BOAT APPROX. SEVENTY-FOUR NORTH TWENTY-NINE EAST. SINKING FAST."
WHAT DO WE DO?
SIR--
WE HUNT THE TIRPITZ.
APPARENTLY.
FROM THE ANGEL: "UNDER ATTACK BY U-BOAT. RATHLIN ISLE AND CORSAIR SUNK TO NORTH. NO SURVIVORS."
WITHIN AN HOUR THE BRIGHTON JOINED THEM.

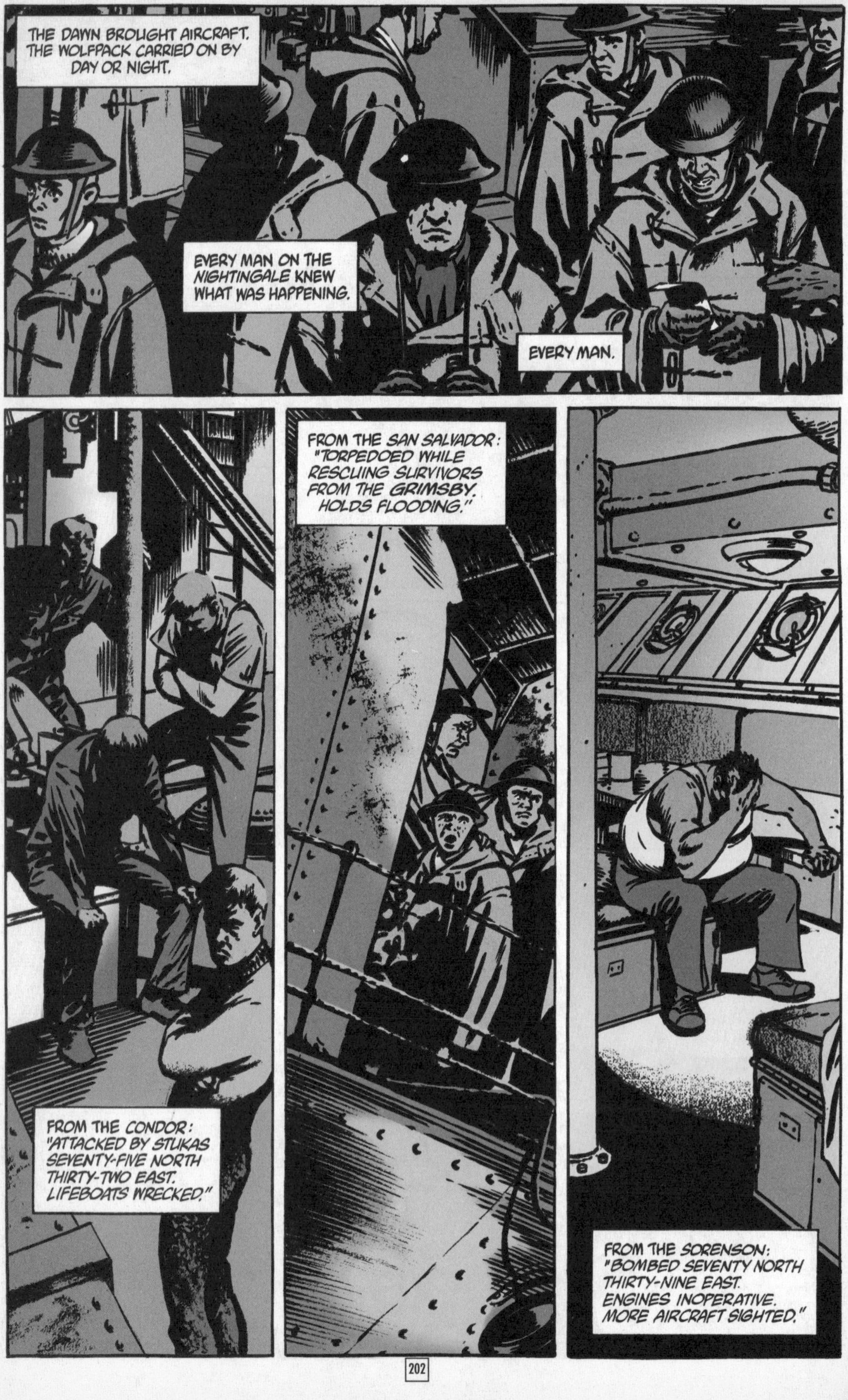
THE DAWN BROUGHT AIRCRAFT. THE WOLFPACK CARRIED ON BY DAY OR NIGHT.
EVERY MAN ON THE NIGHTINGALE KNEW WHAT WAS HAPPENING.
EVERY MAN.
FROM THE CONDOR: "ATTACKED BY STUKAS SEVENTY-FIVE NORTH THIRTY-TWO EAST. LIFEBOATS WRECKED."
FROM THE SAN SALVADOR: "TORPEDOED WHILE RESCUING SURVIVORS FROM THE GRIMSBY. HOLDS FLOODING."
FROM THE SORENSON: "BOMBED SEVENTY NORTH THIRTY-NINE EAST. ENGINES INOPERATIVE. MORE AIRCRAFT SIGHTED."

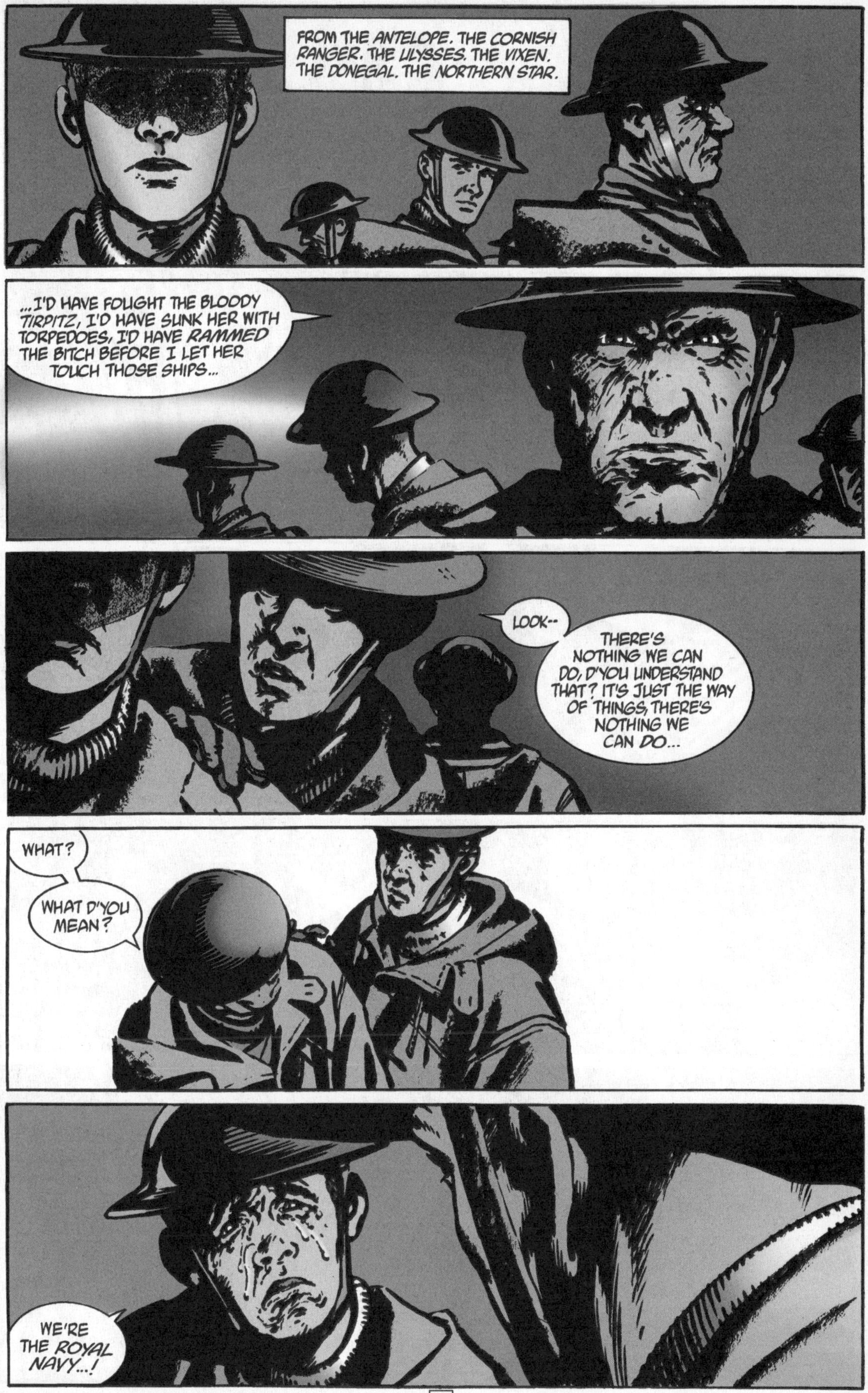
FROM THE ANTELOPE. THE CORNISH RANGER. THE ULYSSES. THE VIXEN. THE DONEGAL. THE NORTHERN STAR.
...I'D HAVE FOUGHT THE BLOODY TIRPITZ, I'D HAVE SUNK HER WITH TORPEDOES, I'D HAVE RAMMED THE BITCH BEFORE I LET HER TOUCH THOSE SHIPS...
LOOK--
THERE'S NOTHING WE CAN DO, D'YOU UNDERSTAND THAT? IT'S JUST THE WAY OF THINGS, THERE'S NOTHING WE CAN DO...
WHAT?
WHAT D'YOU MEAN?
WE'RE THE ROYAL NAVY...!

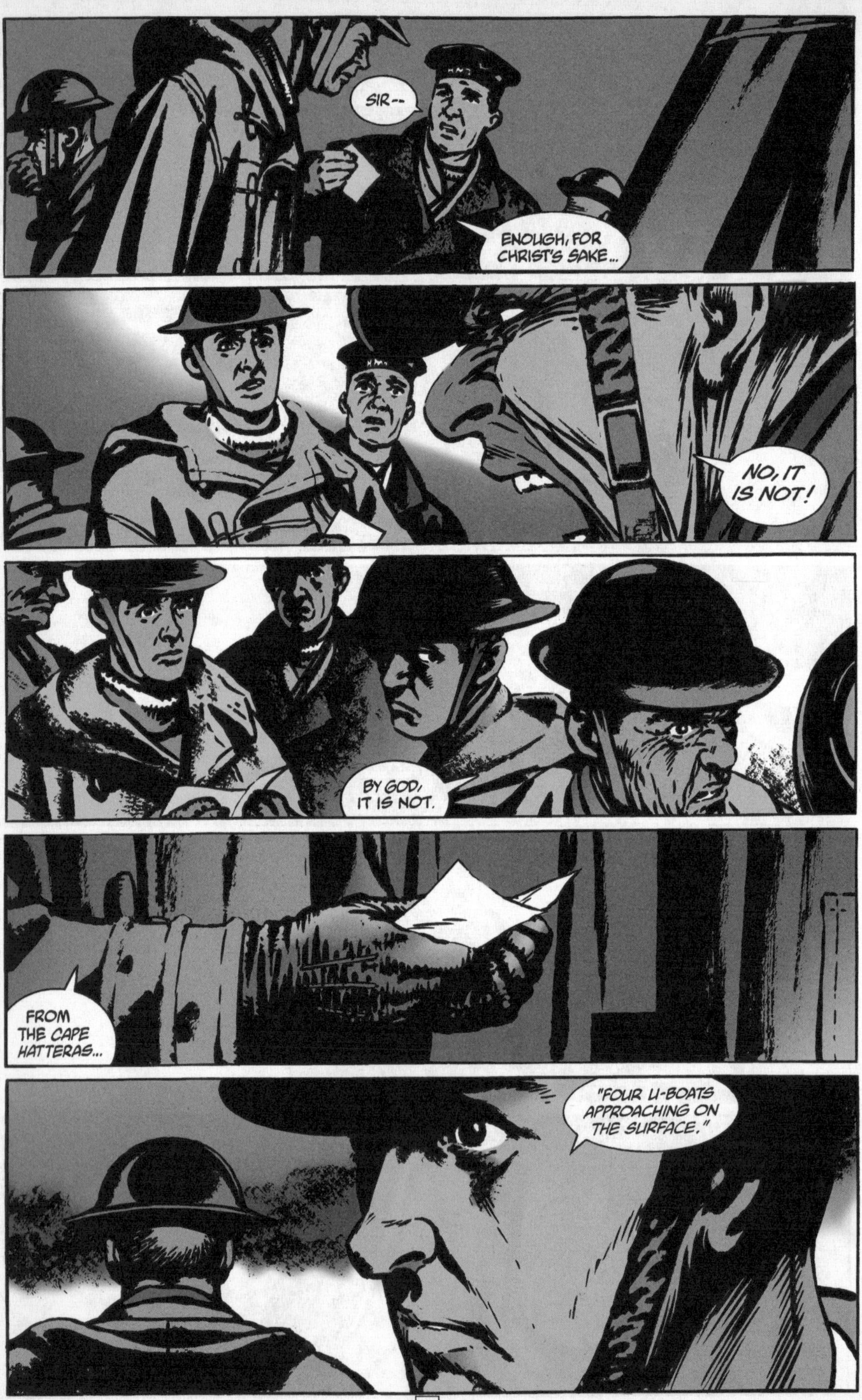
SIR--
ENOUGH, FOR CHRIST'S SAKE...
NO, IT IS NOT!
BY GOD, IT IS NOT.
FROM THE CAPE HATTERAS...
"FOUR U-BOATS APPROACHING ON THE SURFACE."

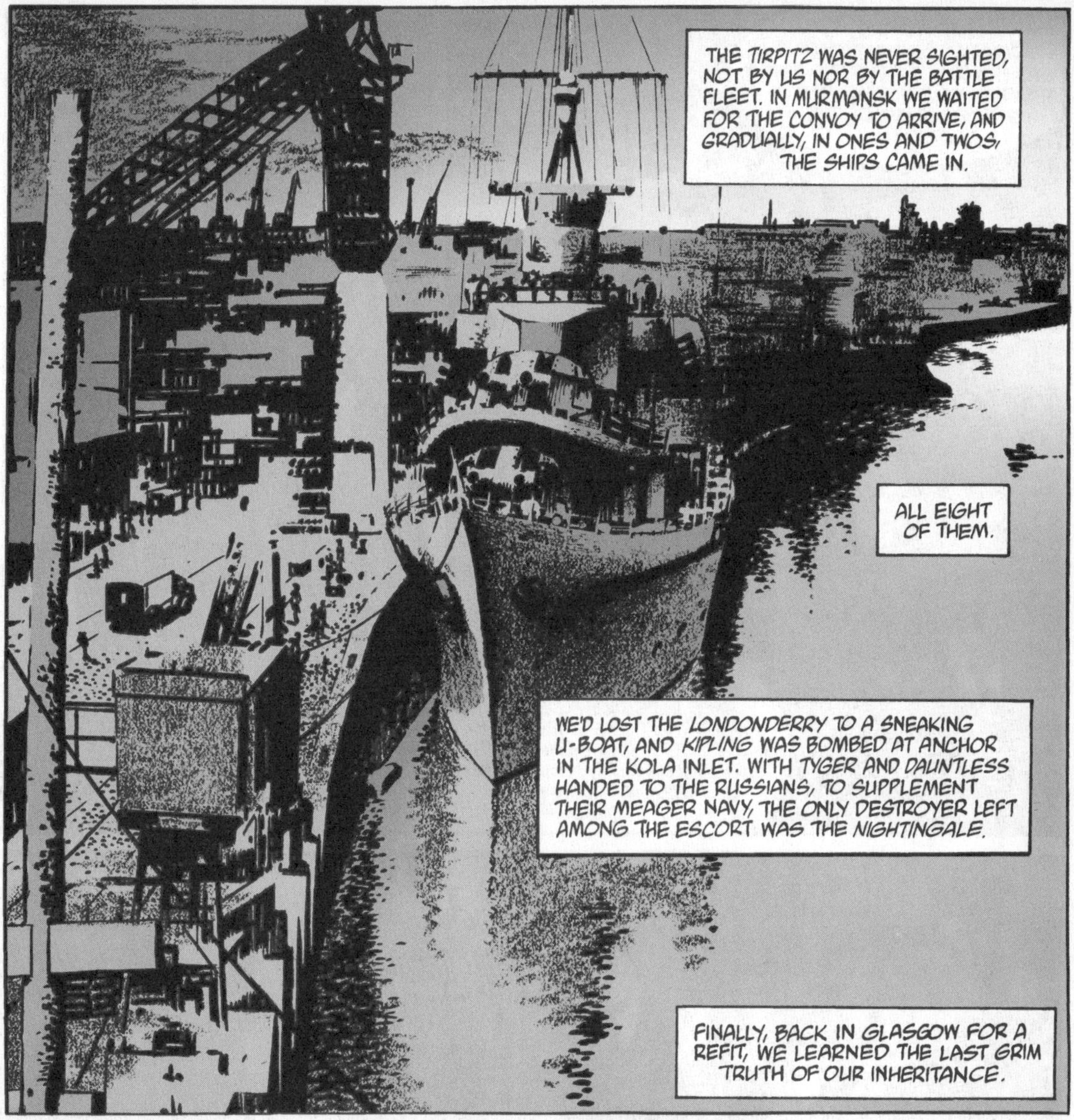
THE *TIRPITZ* WAS NEVER SIGHTED, NOT BY US NOR BY THE BATTLE FLEET. IN MURMANSK WE WAITED FOR THE CONVOY TO ARRIVE, AND GRADUALLY, IN ONES AND TWOS, THE SHIPS CAME IN.
ALL EIGHT OF THEM.
WE'D LOST THE *LONDONDERRY* TO A SNEAKING U-BOAT, AND *KIPLING* WAS BOMBED AT ANCHOR IN THE KOLA INLET. WITH *TYGER* AND *DAUNTLESS* HANDED TO THE RUSSIANS, TO SUPPLEMENT THEIR MEAGER NAVY, THE ONLY DESTROYER LEFT AMONG THE ESCORT WAS THE *NIGHTINGALE*.
FINALLY, BACK IN GLASGOW FOR A REFIT, WE LEARNED THE LAST GRIM TRUTH OF OUR INHERITANCE.

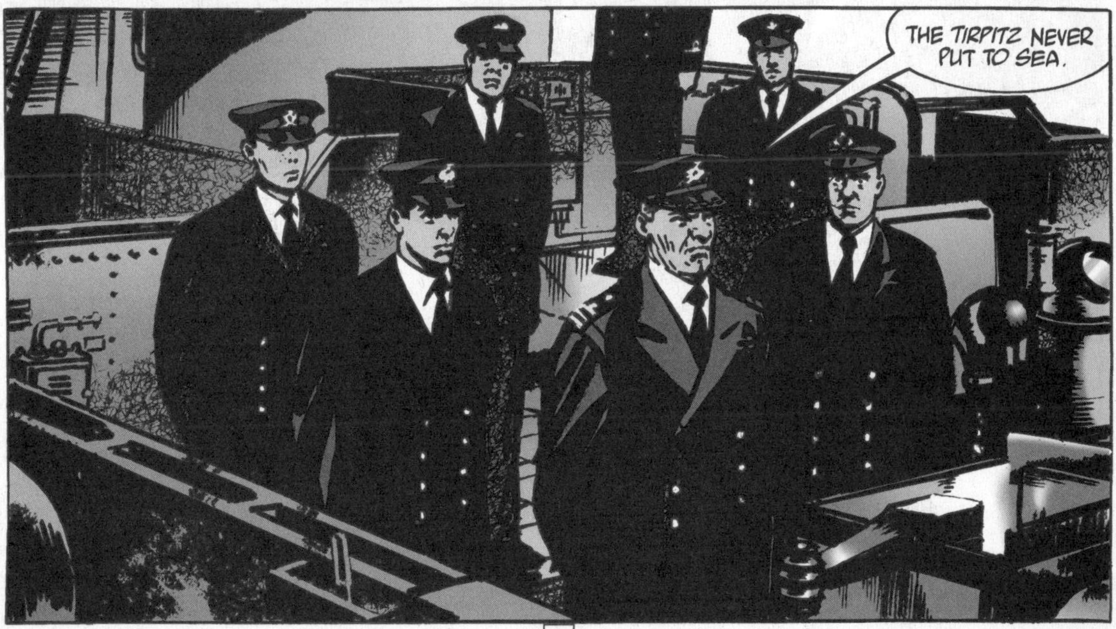
THE *TIRPITZ* NEVER PUT TO SEA.

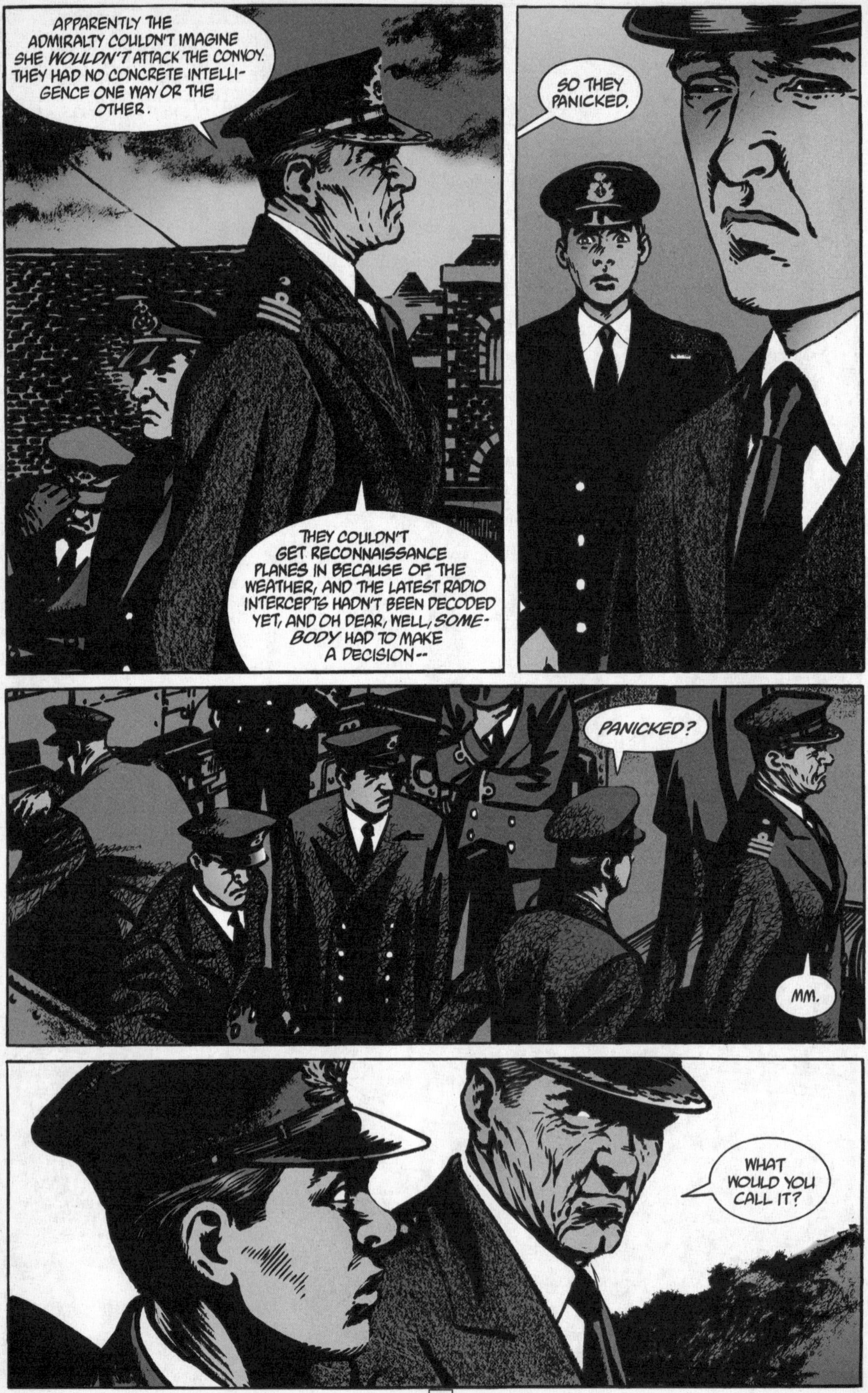
APPARENTLY THE ADMIRALTY COULDN'T IMAGINE SHE WOULDN'T ATTACK THE CONVOY. THEY HAD NO CONCRETE INTELLI- GENCE ONE WAY OR THE OTHER.
THEY COULDN'T GET RECONNAISSANCE PLANES IN BECAUSE OF THE WEATHER, AND THE LATEST RADIO INTERCEPTS HADN'T BEEN DECODED YET, AND OH DEAR, WELL, SOME- BODY HAD TO MAKE A DECISION--
SO THEY PANICKED.
PANICKED?
MM.
WHAT WOULD YOU CALL IT?

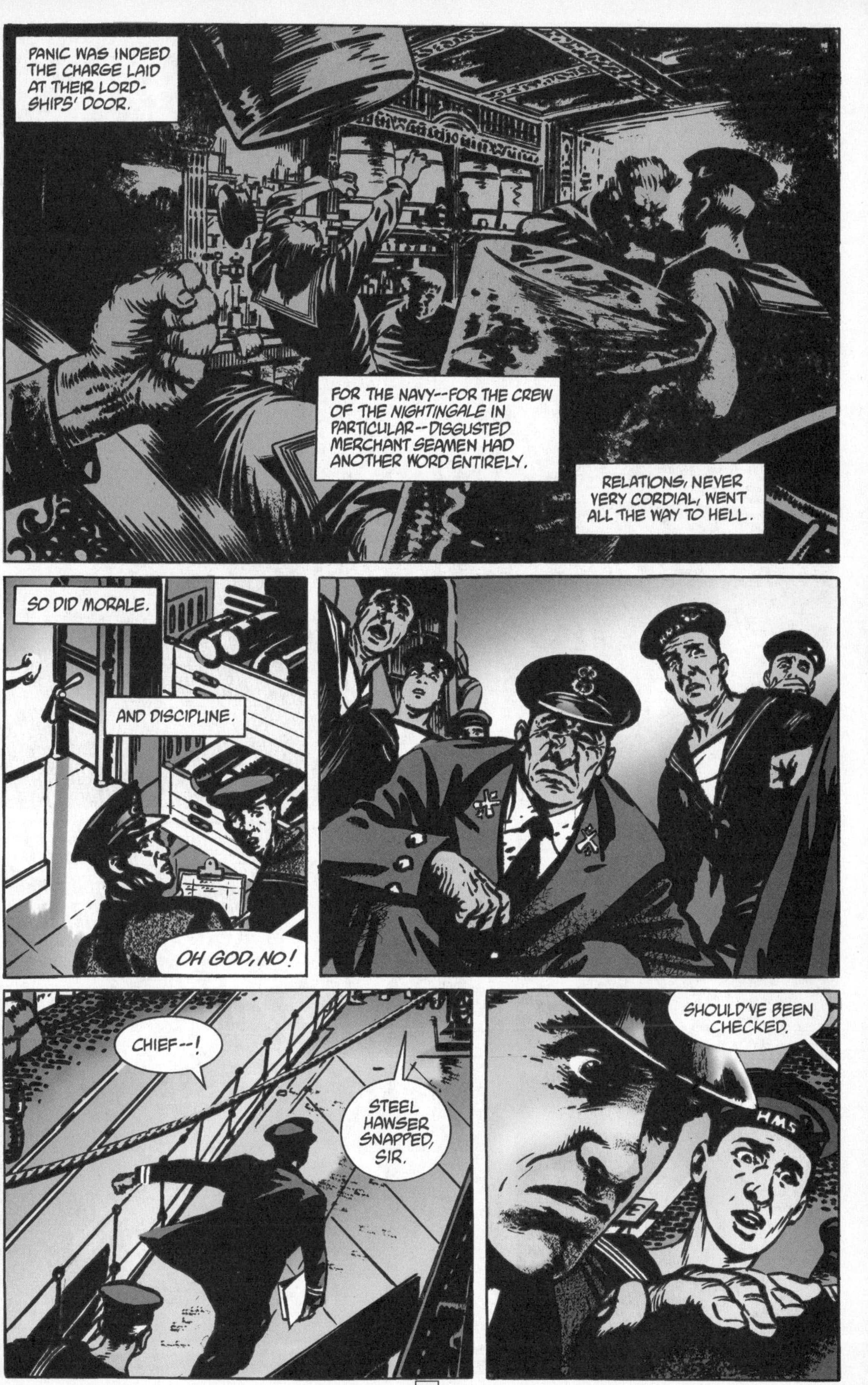

PANIC WAS INDEED THE CHARGE LAID AT THEIR LORDSHIPS' DOOR.
FOR THE NAVY--FOR THE CREW OF THE *NIGHTINGALE* IN PARTICULAR--DISGUSTED MERCHANT SEAMEN HAD ANOTHER WORD ENTIRELY.
RELATIONS, NEVER VERY CORDIAL, WENT ALL THE WAY TO HELL.
SO DID MORALE.
AND DISCIPLINE.
OH GOD, NO!
CHIEF--!
STEEL HAWSER SNAPPED, SIR.
SHOULD'VE BEEN CHECKED.
HMS

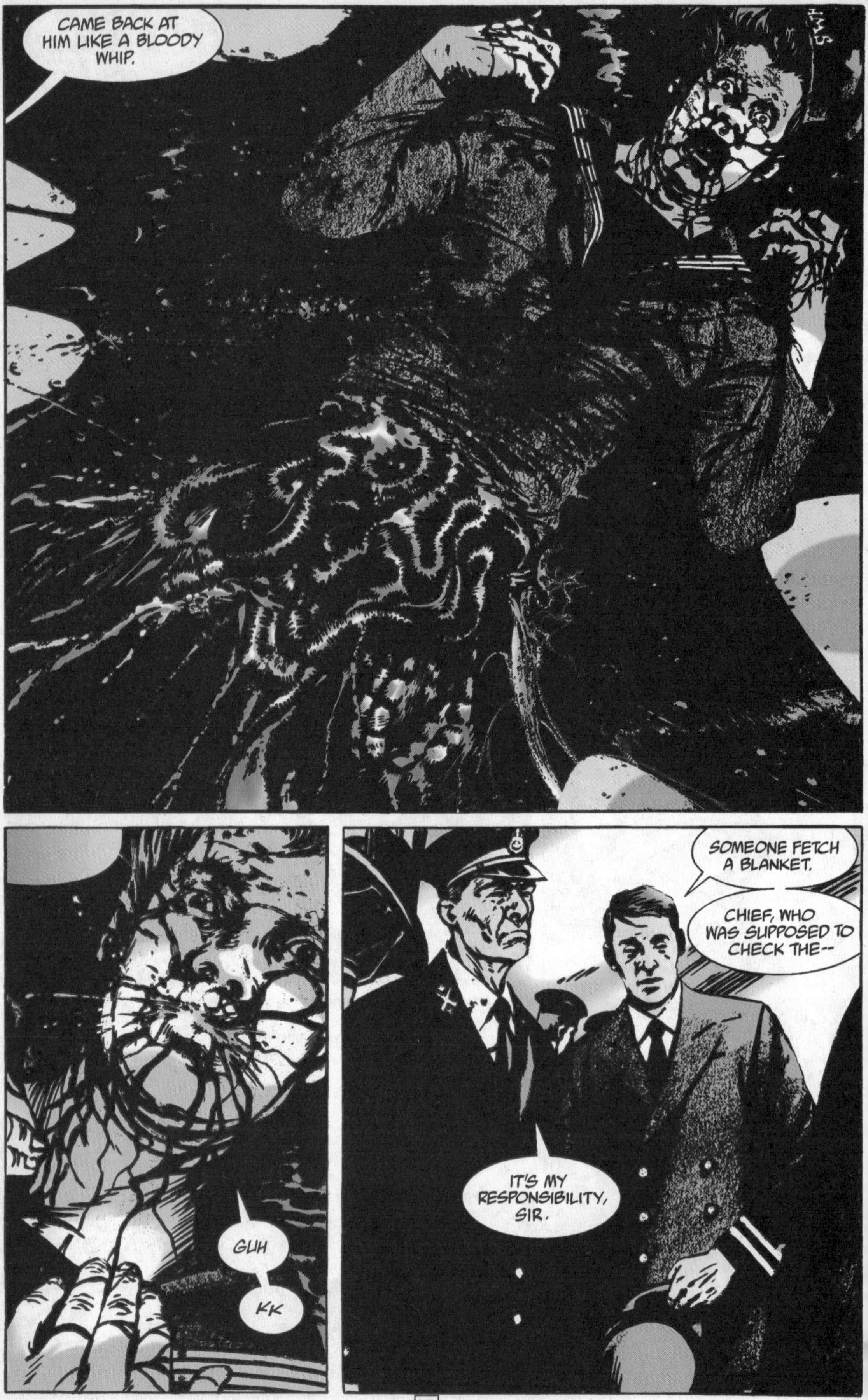
CAME BACK AT HIM LIKE A BLOODY WHIP.
GUH
KK
SOMEONE FETCH A BLANKET.
CHIEF, WHO WAS SUPPOSED TO CHECK THE--
IT'S MY RESPONSIBILITY, SIR.

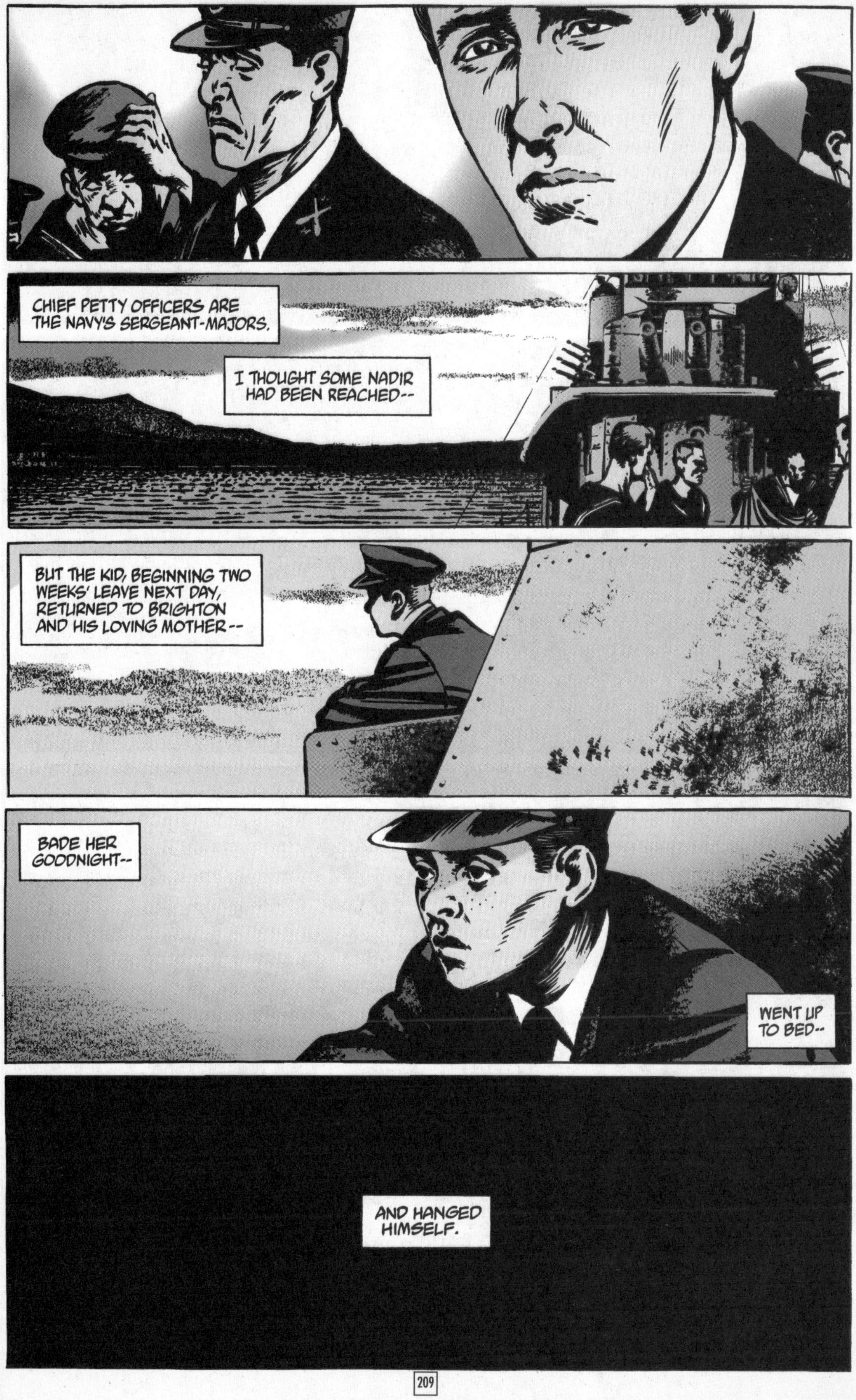
CHIEF PETTY OFFICERS ARE THE NAVY'S SERGEANT-MAJORS.
I THOUGHT SOME NADIR HAD BEEN REACHED--
BUT THE KID, BEGINNING TWO WEEKS' LEAVE NEXT DAY, RETURNED TO BRIGHTON AND HIS LOVING MOTHER--
BADE HER GOODNIGHT--
WENT UP TO BED--
AND HANGED HIMSELF.

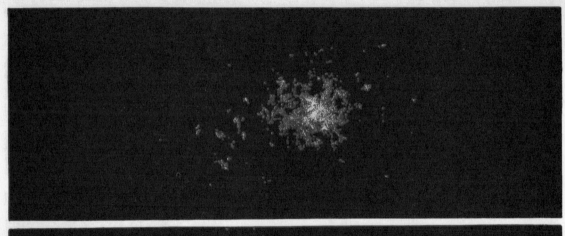

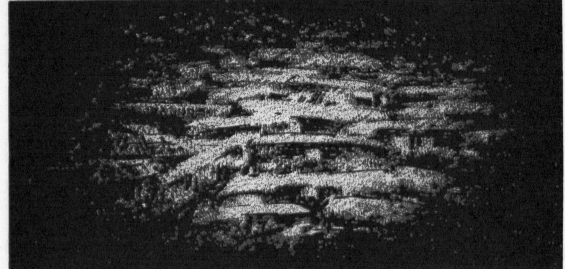

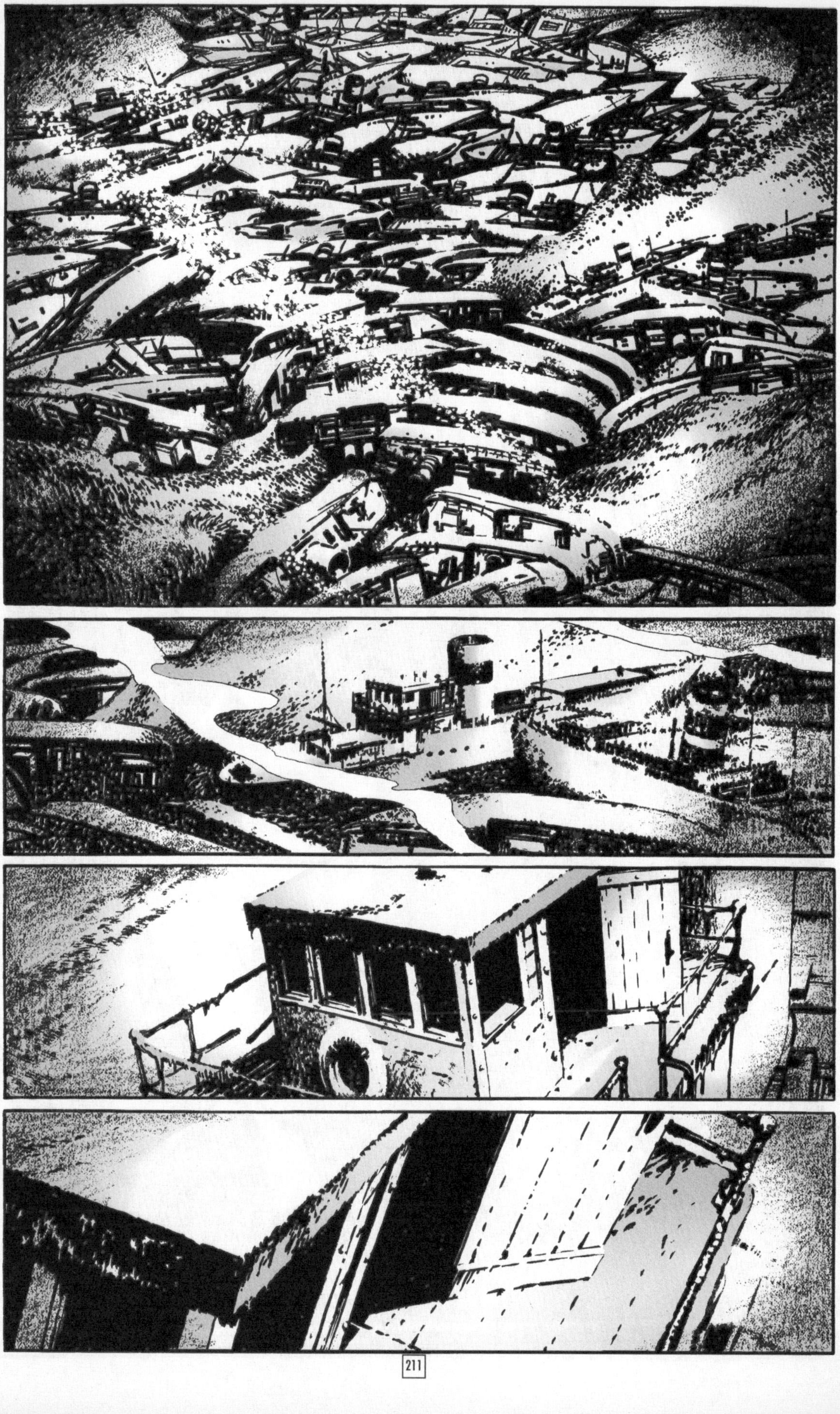

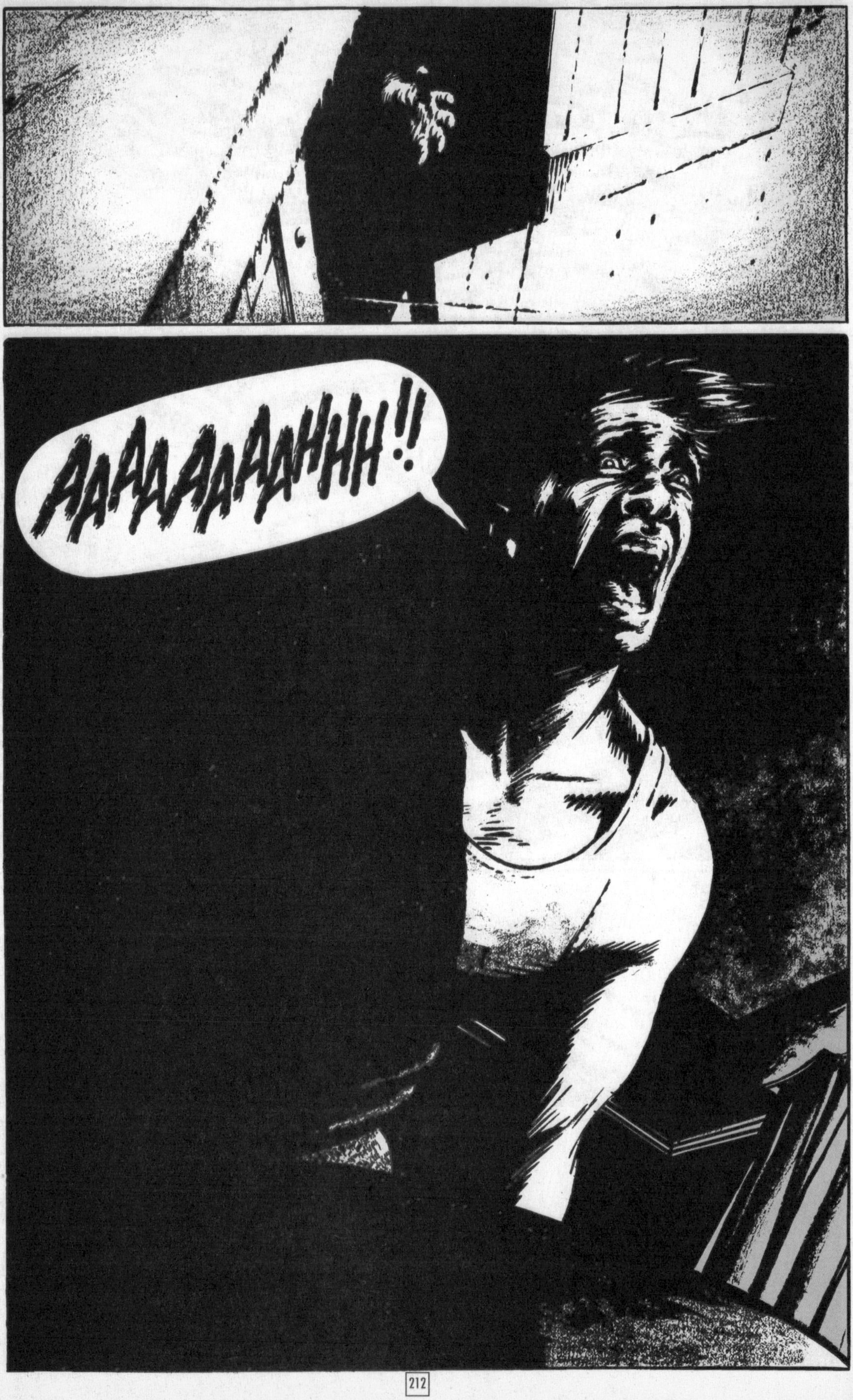
AAAAAAAAHHH!!

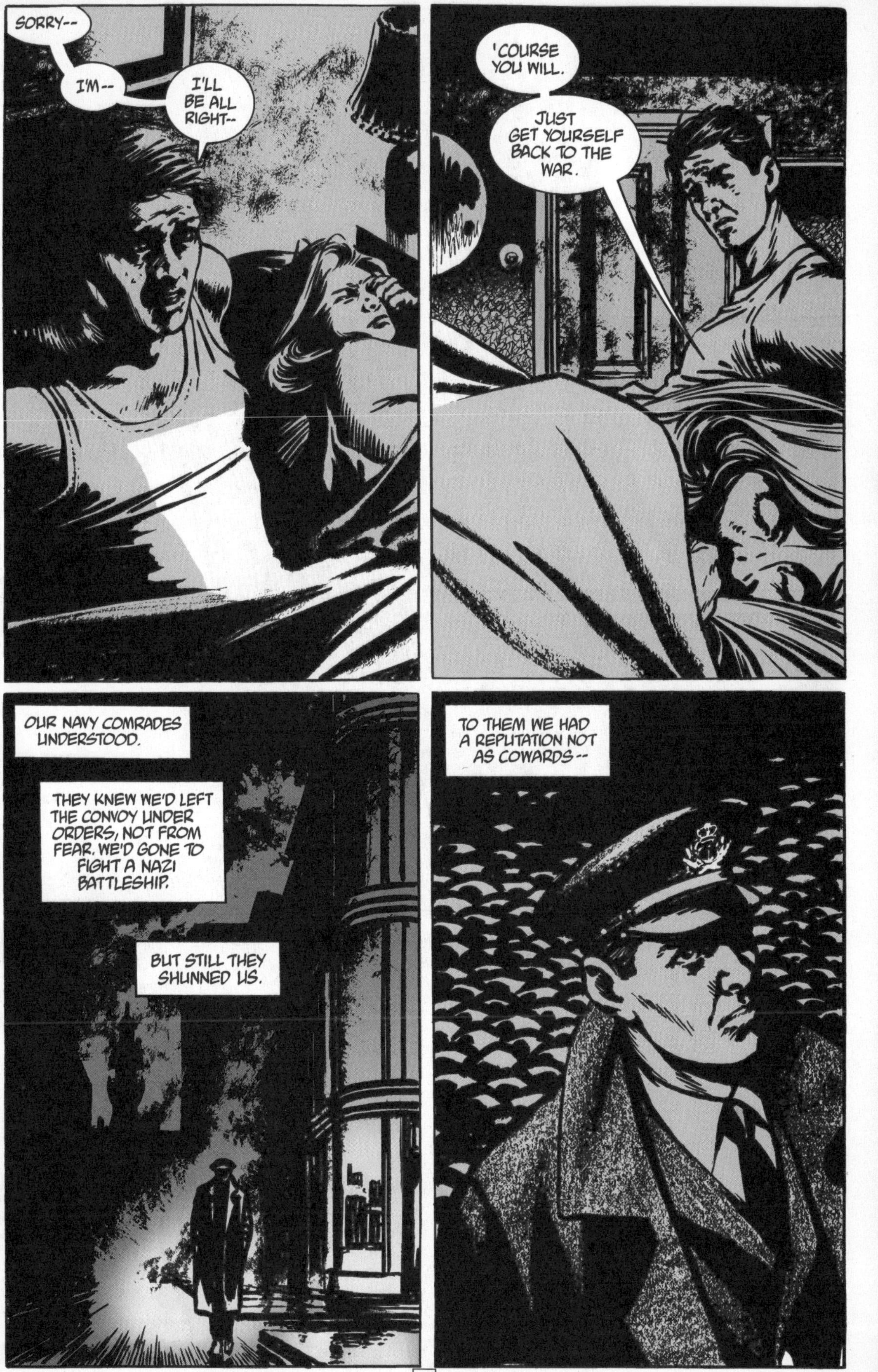
SORRY--
I'M--
I'LL BE ALL RIGHT--
'COURSE YOU WILL.
JUST GET YOURSELF BACK TO THE WAR.
OUR NAVY COMRADES UNDERSTOOD.
THEY KNEW WE'D LEFT THE CONVOY UNDER ORDERS, NOT FROM FEAR. WE'D GONE TO FIGHT A NAZI BATTLESHIP.
BUT STILL THEY SHUNNED US.
TO THEM WE HAD A REPUTATION NOT AS COWARDS--

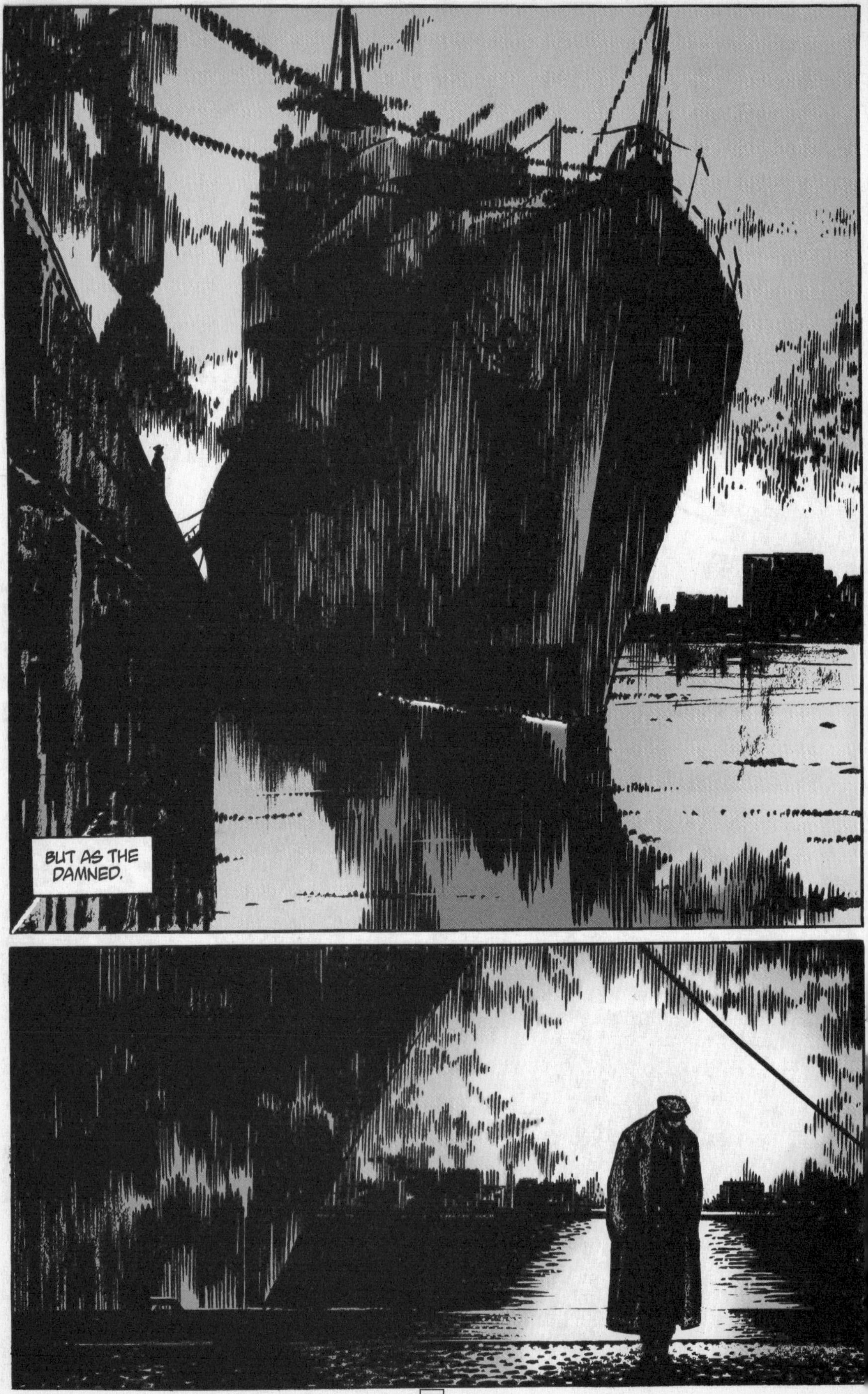
BUT AS THE DAMNED.

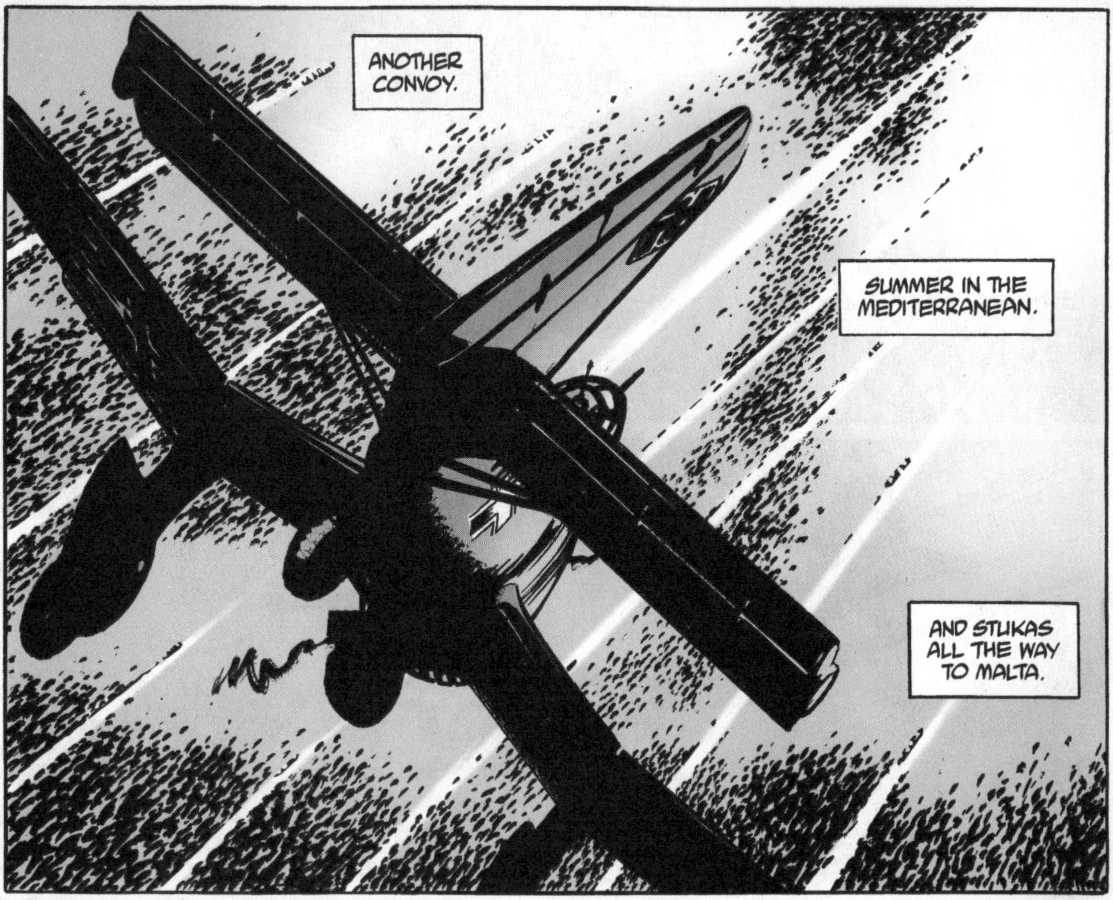
ANOTHER CONVOY.
SUMMER IN THE MEDITERRANEAN.
AND STUKAS ALL THE WAY TO MALTA.

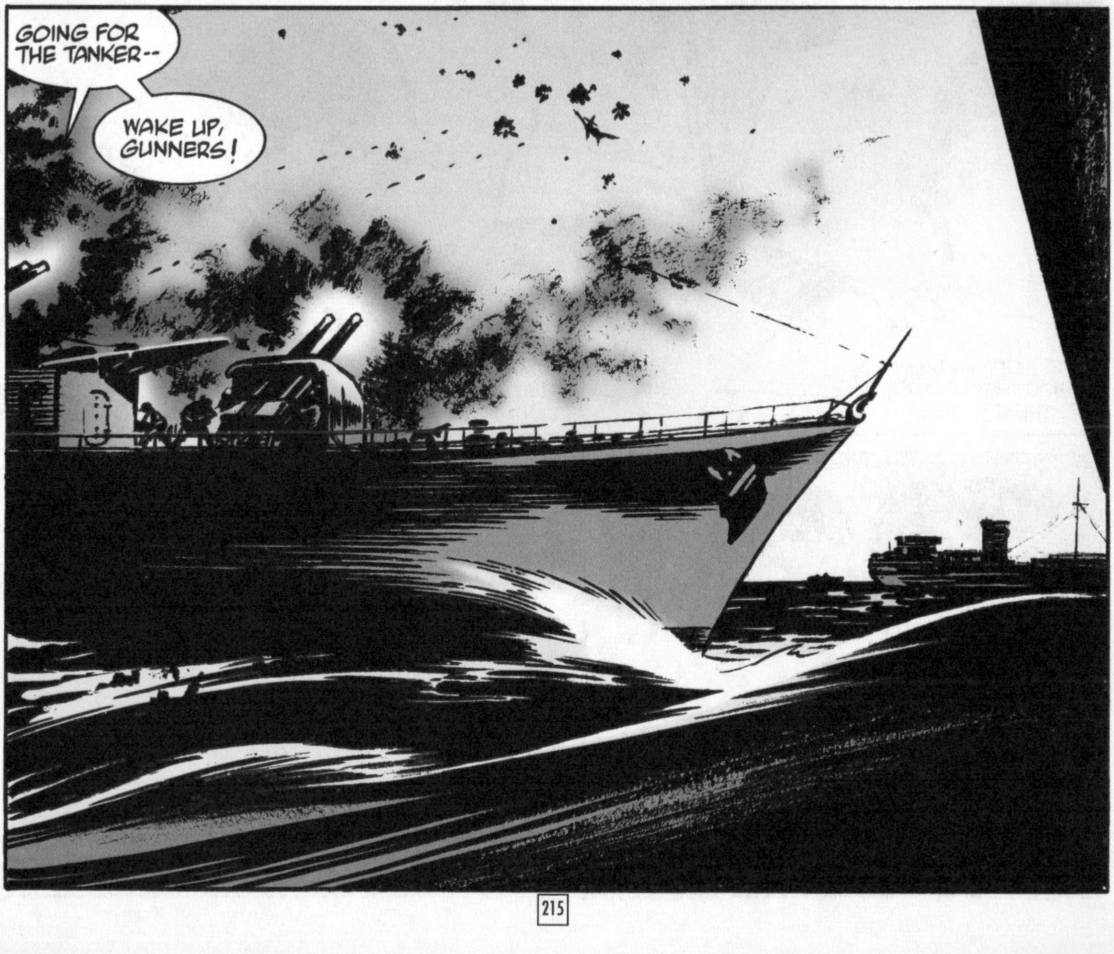
GOING FOR THE TANKER--
WAKE UP, GUNNERS!

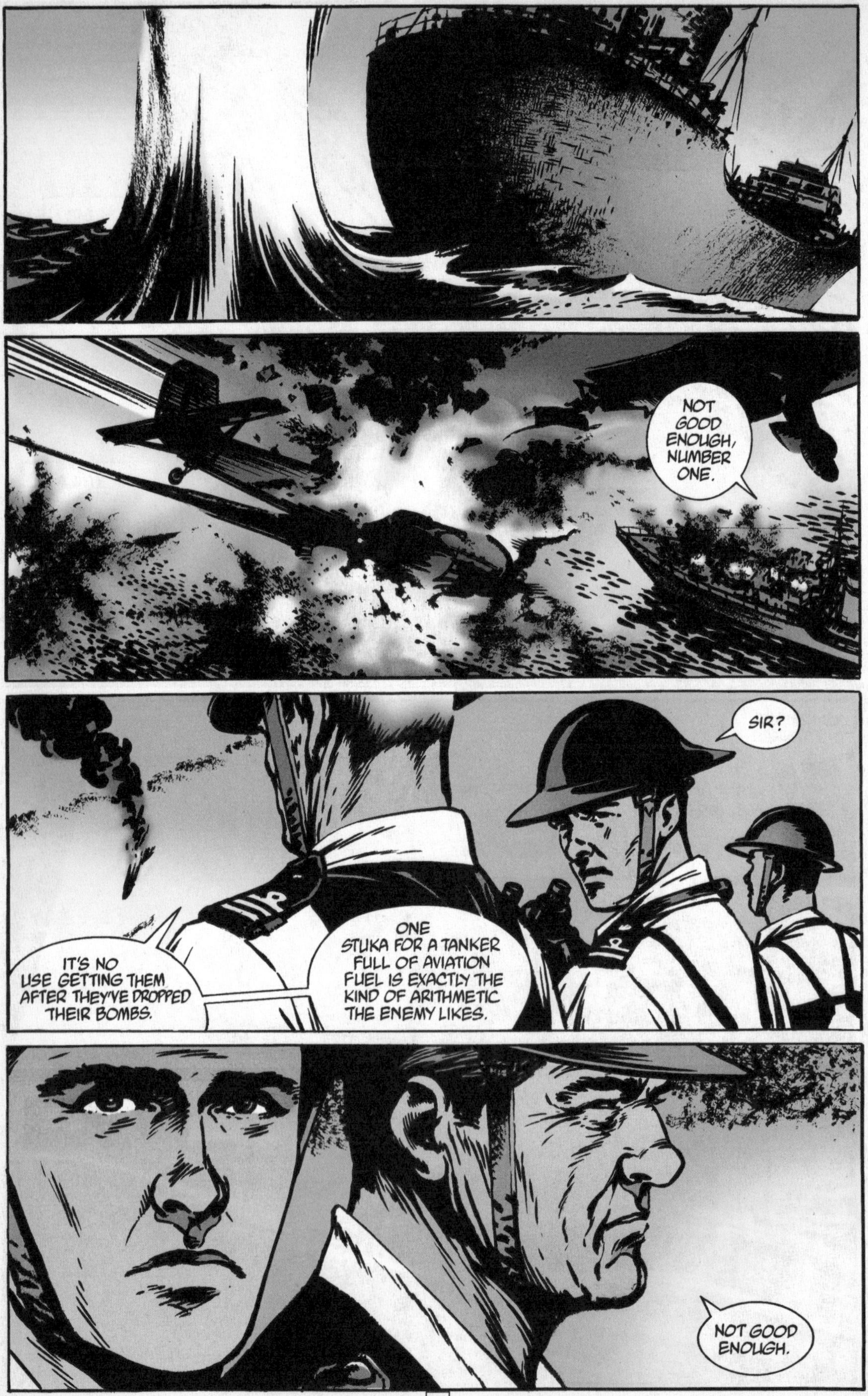
NOT GOOD ENOUGH, NUMBER ONE.
SIR?
IT'S NO USE GETTING THEM AFTER THEY'VE DROPPED THEIR BOMBS.
ONE STUKA FOR A TANKER FULL OF AVIATION FUEL IS EXACTLY THE KIND OF ARITHMETIC THE ENEMY LIKES.
NOT GOOD ENOUGH.

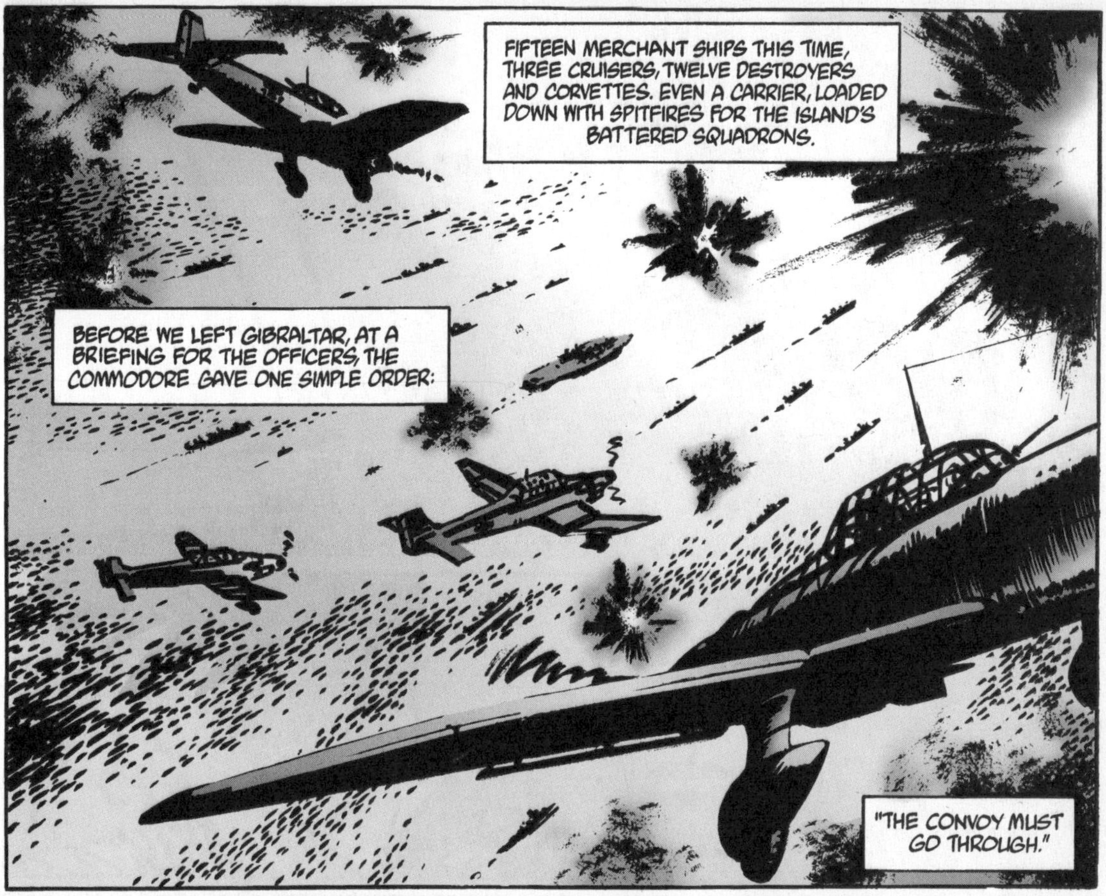
FIFTEEN MERCHANT SHIPS THIS TIME, THREE CRUISERS, TWELVE DESTROYERS AND CORVETTES. EVEN A CARRIER, LOADED DOWN WITH SPITFIRES FOR THE ISLAND'S BATTERED SQUADRONS.
BEFORE WE LEFT GIBRALTAR, AT A BRIEFING FOR THE OFFICERS, THE COMMODORE GAVE ONE SIMPLE ORDER:
"THE CONVOY MUST GO THROUGH."

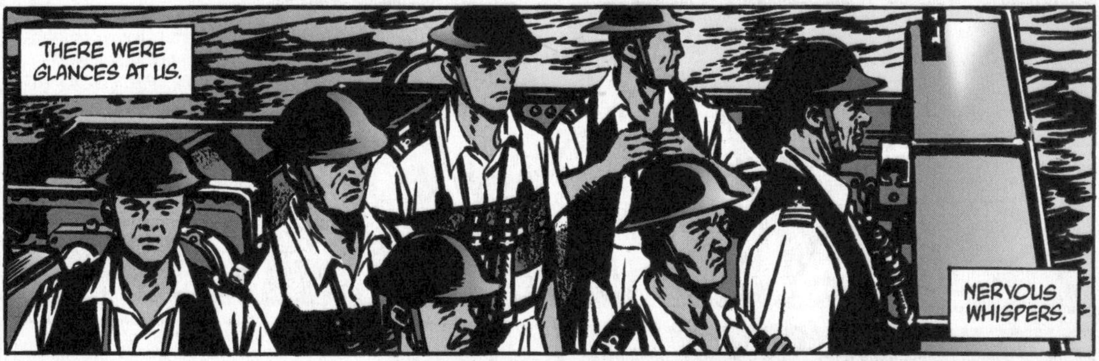
THERE WERE GLANCES AT US.
NERVOUS WHISPERS.

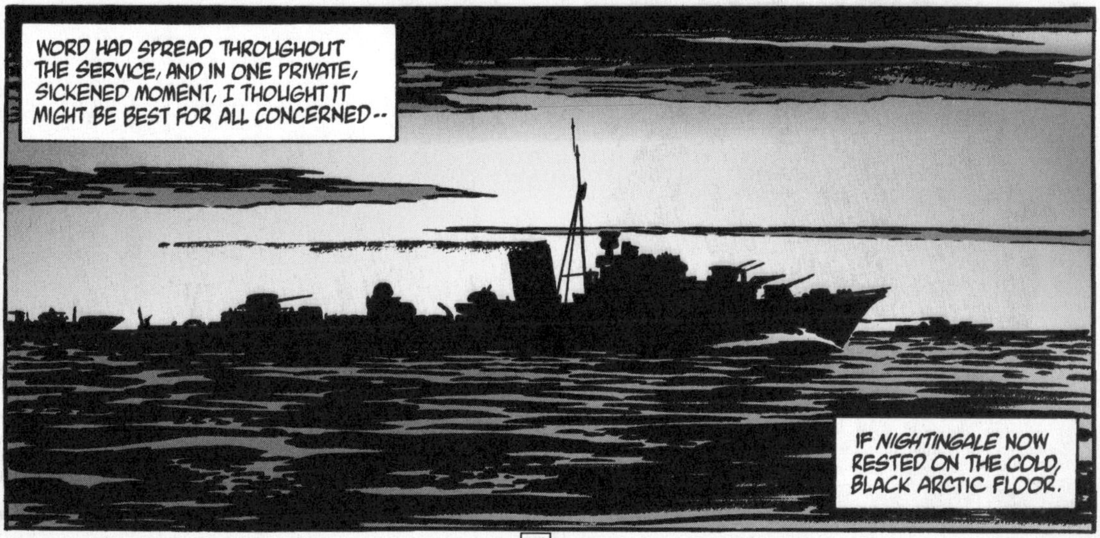
WORD HAD SPREAD THROUGHOUT THE SERVICE, AND IN ONE PRIVATE, SICKENED MOMENT, I THOUGHT IT MIGHT BE BEST FOR ALL CONCERNED--
IF *NIGHTINGALE* NOW RESTED ON THE COLD, BLACK ARCTIC FLOOR.

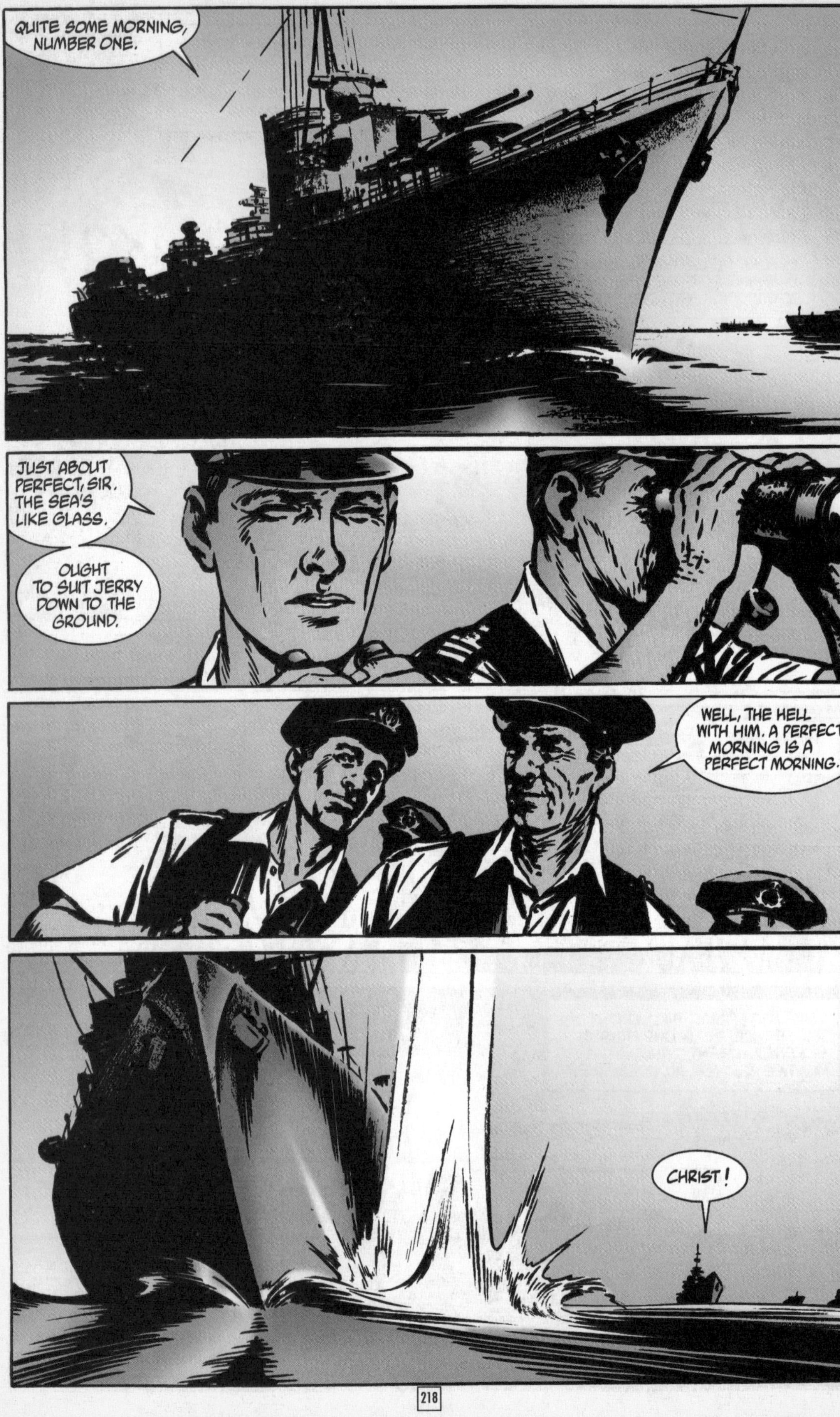
QUITE SOME MORNING, NUMBER ONE.
JUST ABOUT PERFECT, SIR. THE SEA'S LIKE GLASS.
OUGHT TO SUIT JERRY DOWN TO THE GROUND.
WELL, THE HELL WITH HIM. A PERFECT MORNING IS A PERFECT MORNING.
CHRIST!

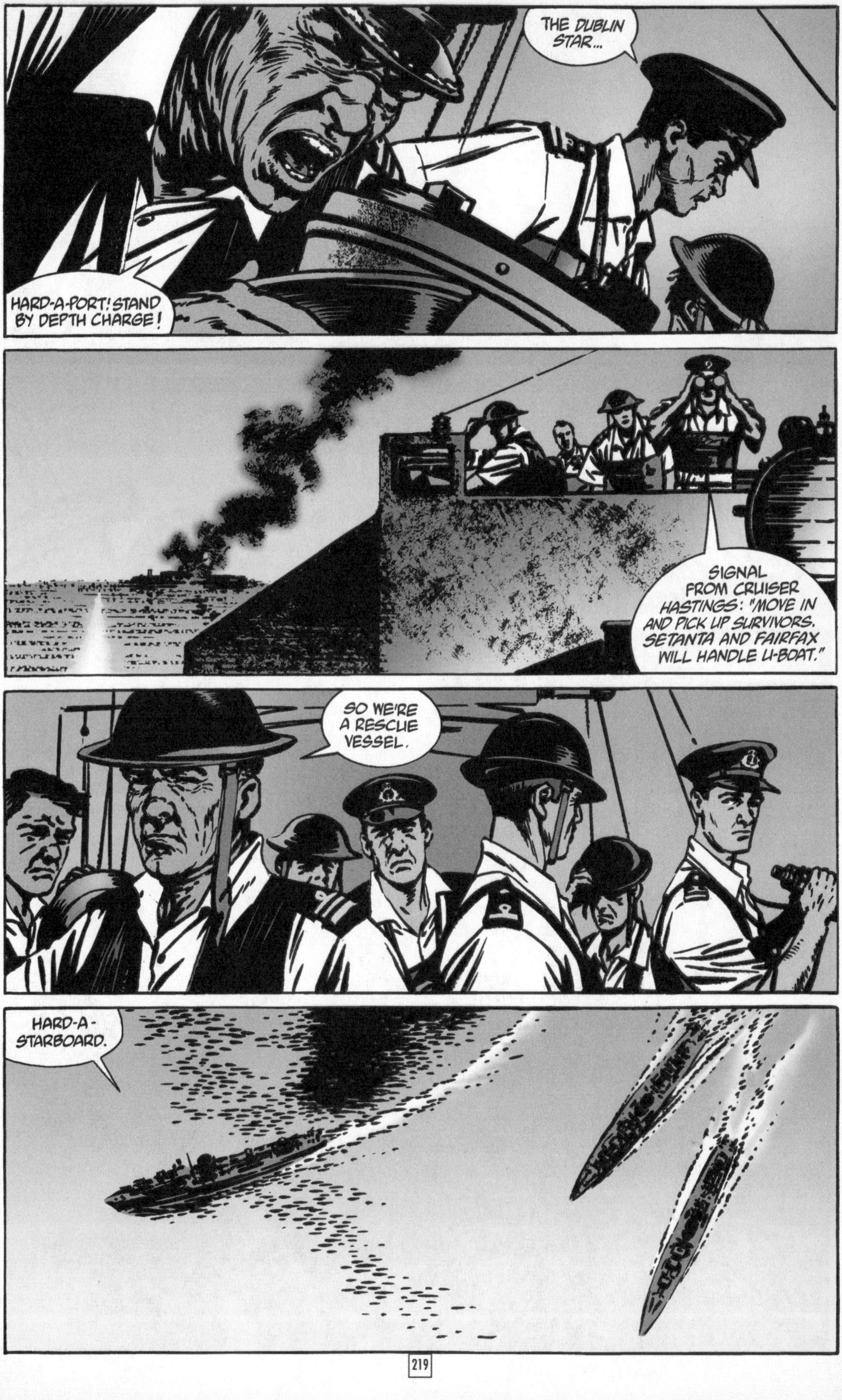
THE DUBLIN STAR...
HARD-A-PORT! STAND BY DEPTH CHARGE!
SIGNAL FROM CRUISER HASTINGS: "MOVE IN AND PICK UP SURVIVORS. SETANTA AND FAIRFAX WILL HANDLE U-BOAT."
SO WE'RE A RESCUE VESSEL.
HARD-A-STARBOARD.

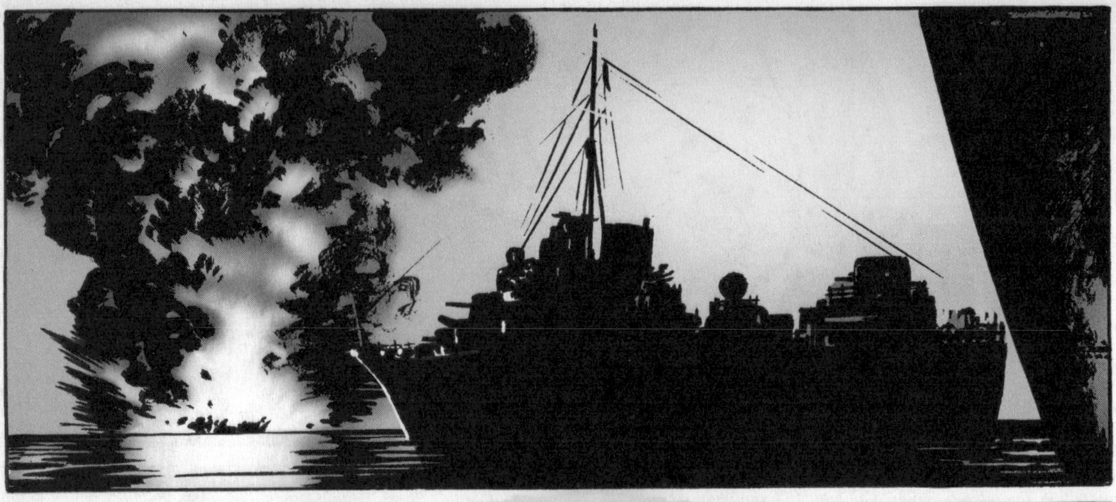

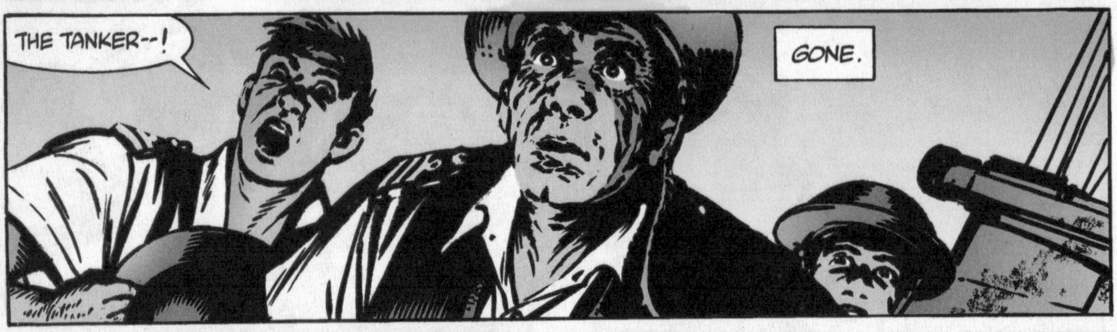
THE TANKER--!
GONE.

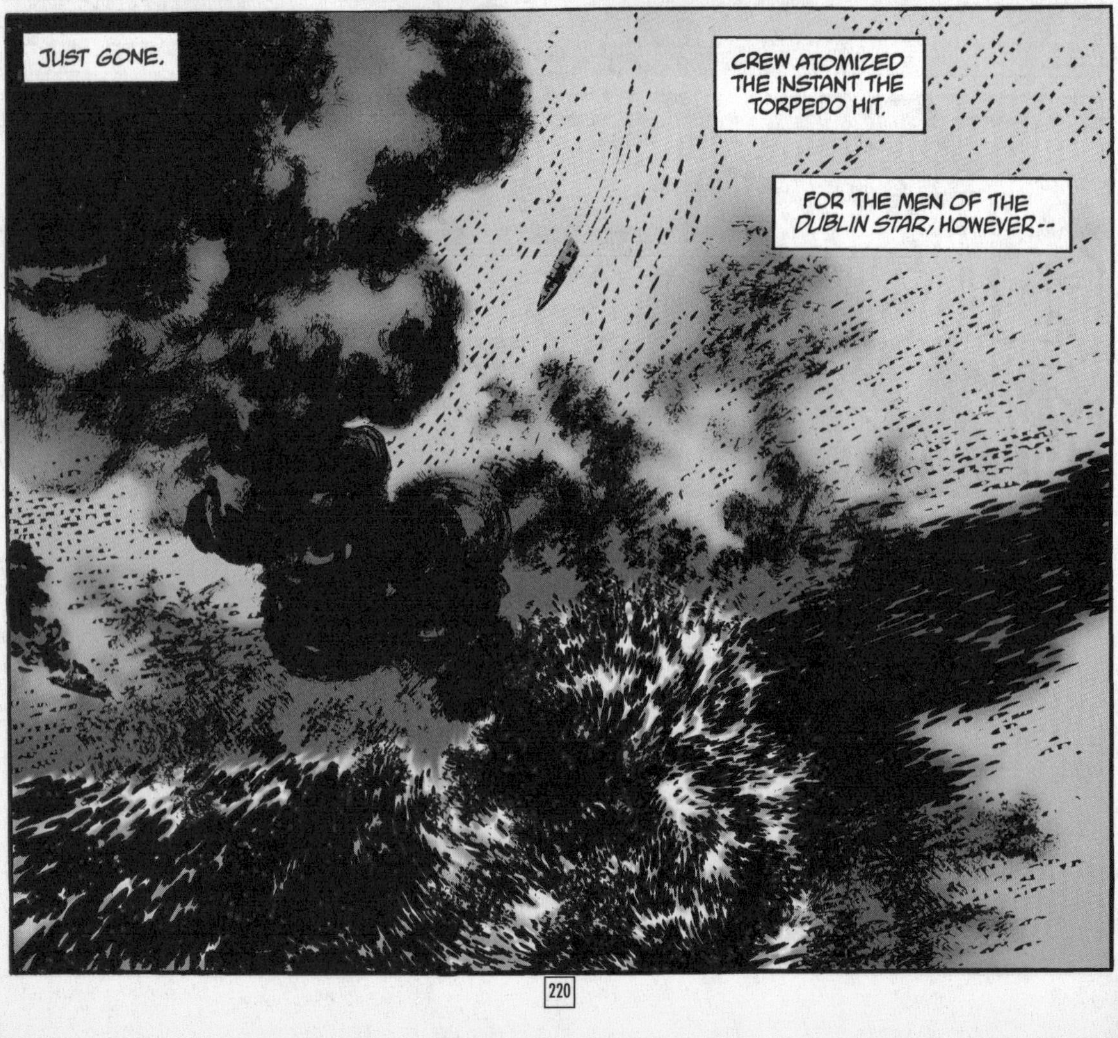
JUST GONE.
CREW ATOMIZED THE INSTANT THE TORPEDO HIT.
FOR THE MEN OF THE DUBLIN STAR, HOWEVER--

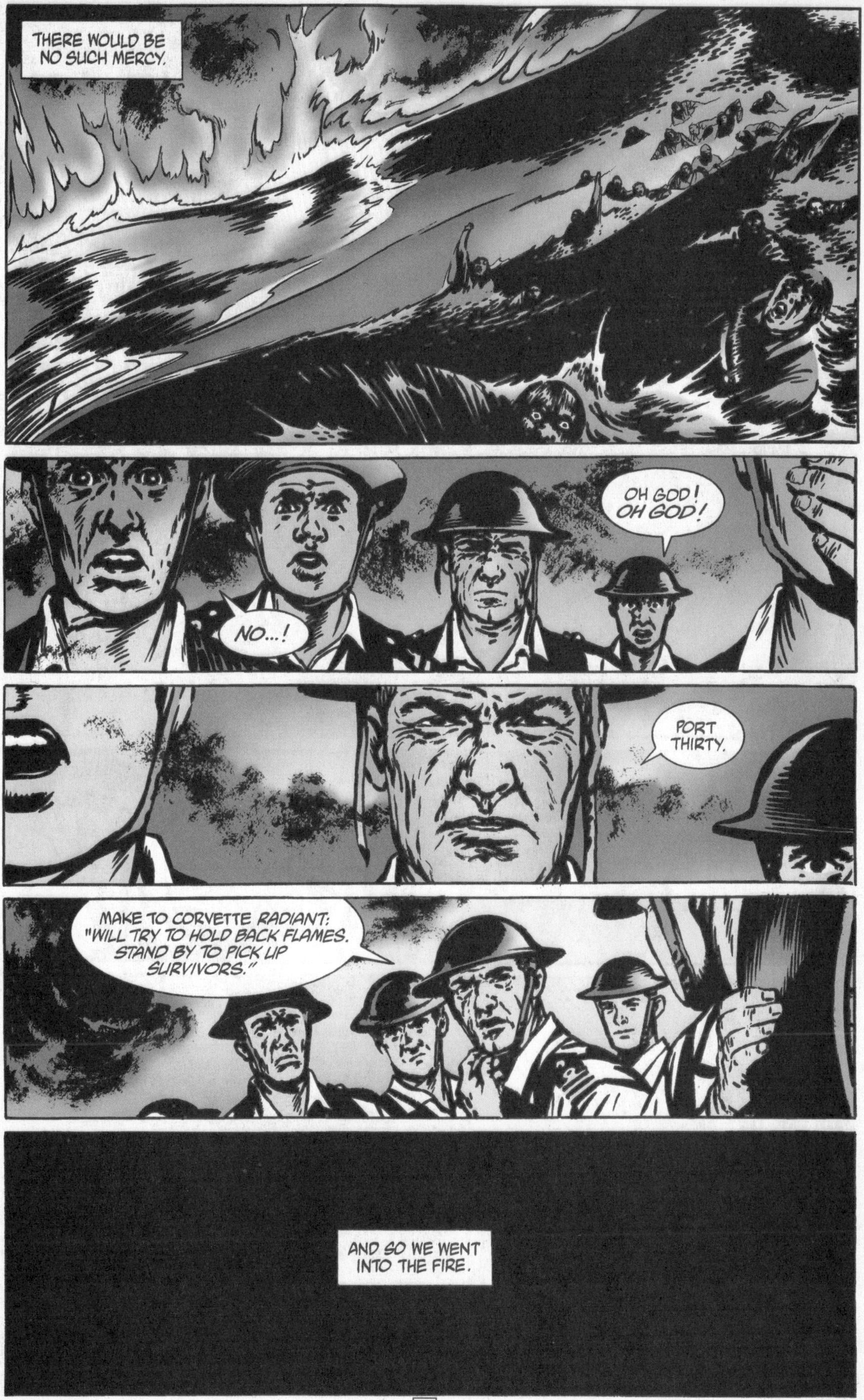
THERE WOULD BE NO SUCH MERCY.
OH GOD! OH GOD!
NO...!
PORT THIRTY.
MAKE TO CORVETTE RADIANT: "WILL TRY TO HOLD BACK FLAMES. STAND BY TO PICK UP SURVIVORS."
AND SO WE WENT INTO THE FIRE.

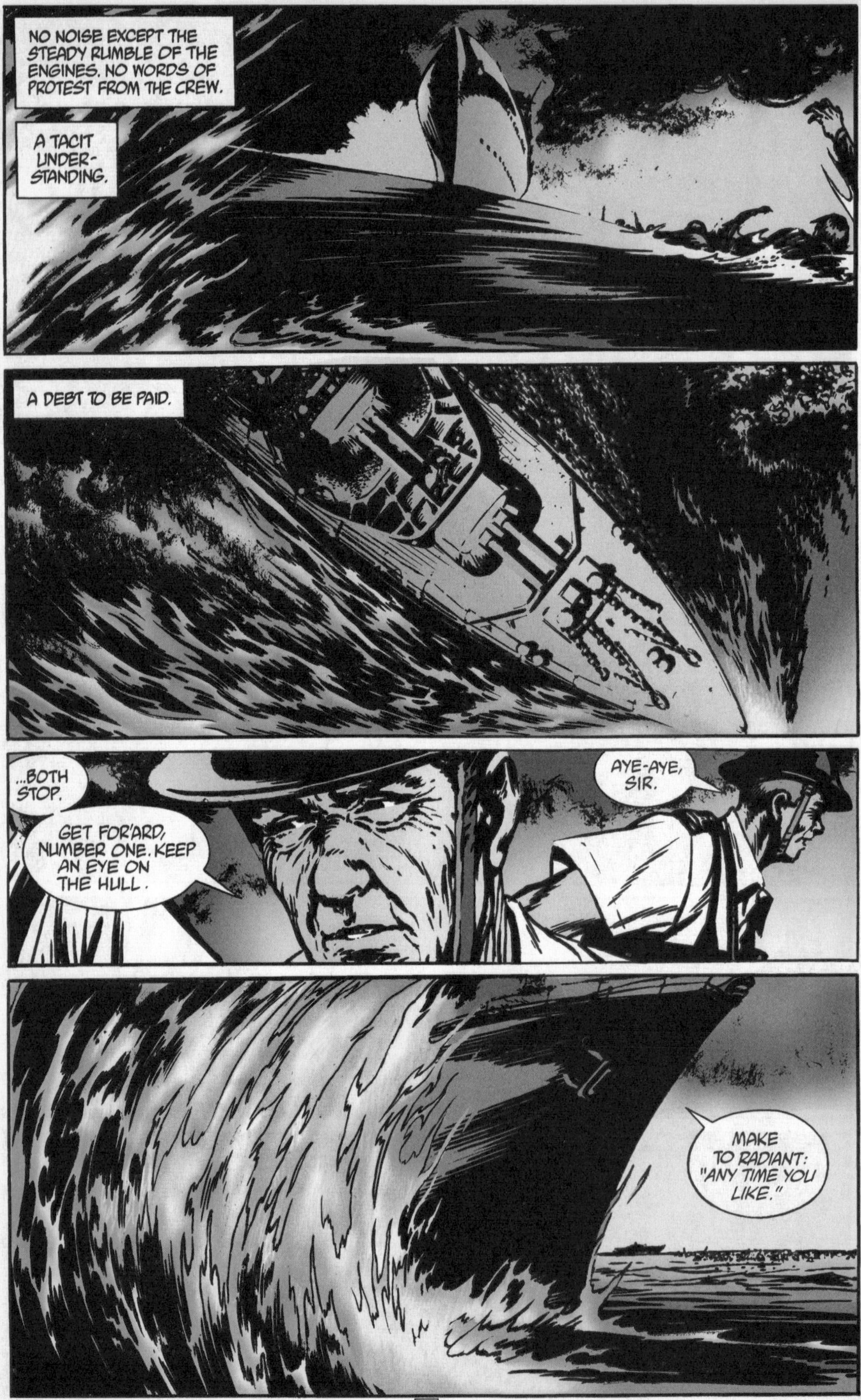
NO NOISE EXCEPT THE STEADY RUMBLE OF THE ENGINES. NO WORDS OF PROTEST FROM THE CREW.
A TACIT UNDER-STANDING.
A DEBT TO BE PAID.
...BOTH STOP.
GET FOR'ARD, NUMBER ONE. KEEP AN EYE ON THE HULL.
AYE-AYE, SIR.
MAKE TO RADIANT: "ANY TIME YOU LIKE."

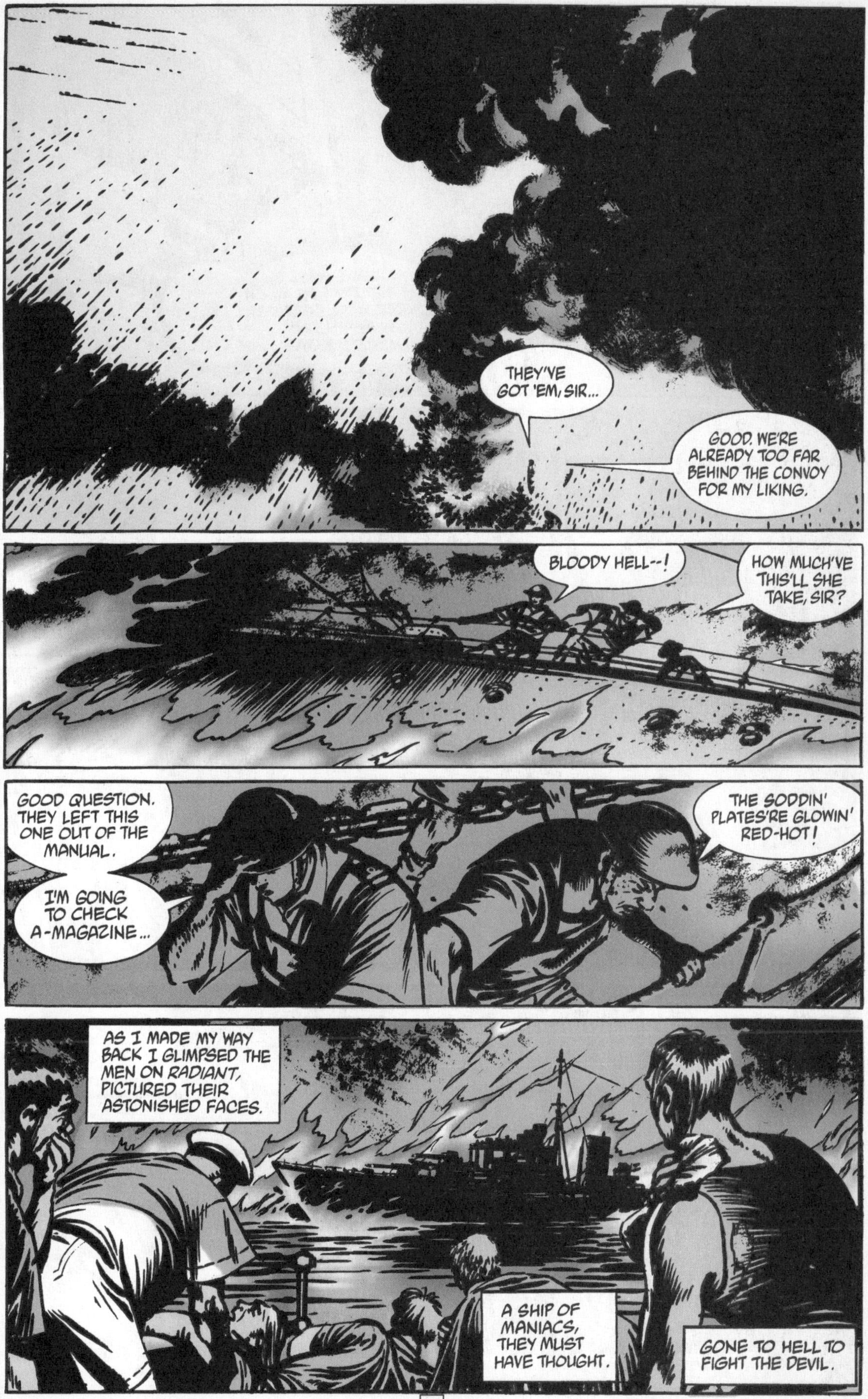
THEY'VE GOT 'EM, SIR...
GOOD. WE'RE ALREADY TOO FAR BEHIND THE CONVOY FOR MY LIKING.
BLOODY HELL--!
HOW MUCH'VE THIS'LL SHE TAKE, SIR?
GOOD QUESTION. THEY LEFT THIS ONE OUT OF THE MANUAL.
THE SODDIN' PLATES'RE GLOWIN' RED-HOT!
I'M GOING TO CHECK A-MAGAZINE...
AS I MADE MY WAY BACK I GLIMPSED THE MEN ON RADIANT, PICTURED THEIR ASTONISHED FACES.
A SHIP OF MANIACS, THEY MUST HAVE THOUGHT.
GONE TO HELL TO FIGHT THE DEVIL.

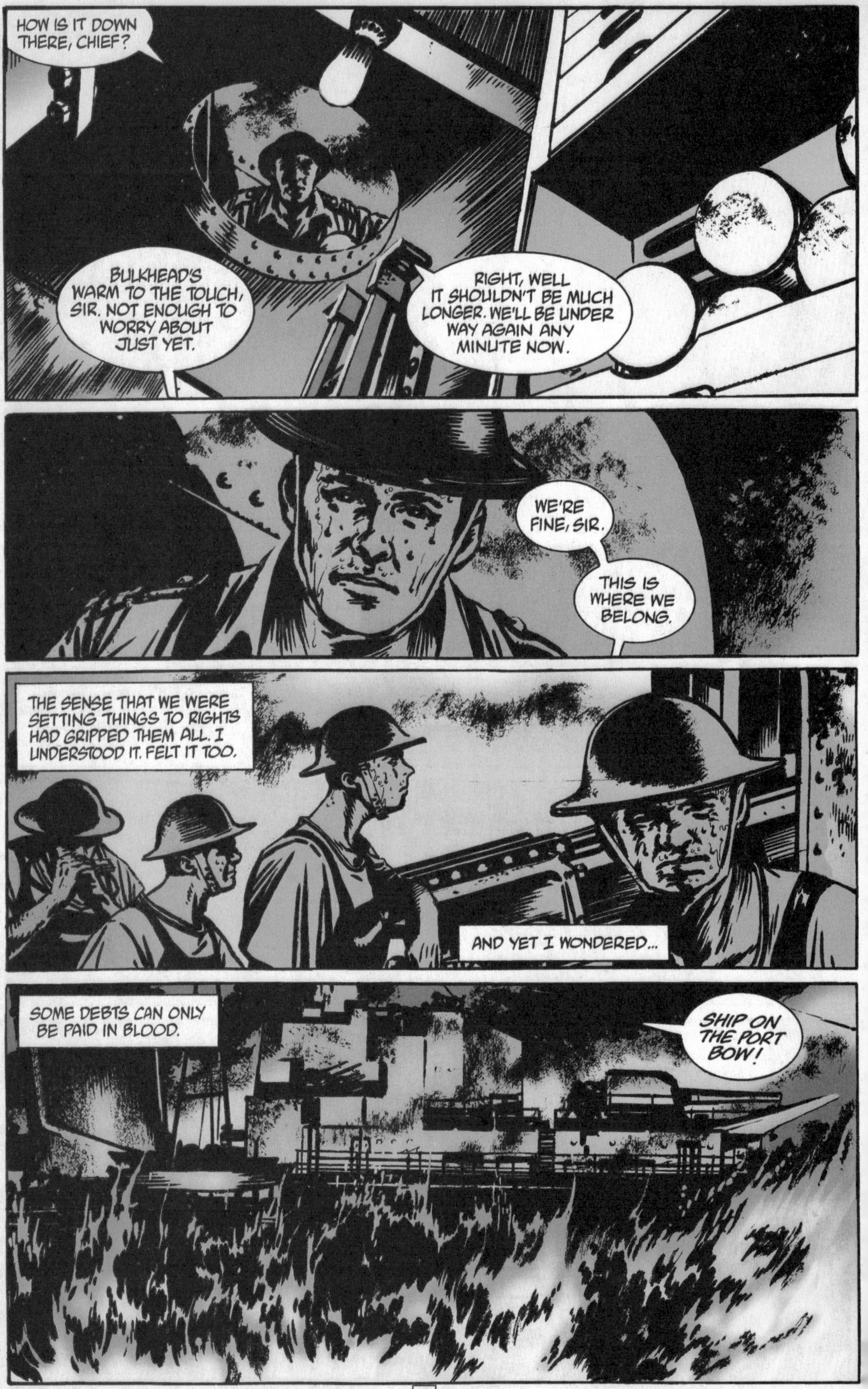
HOW IS IT DOWN THERE, CHIEF?
BULKHEAD'S WARM TO THE TOUCH, SIR. NOT ENOUGH TO WORRY ABOUT JUST YET.
RIGHT, WELL IT SHOULDN'T BE MUCH LONGER. WE'LL BE UNDER WAY AGAIN ANY MINUTE NOW.
WE'RE FINE, SIR.
THIS IS WHERE WE BELONG.
THE SENSE THAT WE WERE SETTING THINGS TO RIGHTS HAD GRIPPED THEM ALL. I UNDERSTOOD IT. FELT IT TOO.
AND YET I WONDERED...
SOME DEBTS CAN ONLY BE PAID IN BLOOD.
SHIP ON THE PORT BOW!

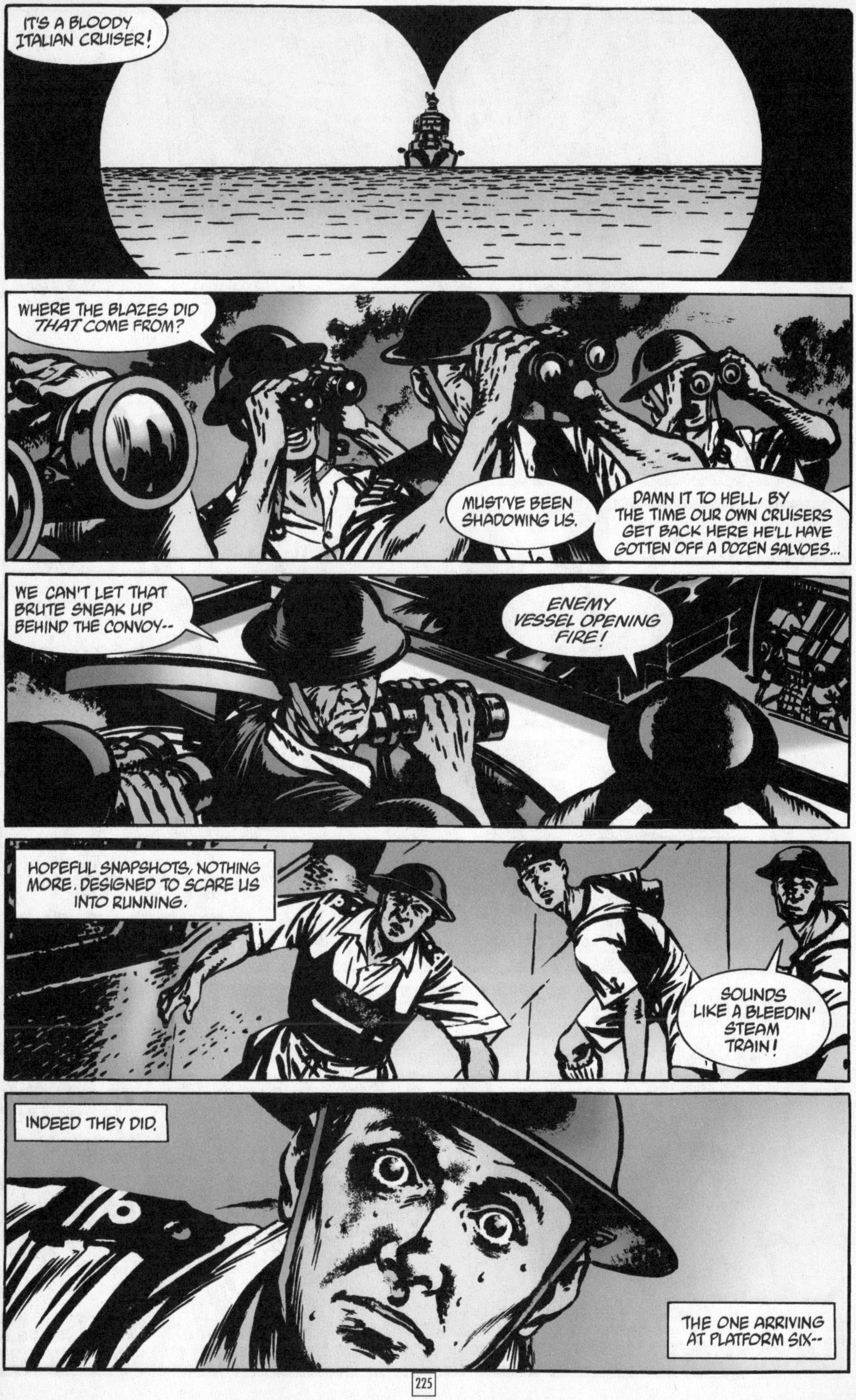
IT'S A BLOODY ITALIAN CRUISER!
WHERE THE BLAZES DID *THAT* COME FROM?
MUST'VE BEEN SHADOWING US.
DAMN IT TO HELL, BY THE TIME OUR OWN CRUISERS GET BACK HERE HE'LL HAVE GOTTEN OFF A DOZEN SALVOES...
WE CAN'T LET THAT BRUTE SNEAK UP BEHIND THE CONVOY--
ENEMY VESSEL OPENING FIRE!
HOPEFUL SNAPSHOTS, NOTHING MORE. DESIGNED TO SCARE US INTO RUNNING.
SOUNDS LIKE A BLEEDIN' STEAM TRAIN!
INDEED THEY DID.
THE ONE ARRIVING AT PLATFORM SIX--

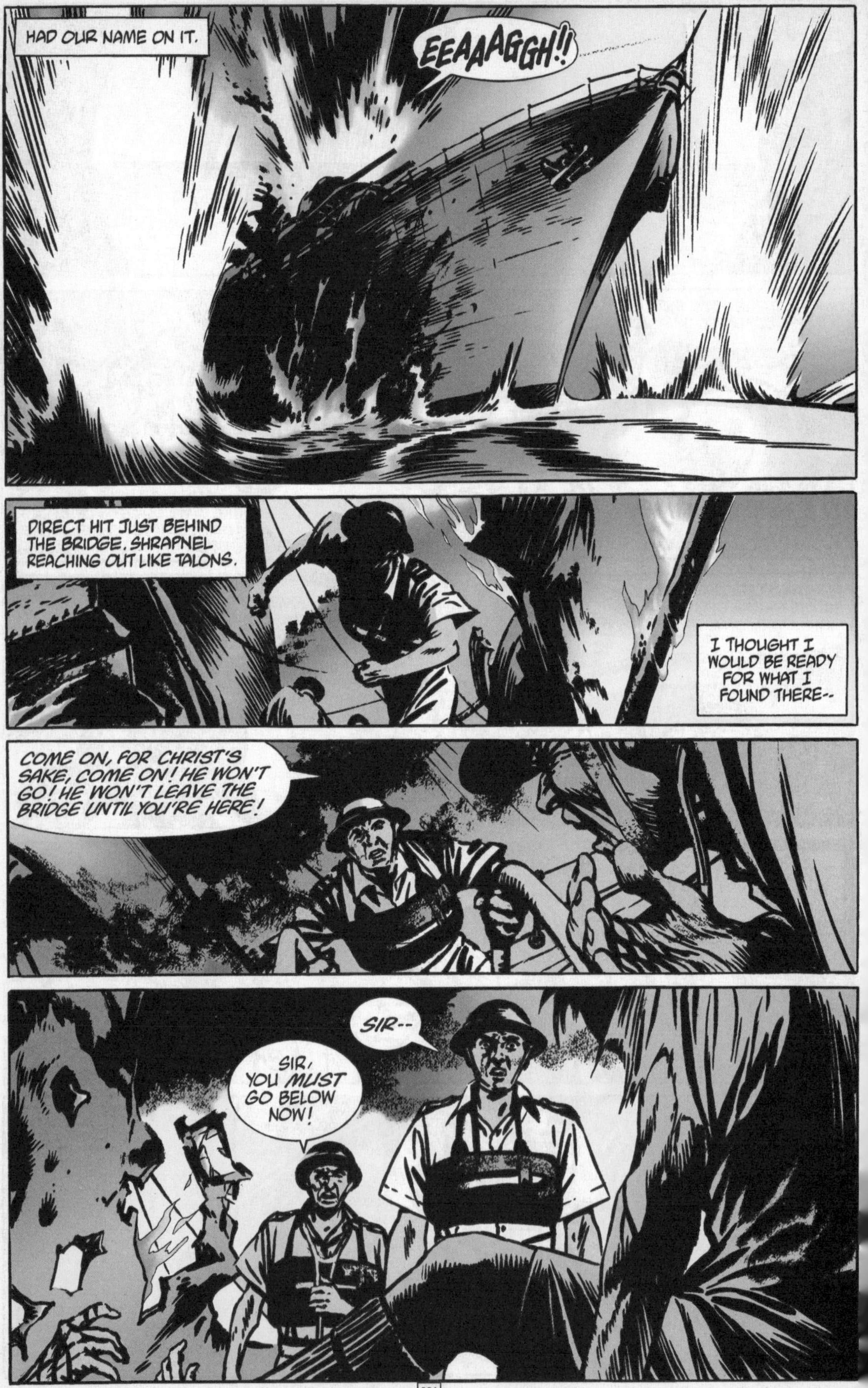
HAD OUR NAME ON IT.
EEAAAGGH!!
DIRECT HIT JUST BEHIND THE BRIDGE. SHRAPNEL REACHING OUT LIKE TALONS.
I THOUGHT I WOULD BE READY FOR WHAT I FOUND THERE--
COME ON, FOR CHRIST'S SAKE, COME ON! HE WON'T GO! HE WON'T LEAVE THE BRIDGE UNTIL YOU'RE HERE!
SIR--
SIR, YOU MUST GO BELOW NOW!

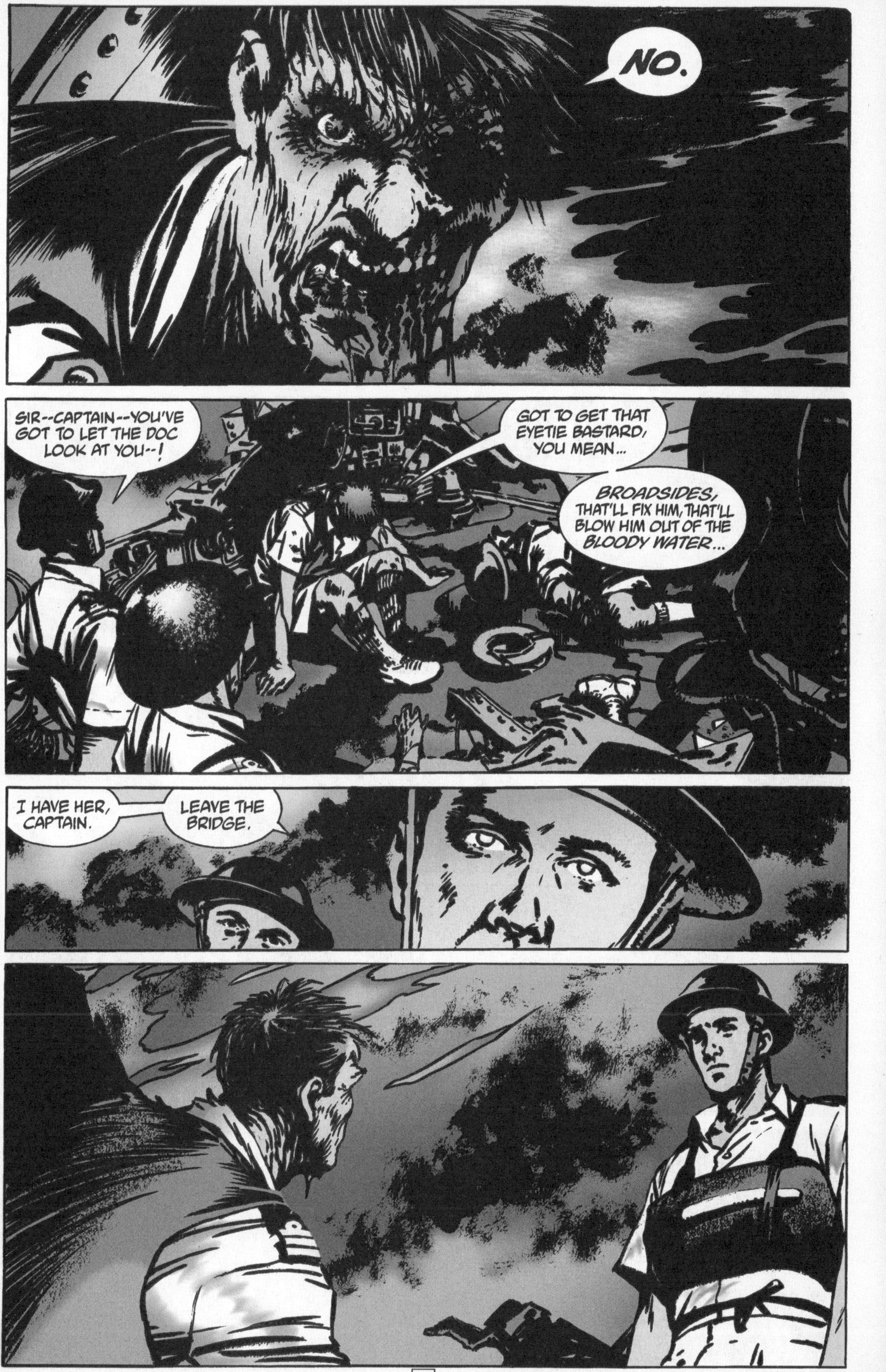
NO.
SIR--CAPTAIN--YOU'VE GOT TO LET THE DOC LOOK AT YOU--!
GOT TO GET THAT EYETIE BASTARD, YOU MEAN...
BROADSIDES, THAT'LL FIX HIM, THAT'LL BLOW HIM OUT OF THE BLOODY WATER...
I HAVE HER, CAPTAIN.
LEAVE THE BRIDGE.

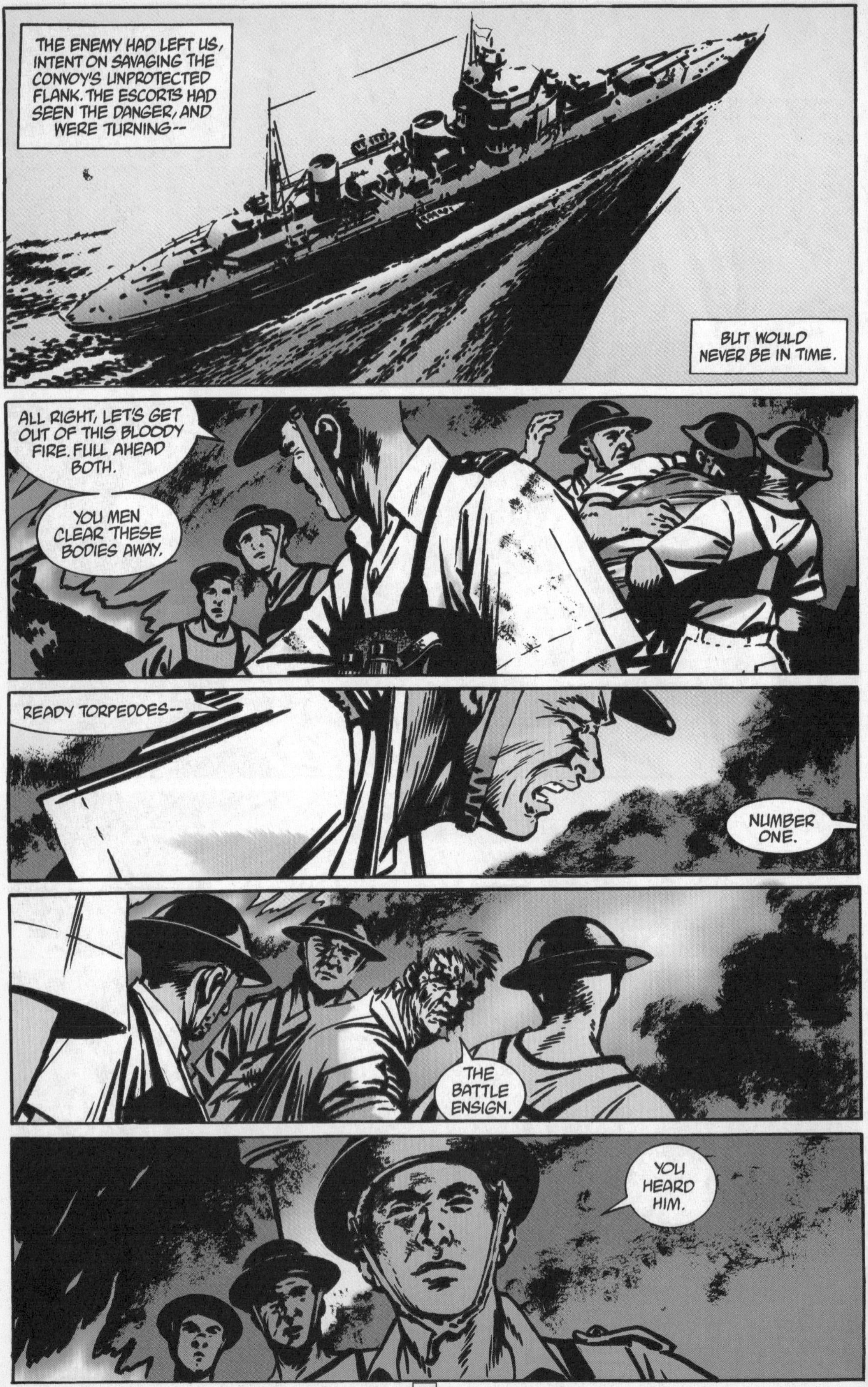
THE ENEMY HAD LEFT US, INTENT ON SAVAGING THE CONVOY'S UNPROTECTED FLANK. THE ESCORTS HAD SEEN THE DANGER, AND WERE TURNING--
BUT WOULD NEVER BE IN TIME.
ALL RIGHT, LET'S GET OUT OF THIS BLOODY FIRE. FULL AHEAD BOTH.
YOU MEN CLEAR THESE BODIES AWAY.
READY TORPEDOES--
NUMBER ONE.
THE BATTLE ENSIGN.
YOU HEARD HIM.

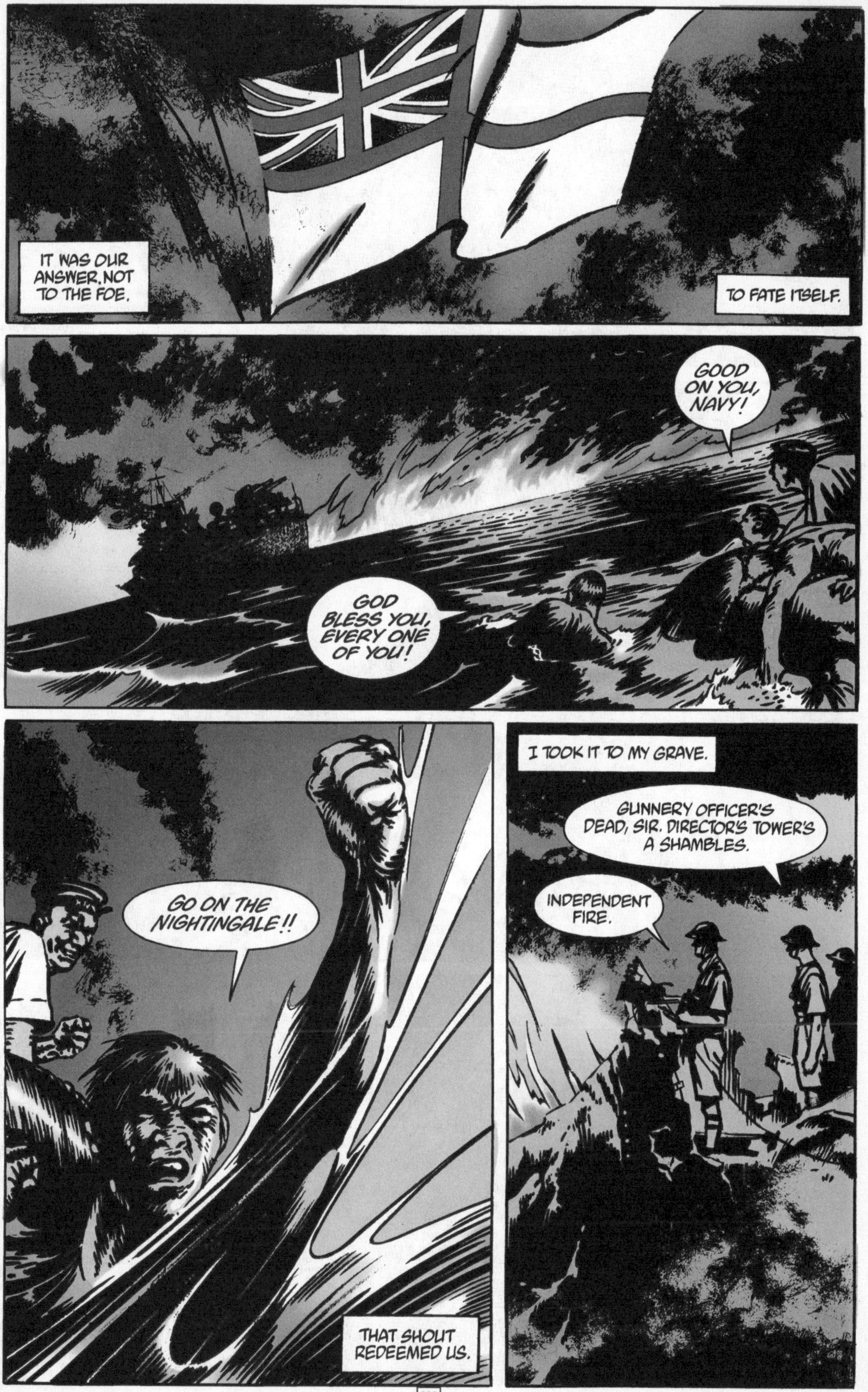
IT WAS OUR ANSWER. NOT TO THE FOE.
TO FATE ITSELF.
GOOD ON YOU, NAVY!
GOD BLESS YOU, EVERY ONE OF YOU!
GO ON THE NIGHTINGALE!!
THAT SHOUT REDEEMED US.
I TOOK IT TO MY GRAVE.
GUNNERY OFFICER'S DEAD, SIR. DIRECTOR'S TOWER'S A SHAMBLES.
INDEPENDENT FIRE.

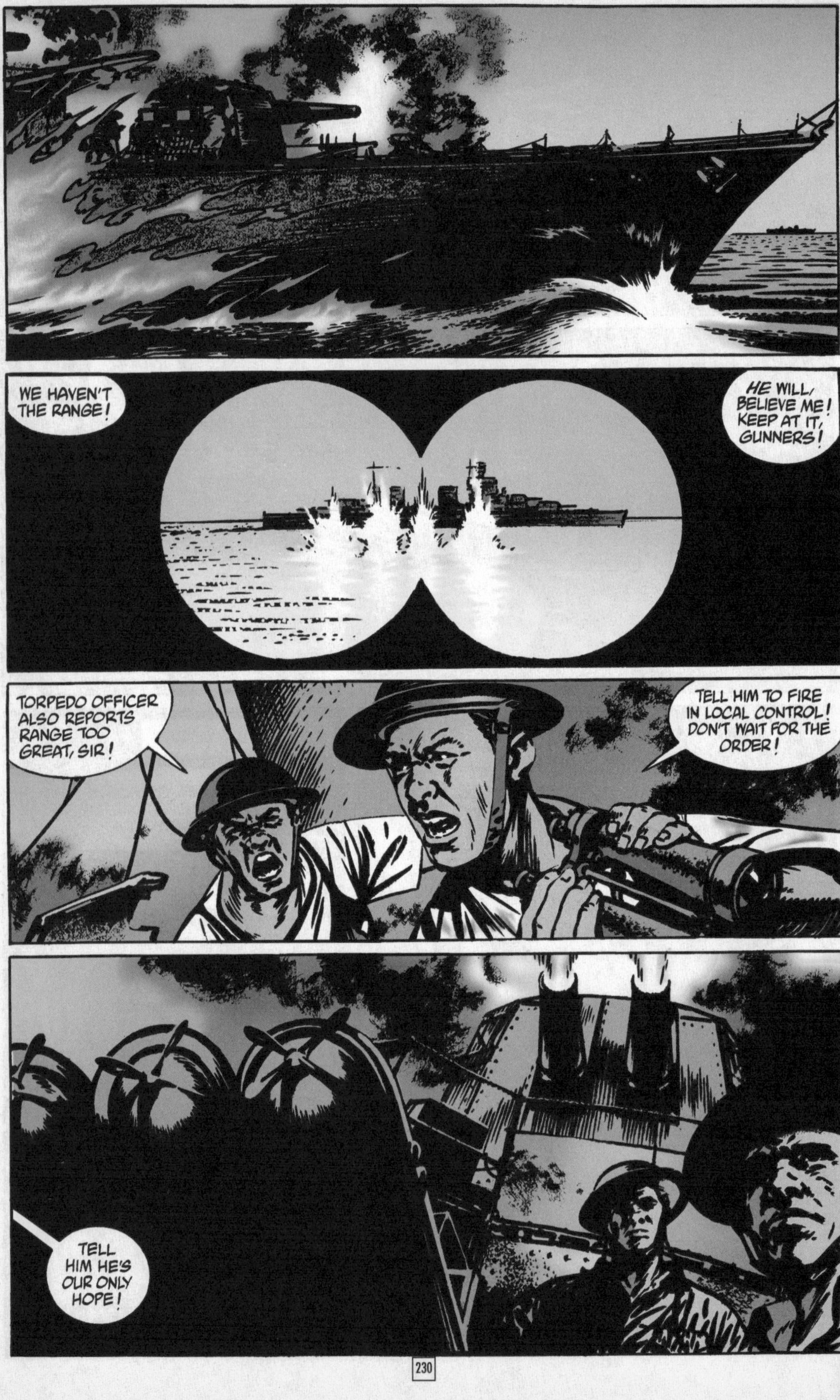
WE HAVEN'T THE RANGE!
HE WILL, BELIEVE ME! KEEP AT IT, GUNNERS!
TORPEDO OFFICER ALSO REPORTS RANGE TOO GREAT, SIR!
TELL HIM TO FIRE IN LOCAL CONTROL! DON'T WAIT FOR THE ORDER!
TELL HIM HE'S OUR ONLY HOPE!

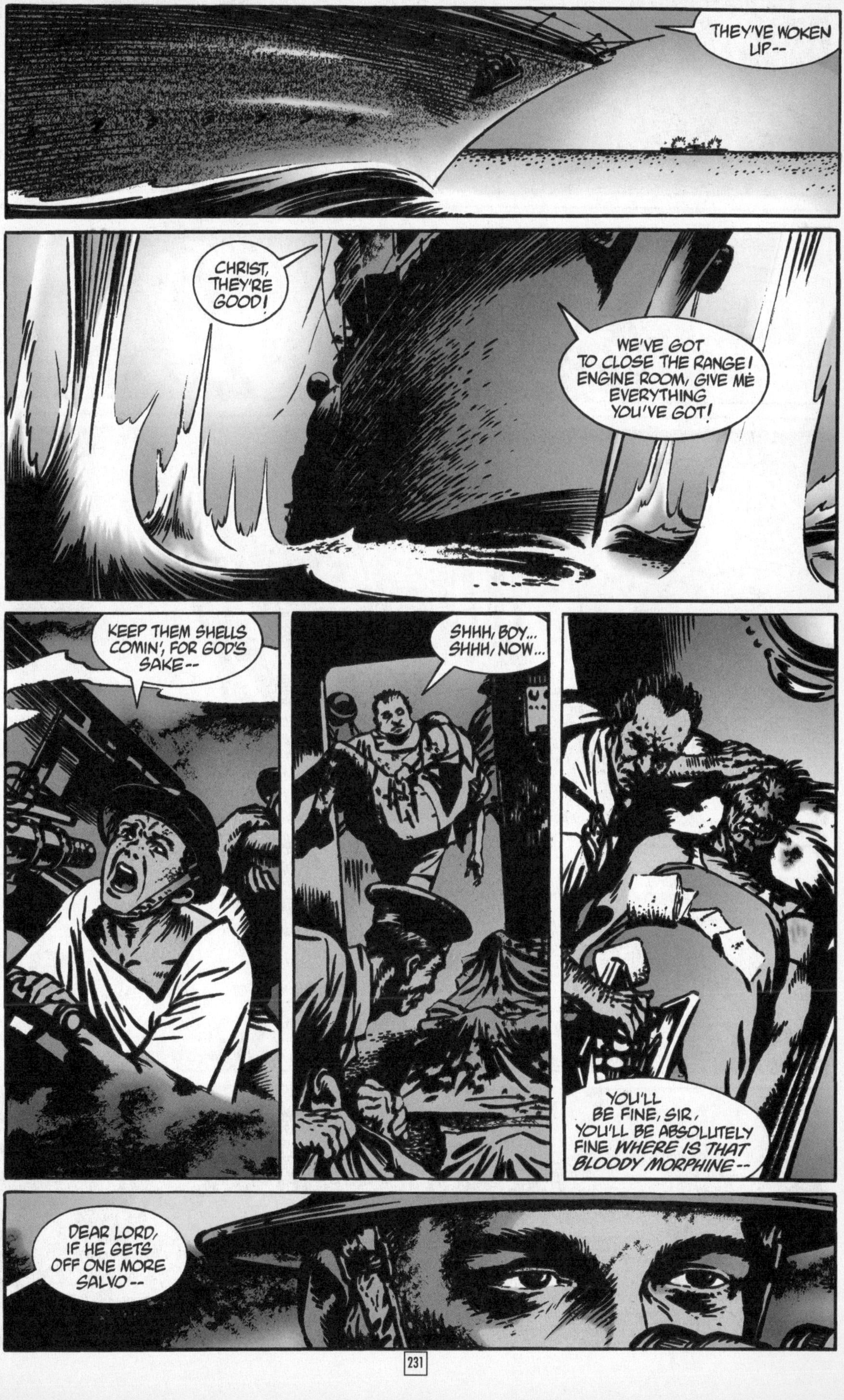
THEY'VE WOKEN UP--
CHRIST, THEY'RE GOOD!
WE'VE GOT TO CLOSE THE RANGE! ENGINE ROOM, GIVE ME EVERYTHING YOU'VE GOT!
KEEP THEM SHELLS COMIN', FOR GOD'S SAKE--
SHHH, BOY... SHHH, NOW...
YOU'LL BE FINE, SIR, YOU'LL BE ABSOLUTELY FINE *WHERE IS THAT BLOODY MORPHINE*--
DEAR LORD, IF HE GETS OFF ONE MORE SALVO--

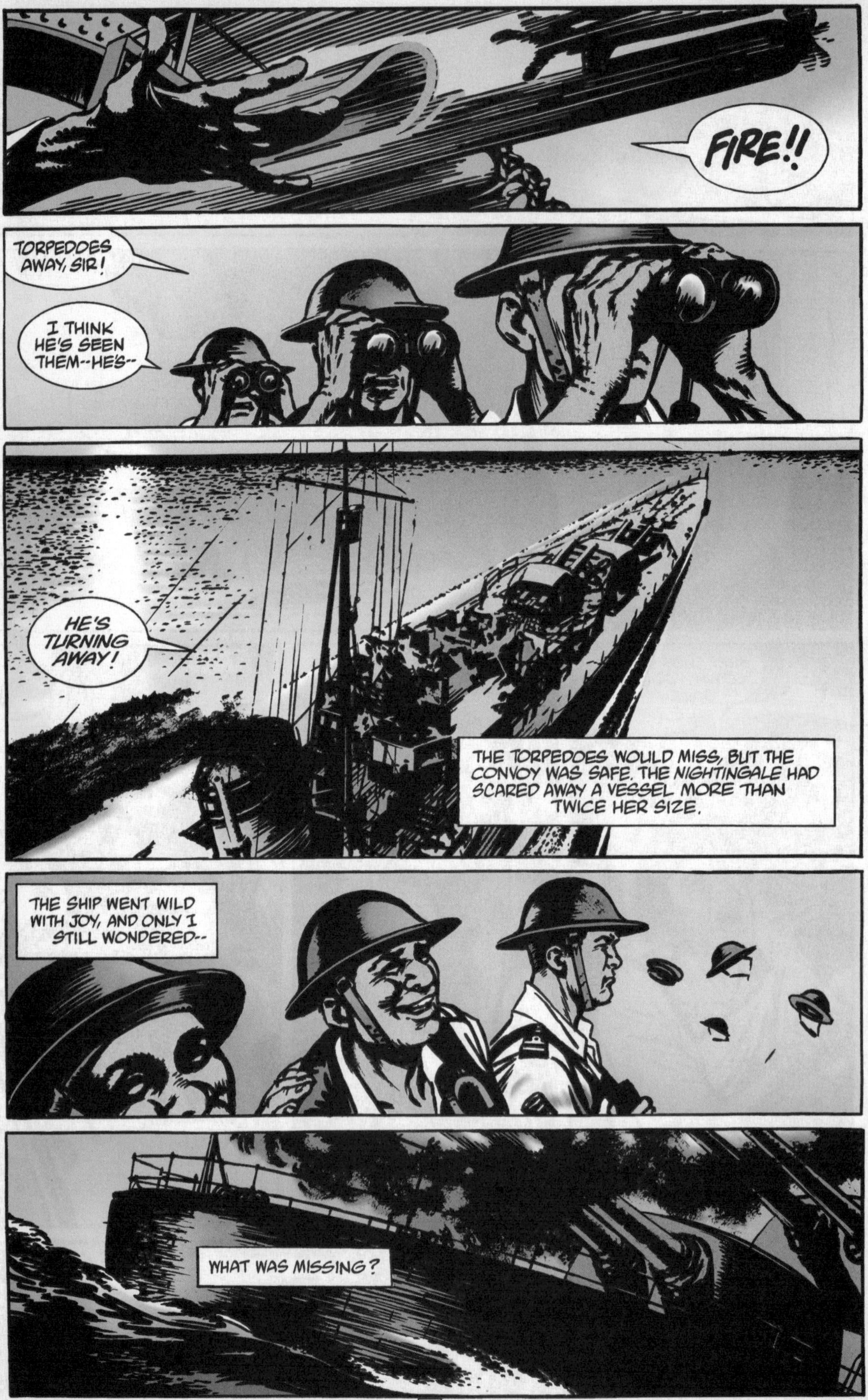
FIRE!!
TORPEDOES AWAY, SIR!
I THINK HE'S SEEN THEM--HE'S--
HE'S TURNING AWAY!
THE TORPEDOES WOULD MISS, BUT THE CONVOY WAS SAFE. THE NIGHTINGALE HAD SCARED AWAY A VESSEL MORE THAN TWICE HER SIZE.
THE SHIP WENT WILD WITH JOY, AND ONLY I STILL WONDERED--
WHAT WAS MISSING?

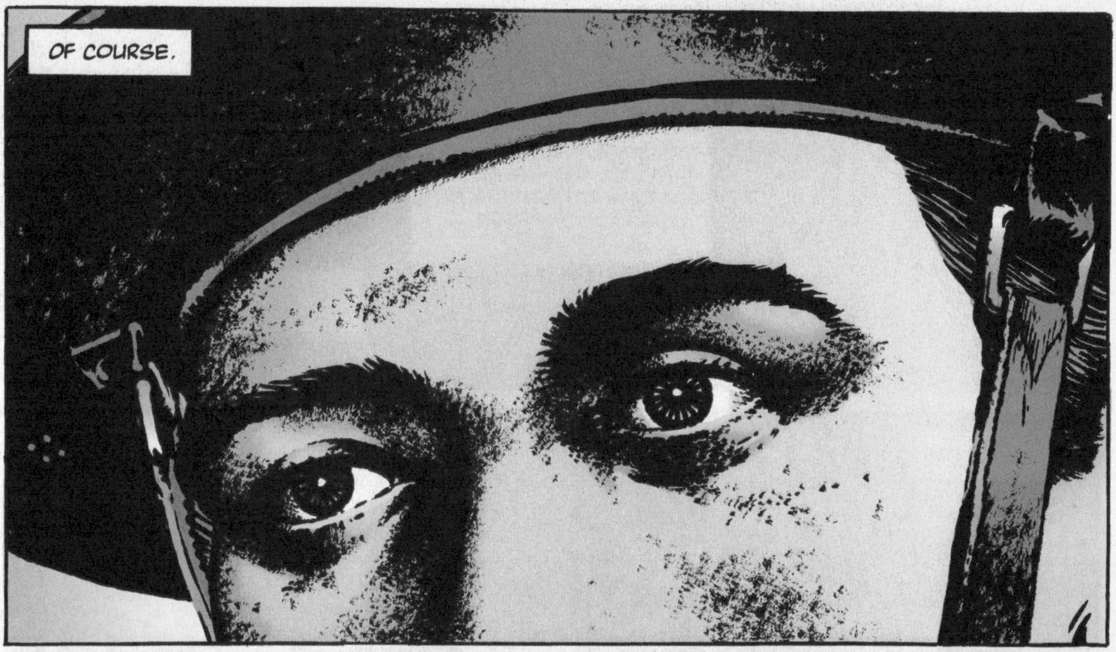
OF COURSE.

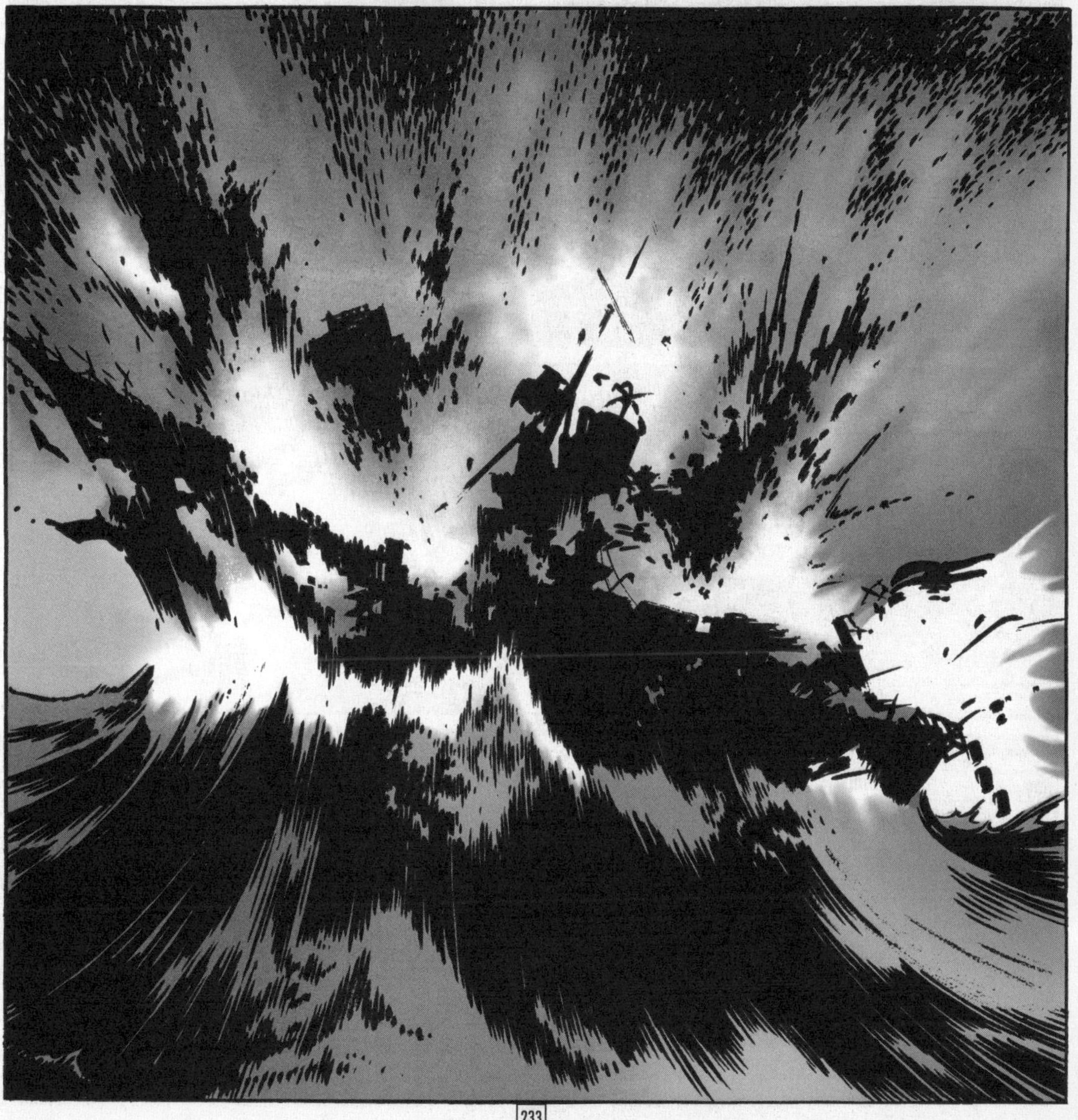

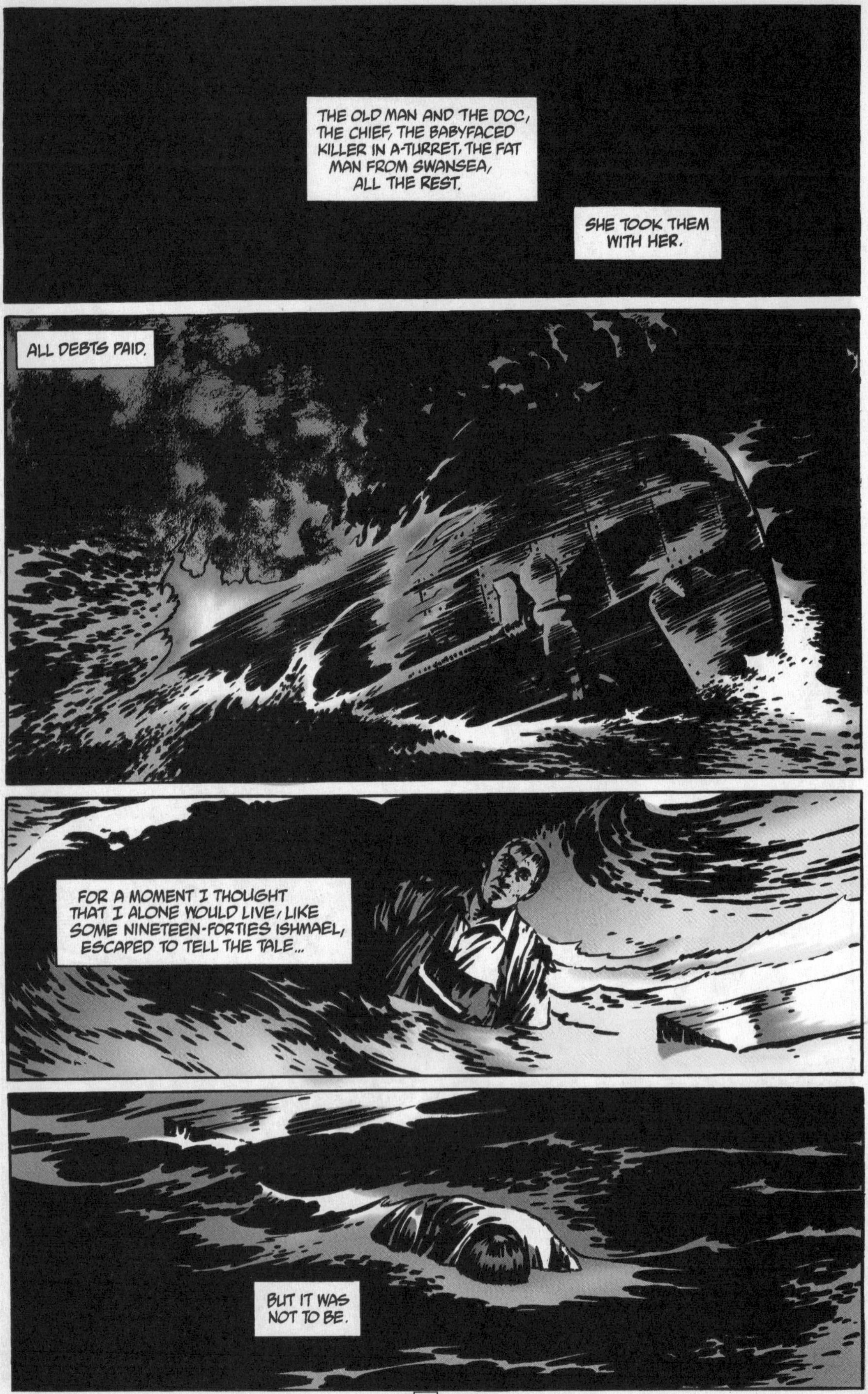
THE OLD MAN AND THE DOC, THE CHIEF, THE BABYFACED KILLER IN A-TURRET, THE FAT MAN FROM SWANSEA, ALL THE REST.
SHE TOOK THEM WITH HER.
ALL DEBTS PAID.
FOR A MOMENT I THOUGHT THAT I ALONE WOULD LIVE, LIKE SOME NINETEEN-FORTIES ISHMAEL, ESCAPED TO TELL THE TALE...
BUT IT WAS NOT TO BE.

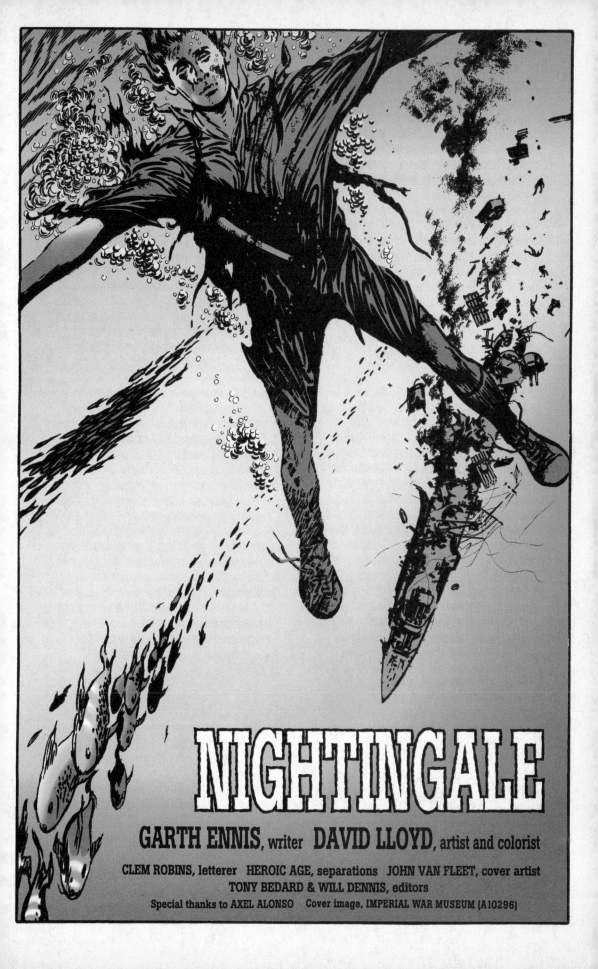

NIGHTINGALE

GARTH ENNIS, writer   **DAVID LLOYD**, artist and colorist

CLEM ROBINS, letterer   HEROIC AGE, separations   JOHN VAN FLEET, cover artist
TONY BEDARD & WILL DENNIS, editors
Special thanks to AXEL ALONSO   Cover image, IMPERIAL WAR MUSEUM (A10296)

The stories you've just read are fiction based loosely around fact. Broadly speaking, the characters and situations are invented while details of weapons, equipment, tactics and so on, along with the general historical context, are as accurate as could be achieved. Artists Chris Weston, Gary Erskine, John Higgins, Dave Gibbons and David Lloyd were as diligent as possible in researching their subjects; their dedication is reflected in the excellence of the artwork they produced. With a little space to spare, I'd like to look at each of the four War Stories in greater detail, and hopefully shed some light on what was real and what was not.

○ ○ ○

The mechanical star of *Johann's Tiger* was every bit as dangerous as the narrative suggests. The Tiger tank was an instant world-beater, a 56-ton monster that could easily make mincemeat of any tank put up against it. It might be outmaneuvered (most Allied tanks were faster), it might break down (overly complex, it was a temperamental beast to maintain), it might be overwhelmed by sheer weight of numbers (its complexity once again its undoing, with simpler American Shermans and Russian T-34s being turned out in their tens of thousands): but in a head-on encounter, the Tiger's opponent was almost certainly doomed. Only in the last years of the war did the Allies field weapons that could pierce its frontal armor, and none of their tanks had sufficient protection to survive a hit from its 88 millimeter gun. There are several accounts of Tigers surviving — and winning — battles with superior numbers of Russia's mighty Josef Stalin tanks; for Johann and company to last as long as they do seems reasonably credible.

In the hands of a skilled crew the Tiger could dominate the battlefield, and frequently did. "Aces" like Otto Carius, *Oberfeldwebel* Knispel and the famous

Michael Wittman racked up incredible scores, sometimes during a single day's fighting. Nothing, of course, could prevent Germany's eventual defeat, and while many *Wehrmacht* and S.S. units bitterly contested every scrap of ground, some disintegration was inevitable. Field Police units like the one Johann encounters were hard at work in 1945, and battlefield executions were alarmingly frequent. For five men to slip through the net — or at least get as far as our motley little band do — would be difficult, but not impossible. For them to have crewed the same Tiger as long as the story suggests would be another matter entirely; Nicolas must have been a skilled mechanic indeed for Big Max to have lasted two years without falling apart.

Regarding language: an *experte* was a fighter pilot of enormous ability, an ace many times over; the *Ritterkreuz* was the Knight's Cross, Germany's highest military decoration; *Jabos* were fighter-bomber aircraft, the bane of Germany's armies once her decimated air force lost control of the skies. And one final point: with Johann's experiences as grim as they are, I originally intended him to be an officer in the *Waffen* S.S., until a little further reading revealed that atrocity was by no means the sole province of that organization. In fact, every German frontline unit would have been involved in such horrors to one extent or another; acknowledging this point is perhaps central to understanding the ghastly reality of the Eastern Front.

○ ○ ○

I first came across *The Ballad of the D-Day Dodgers* some years ago, and indeed, for a variety of reasons, this story was much longer in gestation than the three that accompany it. Something in the injustice of the central accusation — that men fighting in Italy were literally dodging service in Normandy — served as the inspiration for *D-Day Dodgers*: a small injustice, historically speaking, but no less foul for all that. Lady Astor did indeed claim never to have made the offending speech, and in fairness it must be noted that no official record of her having done so actually exists. Whoever was responsible, the story spread like wildfire though the British Eighth Army in the summer of 1944. *The Ballad* followed soon afterwards.

The Antrim Rifles are an invention, though their organization, weapons and tactics are a reasonable approximation of a British infantry regiment's in the latter half of the Second World War. Captain Lovatt's recollection of the Oxford Union debate of 1933 is accurate. His opinions on General Clark and the nature of the Italian campaign are open to debate, although Clark did indeed divert American units into Rome in June of 1944, when his continued pursuit of German forces might have proved more fruitful (Rome was in fact abandoned without a fight). And one small point: Dunn's password, *Yello Man* (also Yellow, Yella etc) is the name of a sticky, honeycomb confection sold in seaside towns along Ireland's North coast, most notably Ballycastle. Too much of it will make you very ill.

As noted at the beginning of the story, the Italian campaign was not quite the picnic that Lady Astor (or whoever) suggested. It was a long, brutal slog against a determined enemy, fought in some of the most inhospitable terrain that any army had to deal with during the Second World War. Salerno, Anzio and the Gothic Line were terrible battles, Monte Cassino was a nightmare, and for the troops to keep going through two miserable Italian winters speaks very highly of them indeed. *D-Day Dodgers* is but one small, utterly inadequate tribute to their courage.

○ ○ ○

The story of the U.S. 101st Airborne Division's journey across Europe has been told many times, most obviously by the historian Stephen Ambrose in his book *Band of Brothers*, and in the excellent TV series adapted from it. *Screaming Eagles* draws heavily on the former (particularly Eddie Brewer's opinions on the army); I can honestly say that the script was written a full year before the latter was broadcast. The characters in the comic are not supposed to suggest the men of the real Easy Company; the reason I chose "Easy" will be obvious from the last line of the story, and there was no 655th regiment in the 101st Airborne.

The American paratroopers who jumped into Normandy on D-Day spent much longer in the front line than they had been led to expect; having been assured that they would simply take their objectives and hand over to ground units advancing from the beach head, the men of the Airborne divisions were not in fact relieved until over a month after the initial drop. The savage, close-quarter battles in Normandy's *bocage* country, the sad failure of Operation *Market-Garden* and the grim autumn fighting in the flooded Dutch countryside are a matter of historical record; the 101st's epic defense of Bastogne has now passed into legend, and rightly so. These men had come a long way from their homes to help in the liberation of Europe. If some of them helped themselves to the plunder thrown up by the defeat of the Third Reich, who can say that they didn't deserve it?

○ ○ ○

Of all the stories in this collection, *Nightingale* draws most heavily on actual historical incident. The supply convoys that ran from Britain to Russia were always vulnerable to attack by submarine or aircraft, but from these threats their escort vessels could provide at least some protection. What destroyers and corvettes were supposed to do against a battleship was something else entirely, and the dread of an encounter with the *Tirpitz* weighed heavily on every sailor's mind from the moment his ship left port. In the summer of 1942, with convoy PQ-17 on its way to Murmansk, the British Admiralty — believing that the German battleship was indeed on the loose — gave orders for the merchant ships to scatter. The U-boats and bombers had a field day. The *Tirpitz*, meanwhile, had not even weighed anchor.

Among the escorts was the destroyer H.M.S. *Ledbury*, commanded by one Roger Hill. Being forced to stand helplessly by while his disparate charges were massacred affected Hill deeply, and on *Ledbury*'s next assignment he was granted an opportunity to square the account. Operation *Pedestal*, a British convoy intended to relieve the pressure on the besieged island of Malta, saw some of the fiercest fighting of the war at sea: German and Italian aircraft harried the Allied vessels mercilessly, almost from the moment they entered the Mediterranean. Losses were appalling, and when he saw a doomed ship's crew floundering in the water, surrounded by an inferno of blazing petrol, Hill sensed that his hour had come. *Ledbury* went into the flames.

Some of her sailors lowered themselves on ropes tied around their waists to reach the men in the burning waters, others climbed down scramble-nets to pull the wounded to safety. Hill described his men as "marvellous." Later, when *Pedestal*'s few survivors had struggled into Malta, another officer asked him if he knew anything about a destroyer that had reportedly risked fiery doom to rescue a number of shipwrecked sailors. No, Hill replied, he didn't, but it sounded bloody silly to him.

A glance at a map of Norway and Northern Russia will give some clue to the tribulations that awaited the crews who made the Arctic run. Over half the voyage took place inside the Arctic Circle, and the pack ice

forced the convoys closer to the coast — well within range of German aircraft. Summer's endless daylight left little hope of evading detection; winter brought conditions so wretched they defy description. Yet still the convoys went: merchantmen and escorts, smashing their way through waves like mountains, the spray freezing as it crashed down on bridges and gun turrets that lay open to the elements. The enemy waited with Stukas, submarines, surface raiders and torpedo bombers: and still the convoys went.

o o o

Perhaps the true drama of any war story lies in its basis in reality, more so than that of any other genre. Whether the stories themselves ring true or not, we know that these things happened once upon a time. We know that the battles were real, that the effect they had on our world was real, that the people who fought and died in them were very real indeed.

— Garth Ennis
February, 2004

BIBLIOGRAPHY

JOHANN'S TIGER
- *Tiger Ace*, Gary L. Simpson, Schiffer Military History 1994
- *Tiger Tanks*, Michael Green, MBI Publishing Co. 1995
- *Frontsoldaten*, Stephen G. Fritz, The University Press of Kentucky 1995
- *Russia's War*, Richard Overy, Penguin Books 1997

D-DAY DODGERS
- *The Face of Battle*, John Keegan, Penguin Books 1976
- *The Second World War*, John Keegan, Pimlico 1989
- *The Sons of Ulster*, Richard Doherty, Appletree Press 1992
- *The Voice of War*, Ed. Victor Selwyn, Penguin Books 1995

SCREAMING EAGLES
- *Six Armies in Normandy*, John Keegan, Pimlico 1982
- *Band of Brothers*, Stephen E. Ambrose, Touchstone 1992
- *Citizen Soldiers*, Stephen E. Ambrose, Touchstone 1997

NIGHTINGALE
- *Convoy*, Paul Kemp, Cassell & Co. 1993
- *Destroyers*, Antony Preston, Parkgate Books, 1998
- *For Five Shillings a Day*, Dr. Richard Begg and Dr. Peter Liddle, HarperCollins 2000
- *Malta: The Spitfire Year*, Christopher Shores, Brian Cull and Nicola Malizia, Grub Street 1991